COPING WITH CHANGING VALUES

ROBERT B. NORDBERG

THE ROSEN PUBLISHING GROUP, INC.

NEW YORK

Published in 1983 by The Rosen Publishing Group, Inc.
29 East 21st Street, New York, N.Y. 10010

First Edition

Manufactured in the United States of America

Library of Congress Cataloging in Publication Data

Nordberg, Robert B.
Coping with changing values.

Summary: Guidance for developing a personal philosophy and set of values during a period when drastic changes are occurring in traditional institutions such as marriage, family, and education.
1. Youth—Conduct of life. 2. Values—Juvenile literature. [1. Conduct of life. 2. Values] I. Title.
BJ1661.N67 1983 170'.2'0223 82-22965
ISBN 0-8239-0596-9

About the Author

Robert B. Nordberg is a Professor of Education and former Dean of the School of Education at the Marquette University School of Education in Milwaukee, Wisconsin. Before joining the faculty of Marquette, he was Director of Counselor Education at Catholic University of America. He served as a cryptographer in World War II and the Korean War.

Dr. Nordberg holds a bachelor's degree in psychology and a doctorate in education from the University of Denver, and a master's degree in psychology from the University of Colorado. He is a member of numerous professional organizations, among them the National Catholic Guidance Conference, of which he is a past member of the Board of Directors. He is currently President of the Marquette Chapter of the Fellowship of Catholic Scholars. He is also Consulting Editor for *Counseling and Values*.

Among his writings are the books *Guidance: A Systematic Introduction; Philosophy and Education: A Total View,* written with A.M. Dupuis; and *Methods of Research in Education,* written with J. E. Wise and D. J. Reitz. He is author of two correspondence study manuals for the University of Minnesota, and of numerous articles for reference works, textbooks, and anthologies. He has also written articles for scholarly journals such as *American Behavioral Scientist, Educational Forum, Catholic Educa-*

tional Review and *Journal of General Psychology;* popular-level articles on mental health; and many reviews of fiction and nonfiction books. One of his articles was broadcast by the Voice of America as an example of American culture. Dr. Nordberg is also active as the director of miscellaneous seminars, institutes, and workshops and has lectured on television.

Preface

In 1972 I gave a talk at the national convention of the American Personnel and Guidance Association, suggesting that psychedelic drugs, biofeedback, popularizations of Yoga and Zen contemplation, astrology, suburban witchcraft, and some other phenomena of the times were best regarded as latter-day searches for mystical experience. The thought was fairly new then, although it has long since become a cliché. To my delight, Richards Rosen Press expressed interest in publishing the talk in expanded form as a book. This they did, under the title *The Teenager and the New Mysticism*.

Unless you count an Italian translation of a text on educational research, that was my last book for almost ten years, for I drifted into academic administration and spent some years as a Dean. In 1981, being done with deaning and on sabbatical leave, I learned happily that the same publisher was interested in a text for young people on coping with changing values. This topic, while broader than the previous one, offered continuity with it and was of considerable interest to me. Accordingly, the main project of my sabbatical year has been researching and writing this book. I hope you find it of interest and value and would be pleased to hear from you about your reactions.

At least three persons ought to be thanked: My wife, Beverly, whose contributions to my existence and functioning are too pervasive to enumerate; Ruth Rosen, who has always been pleasant and effective to work with; and my graduate assistant, Mr. Sundar Ramaswami, who helped in reviewing the manuscript and in other ways.

Robert B. Nordberg

Milwaukee, Wisconsin

Contents

Chapter I

The New World Upon Us

A police official in New York City was quoted recently as saying that not only is there more juvenile crime than ever before, but there is a new attitude toward it by the offenders. We have made, he said, some kind of qualitative leap. So it is in many spheres. Sociologists speak of the mores of a society, the customs and manners that people regard as morally binding. Sometimes the mores coincide with the law; sometimes, not. If the laws were enforced as strictly as the mores are, it would probably be a better world. We speak, too, of values, those things considered valuable or desirable by an individual or a society.

Alvin Toffler had much impact through a book called *Future Shock*. The gist of Toffler's message was that while mores and values are constantly changing, we live in a time when this is happening at an accelerated pace—indeed, at an *increasingly* accelerated pace. The result is something akin to jet-lag. We can't cope with it. Our consciences and our nervous systems can't quite keep things sorted out. It is puzzling to your parents, for example, if they have paid your way through college on the assumption that the diploma would be your ticket to social and economic advancement, to be told that you wish to be a house painter or a carpenter so you can keep in touch with the common man. People who practiced sexual restraint with great difficulty are now told by some liberal clergymen that anything goes, inside marriage or outside. Movie starlets on talk shows tell us that marriage is only a scrap of paper. (Later, they may sue for palimony.)

A young man, a good student, not long ago talked with an academic administrator. As the culmination of his teacher-training, the young man found himself doing practice teaching in one of the schools where, at best, the teacher can only keep order. The faculty seemed to have given up hope of actually providing the students with a high school education. "This is not what I've spent sixteen years getting ready for," the young man said. The administrator understood the problem. Yet he also pointed out, "You may find yourself hired by just this sort of school. It wouldn't hurt to have a little experience in one." A compromise was reached. The student would spend half a term in this blackboard jungle, the other half in a school where there was still real concern with verbal and mathematical literacy.

Perhaps you see most of the social changes as for the better. They certainly represent big changes. The movies from the 1930's and '40's that we see on television portray quite a different world. Hollywood took minimal notice that there were two sexes. Homosexual liaisons or attractions were not even hinted at. A man and woman could not be shown in bed together unless one of them had a foot on the floor. Fred Astaire and Ginger Rogers might have aroused more erotic fantasies by dancing together than some pornographic films do today, but symbolism always kept the audience at one remove. What Buck Rogers and Wilma Deering did during dull interludes on those long journeys through space, or how literally to take the proposition that the lovely Margo Lane was the Shadow's "constant companion" were not hinted at.

The good guys always won. Stories always had an ending. The only question was when and how the bad guys would get their comeuppance. In international relations, Americans were *of course* the good guys. The Russians were honorary good guys because they were our allies. We would worry about that later. The F.B.I. was the friend of all law-abiding citizens. During the five years after World War II, Americans accommodated themselves to many new ideas. It was clear that the United Nations was not going to lead all nations to peace and justice. The nation learned that we were in a nonshooting war with the Soviet Union with no end in sight. Radio started giving way to television as the chief medium of home entertainment. Still, popular values were mostly intact. The staid and proper Rudy Vallee had given way to the slightly risqué Bing Crosby as king of the crooners. Then Elvis Presley dethroned Crosby. Presley was something else. He gyrated suggestively, despite his statement to a reporter that "I don't do no dirty movements." He was polite enough in public, but one sensed that he was in some sense primitive, hostile to the Establishment. The Beatles gave adults the same sense that they were being mocked, as it were, by their own children. By now, of course, there are so many rock'n'roll groups imitating one another's dress and vocal styles that only ardent devotees try to keep track.

By the mid-1960's, it was evident even to the casual observer that a revolution of some sort was under way. The American military involvement in Vietnam was strenuously protested by many. College campuses were taken over by students, sometimes in violent and disruptive ways. One began to hear talk of the counterculture. A rhetorical style developed that seemed shrill and irresponsible to some, but plainly inflamed others.

Most of the older generation were vastly puzzled by all of this. Were not the young protesters extremely naive?

Did they think, for example, that the Russians would throw away their nuclear weapons any time soon? Did they not see that, alas, this is a world where armies and navies—yes, and cloak-and-dagger agencies—are necessary? Was not their talk of anarchy the most adolescent kind of romanticism?

Even if one grants all of that, however, the protesters had a point. They were trying to tell the country something, and the country did not listen until it had the demonstrations and the violence. The agitators and marchers were saying, in part, that Americans are *not* always the good guys. There is a kind of osmosis in warfare whereby the winners gradually take on some characteristics of the losers, so that nobody wins in any clean, clear sense. America had drifted far from the ideals of the Founding Fathers. Twice since World War II we had gone to war to side with one corrupt regime against another. The Central Intelligence Agency was being increasingly misused to spy on innocent people and even to pursue partisan political ends. Then, of course, there were all of the shocking revelations about the Nixon administration, its substance and its tone. A President who had publicly expressed his joy that Dwight D. Eisenhower had restored dignified language to the White House, after the occasional "damn" and "hell" of Harry S. Truman, talked in private in ways that reminded one of the old saying: "There's cussin', and then there's cussin'." To this day, many Americans cannot muster much confidence even in the good intentions of government. It seemed that we had hit bottom. One began to understand the complaints of the counterculture.

Technology has had much to do with the changes. Applied science cannot, in itself, tell us what we ought to value, but it usually reflects what we *do* value and leads, in turn, to new goals and priorities. Television was the first major invention that the public was prepared to believe in before it materialized. The man on the street did not seem to doubt that it could be done, although electronics engineers were aware of a sufficiency of problems. When the blank screen was there, ready to be filled, the question arose: what shall it be filled with? The answers, of course, came from contemporary American culture. A few adjustments had to be made. Groucho Marx discovered, for example, that the frantic pace of Marx Brothers movies did not translate well from the large theater screen to the tube in the living room. (The early TV screens were even smaller than those we have today.) Thus, he adopted a more sedate pace for his popular quiz program. Basically, though, there was never much doubt about the bill of fare. Whereas England's B.B.C. had assumed from the beginning that the point of radio and television is to educate, to elevate public taste, commercial broadcasters in the United States assumed that the point is to get as large an audience as possible—not in an uncertain future, after months or years of exposure to high-quality programs, but *tonight*.

Although television took its programming from the current culture, it also influenced that culture. Millions of non-Catholic Americans formed their impressions of the Catholic Church chiefly from the televised talks of Fulton J. Sheen. The norms for comedy were largely established by a few holdovers from vaudeville and radio such as Milton Berle and Jack Benny, who successfully adapted to the new medium. Other comedians such as Fred Allen, whose humor was more intellectual than visual, fell by the wayside. They weren't funny to watch.

Another technological development was "the pill." Here, at last, was a birth-control device more effective than the rhythm method and less cumbersome than some other methods. It happened to come along when the Roman

Catholic Church, a major advocate of leaving the procreative act open to the possibility of procreation, had undergone a major council that left many people with the vague impression that former moral strictures no longer applied. Use of "the pill" became widespread, scarcely less among Catholics than among other people. Sex outside of marriage became less threatening.

Patterns Among the Changes

This description of the revolution in progress is deliberately simplified. Only in this way can one get some sense of the overall contours of what is happening. As those contours appear, one also sees patterns among them. Above all else, there is a drift toward subjectivism, the viewpoint that there is nothing definitive outside the individual to tell him/her what is true, what is good, what is beautiful, what is worth doing, what life "means." This subjectivism takes many philosophical forms: Existentialism, Phenomenalism, Positivism, Pragmatism, Linguistic Empiricism, and so on. Each such system, of course, offers its own arguments and differs somewhat from the others in its conclusions. Nevertheless, they hold in common the basic premise that knowledge reduces to the subject knowing. They all minimize tradition and authority. They all tend to assume that man is infinitely perfectible on the natural plane. Some form or forms of environmental manipulation can bring us to Utopia: perhaps education, perhaps psychotherapy, perhaps redistribution of the wealth, perhaps this or that political blueprint, but something!

We are speaking of a loose tendency here. Subjectivism cannot be equated with liberalism (in the classic, nineteenth-century sense), nor objectivism with conservatism. Nevertheless, many of the same currents do dart in and out. Related are ethical and aesthetic pluralism. Most Americans are not unnerved by the proposition that there is room for debate about what is good art. This attitude has always been part of our culture, somewhat inconsistently with some other beliefs. Ethical pluralism and its first cousin, ethical relativism, are newer in our thinking. We are sometimes told nowadays that one cannot apply the same ethical norms to all races or to both sexes. An employer who was told that he must hire a black applicant over a white applicant who was better qualified said, "I don't understand the principle involved here. If it is immoral to consider race for hiring and promotion when the potential beneficiary is white, why is it not immoral to do the same when he is black? Either race is a legitimate issue in these matters or it is not." The reply was that we cannot apply the same ethical norms to disadvantaged people. Such a statement would not look good in an essay on ethics, yet we must have some means to overcome the injustices of the past.

We must not overstate the novelty of what is happening. It was in another generation that the Spanish philosopher José Ortega y Gasset wrote *The Revolt of the Masses*. There, he reported that the common man, who once felt constrained by traditions and norms, now felt free to look only within himself for guidelines. A visitor to a distinguished art gallery was once passing flip judgments upon some masterpiece on exhibition. Finally, a guard could abide it no longer. "Sir," said he, "these pictures are not here to be judged by you. They are your judges." Ortega felt as the guard did. Most people today would be on the visitor's side.

College and university professors detect among today's students much of the attitude displayed by that visitor. They do not feel on trial in the face of Shakespeare, Poe, Plato, or Joyce. Those people are on trial before *them* The cultural state that students bring to this task of evaluating classics is often a bit primitive. As everyone knows, average scores on standardized achievement tests have basically been going down since the mid-1960's. Perhaps the curve is now bottoming out. Why has the curve been going down? One major reason is that most of you in high school or college today feel qualified to make your own judgments of what is worth learning. Again, subjectivism.

Indeed, we could hark back to ancient Rome and quote statesmen of that day that the younger generation was going to the dogs. Civilization has its ups and downs. No particular solace or solution is to be drawn, however, from the fact that there have been troubled times before. We must address the special troubles of *our* time. These include the sudden sense that earth's resources are limited and that those limits are not far off; the ever-present prospect of nuclear war; worldwide problems of inflation, unemployment, and unstable economies; the competing claims of the Women's Movement, civil rights, and so on; machines that check your credit rating while you stand in line at the supermarket; a drastic disintegration of family life; schisms and demoralization within religious bodies; and, as an erstwhile politician put it, "the packaging of Presidential candidates like breakfast cereals."

What Toffler called future shock is called, in academic circles, cultural dislocation. It is the tug-of-war in the mind and emotions of the individual person as he/she is pulled this way and that by confusing forces. There are always conflicts within a culture, of course. We are told to turn the other cheek, and we are offered assertiveness training. We are told to love our neighbor as ourselves, but we are expected to succeed by one means or another. For every proverb, there is another one to give the opposite advice. We say "Look before you leap," but we also say, "He who hesitates is lost." We say, "It's a wise father that knows his own child," but we also say, "Like father, like son."

In times of rapid transition, this element of internal contradiction has added to it a deep uncertainty about where things are going and why. Some see in our current *levée en masse* a purification, a return to a simple morality arising out of genuine respect for human beings. Others see the downfall of all that sustains civilized usage. Oddly, there is among both groups the occasional sense of Armageddon as imminent.

The individual, facing all of this, must adjust and survive. Indeed, to "adjust" is far from the whole problem. It is not just a matter of adapting to circumstances. During the witch trials in Salem, the person who accused his neighbor of witchcraft before his neighbor thought to accuse him was admirably "adjusted," but he was not behaving very ethically. The problem is to adjust and still to have some personal wholeness, some sense of where one is going with some conviction that one ought to go there. When one can function in a situation with at least moderate success and without exhausting one's resources early on, one is said to be coping. To cope is, in absolute terms, a modest enough goal, but it is often as much as we can hope to do. As G. K. Chesterton somewhere said, "If a thing is worth doing, it is worth doing badly." This book is about coping: dealing adequately, perhaps even well, with the tendency of things to break within a month of the time you buy them, with the cab driver who insults you as he extends his hand for a tip, with feeling within ten years of entering a vocation that you must get out of it for your sanity, with new notions of right and wrong, with the coexistence of electronic computers and astrology columns, with clergy who have always told us what to do and now announce that they have no answers, with your parents who find us too liberal, with being alive in America in the 1980's.

One caution: the writer fancies himself an honest man and takes you to be a mature person who wants the truth and is entitled to it. Thus, there will be none of the magic formulas that are almost obligatory in self-help books today. Utopia is not promised. Nirvana is not around the corner. Life is difficult and will continue to be so. Some of us think it was meant to be so. It is usually, however, *manageable*. We can usually do better than we are doing. That, gentle reader, is my hope for you and for me.

For Further Reading

Allen, Bem P., *Social Behavior—Facts and Falsehoods about Common Sense, Hypnotism, Obedience, Altruism, Beauty, Racism, and Sexism* (Chicago: Nelson Hall, 1978), pp. xxxv, 226.

Brandon, Samuel G. F., *Time and Mankind; an Historical and Philosophical Study of Mankind's Attitude to the Phenomena of Change* (New York: Hutchinson, 1951), p. 228.

Canning, Jeremiah W., ed., *Values in an Age of Confrontation* (Columbus: C. E. Merrill, 1970), pp. x, 206.

Hodges, Harold M., *Conflict and Consensus; an Introduction to Sociology* (New York: Harper and Row, 1971), pp. xviii, 587.

Lippitt, Ronald, *et al.*, *The Dynamics of Planned Change; a Comparative Study of Principles and Techniques* (New York: Harcourt, Brace, 1958), p. 312.

McReady, William C., *The Ultimate Values of the American Population* (Beverly Hills: Saga Publications, 1976), p. 213.

Chapter **II**

Changes at Home: Marriage

Values are changing so fast these days that we can't keep up. It is hard for the individual to adjust and survive. Thus we have argued. The next few chapters will look at these changes in various aspects of our lives: at home, at school, at work, and in society. The changes at home include the desanctification of marriage, a decreasing role for the family and decreasing reverence for it, and a steady rise in divorce rates.

The older generation probably grew up taking marriage for granted as a part of the natural order, rather as one takes fireplugs and drugstores for granted. It was taken for granted that every woman would get married if she could. The occasional man who clung to his bachelor status was regarded as a bit peculiar. Divorced persons sometimes felt so disgraced that they left the community to build a new life elsewhere.

Currently, many people are taking a new look at marriage. They are defying the conventions and, sometimes, the laws in the matter. They do not see that what they may be doing in the long sweep of history is giving a new form to an institution that has had many forms. The institution of marriage, which some contemporary savants are prepared to dismiss so lightly, has been a universal of human history because of its many personal and social functions. It provides for the care and guidance of children, regulation of lines of descent, sexual gratification and control, division of labor between the sexes, companionship, status, and affection. The specifics of this arrangement depend upon various characteristics. Social class boundaries, for instance, sometimes place limits on the selection of a mate. The women's movement in the United States has tended to redefine the role of the wife. Attitudes toward divorce and remarriage are often shaped by religious beliefs.

"Just Molly and me, and baby makes three," run the lyrics of "My Blue Heaven." Family life has not always and everywhere been like that. Many societies have had a clan system headed by a patriarchal chief. When a woman married, she left the clan into which she had been born and entered the one to which her husband belonged. No woman could be taken away from her clan without the consent of her chief. No man could marry without the consent of his chief. Marriage, thus, could be regarded as a transaction not simply between two persons, but between two clans. The termination of a marriage likewise involved cooperation of the two clan chiefs.

This tradition was practiced among the Jews as well as the Germanic peoples at the time of the rise of Christianity. It had undergone long development in which Greek and Roman customs had been incorporated. The Christian Church posed four conditions for the state of marriage: (1) it must involve a union of two sexes; therefore, there cannot be a homosexual marriage; (2) it must be a permanent union, breakable only by the death of one or both spouses; (3) it must be an exclusive union; therefore, extramarital acts are forbidden; and (4) its permanent and exclusive character must be guaranteed by a contract; therefore, merely living together without a mutual and binding commitment is concubinage, not marriage.

These four conditions, of course, were stated as the ideal. Infidelity did not mean that a marriage had ceased to exist, although it was more likely to lead to separation if it were the wife who was unfaithful. Prostitution has existed in societies dedicated to monogamous marriage, and the right of men to keep mistresses has often gone unchallenged.

Is matrimony a spiritual or a secular matter? Church and State have typically disagreed about that. The State gradually came to exercise a dominant role. In many places, legislation recognizes common-law marriages: those in which the partners have lived together for a certain length of time and consider themselves married, although they have not gone through an official ceremony. There have also been disputes over the form that such ceremonies should take, relating chiefly to the spiritual-secular issue. In the Soviet Union, for example, only a civil wedding is recognized. A couple are married when they register as man and wife with the officer of civil status. There are still a few places where the ceremony must be religious to be recognized. Vatican City, as would be expected, is one of them.

Patterns of family organization have varied according to circumstances. In the industrialized, urbanized, Western world, the typical pattern has been the nuclear family: a married couple and their children. "And though it's big enough for you and me, someday we'll make it tea for three," run the coy lyrics of "Dream House," another popular ballad. In some countries, especially in the Orient, marriage is usually part of an extended family system including parents, aunts, uncles, grandparents, and possibly more distant relatives.

The two systems work quite differently. Under the extended family system, marriages are usually arranged, the assumption being that marriage leads to love rather than vice versa. Anyone who has been in Shakespeare's "world-without-end bargain" for many years will recognize the truth in this. Romantic love does not last forever. There is a deeper kind of affection that comes from shared joys, sorrows, responsibilities, and achievements over the years. In making marital arrangements under the extended family system, consideration is given to the socioeconomic aspects. Having many children is normally considered advantageous. The man is recognized as head of the house. Prestige and influence attend the aged. It is taken for granted that the elderly will be cared for within the family circle.

In the nuclear family system, people choose their own mates as a rule; love is regarded as a cause of marriage rather than its consequence; marrying across class lines is less frowned upon; and no special status attaches to having a large number of children, which may even be considered undesirable. Nowadays, many people wish to combat the population explosion by having only one or two children or none. Ironically, it is usually those who are in a position to do the most for their children who take this stance. In the nuclear family system, the husband is no longer regarded as the head of the home, but as an equal with his wife. (Not everyone sees it that way, to be sure!) The elderly are not accorded much special respect, if any. If Grandma needs special attention, she is more likely to find herself in a nursing home than in the bosom of the family. Relatives may not see each other or communicate for many years. A card during the holiday season often suffices to serve notice that everyone is alive and well.

The system of arranged marriages still prevails in much of the world, but it has been gradually breaking down. Increasing numbers of young people feel that a husband and wife ought to know each other before marriage. In some countries, a compromise system has evolved. A young couple find each other as marital prospects, then seek parental approval of the choice. This shift was especially noticeable after World War II in Japan, where parents had previously contracted all marriages.

Where marriages are not arranged, there has usually been a pattern of dating and courtship. This custom provides an opportunity for a man and woman to get to know one another and judge the extent of their compatibility, although it has usually been pursued without much conscious thought to its aims. Dating has usually started in high school in the United States. In other countries it starts later, except in groups.

The "date" as an institution seems to be disappearing from American life, or at least changing its form. You are not likely to show up, formally dressed, with candy and flowers, to escort a girl to the movies. You, if a girl, are likely to be wearing blue jeans for the occasion. Perhaps the rising divorce rate convinced people that the system of dating and courtship was not meeting its purposes effectively. The shrinking globe has also brought complications. Many Oriental men come to the Western world to study. They may then return home and marry a girl chosen by their parents. The wife thus chosen may have less education than her husband. She may feel ill at ease in mixed social situations. Her husband may wish her wifely role to be as it is in the West, while she prefers to cling to the Oriental pattern. All of this, of course, places strains on the marriage.

We can understand the matrimonial union better by recalling that a human being, at birth, is probably the most helpless of creatures. A newborn baby, left to fend for itself, would soon perish. Thus, there would be no continuation of the species without some special arrangement to care for the young. The mother, being typically less powerful than the male, is not fully equipped to protect the infant from all forms of dangers.

Marriage also channels the inheritance of possessions. Even primitive societies have acknowledged private ownership of certain economic goods such as horses, axes, and construction tools. These were either passed from fathers to sons or inherited within the broader kinship group.

Divorce

I Do, I Do, For Now! is the title of a recent play. Marriage is ostensibly for life, but it is often otherwise. Divorce is the legal dissolution of a marriage in some way other than through the death of one or both of the spouses, so that both parties are legally free to remarry after some specified length of time. They may be barred from remarriage in some other way, of course, such as religious beliefs. Divorce is not to be confused with annulment, which is a legal declaration that there was no valid marriage.

From the rise of Christianity until the eighteenth century, a divorce *a vinculo matrimonii* (permitting remarriage) was generally not obtainable. One could sometimes get a divorce *a mensa et thoro* (separation from board and bed), which permitted no remarriage. Complete divorce has become increasingly common in the nineteenth and twentieth centuries.

Marriage and divorce laws are left to the states by the Constitution of the United States. The acceptable grounds for divorce have always varied from one state to another, ranging from incompatibility (which can easily be alleged) to no grounds at all. There is a slow movement toward uniformity. Like marriage, the undoing of a marriage affects people beyond the husband and wife. Nevada, with its law permitting divorce after a six-week residency, has been viewed critically by many people who feel that the norms should be about the same everywhere. Should the termination of a marriage be easier for those who can afford a trip to Nevada? Occasional efforts have been made by other states not to recognize Nevada decrees, but the U.S. Supreme Court has upheld their validity in view of the "full faith and credit" clause, Article Four, of the Constitution.

The ratio of divorces to the population in the United States has risen steadily and, in recent times, swiftly. In 1867 the rate was .3 divorces per 1,000 population. In 1946 it was 4.3 per 1,000 population. Today approximately one marriage in two is destined to fail unless the trend reverses itself. About half of divorced couples have children. The rising number of marital failures has brought about an increased realization of the importance of training engaged couples in the responsibilities of married life. Counseling services have also been set up in connection with divorce courts. A study of couples who received counseling in one year in Los Angeles County showed that half of them became reconciled.

Family disorganization can come about, of course, in other ways, some of which we shall look at later: the death of one or both parents, desertion, or a kind of demoralization and abandonment of responsibilities within the home. It should be recognized, too, that the factors that destroy a marriage are often not those cited in a court to satisfy the law. The real reasons often do not become known because they are so personal and intimate that people prefer not to reveal them. Sometimes, too, the parties do not really understand why a marriage has "gone sour." "A slow leak" was the explanation offered by a friend of the writer. Family life is no longer as unified as it once was. Women with careers may feel less inclined to make the sacrifices necessary to keep a marriage going in some cases. The rise of an attitude of individualism, "do your thing," is clearly not conducive to the kind of forbearance a marital union may need. The decreasing influence of religion has also been a factor.

The causes mentioned so far are social. There are also basic psychological causes. A husband and wife may simply be unsuited to each other sexually, intellectually, or in other ways. Their interests may be so different that, after the bloom is off the romance, they no longer find much pleasure and companionship in one another's company. There may be quarrels over money. The two families from which they come may not get along. It is significant that every comedian has a supply of mother-in-law jokes.

Divorce is often talked about as a cause of family disintegration. *It is a result of family disintegration, not a cause*. The problem, to put it another way, is not to keep people from getting divorces, but to keep people from *wanting* divorces. To make divorce (even in the sense of separation of board and bed) impossible is to lock the barn door after the horse has been stolen.

"A Scrap of Paper"

With this background, we can see why the marriage contract has become, in many people's eyes, "a scrap of paper." In a popular song, a man tells a woman that she is "gentle on my mind" because he can pack up and leave any time he feels like it without further complications. Somehow, the song makes this attitude seem to be a virtue. "Without a marriage certificate, what's missing," young people ask, "so long as a man and a woman care about each other?" What is missing, of course—aside from religious sanctions—is commitment: a pledge and intention of staying with each other, facing life's problems together, and looking to each other's needs. It has become increasingly plain, to be sure, that this commitment is often missing even when a couple promise before a clergyman or civil official to love, honor, and cherish one another "till death do us part." A prominent actress, two decades ago, told reporters in an interview about her forthcoming nuptials, "When a girl is getting married for the fifth time, she thinks very carefully." An observer commented, "The first four times, of course, she lets the chips fall where they may."

We should not suppose that all of those who have a de facto marital relationship without being legally married have unworthy reasons. Some people are not legally free to marry, but consider themselves morally free. Some do not wish to reduce the amount of Social Security payments they receive. Some are just being fashionable. Some sincerely question the merits of a lifetime commitment. Some see marriage as irrelevant unless there are children.

In light of the varied forms of marriage in different times and places, we can recognize that those who think they are overthrowing the institution are more nearly redefining it. Of late, courts are being asked to provide the equivalent of alimony in some such cases, even though the former partners were never legally or religiously spouses.

Forging an Attitude

Whether directly involved or not, anyone nowadays needs to forge a set of internally consistent attitudes on this whole subject. What do I believe about marriage? Do my beliefs on this subject match my other beliefs? On what grounds do I hold them? Are my convictions about marriage (and alternatives to it) chiefly the product of reason? Of faith? Of emotion? Of prejudice? Having asked and answered these questions, do I want to modify my beliefs?

There is also the issue of whether one's views on the matter should be used to judge others. A brief consideration of abortion may make this clearer as a comparison. Some people believe that direct abortion (any deliberate destruction of the product of human conception) is murder. Even murder has its complications. It is generally held that the State has the right to take the life of a condemned criminal when this is necessary for just purposes. Soldiers are told that it is moral to kill the enemy. Killing in self-defense is usually held to be acceptable. Nevertheless, we all understand what murder is: unlawfully killing another person with malice aforethought. No one—no ordinary citizen and no legislator—says, "*I* don't believe in murder, but it's OK for my neighbor to kill people if he wants to, because his beliefs may be different from mine. It's certainly not something the *government* should be nosing into." We expect the government to treat murder as a capital crime. If abortion is murder, why do we not apply to it the same expectation?

The answer, of course, is that some people do *not* think abortion is murder. The disagreement essentially reduces to a question of when human life begins. There has been testimony by biologists that there is evidence of animate processes in an organism from the moment of conception. That does not really answer the question, though: when does a fetus become a human being? This is not a question to be resolved by observations or experiments. It is a theological or philosophical problem. Regardless of what position is taken, there are likely to be gray areas, difficult situations to resolve. There is the difference, for example, between induced abortion and the passively permitted evacuation of a fetus before it is able to survive outside the womb. This latter may be a side effect of a legitimate medical procedure. Again, the distinction between abortion and stillbirth has not always been agreed upon. Medical ethics and the law in most countries permit induced abortion when the mother's life, health, or reason is in danger from continuation of the pregnancy. No clear philosophical position seems to be involved in the decisions of the U.S. Supreme Court about the circumstances in which direct abortion is permissible. If one believes that a fetus becomes human at the instant of the implanting of a spiritual soul, a new controversy arises: when does *that* happen?

If the topic were murder, considered as such, the writer would have no hesitancy in telling you that he is "against it" and that he believes the penalty should be severe. Yet he sees abortion as murder, but only with some trepidation can he bring himself to tell you that, and he is not sure what the penalties ought to be for physicians who perform abortions. Is this a philosophical inconsistency, or a wise recognition of a legitimate distinction?

Similarly, with attitudes toward sexual matters, marriage, and divorce, one must ask: Should others be bound by my beliefs? Should I be bound by theirs? Many a mother and father with conservative beliefs and practices in this area have found themselves dealing with sons and daughters of liberated persuasion. The language is having an equally hard time in adjusting. We read such coy expressions as "live-in boyfriend" and "close companion." One columnist had heard "um . . . er" used so often in this context that she suggested that it become an accepted designation. It is less than clear why we no longer use such terms as "mistress," "kept woman," "paramour," and "concubine."

The point finally at issue here is whether morality is an objective thing, the same for all persons in all times and places, or something for each individual to decide. In any case, it is one thing to develop a philosophical position and quite another to deal with the emotions and mental sets conditioned by our upbringing, our expereince, and our culture.

"Adjusting"

In looking at each of the areas of changing values, we shall talk about coping with the changes. To cope, as has been noted, is to get along adequately while dealing with problems. Two special modes of coping will be examined in each case: adjusting to conditions and combatting them.

What, then, is it to adjust? It is to adapt oneself to realities in such a way that a balance is achieved and maintained between one's own needs and social demands. During certain phases of life—adolescence is perhaps the case par excellence—this process is especially active and difficult. Nevertheless, it is never finished until death. Each new day brings changes in the world, demanding some degree of change in oneself. Whether adjustment and mental health are interchangeable is a debatable point. Certainly, there is a difference between adjustment and conformity. To conform is to "give in," to behave and think as others around us are doing. To adjust is, again, to satisfy both society and oneself, or to come close enough to doing so that one is acceptable both to self and to others.

A simple situation will illustrate what is involved in adjustment. A girl is thirsty. This means two things. It means, objectively, that she is deficient in water. Subjectively, it means that she has a desire to drink some water. (It could mean the latter without the former. A hypnotized person can be made thirsty by suggestion, for example.) If a faucet and a glass are handy, if the glass is clean and the drinking water is sanitary, and if the girl has normal use of her hands, there is no problem. She fills the glass with water and drinks it. Suppose, however, that the girl's arms are in a sling, or that she is blind, or that no clean glasses are at hand, or that the faucet is broken, or that the plumber has temporarily shut off the water supply, or that the city's reservoir has been contaminated. Habit then ceases to rise to the occasion. The girl must find an unusual way to meet her need. She must adjust.

Life is like that. We have drives, needs, goals. The world sometimes makes it easy to satisfy them, but sometimes it sets up blocks and frustrations. The choice then becomes: adjust or go without. Occasionally, the choice is: adjust or die. Indeed, biological death can be appropriately regarded as the final inability of the organism to cope with all of the demands upon it. Besides such internal drives as hunger, thirst, and sex, we all have social drives for self-esteem, security, love, independence, acceptance, and at least a touch of adventure and variety.

Suppose that you are a college student, Jane, who has been sharing an apartment with another student, Stanley. The two of you care about each other, but you have no specific plans for marriage. It is something you want to decide about later. Meantime, you have been invited home for Thanksgiving weekend. You want to bring Stanley with you. You take it for granted that you and Stanley will sleep in the same bed, because that is what you do regularly and your parents are aware of it. They have expressed their disapproval vaguely, but they have left the impression that they regard this as properly your choice.

You telephone home and announce that you would like to bring Stanley with you. Mom says "Fine!" You both arrive. Dad says, "I'll take care of your luggage. Stanley can use the guest room." You resent this as hypocrisy. Your parents know that you and Stanley are lovers. Why go through a pretense of denying what everybody concerned knows to be a fact? Furthermore, you *want* to sleep with Stanley. It seems that making love in your own home would add something sacred to the relationship. Your parents, however, understand none of this.

"Stan and I thought we'd both use my room," you say tentatively.

Mom wrings her hands nervously and comments, "That doesn't seem quite right. Would you mind using separate bedrooms while you're here?"

Stan, conscious of his status as a guest, says that he wouldn't mind. "*I* would mind," you add. "Look, Mom, you know perfectly well that Stan and I sleep together every night of our lives. Why should it be different here?"

There are various answers that Mom could give. She might say, "Look, Jane, your father and I like Stanley, but you know we don't believe in this sort of thing. What you do someplace else is your business, but you shouldn't ask us to condone this kind of arrangement in our own home." If you protest that you are not asking that the arrangement be condoned, merely that it exist, Mom or Dad could reply reasonably enough that they feel answerable for what happens under their own roof.

What, Jane, is it reasonable for you to say and do? You could say, "I love Stanley. If he isn't welcome to stay here and share my room, we'll both go right back to where we came from." This creates a dilemma for your parents. They must either back down, lose face, and put up with a situation they actively resent, or incur the lasting wrath of the daughter they love very much. Even if they agree to you and Stanley sharing a room, the visit is likely to be a tense one.

You could say, "Well, Mom, I can't understand your attitude. You've continued to write to me, send me money, love me, knowing about Stan and me. Now you want to play a game that what you know is true isn't true. Nevertheless, it's your house, and I don't want to embarrass you or Dad or to put you in the position of seeming to approve what you don't approve. Stan and I will use separate rooms. It's not that big a deal."

Your parents would have done well, of course, to have an understanding with you on this point before you and Stanley arrived. You would have done well, also, to seek such an understanding. Since nobody did, however, there is a direct clash of motives. Something and somebody must give. Try to understand that parents are usually not stark realists about their children. They like to believe the best (as they define the best) that the facts allow, and perhaps even a little better. You must decide how far and in what circumstances to humor this tendency.

Try to be conscious of your motives in the situation, too. Perhaps you are testing your parents, seeing how unconditional is their love for you. Sometimes we want other people to set limits for us, even if we would never admit it.

Suppose you are a girl who is "propositioned" and who wants to be a virgin on her wedding day. Suppose you are a young man who would like to observe chastity but feel that girls expect and desire sexual activity nowadays. One question to ask oneself in all of the kinds of situations discussed in this book is: Am I reacting too much by habit and association? We often find ourselves reacting in a certain way for no better reason than that this is how we learned to react as small children. Suppose that your girlfriend considers it more important to get the birthday gift she wants, chosen by herself so everything about it will be just right. You may be intellectually convinced that there is nothing wrong with this. Yet if birthday gifts were always surprises when you were a child, you may find it hard to make the change. A Catholic who has spent a good part of his life abstaining from meat on Fridays may have the reaction voiced by one man when this requirement was rescinded: "If the Pope wants to go to hell, let him!" We have to ask ourselves in tight situations: Is it reason or habit talking?

Try this: On a large sheet of tablet paper, make four headings: What do I want in this situation? Why do I want it? Considering why I want it, do I still want it? If so, what is the best way to get it? The writer has often found this a useful way to clear his head. It calls for more honesty with oneself than we sometimes indulge. One may say, for instance, "I want the good of the operation," when that answer ought to be augmented by another: "I want to take one or two of my colleagues down a peg." The second part calls for the psychological scalpel to go even deeper: Why do I want these things? Don't manufacture shoddy motives, but don't deny them if they are there either. You may find that you have some good reasons and some not-so-good ones. Then comes an important step: Now that I have taken a harder look at the situation and at myself in it, should my goals be modified? Is there a way to pursue the worthy motives and abandon the unworthy ones? When you have done all of this, the goal should be out there in front of you, in reasonably plain sight. The question then becomes: How best can I get from here to there? We often behave with self-defeating indirection. Any fan of the soap operas must occasionally have such reactions as: "If you love her, why don't you tell her you love her?" "If you're being blackmailed, why don't you refuse to pay the blackmailer and prepare to pay the price?" "If you think your wife is being unfaithful to you, why don't you ask her?"

Sometimes, of course, we may find that, at bottom, we want something for no apparent good reason but are unable to stop wanting it. Someonc may crave fame and recognition, knowing full well that it is an empty bubble but unable finally to give it up as a goal. If a goal survives in the face of every attempt to reason it away, one must deal with it somehow. Consider so simple a matter as playing solitaire. Why do you care whether you win or not? Nobody else will know. There are no prizes for winning, no penalties for losing. The outcome, moreover, depends much more on the shuffling of the cards than on skill. A confirmed solitaire player, nevertheless, usually keeps at it until he wins. When this finally happens, he regards that happy outcome as simple justice. The other cases were the bludgeonings of chance. Poor logic! Suppose, though, that you are fully convinced of the insignificance of winning or losing at solitaire but find that you still want very much to win. Avoid the game or play until victory comes!

When we know what our convictions are—when we have asked such questions as "Am I reacting more from habit than from reason?" and still our attitude is the same—then there can surely be no happiness in compromise. The girl who is propositioned (or perhaps simply finds an attempted seduction in progress without benefit of prior discussion), if she does not want this, must avoid it. Usually, this can be done tactfully. One can quietly disengage, jump up and ask one's boyfriend if he would like a cup of coffee, or simply say something like, "We'd better ease up. I'm getting carried away." The boyfriend will then feel flattered about his desirability instead of simply frustrated in his designs. Tact will not always do the job, of course, but it should be attempted.

What of the young man who prefers not to act as Don Juan but feels it is expected of him? He needn't raise the issue unless the woman with him does. Since men are customarily expected to be the pursuers, he has an advantage. He can simply not pursue. Men and women both need to realize, of course, that the time to stop making love is before it starts. The flesh has its own logic, which becomes less resistible as things move along.

Adjustment to divorce is a very big thing. The amicable divorces that one hears about are probably very few. Typically, there is bitterness on both sides, a tendency to blame one's partner for the marriage's going bad, an unwillingness to admit that there was fault on both sides. There is also the feeling of having failed. There are the numerous practicalities of daily life in which one has learned to rely on a husband or wife. There is the difficulty of socializing with people who were friends of both. There is the disposition to want one's friends to take sides.

If your parents are getting divorced or have recently done so, they may well be so caught up in adjustment problems that they are not as able as they might be to help you make your own adjustments to the situation. Psychotherapists often find that young children blame themselves for the separation. "There must be something wrong with me or they would have stayed together," goes the reasoning. These guilt feelings can continue to plague you long after you have ceased being conscious of them. It is hard to realize, sometimes, that many unfortunate events are not anybody's fault. It would be possible, at the other extreme, to use the divorce of one's parents as a psychological crutch, a convenient rationalization whenever things are going poorly.

You might find it necessary and helpful to say to Mom or Dad, "Look: I love both of you. I respect both of you. I'm very sorry that this has happened. You don't need to doubt my feelings about you, but please don't make things harder for me by saying nothing but negative things about my other parent." You may have to do the same thing with friends and relatives of your parents. Make it clear that this is a situation in which you do not wish to take sides.

Fighting the Culture

Only a relative handful of persons ever contribute anything to the mores and folkways of their societies. This is not necessarily because one has nothing valuable to contribute. It is likelier to be because society does not want anything contributed. Social customs and attitudes usually change slowly and in response to a whole complex of forces. Rarely does an individual sway the mass in such matters. When someone does, it is probably because the time was ripe for it and an articulate spokesman came along.

If, then, you decide that on a particular matter your goal is not to "adjust" but to resist, not to follow the mores but to change them, you must recognize at the outset that you are swimming upstream against a very strong current. Even if you persuade no one, nevertheless you will have the satisfaction of knowing that you did what you believed was right. Few things in life can bring such peace of soul. If you persist, moreover, you are likely to have a few imitators. Suppose that, in the area where you live or work, people have gotten in the habit of ignoring the traffic lights, with the result that neither drivers nor pedestrians can proceed properly, and there is some danger to the latter. You can ignore the traffic light as those around you are doing, or you can follow its directives. If you obey the light, you will probably find one or two other persons around you each time who decide to do as you are doing. Most of us are much braver when someone in the immediate vicinity is setting an example.

Sociologists sometimes describe people as belonging to one of three types in their attitudes toward change and conformity: inner-directed, outer-directed, and tradition-directed. The inner-directed person behaves according to what his conscience tells him and is not particularly uncomfortable if that is out of harmony with what those around him are doing. The outer-directed person follows the crowd. Observation quickly makes clear how many people are of this sort; most people seem to be very uneasy if they are not conforming to what people around them are doing. The tradition-directed person, of course, does what people have generally done in the past. If you are an inner-directed sort of person, you will find it relatively easy to fight the society you live in when you disagree with its directions. If you are outer-directed, you may pay a price in conflicts between what you do and what you feel you ought to be doing. If you are tradition-directed, you may easily fail to perceive changes in conditions, the new occasions that teach new duties.

For Further Reading

Achtenmeier, *The Committed Marriage* (Philadelphia: Westminster Press, 1976), p. 224.

Belgum, David R., *Why Marry? Since You Don't Need a*

License to Love (Minneapolis: Augsburg Publishing House, 1972), p. 95.

Carin, James, *Mating, Marriage, and the Status of Women* (New York: A.M.S. Press, 1976), p. 181.

Kohut, Nester C., *A Manual on Marital Reconciliations; a Socio-Legal Analysis of Divorce for the Unbroken Marriage* (Chicago: Adams Press, 1964), p. 100.

Mason, Pamela, *Marriage Is the First Step Towards Divorce* (New York: P. S. Eriksson, 1968), p. 184.

Chapter **III**

Changes at Home: The Family

In looking at marriage, we saw the difference between the nuclear and the extended family. Some form of family is found in every society, despite such differences. The institution was already established when recorded history began. A family is a group of persons related by blood or marriage, usually living under one roof. A household is not necessarily the same thing. A group of students living in a commune, for example, form a household. At the heart of the family as an institution is the parent-child relationship.

When one considers all the perils that beset the duration and functioning of any particular family, it is perhaps surprising that the institution has been as stable and universal as it has been. That stability derives in part from flexibility. Familial patterns in a given society at a given time tend to adapt to the needs of that time and place. As with marriage, therefore, changes that seem to be weakening the institution can be regarded from a broader perspective as keeping it alive.

The general trend of many modern developments—the decreasing difference between jobs available to men and to women, for example—has been toward making the individual members of a family less dependent upon it. This trend, of course, makes it harder to maintain the stability of the family.

A large part of what a society tends to regard as moral is devoted to keeping familial patterns intact. To look at it another way, when we talk of Utopia, of peace on earth and good will among men, we are talking of extending the characteristics of a family to all of mankind. (Considering the tensions and violence that crop up within families occasionally, perhaps mankind has already accomplished that!)

Practically speaking, adulthood has been reached when one is no longer directly and strongly dependent upon the family. Much of the storminess of adolescence derives from the healthy if sometimes clumsy efforts of the teen-ager to reach out toward such independence. One does not, after all, grow up in a single day. The period of courtship and marriage often overlaps this reaching for independence or can be regarded as part of it.

"In my very own self," wrote D. H. Lawrence in *Apocalypse*, "I am part of my family." The tension between this attitude and individualism accounts for some of the strains of family living. The stress has been increasingly upon individual freedom. Even among those who stress social over individual values, there have been some who have maintained that there are better ways to achieve them. In Plato's ideal society (written about but not attempted), children would be taken from their parents at birth and raised by the State. The Chinese Communists tried something of the sort, raising children in communes. The experiment did not work and was abandoned. The Chinese government still tries to decrease the role of parents and increase that of the State in raising children. Where privacy of the home is regarded as sacred in the West, it may be seen in Communist countries as a potential conspiracy against the State.

Our family backgrounds are major factors in making us

who we are psychologically. Our interests and attitudes almost invariably reflect those of our parents, either because we copy them or because we rebel against them. One also gets or fails to get a sense of security in the family circle. Even the family name helps to confer a sense of identity. Today, many people such as actors and actresses change their names for business reasons. John Sullivan became Fred Allen; Isadore Iskowitz became Eddie Cantor. Sometimes, no last name is used, as with Ann-Margret and Cher. Lucille Lesueur became Joan Crawford; Jack Kubelsky became Jack Benny; Frances Gumm became Judy Garland. Sometimes the children of those who have changed their last names revert to the previous family name to get a stronger sense of roots.

The home has lost much of its former role as the central social unit. The Sunday afternoon "musical," for instance, is unknown to the present generation. Time was when the villages in which most families lived were small. There were few houses other than those occupied by families. The home thus tended to become the center of social and recreational activities. Community undertakings such as holiday ceremonials might occasionally compete with the home, but participation in them was largely on a familial basis.

As villages gave way to cities, a new situation developed. There was no particular identification with "the land," no special expectation of living all of one's life in a single place. There was a specialization of labor, but largely on an individual basis. Industrialization made further changes. More space and workers were needed than could be found in the household. Production began to take place in factories instead of in homes. About the only economic functions remaining in the home are cooking, housekeeping, and maintenance, and even portions of these functions are often given up to outside sources. Not many women bake their own bread any more, and you would look hard to find someone who still makes soap for the family. Fast-food establishments often relieve Mom of cooking lunch or dinner. Clothes are sometimes sent to the laundry or laundromat. Socks may be thrown away as an alternative to darning them. These changes probably have more to do with the family size than is generally realized. Relatives and children (including married children) are no longer needed to carry out the economic functions of the household. The development of contraceptive methods and the widespread acceptance of them have also contributed to decreasing the size of the family.

Some other traditional functions of the family have likewise been gradually assumed by other agencies. Education is mostly left to the schools. Religious formation is mostly left to the churches. Community recreation centers help to keep youth amused and diverted. Policemen protect them, not parents. The home should cooperate in all these matters, of course. In practice, however, its role is usually minimal. What is left? Is there anything that can be done better in the family than anywhere else? Yes: loving. The vital need for love is seldom met as well anywhere else. Even Lady Macbeth spoke of "How tender 'tis to love the babe that milks me." Thomas Jefferson's comment is well known: "The happiest moments of my life have been the few which I have passed at home in the bosom of my family." Parental love and acceptance acquire increased importance for children who are uprooted every few years. The average family in a very large city moves about every two years. Children must then adjust to new schools and find new friends. If both parents are working and not much disposed to sympathize with their children's problems in such free time as they have, the situation can be serious.

Desertion is a major cause of family disorganization. It is sometimes called "the poor man's divorce." Many children grow up not knowing who their fathers are and without any kind of paternal influence. The relationship of divorce to number of children in the family is the opposite of that of desertion. Divorce is less likely to occur in families with children than between childless couples. Desertions, by contrast, are more common where there are children than where there are not. Desertion is largely an urban phenomenon. Few desertions are reported in rural areas.

Family disorganization can also occur when parents' attempts to retain a way of living are counteracted by outside influences. First- or second-generation immigrants often cluster in one part of a city. They keep the cultural patterns of their forebears, sometimes because they want to, sometimes because they have little occasion to learn other ways. Then little Lucy and Fred come home from school having learned different ways of speaking, thinking, dressing, eating, playing. The youngsters may be ridiculed at school for their alien ways. If they try to change to become accepted at school, they find themselves less accepted at home. Fortunately, recent years have seen a trend toward respecting divergent cultural patterns and recognizing that no one of them has better claim than any other to represent "the American way of life."

Another force that can work toward family disorganization is the two-career family. The typical pattern until recent years was this: The man spent part of his youth preparing for a vocation. Then he started working at it. For quite a few years, he concentrated on rising in his work—climbing the corporate ladder, or whatever. Then his yearnings turned toward retirement. Often he had to retire to discover that what he really liked best was being on the job. Meanwhile, the woman who had married him had grown up assuming that her role would be that of homemaker. If she took paid employment, that was understood to be transient, perhaps to help in a financial pinch, perhaps to get a bit of occasional variety.

All of that is, of course, quickly changing. In part, this is happening because of economic pressures. Two incomes are often needed nowadays to keep a modest amount of money in the bank. Another factor is that women tend to find the provinces of wife and mother insufficiently fulfilling. "The pill," an oral contraceptive, also made it easier for women to determine how many children they would have. People are also becoming more responsive to problems of overpopulation. Zero population growth is regarded by many as a worthwhile social goal. Sociologists' predictions of a few years ago on population trends are not panning out because people are having fewer children.

Adjusting

Family functions and relationships in the two-career situation are bound to be somewhat different than when Dad was facing the "jungle out there" and Mom was at home baking bread and fighting "ring around the collar." Slightly over half of contemporary American households involve two-career families. Sometimes both husband and wife are highly trained professionals. Sometimes one is, sometimes neither. Sometimes the wife enters the labor force while her husband, disenchanted with his career, tries to work into something else. In some cases, the husband fails to recognize or will not accept that he needs to make some adjustments after his wife goes to work. She may not like putting in a busy day on the job, then coming home to all of the chores and responsibilities that she had before she was "working." The husband may feel that, since his wife went to work, much of the interest she used to take in him and in their children has been switched to her career.

Curiously, even though the majority of families now involve two-career patterns, institutions and folkways are still mostly attuned to the former pattern. A school may schedule an activity involving parents for the afternoon, figuring that the mothers will be able to come. The furnace repairman may tell you that he can come at 10 a.m. on Thursday, figuring that the housewife will, of course, be home. Perhaps Dad still wants to read the evening paper at 5 p.m. and to sit down to dinner at 6. He may also resent giving certain kinds of help, not because he is averse to work, but because he feels it is unmasculine to take out the garbage, vacuum the rugs, iron a shirt, or clear the dinner table.

"Housekeeping"—caring for property, managing it, equipping it—is a complex business. Yet it often goes forward with little conscious thought. It comes to be understood that Mother will do this, Father will do that, Sister will do the other. If Mother takes a job, some new understandings may be needed about who will do what at home. Different assumptions may be held, too, about what constitutes a neat, organized, adequately functioning household. Perhaps Father doesn't care how the clothes are arranged in the closet, but he can't stand seeing the daily newspaper in disarray. With Mother, it may be the other way around. Hurt feelings or chronic irritation can easily result if these things are never talked about—or, for that matter, if they are talked about in a carping, negative, nagging way. There is no set of rules laid down in heaven for housekeeping. Every family must devise a system that works and satisfies everybody. While it is widely believed that working couples divide the domestic chores about equally, survey evidence indicates that this is not done in most two-career families. In most cases, women still do the bulk of the housework. When there is a division of labor, it is usually along traditional lines: women wash the dishes, cook, sew, clean, and take care of the children, while men do heavy work such as moving furniture and take care of the yard and the car. Men often recognize the need to do more around the house, but they say they "feel silly" doing dishes or vacuuming the rugs. Various appliances, of course, have made some of these tasks easier than they used to be.

Sometimes, a woman who has taken a job is not satisfied with the results of her husband's housekeeping efforts, even if he is perfectly willing to make them. Dad may sweep the dirt under the rug, figuring that is the whole point of having rugs. He may leave the clean dishes on the sinkboard on the grounds that, after all, they'll be needed again to set the table in a few hours. Thus, Mom may continue to do some things by choice while Dad watches television or reads the paper. Here again is something that should be talked about.

Most married women formerly felt that, if they were to take employment, it should be after the youngest child was old enough to get along by himself during the day. That attitude is now much less widespread. Women sometimes take maternity leave, then go back to the job within a few days after the birth of the baby. Others decide not to have children because they want to devote most of their time and attention to their career.

You, as a young person, may not understand the confusion over the changing sex roles that your parents experience. If Mom is employed, it may seem to you at times that Dad is rather inconsiderate of her rights and needs, and you may be right. Just remember that he does not deliberately set out to be. He just never got around to forming new habits. Remember, too, that Mom is not being unreasonable when she asks you to carry your part of the housekeeping load. If Dad should not be let off the hook, neither should you!

Because of today's two-career situation in most families, you may have grown up receiving less time and attention from your parents than children need and are entitled to. Time is not the only problem. It may be difficult for your father, for instance, when he gets home from the office, to switch his mind from the thousand details of his job to the fact that you need a new gown for the senior prom or to listen to your ideas about the world in general. In his mind, he is "out there" every day working partly for you, so you should be slow to draw conclusions from his hasty retreat into the newspaper when he gets home. It might help to give Mom and Dad some advance notice when you want to talk about something that is important to you: "Dad, I know you're tired and busy, but could we talk for about half an hour later this evening? I need your help with something." Chances are, Dad will be at pains to make himself available.

If your parents are or have been on the brink of separation, they have been going through a tense period of difficult decisions: whether to separate, whether to get a divorce, how to break the news to you, what attitude to take about child-support money, who should have custody of the children, and so forth.

You may feel that your task in the situation is to help the two of them to stay together. You may feel, on the other hand, that their relationship is so bad that your influence should be exercised toward encouraging a separation. Both attitudes are very questionable. After all, the marriage existed before you did. The causes of the friction are almost certainly complex and deep. If you have a pronounced and well-advertised viewpoint on the subject, this may simply make it more difficult for Mom and Dad to look at the matter objectively. Besides, your viewpoint may be wrong. We are dealing mainly with feelings here, and "the heart has reasons of its own, which the reason does not understand." The best thing that you can do, probably, is to be supportive of both of your parents during this tense period. Listen to them, show them that you care, help them (if they seek such help) to sort out their own feelings. Reassure them that you want them to do whatever their own consciences lead them to do. That may be a very difficult role for you to play, given your own emotional investment in the matter, but it will be the most useful role in the long run for all concerned, including yourself.

This does not mean that you are not entitled to be part of the family dialogue if a separation is being contemplated—or, for that matter, a reconciliation. Some things will be for Mom and Dad in private, of course, but not everything. Don't give them advice, but don't hesitate to remind them, if necessary, that you want to know what is going on.

If your parents are divorcing, you may have some fears associated with the uncertainties about what lies ahead for them and for you. Remember that they share these uncertainties. In most cases, they haven't been through it before, either. Again, don't start believing that what has happened must somehow be your fault. At the same time, don't hesitate to tell Mom that you don't like to hear it portrayed as all Dad's fault, or vice versa.

The need to blame someone in such situations seems almost ingrained in human nature. Nevertheless, legislation may have abetted it in the past. Divorce laws typically demanded that one party be the accuser and the other, the accused. To be the accused was, of course, to be at fault.

The no-fault divorce laws that are being increasingly adopted by the states may ease this pressure by recognizing that divorce is not solely due to the deficiencies of one person.

Preserving Family Life

Many people believe, on religious or other grounds, that marriage is dissolved only by death and that those whose marriages are experiencing turmoil should solve the difficulties in some other way than by separating.

Some marriages appear beyond salvaging. Love, alas, cannot be turned on or off like a faucet. If love has been replaced by indifference or by hatred, and if efforts to recapture the former feelings get nowhere, there seems to be little gain in continuing to live together. This is sometimes done "for the sake of the children," but in cases where husband and wife simply cannot get along peacefully, it is problematical whether the children gain by their staying together. The Catholic Church, as strong an advocate of the sanctity of marriage as remains in today's world, recognizes that separation is sometimes the only answer.

Many husbands and wives who could profit from marital counseling avoid it because they were raised to believe that someone who cannot solve his own problems is seriously deficient. Perhaps they do not understand what kinds of psychotherapists are available (psychologists, psychiatrists, counselors, and so on), what training each has, and what each does. If your own efforts to function as a neutral sounding board have failed, it might be a valuable service for you to encourage your parents to seek psychotherapy. Not all of the psychotherapist's success traces to his training and expertise. Much of it can be credited to the fact that he does not have the previously existing emotional involvements that a member of the family has.

Positive and negative feelings toward someone can prove to be two sides of one coin. Much mischief has been worked by the adolescent notion that marriage should be or can be a permanent honeymoon. Conditions change and people change. Once past the stage of being "in love," we begin to see the loved one as the individual human being that he/she is. In the first stages of infatuation, one is usually blind to this. Other people note physical or psychological resemblances to Cousin Bill or Aunt Clara, but these strike us as ridiculous. The loved one is the sun, moon, and stars. Comparisons are pointless. This curious delusion doubtless has its function in nature's scheme. Fortunately, it seldom lasts long. In the movie *The Best Years of Our Lives,* a young woman with marital troubles upbraids her father when he gives advice, saying that it's easy for him to talk, since he and her mother have always been like sweethearts. Father assures daughter that he and her mother have had to fall in love with each other at least six times.

Few things in life can approach the beauty and satisfaction of a marriage that has endured through the better part of a lifetime with peace and love prevailing most of the time. It must be worked at, however. Many of those who declare themselves "not cut out to stay with one person" probably have not given much effort to the project.

For Further Reading

Leslie, Gerald R., *The Family in Social Context,* 3d ed. (New York: Oxford University Press, 1976), pp. viii, 815.

Minuchin, Salvador, *Families and Family Therapy* (Cambridge, Mass.: Harvard University Press, 1974), pp. viii, 268.

Rapoport, Rhona *et al.*, *Fathers, Mothers, and Society: Towards New Alliances* (New York: Basic Books, 1977), pp. viii, 421.

Rodgers, Roy H., *Family Interaction and Transaction: the Developmental Approach* (Englewood Cliffs, N.J.: Prentice-Hall, 1973), pp. xiii, 273.

Scanzoni, John H., *Sex Roles, Women's Work, and Marital Conflict* (Lexington, Mass.: Lexington Books, 1978), pp. xiii, 175.

Chapter IV

What Happened to Education?

Vignette Number One: A young man has completed his teacher-training except for practice teaching. He has been assigned to a high school where about a third of the students are absent on any given day, no serious attempt is made to enforce the laws on school attendance, vandals who may or may not be students at the school roam the halls seeking to make mischief, few students seriously attempt to learn, and most of the teachers have stopped trying to do more than maintain order. The odor of marijuana is always in the air. The student has a good academic record. "I didn't spend four years preparing to be a guard," he tells an administrator at his university. "Please assign me to a school where some learning is going on." The administrator reflects that, regardless of where the young man does his practice teaching, he may later find himself faced with a choice: to teach at a school such as this one or to earn his living otherwise than by teaching.

Vignette Number Two: A middle-aged professor sits in a faculty dining room, talking with a small group of colleagues. His face has the glazed appearance it acquires whenever he thinks about current conditions. "I can't understand it," he says. "This boy actually said that Hitler was the ruler of Russia. How did he get admitted to the university?" One or two of those present share his outrage. The others, inured to the situation, are disposed to treat it as a joke. One of them, a philosopher, challenges: "Prove to me that Hitler was *not* the ruler of Russia. Whatever your argument is, I'll demolish it." The others fall to telling with high glee about recent examples of blank minds exhibited by *their* students. The one who can produce the most outrageous example will be understood to be the winner of the game. The professor who lodged the complaint sits staring at nothing, immune to this levity. "I just can't understand it," he repeats to anyone who may be listening.

Something, certainly, has happened to education. It is, like all social trends, very hard to describe accurately. One cannot make valid categorical generalizations because many schools, many students, and many teachers are doing better than ever. Statistics can be cited, but they do not give the human flavor of what is going on. One can tell anecdotes, but their typicality can always be disputed. Here and there a relevant statistic does demand attention. For example, average scores on college entrance tests have been engaged in a slow, steady downward movement since the mid-1960's.

Educators are generally inclined to see this development as a decline in academic achievement. So it is, but it can also be viewed in another dimension: *education is not valued by most people as much as it used to be*. What produced the change? That is debatable. Some critics blame the philosophy of the late John Dewey. Dewey was a very influential educational theorist whose influence was at its peak in the 1930's and '40's. He was of the school of thought called Pragmatism, which holds that a true idea is one that "works." Most of us think a true idea is one that corresponds with some reality, but the Pragmatists did not believe that human beings are in a position to make statements about reality. In education, Dewey emphasized having a relevant curriculum, motivating students, and operating schools democratically. The Progressive Education movement hailed him as its major prophet, although Dewey did not approve of some of the things that happened in that movement. In practice, Deweyism tended to mean letting students determine the curriculum. That tendency certainly helped the learners to see the practical bearings of what they were being taught. On the other hand, some people felt it was akin to letting the inmates run the asylum. In any case, it is unlikely that most teachers perform as they do because of any abstract system of thought.

If we can point to any one factor with confidence, it is surely the counterculture. In the mid-1960's, for whatever reasons (the Vietnam War is usually cited as the major one), there developed a culture of the young with attitudes and mores that ran counter to those of the established order of society. There was a pattern to this counterculture. It rejected reason. Science, philosophy, theology, and logic were tossed out the window in one large heave. Love and mystical experience were offered as the chief substitutes. If everybody would just love everybody else, so the thinking ran, all problems would be solved. Love, unfortunately, will not program a computer or develop a vaccine against tuberculosis. It is begging the question, moreover, to prescribe universal love and good will among men, since nobody has ever found a way to produce this condition.

The counterculture also had strong overtones of reasserting the importance and rights of the individual. A polite prose piece of the time was the "Gestalt Prayer," which advocates, in effect, ignoring the needs of others. A magazine called *Self* became popular. A generation seemed to be saying, with Walt Whitman,

I celebrate myself and sing myself,
And what I assume you shall assume.
(*Song of Myself*)

This attitude was logically incompatible with the theme of universal love; but, to repeat, the movement was not strong on logic.

One important product of this situation was the conviction that an education is to be judged by the educat*ee,* not by the educat*or*. The claim had its merits. People learn best, apply best, and remember best when they are intrinsically motivated—when, that is, they value what is being learned for its own sake, not simply as a way to gain the rewards and avoid the punishments that a teacher is empowered to bestow. Skilled teachers have always understood the importance of trying to lead students to this kind of motivation. All of us, probably, can remember subjects that a teacher tried to sell us without explaining how, when, or why the material would relate to anything in our lives. Nevertheless, to suggest that the modestly educated know what is worth learning better than do the highly educated verges on self-contradiction.

A generation looked at its curriculum and pronounced it "irrelevant." It was the educational catchword of the decade. It meant, of course, that the studies being required of youth did not apply to their present and future needs as judged by themselves. Other factors were undoubtedly at work, but this mass rejection of the curriculum by its intended clientele was a major one. This premise of "customer control" was illustrated recently when a group of college students demanded that a course in astrology (for which no scientific support has ever been found) be offered for academic credit.

Revamped curricula were one harvest of all of this. Another was a drop in academic achievement. A third was a drift away from the liberal arts among college students, into vocational training. What, exactly, are these liberal arts? The name stems from the intent to devise a course of studies for free men. Plato had advanced the outline in *The Republic*. It became a reality in the Middle Ages as the basis for more specialized studies in law, medicine, and theology. The seven liberal arts were divided into the trivium (grammar, rhetoric, and logic) and the quadrivium (mathematics, geometry, astronomy, and music). "Grammar" included literature. There have been changes in the liberal arts pattern during the succeeding centuries, of course, and rightly so. Still, the essential idea has remained intact: a course of verbal and mathematical studies designed both to sharpen and deepen the intellect, a broad and deep preparation for living.

Notice: for *living,* not for *making* a living. Over the long haul, liberal arts graduates tend to be successful by conventional standards. Nevertheless, the studies leading to a BA degree do not usually prepare one to enter any specific profession. (A notable exception is that a liberal arts student can usually take teacher-training as an undergraduate.) Liberal arts colleges, both the independent ones and those within universities, have had to scramble in recent years to keep enough students. Typical of the criticisms of their offerings has been a book by Caroline Bird, *The Case Against College* (see chapter bibliography). Mrs. Bird looks at costs and concludes that college is "the dumbest investment you can make." Alternatives to college are considered: apprenticeships, trade schools, the armed forces, and others. The major thrust of the author's argument appears to be that a liberal education is not vocational training. Almost any educator would respond along the line of, "Of course not! But who ever said it was?"

Many "alternative" schools were established during the late 1960's and early '70's. Many books appeared that denounced conventional schools in strong terms. Jonathan Kozol, John Holt, James Herndon, and Paul Goodman were among the better-known authors. Books of this sort had a characteristic tone. Whatever it was, it was not moderation. To those who felt that drastic and swift reform was needed, such volumes may have struck exactly the right note. Many people felt, however, that these works were more polemical than analytical, that they were weak in defining, qualifying, demonstrating, and the other conventional usages of responsible scholarship. Most of the "free" or "alternative" schools have closed by now. Books of the Total Reform Now mood still appear, but less often, and they seem to attract less attention.

Organizations must surely produce ambivalence in every reflective person. On the one hand, it is no great trick to demonstrate stupidity, lethargy, and mindless bureaucracy at work in any school, hospital, library, university, business, factory, bank, or other human institution. Actions that were once appropriate means become ends, mindlessly pursued. It is very easy to say, "All of this must go immediately!" The trouble is that nobody has found a way to make organizations daily models of lucidity and high efficiency. Liberals and conservatives differ as to the reasons for this. The liberal thinks it is because the right approaches have not been found and tried yet. The conservative thinks it is because human nature is basically flawed. The radical is a liberal with a difference: he wants sweeping action *right now*. As has often been pointed out, he/she almost never offers even a vague suggestion about what ought to replace existing institutions. How the world looks does depend greatly upon where you sit. The writer has been a professor and an academic administrator. As a professor, he sometimes felt that "the administration" consisted of persons poorly acquainted with the problems of the faculty, less than wholly dedicated to the institutional goals proclaimed on ceremonial occasions, and preoccupied with secondary issues. As an administrator, he sometimes felt that some faculty members tended to have stunted perceptions of the operation as a whole, that it is mostly the sacrifices and hard work of administrators that keep a college going. There is a touch of truth in both viewpoints. Those who have not functioned as classroom teachers should be slow to criticize those who do. It is not easy to be creative and effective with a large group of students, six hours a day, five days a week. Teachers, on the other hand, should recognize their continuing obligation to improve or, failing that, at least not to deteriorate. The teacher does have the satisfaction of doing the one job without which the world would revert to barbarism in a generation.

Adjusting

Since one-person crusades seldom get far, teachers, students, and parents of students must do much adjusting to schools, colleges, seminaries, and universities as they are. Gifted students, for example, have special adjustments to make. If you are a student of exceptionally high measured intelligence, some intensity of drive, and a tendency to look for causes and relationships more than most people seem to, you have probably noticed that people react to this in various and sometimes strange ways. Some parents of a gifted child want to put him or her on display before the entire world. Others seem embarrassed and try to create the impression that their youngster is typical in every way. Still others become excessively anxious lest the educational system fail to develop fully the potentialities of their child. You can help in all such cases by encouraging your parents to take a more relaxed, matter-of-fact attitude toward your special abilities. (This, to be sure, may be very hard to do.)

A highly intelligent boy in a junior high school science class was asked to take his turn one day at going to the microscope, looking carefully, and describing what he saw. The teacher's point, of course, was to help the students to develop observational and descriptive skills. Only one thought was in the boy's head, however. He did not wish to do a better job than his classmates and thereby add to his reputation as being "different" and "a brain." Therefore, he gave a silly, smart-alecky description of what he saw through the microscope and started returning to his seat, smiling at the appreciative titters of a few boys and girls. "Just a minute," the teacher's baritone voice rang out. "Go back to the microscope." The frightened boy, not knowing what was up, did so. "You," the teacher told him, "are a student of exceptional ability, but you try to pretend to be otherwise, so people will like you. These other kids sitting here are just as insecure as you are, and they will like you better if you are yourself. Now, look through the microscope again and tell me what you really see." Although the boy was somewhat discomposed by the teacher's words, he also was strangely exhilarated. "Yes," he thought to himself, "I do have some brains, and I do try to hide it." He peered carefully into the microscope, described what he saw with precision, and walked quietly to his seat, feeling somehow like a new and vindicated person.

You can be yourself, of course, without conveying the impression that other people are at fault for being *them-selves*. In any case, trying to hide a trait has a way of calling attention to it. A girl who is considerably taller than most of her classmates will be better received if she "walks tall" than if she slouches around trying to appear to be five feet tall. It would not work out well, however, if the tall girl were to limit her circle of acquaintances to other tall people. Whatever your physical traits, your intellectual gifts, your interests, you will do well to mix with a variety of young people and to respect them all as individuals. Suppose, for instance, that football bores you to distraction. You don't have to jump up and down and wave a pennant and cheer, but you can attend a few games with your friends. You might even get interested in the game!

Swimming Upstream

Suppose you feel, after careful consideration, that you simply must fight the culture on the deterioration of education. Suppose that this is akin to a holy cause for you. Then, certainly, you must follow the promptings of conscience. The only question is how. There is this paradox in education and in prophecy: to the extent that one is "far out" and shrill, one is likely not to be listened to. To the extent that one is in line with custom (and therefore *is* listened to), it is likely to be because one has nothing startling to say. Teaching is taking people from where they are to where they should be. The most popular teachers are often those who take students from where they are to where they are—who, that is, take them nowhere, merely reflect back to them the folkways in which they have been swimming since birth.

The voice crying in the wilderness sometimes serves a very valuable function in awakening the rest of us. Somewhere there must be that first voice to cry out that the emperor has no clothes on. Don't forget, though, that the crowd became very angry at the child who cried out with that message. As a rule, those who accomplish the most are probably those who are far enough from dead center that they have something unusual to say, but who manage to say it in an appealing way. Part of that appeal is nearly always *letting people save face*. Nobody likes to be told that he/she is stupid or knavish. Nobody will consciously entertain a self-concept as being stupid or knavish. Most of us will go to just about any length of rationalization to avoid entertaining such distressing thoughts about ourselves. Thus, "a slice at a time" may well be the best approach to educational reform, as it is to other kinds.

The late Robert Hutchins was something of a prophet in his time as president of the University of Chicago. Hutchins shared many of the ideas of a leading contemporary philosopher, Mortimer Adler. Indeed, he learned many of them from Adler. Hutchins, however, was more of an administrator than Adler. But was he? Opinion is still divided on that. Hutchins wanted to pull the University of Chicago away from the influences of pragmatic and existentialist philosophers, back toward more classical conceptions of scholarship. He was a very witty and articulate man and seldom missed a chance to employ these gifts in the cause. Hutchins did not intend to wait around longer than necessary for his reforms to come to pass, either. As a result of all this, he became a figure of much controversy, later leaving the university for one of those foundation presidencies that seem to exist partly to keep former university presidents gainfully employed. Scarcely had Hutchins departed when some of his critics at the University of Chicago went to work undoing much of which he had done. Would it have been better if he had been more quiet and temperate in seeking his goals? That is very difficult to say. Such, at any rate, is the choice everyone must make who chooses to swim against the current.

If you choose to be an outspoken critic of the school or college that you attend, you can be confident that not everyone will be pleased. Yet students are often listened to by academic administrators with respect and admiration when the students show that they have carefully considered what they have to say. If you find the courage to speak up, some others will probably be helped by your example to do the same.

For Further Reading

Bhaerman, Steve, and Denker, Joel, *No Particular Place to Go: the Making of a Free High School*, 2d ed. (Carbondale, Ill.: Southern Illinois Press, 1982), pp. xvii, 245.

Bird, Caroline, *The Case Against College* (New York: David McKay, 1975), pp. x, 308.

Gallagher, Buell G., *Campus in Crisis* (New York: Harper and Row, 1974), pp. ix, 288.

Kozol, Jonathan, *On Being a Teacher* (New York: Continuum Publishing Corp., 1981), p. 177.

Owen, David, *High School* (New York: Viking Press, 1981), pp. xii, 262.

Turner, Joseph, *Making New Schools* (New York: David McKay, 1971), p. 302.

Chapter V

Changes at Work

"Work" means many things. In this chapter we shall think of the world of work as including the activities by which people earn their livings and the whole realm of business, industry, and the professions. Here, too, changing values confront us in many places. Among the topics we shall consider are declining standards and self-expectations in the work force, low productivity, the impact of the women's movement, the decline of the work ethic, and a relatively new phenomenon called "burn-out."

"Efficiency" is sometimes taken to mean simply performance level, but it means, more specifically, performance level in relation to energy used. Similarly, productivity, as economists talk about it, is the ratio of the output of goods and services to the input of the factors producing them. Any kind of input can be used as the denominator of a productivity ratio. Labor is the most commonly used denominator because it represents, as a rule, the largest input. Typically, labor absorbs from two-thirds to three-quarters of the gains from economic activity. Productivity of labor is considered an important yardstick of a nation's economic health. After all, a rise in labor productivity tends to mean the availability of more goods and services per worker than before. This condition, in turn, creates a potential for a better standard of living for workers and their families. In countries where we see high wages in terms of purchasing power, we also see high labor productivity.

Steady increases in labor productivity tend to be accompanied by decreases in the number of hours in the workweek. In 1850 a 60-hour week was common in this country. A century later, 40 hours was the usual pattern. People tend to produce more when they are not working for excessive lengths of time. Thus, there were compensatory gains in the movement toward a 40-hour week. Today, however, a common complaint among employers is that too many employees take two or three hours to do an hour's work. It is significant that, while salaries of automobile workers in the United States have continued to rise through the years, Americans are now showing a preference for foreign-made cars. In 1982 the auto workers' union negotiated with major manufacturers a revised contract under which employees would get less than before but the manufacturer would be able to stay in business in competition with imported cars.

An extensive literature has grown about how to motivate employees to be more productive. Everything from Christmas bonuses to recognition ceremonies for outstanding performance has been considered in that effort. The newcomer to this problem might be startled to discover that the employee is not expected to motivate himself. A motive, after all, is within the person. It cannot simply be placed there by somebody else. What another person can sometimes do in that respect is to show us that what he/she wants from us is a means to something that we want for ourselves. One mark of a professional, incidentally, is that such a person supposedly does not need and might even resent being "motivated" by another. "I think of myself as someone who always does a good job," one woman said. "Deserving that opinion of myself is more important to me than any incentives that anyone else could provide."

Breakdown of the Work Ethic

Why do so many workers expect less of themselves these days? To understand what has been partly lost, we need to look at something called the Protestant work ethic. It is poorly named, since it derived only from certain segments of the Protestant community: the Calvinists and others who shared their doctrine of predestination. According to this doctrine, God has eternally chosen those who will be saved. (This must be distinguished from God eternally *knowing* who will be saved.) Human free will was thus put aside as being no factor in salvation. Those thus eternally chosen were called the Elect. One could do nothing to *make* himself belong to this group, since God had irrevocably decided on the matter. What one *could* do was to *demonstrate* membership in the Elect by showing certain external signs. Prominent among these was that one's worldly affairs would prosper. Thus, men and women worked hard to acquire a generous supply of this world's goods, seeking thus to make manifest that God's favor rested upon them. So, at least, goes a widely accepted theory.

There are, of course, many reasons why people work: to obtain the material necessities of life, to provide for their children's future, for various comforts and conveniences beyond the necessary, to express themselves, to achieve a sense of identity, because the work is enjoyable in itself, to serve society, to enjoy prestige, and others. In the early period of America's history, there was a shortage of chances for the more luxurious reasons such as enjoying what was being done, but there was no shortage of practical reasons. There was a great wilderness to be conquered if the people were to survive. Building homes, clearing land for cultivation, and providing clothing, all with the equipment then available, were formidable tasks.

Ablebodied persons worked from morning to night. Work became a central theme in many American folkways. It came to be valued for its own sake. "The devil finds work for idle hands to do," people reassured one another. A man wanted a home and land for his family and himself. If, beyond that, he could own a store or a factory, so much the better.

This dawn-to-dusk work schedule tended to continue on the farms after city workers began to enjoy an easier routine. At first it was taken for granted that factory hands would put in from twelve to sixteen hours a day. Long and sometimes bloody struggles were required to get to the eight-hour day. Children were expected to do their share at home. Sometimes they were hired as cheap labor. Since most Americans could find plenty for their children to do at home, child labor never became the major social problem that it was in England.

As industrialism developed, more and more of the population did not have large tracts of land. The trend toward bigness and consolidation likewise decreased the number of small-scale entrepreneurs. A new perspective began to develop in which labor and capital each saw the other as an enemy. Employees often felt that they were being exploited so that stockholders of giant corporations could show a profit. Employers often saw labor unions as grasping and irresponsible. Unfortunately, there was considerable truth in both viewpoints.

For whatever reasons, the worker who takes such pride in his craft that he will not let shoddy goods or services come from his hands has ceased to be typical. Your parents might have grown up in a home where one toaster served throughout their childhood, as did one pair of scissors, one eggbeater, one alarm clock, and so on. Today one buys such items expecting to replace them within a year or two. The professor of a generation ago usually identified strongly with the college or university where he served. He wanted and expected to stay there throughout his career. He usually taught a full load of classes and did his research and writing "on the side" as a means of advancement and of community service. Today's professor is more likely to identify himself with a specialty than with an institution. He/she wants a reduced teaching load for almost any special assignment that may come along and sometimes sees the college or university as an antagonist to be "ripped off" now and then. Universities find themselves confronted with faculty requests for programs for faculty development; whereas previously professors would have been insulted to be told that their professional development was anybody's business or responsibility but their own.

The Women's Movement

"Frailty, thy name is woman!" said Hamlet. While woman's role has varied from one society to another and one time to another, women have typically been looked upon as weak, emotional, unsuited for higher learning, and meant by God and nature to play subordinate roles. In the 1880's—only a century ago, please note—a memory book for young women, popular in the schools of that time, contained various questions such as "What is your favorite poem?" "What is your favorite flower?" One question was, "What is your favorite trait in a woman?" The answer written oftenest by far was, "Obedience," and the young ladies themselves were giving that answer. At that time, as we have noted, farming was the principal occupation. Women seldom worked outside the home. They were economically dependent upon their fathers and husbands. Perhaps, considered in that light, "Obedience" was not a surprising answer.

Of course, as *Life With Father* reminds us, many women have mastered the art of dominating while appearing to submit. Nevertheless, obedience and subordination on women's part were much commoner than they are today. The position of women in families has usually correlated highly with the economic functions they performed. There are other variables, of course, such as whether a particular woman has a dominant personality, and whether her husband likes to surrender what some men consider the prerogative to direct. A century ago a married woman could not bring a lawsuit nor execute a deed without her husband's concurrence. She had no control of her personal property. Women have always played an inferior role in religion. Until recently, if a woman became the head of a government, she did so by birth. A married woman who seeks to open a charge account in her own name may still find that her husband is asked to cosign, even if the woman is bringing home most of the bacon.

We speak of the women's movement as if it were entirely the product of the two decades since Betty Friedan wrote *The Feminine Mystique*. Actually, women's lot has been gradually improving for at least the last century. The revolution is reflected in such changes as women's suffrage and repeal of laws that permitted a husband to dispose of his wife's earnings. Within the past generation, however, this movement has shifted into high gear. It has become articulate, determined, and organized. In the world of work, it stands for women's right to hold all kinds of jobs for which they prove qualified and to receive equal pay for equal work. In the psychological sphere, it stands for shattering the stereotype of what women are and what their roles in the family and in society ought to be. In politics, in the arts, in business, in technology—in short, everywhere—women are demanding to be considered and rewarded on their merits.

Like most revolutions, this one has gone too far or lost its sense of direction at times. Betty Friedan complained that it has become a Hate Men movement. Attention to small points of language has been given an emphasis that seems absurd when compared to the larger issues—equal pay for equal work, for instance—that are still so far from solved. Writers perpetrate such grammatical lapses as "A person should mind their manners" because they would rather give a singular antecedent to a plural pronoun than be guilty of saying "his manners," "her manners," or the rather tedious "his or her manners." "Ms." has become an accepted, sometimes demanded, term of address, even though nobody knows what word it stands for. Forgotten is the meaning of the suffix "man" as "one who," as in "workman." One writer suggested in all seriousness that it is arbitrary to refer to Jesus Christ as a man. At one meeting there was an angry objection to the use of the term "chairman," while at the same meeting "chairwoman" went unremarked. Soon we shall be faced with such aberrations as "See if the personperson left any person in the personbox." (See if the mailman left any mail in the mailbox.) Well, revolutions do have these silly sides, and there is no doubt that English usage has been slanted to favor males. Some writers have taken to using masculine and feminine pronouns alternately in referring to such indefinite entities as "the reader." Perhaps we need a new English word for "him or her," another for "he or she," and still another for "his or hers." Then, perhaps, we could get on to more pressing problems, before the leaders of Men's Lib get around to demanding, for example, that a famous classical hero be renamed Ben Him.

Predictably, there has been some backlash to the women's movement. Phyllis Schlafly has been a leader of those who have seen menace in the proposed Equal Rights Amendment and who feel generally that things were better before womankind became so militant.

We are considering the women's movement chiefly as regards its economic bearings. In 1979 the median salary for women professional and technical workers was $13,700, 64.3 percent of the median for men. (The median is the middle value, the point above and below which an equal number of cases can be found. It is often a more meaningful statistic than the average or mean, because the median is less influenced by extreme cases.) Some additional medians for occupational groups of women are given in the table below, which is derived from the Women's Bureau of the U.S. Department of Labor.

Occupational Group	1979 Earnings	Percentage of Men's Earnings
Nonfarm managers and administrators	$11,698	53.6
Clerical workers	9,853	59.6
Sales workers	8,910	52.1
Operatives (e.g., transport)	8,579	57.4
Service workers	7,486	62.7
All occupations	10,168	59.6

Generally, then, women are earning less than two-thirds of the salaries given to men in corresponding occupations. We are only about a generation removed from an era in which female teachers were paid far less than male teachers and a woman in an office or a classroom was often regarded as cheating some man out of a job. Today, the standard pattern in virtually all public and most private school systems is a salary scale based on education and experience, with sex playing no role. In universities, where salaries are usually determined by a merit system, one almost invariably sees female professors of any given academic rank averaging far below their male colleagues in salary. Also, far fewer women reach the senior ranks and become tenured. In the teaching profession, there is still a widespread assumption that men belong in colleges and universities and women belong in elementary schools, while secondary schools can reasonably be populated by both genders.

"You've come a long way, baby," but you are still called "baby"!

Burn-Out

Graham Greene wrote a novel called *A Burnt-Out Case*. Later, in technology, "burn-out" became a term for cessation of operation of a jet or rocket engine. Perhaps from one of these sources, we now have "burn-out" as a name for a debilitating psychological condition brought about by prolonged stress on the job. Its symptoms include ineffectiveness in performance, a powerfully felt need to get into a different line of work, lowered resistance to illness, depression, pessimism, decrease of energy, and chronic fatigue.

Is this a new kind of illness? Yes and no. The symptoms have all been familiar to physicians and psychotherapists for a long time. Many of them are the customary signs of clinical depression. What is relatively new is the centering of these symptoms so directly on one's career, along with the increasing numbers of those who spend years preparing for a vocation only to find, after practicing it for a few years, that they want out. Some researchers have concluded from studying hundreds of cases that, ironically, burn-out tends to affect those who were once very idealistic and enthusiastic. If someone enters a profession with a cynical attitude, the odds are better for endurance than if one has a powerful desire to serve others and to achieve. To put it another way, you can't burn out unless you were once on fire.

The causes of burn-out are partly in the victim and partly in the situation. A job that applies constant pressures is usually the main external factor. Internally, the problem is one of balancing a work situation that does not meet one's needs well against the need to earn a living and to stay in one place for a reasonable length of time. Given that we are on earth once, it scarcely seems wise to devote a whole career to a situation in which one is miserable. This does happen. Retirees are sometimes heard to say, "I hated every minute of it." At the other extreme, everyone who hires people learns to be skeptical about the applicant who never stays in one position for more than a year or two. If many positions that looked good turn out otherwise, it is unlikely that "Everybody's out of step but Johnny."

Adjusting

Preachments at or about workers with low self-expectations are unlikely to help. The writer's wife was disgruntled one day when a huge truck stopped in an illegal parking place. "You can't park there," she told the driver. Looking around meditatively, he replied, "Obviously, I can, since I just did." The historical factors that have contributed to an attitude that an employer is someone to be taken advantage of are not going to yield to a maxim or two. Both consumers and employers can quietly insist on getting their money's worth.

When you enter the job market, you will do so with one

attitude or another about what sort of employee you want to be. No matter what that attitude is, you may find that it doesn't please everybody. If your idea is the old-fashioned one of "a day's work for a day's pay," you may find that some of your fellow workers resent your efficiency and productivity. A young reporter who exhibited zeal in covering stories was quietly taken aside by an older colleague and told, "Slow down! You may work yourself out of a job!" It is all but certain that if you belong to a union, the union will not appreciate your concern to give the employer his money's worth. On the other hand, if you try to match your pace to the lowest common denominator, your superiors will not mark you for advancement and reward. A young postman told of getting back from his rounds earlier than his co-workers, with the result that he was given a larger route. Perhaps he *should* have been given a larger route, but so should they!

The advice is surely easier to give than to take, but: follow your conscience. Behave as you would expect someone in your position to behave if you were the employer. You don't need to argue with someone who tells you to slow down and make more mistakes. You can, for example, make a joke out of it: "I guess I'm just new and eager." Suppose, however, that you find that no effort is made to reward merit. A college student took a job typing bills of lading for a large truck line. The beginning hourly wage was modest, but he was told that his work would be monitored and that merit raises would be forthcoming if earned. After many months of doing his best, doing accurate work at a considerably faster rate than any of his co-workers, he learned that no one kept any record of this, that the personnel people never asked and were never told how well any typist was doing. He then had to decide: Why am I doing my best? If it is for rewards, I might as well relax, because there are no rewards. If it is so I can go home at night feeling comfortable about myself, I should go on as I have been doing. He chose the latter. He never got a raise; but, presumably, it would have been a strain on his temperament to goof off as he saw others doing.

If you join a union, remember that it is supposed to represent you as much as any other worker. Time was when labor unions brought the typical worker from poverty to a decent standard of living and conferred upon him a dignity not felt before. Today, some fine things are still being done by unions, as when labor and management can plan cooperatively for times of economic pinch. It is also a sad fact that labor-management relations too often have been conducted at the level of a cat-and-dog fight, with neither side caring much about the needs and rights of the other side, and with union meetings characteristically dominated by the person with the loudest voice. Too many union presidents are like the one who said in a television interview some years ago, "No matter how much they give us, we'll always want more." Don't hesitate to use your influence to help to make your union what you think a union should be. At the same time, remember that a young new employee, speaking as a lone voice, seldom brings on any revolutions.

There is a healthy aspect to the demise of the old idea that work is valuable for its own sake. Surely we have a telos more exalted than keeping busy! Many people are so wanting in inner resources, however, that when there *is* leisure they don't know what to do with it. One of the chief uses of electronic wizardry is to keep us pacified and distracted when there is "nothing to do," perhaps by watching a game show or situation comedy on television, perhaps by shooting down imaginary invaders of earth in a space game.

The women's movement also presents its share of adjustment problems. Attitudes on such subjects go deep and are more the product of conditioning and experience than of reason. Many men have purchased misery for themselves by being unwilling or unable to rethink their beliefs about women's roles. Some men whose attitudes on most subjects are very liberal are somehow unable to live comfortably with the thought of a working wife. Men with such reactions ought to introspect, try to discover the motives at work within themselves. A husband may find, for instance, that he feels like a failure as a provider if his wife is also gainfully employed. That is an illogical conclusion. When it is recognized as such, it can be more easily dismissed.

Those who hire and fire, promote and give raises need to learn (if they have not learned) that everyone is to be judged on merit, man or woman. There may or may not be *tendencies* for men to do better in certain occupations and women in others—the point is still under investigation—but one thing is clear: *one must judge the individual case*. A woman who does not get the job, promotion, or raise that she sought should, of course, seek justice if it is clear that injustice has prevailed. On the other hand, anyone who fails to get some desired good should be careful not to assume automatically that discrimination was at work. A person who belongs to a minority or other downtrodden group has a rationalization readily at hand: I didn't get what I wanted because I am a woman . . . because I am black . . . because I am Catholic . . . because I am Jewish . . . because I have radical political views. Maybe so; maybe not. Often, one can find others in the same category as oneself, employed in the same place, who have fared better.

There is also a difficulty for the woman who is quite

happy with the role of wife and mother and seeks no other. Some people will tell her that she is a traitor to her sex. She should realize that she has a right to her preferences and that the values she is emphasizing are very important ones. Again, there are some of us men who verbally accept the era of career women, but who don't help out around the house more than we did when our wives were not employed.

Eliminating the residue of past errors or biases is a complex problem. A rather elementary principle of ethics is that *you don't undo one evil by committing another.* Two wrongs don't make a right. Yet exactly that kind of dubious ethics is often advocated and practiced in regard to civil rights, women's rights, and so on. When one began to see employers hiring blacks over better qualified whites, universities admitting blacks in preference to better qualified whites, the phrase "reverse discrimination" began to be heard. One man commented, in an attempt to dismiss the phrase, "As far as I'm concerned, you can't reverse a process until you've stopped it." That was clearly not good reasoning. There can be individual instances of discrimination in a given direction even if the statistical pattern is still in another direction. The answer is simply not to discriminate at all, but that simple answer has proved startlingly elusive. Of course, the matter is very complex. There are many legitimate questions about how best to determine someone's qualifications for a job, for admission to an academic program. Again, race, religion, or sex might well be a legitimate part of the qualifications for a particular position. For example, being black would, other things being reasonably equal, be a clear asset to a physician practicing in the black community and hence might be a legitimate consideration in admissions to a medical school. The key thing, again, is to consider only what is demonstrably relevant. Again, *weigh each case on its merits*. It's that simple!

Finally, burn-out presents some special adjustment problems. Sometimes the only answer for the victim is to get into another line of work. Sometimes it is necessary to stop all employment for awhile. Sometimes a vacation and serious thought about one's situation will work wonders.

The sufferer must ask, "Are my expectations unrealistic? Are they unrealizable anywhere?" One can still write a best seller by arguing that schools should be perfect, that hospitals should be perfect, or whatever. One can still "expose" any human institution as a sea of mediocrity. Common sense suggests that there must be sufficient reasons why human institutions are always this way. Some enterprises are conducted better than others, of course. The question for the affected person is, "Are my expectations within the realm of the possible?" The doctor who writes a book exposing medicine—how are his patients doing? The educational expert (often self-appointed) who finds nothing good in the schools—what is his track record in educating others? On the other hand, one should not despairingly resign oneself to current local conditions without reasonable efforts to determine what has happened elsewhere, what is workable.

Fighting the Culture

At work, as at school and in other places, one can examine the situation and say, "No! I will not accept this state of affairs. I don't mean to adjust to it. I mean to work against it." Perhaps there is something to be said for the lone crusader who goes down in flames—the usual fate of lone crusaders. This person may be the one who galvanizes the rest of us into commitment and action. The important thing is to know how it is likely to end before taking the leap, and to decide whether one wants to pay that price.

A man who got reasonably good secretarial jobs in his youth, just on the basis of a high school education with commercial emphasis, now has occasion to hire, fire, assign, and promote secretaries. He learned shorthand in high school and used it in his office jobs. He now finds that most applicants for secretarial jobs in the institution where he works cannot take dictation. It would not do, in his day, to turn in a letter or report with typing errors. Now he hears from colleagues that they often must wait for weeks to get something typed and that, then, it is full of errors. "Give it back to be retyped as many times as necessary," he told one colleague. "I'd be retired before anybody did it right," the colleague replied.

What is the man to do? He can tell secretaries that perfection of copy is expected in these offices, and reasonable promptness in turning out work. If they fail to produce this and are fired, others will be found after a search lasting weeks, and they, probably, will do no better. Nevertheless, the only answer to such a situation—insofar as there is an answer—is to insist in a quiet, dignified, friendly way that things must be done correctly and on time.

If your teachers assign you homework and expect it to be submitted neatly, on time, free of spelling errors, and so forth, it may seem that they are preoccupied with trifles more than with the subject matter. Yet part of what they are probably trying to do is to prepare you for habits of efficiency and organization in your working years that lie ahead. "Being organized" is not a quality that leaps magically into your lap when needed. It begins in first grade or before.

Grade school teachers often give such rewards as Snoopy

stickers to pupils who submit good work. Piano teachers have been known to use similar devices. One's first reaction might be that this relies on extrinsic motivation; that is, the pupil is not doing the thing as an end in itself. It often happens, though, that those who receive such token rewards for writing essays or playing the "Minute Waltz" learn to love writing essays and playing the "Minute Waltz" quite aside from any rewards or punishments. In the long run, however, it is better when we can manage to motivate ourselves. Suppose that a man who is mowing his lawn derives no satisfaction from the activity and does not especially care how his house and yard look. He is putting his house up for sale, though, and he wants prospective buyers to be favorably impressed. Such a man is extrinsically motivated. He is not likely to mow under the hedges where it will not show. He will not trim along the edges of the grass unless he thinks prospective buyers are going to look there. Suppose, contrariwise, that the man likes taking care of his yard. It is fun. It brings him into closer communion with nature and himself. It pleases him to know that, if Superman with his X-ray vision should come along, Superman would know that the grass was mowed underneath the rose bushes. Such a man is intrinsically motivated. He will do a good job, quite independent of selling his house or other such outside considerations. Blessed is the employer who can get his employees intrinsically motivated. Blessed are the employees who *are* so motivated and do not need to be gotten that way.

Suppose you feel that the women's movement has gone too far in some respects or is off on questionable tangents. Suppose you feel strongly enough about this that you cannot accept the status quo in silence. Then you must speak and act—but not shrilly, not fanatically, not irresponsibly. Make your case quietly with facts and reason. Avoid any sort of name-calling or jokes in poor taste. Give examples. Help people to see that your position is something better than the product of emotion and prejudice.

Reason has not always prevailed in this matter. We hear fairly often, for instance, that no man makes advances to a women without some clear signal that they are welcome, and that women who wear revealing clothing are "asking for" rape. Both propositions are nonsense. Some men are less than expert at detecting whether their advances are welcome or not, and some do not care. A person who cannot see an exposed thigh without losing control needs to be institutionalized. This is not to say that modesty has ceased to be a virtue, but somebody or other off in Paris decides how high hemlines shall be this year, and cleavages how low. The rest of us live with it.

Those who fight for justice for women and minorities must walk a tightrope. One should neither tolerate injustice lightly nor see it where it does not exist. Past inequities should not be tackled by creating new ones. Inequities should be tackled on a case-by-case basis. We could all do with a bit more humor on the subject than is usually to be found. We should be very slow to apply emotional tags such as "racist" or "chauvinist" to a person or a situation, using them only when they clearly apply. Even then, facts might be more to the point than adjectives.

For Further Reading

Cherrington, David J., *The Work Ethic: Working Values and Values That Work* (New York: AMACOM, 1980), pp. x, 288.

Daly, Mary, *Beyond God the Father—Toward a Philosophy of Women's Liberation* (Boston: Beacon Press, 1973), pp. xii, 225.

Denison, Edward F., *Accounting for Slower Economic Growth in the United States in the 1970's* (Washington: Brookings Institution, 1978), pp. xiv, 212.

Goldberg, Lucianne, *Purr, Baby, Purr* (New York: Hawthorne Books, 1971), pp. xiii, 174.

Goodwin, Leonard, *Do the Poor Want to Work?* (Washington: Brookings Institution, 1972), pp. xiv, 178.

Chapter VI

A New Culture?

We have looked at changing values in various parts of our lives: at home, at work, at school. This chapter will look at similar alterations in the society as a whole. A group of persons is a society to the extent that its members are held together in a relatively permanent relationship, bound by understanding and agreement, working together to attain their common needs. Because of different viewpoints, there are societies within societies within societies. Thus, we may speak of "New England society" or "American society." Any such group is said to have a culture—that is, a pattern of behavior, along with material objects such as tools, weapons, buildings, and types of clothing. Again, with shifts of viewpoint, we can speak of cultures within cultures within cultures. This is the sort of thing people have vaguely in mind in speaking of "the American way of life" or "the traditions of the South."

It is our lot to live in a time of relatively rapid cultural change. For upward of two centuries this country had a strong sense of progress, both as an accomplishment and a goal. With the Korean and Vietnamese wars, with endless monetary inflation, with overpopulation, pollution, and a Cold War with no end in sight instead of the Utopian world that was expected to follow World War II, we have come to see that problems do not always have solutions, that no nation or society is invincible.

As we look back over our national history, we might ask whether what seemed to be progress always was. We cleared the wilderness and produced farms where once wild beasts roamed. In doing so, however, we brought more floods and more destruction of the soil. We get around much faster than our grandparents did, but are we happier or healthier for it? We are richer materially than they were. Are we also richer spiritually? The size of our federal government has been growing constantly since the 1930's. Depending on whom you ask, this growth is progress or deterioration. Progress is change for the better, but what is better? Our next chapter will look at that.

Some of the general changes that have been taking place are these: a switch by many young people from a goal orientation to a role orientation, different moral standards, a lack of civility in many quarters, a deep cynicism about government, challenges to orthodox religions, and a widespread rejection of science and rationality in favor of pseudomysticisms and superstitions.

Goal and Role Orientations

We have seen how, in the settling of the United States, people routinely wanted to have a home and land. Goals of this sort continued, essentially intact, for those who are now the older generation. Meantime, here is a drama of the sort played out many times. John is an unskilled worker, a member of the upper-lower class, perhaps an immigrant or the son of an immigrant. By hard and unremitting work, he acquires a small home for his family and himself and moves into the lower-middle class. His son, William, goes to college, enters one of the professions, enjoys more of this world's goods than his father had, and becomes a member of the upper-middle class. *His* son,

Fred, goes to a fancier college than William could have afforded or would have aspired to and has somewhat more polished tastes. William, who paid his own way through college, also pays Fred's way. Fred sees this as the natural and proper way for things to happen. William doesn't mind, though, because he foresees higher achievements for Fred than he, William, ever dared to expect for himself. The things William has in mind for Fred don't happen, however, because Fred doesn't want them to happen. After coming home from Princeton or Columbia, diploma in hand, Fred announces that he wants to be a truck driver or a house painter so he can stay close to the pulse of the people. William goes off by himself and starts butting his head against the wall.

What has happened? Sociologists express it sometimes as a switch from being *goal*-oriented (as William is) to being *role*-oriented (as Fred is). Fred cares more about the sort of person he is than about what he has, either in possessions or status. This sort of difference can be viewed in a positive or negative light. On the positive side, it is a step away from materialism and acquisitiveness. On the negative side, it may be more romantic than realistic. Where are tomorrow's dentists, lawyers, and electrical engineers to come from if we are all off smelling the flowers? Again, it may be the brave music of a distant drum. It's easy to be contemptuous of mere money if Mom and Dad are sending a weekly allowance.

Along the way in elementary school, you passed from being influenced primarily by your parents' values to being influenced mainly by your peers. Thus, as you look at your parents' values now, they may seem strange to you. In any case, things will go more smoothly between you and them if you keep in mind that they acquired their basic outlook early in life, just as you did, and that they perceive in terms of largely unconscious value judgments, just as you do. To you, some things that they want may seem vulgar and philistine. To them, some of what you want may seem romantic and ill considered. Communication will not necessarily resolve the difficulty. Indeed, it may serve to lay bare an irreconcilable difference. In any case, everybody will be clearer on where the differences lie, and they can be faced with good will.

Changing Moral Standards

Morality as a way of behaving is conformity to some standards of right conduct. Morality as a subject is the study of what those standards should be and why. It is a branch of philosophy and, for those who believe in God, theology. When we go beyond workaday judgments about what is good and bad, when we ask why something is good or bad, we quickly find ourselves in a metaphysical maze. Some philosophers even deny that ideas of good and bad have any meaning. Among those who do consign meanings to such statements, there is great disagreement about what makes an action good or moral.

At a more practical level, however, we find considerable areas of agreement. The German philosopher Immanuel Kant said, "Act as if the maxim of your action were to become by your will a universal law of human nature." If you push ahead of your proper place in line at the supermarket, the maxim of your action is that it is all right to do this. The question then becomes: Would you want to live in a community where everybody tried to shove ahead of everybody else in the grocery line? If you disregard the traffic light because you see no other cars around, the maxim of your action is that it is all right to disregard traffic lights when no other cars are around. Again, the question is: Would you want to live in a society where every driver went by that rule? What is in one rendition called the Golden Rule can be found with about thirty expressions in many religious and ethical systems: "Do unto others as you would have them do unto you." Whatever speculative difficulties there may be, most of us have a pretty good idea of what that is. I should not interrupt other people who are speaking unless I have no objection to being interrupted. I should not cheat if I have any objections to other people's cheating. I should not lie unless I am perfectly content to live in a world where everybody lies.

That maxim does not take care of all ethical questions, of course. It is just a workable guide to everyday living. As such, nevertheless, it can be very effective. We shall look at a seeming decline in moral standards in that light, since a more philosophical approach would get us into one or another system of thought that would need a lengthy book to defend it.

Many habitual criminals have a curious intellectual blind spot. They can perceive themselves only as victims and recipients of actions, not as causal agents. A defendant in a murder trial may whimperingly tell the court, "I'm at your mercy!" This same defendant, typically, expresses no remorse over what he did to somebody else. There is always a rationalization: "I thought maybe he was going to come at me with a hidden knife." "Society has wronged me since I was a small child, and somebody had to pay." Did the victim have a knife in evidence? No. Was the victim "society"? Had the victim ever done anything to wrong the murderer? No. Those points, however, pass by without comment.

Such behavior is immoral in a practical sense (as well as in most formal ethical systems) because it follows a pattern which, if generally followed, would be destructive of social living. The person who does these things would not want to live in a society where everybody did the same. He excuses himself, though. His case is special. He does not think about what would happen if we all regarded our own cases as special, exceptions to ethical rules.

Sexual looseness can be viewed in the same light. Until recently, and still among many people, the pervading male attitude is that a man wants his wife to be a virgin, but he has no expectation of being one when he approaches the altar. Again, many men have considered it acceptable to have mistresses but have expected absolute fidelity from their wives. Suppose, however, that a couple agree to practice "open marriage"—or, to put it another way, flagrant and continuing adultery. That larger question remains: What would happen to the social fabric if this were everyone's standard? One of mankind's favorite myths is that sex can be compartmentalized, that one can pursue it with no emotional or social complications. The human organism operates as a unit. Our sexual behavior cannot be so tidily dichotomized from the rest of our behavior. A student at a religiously oriented university who was charged with prostitution said that she had needed the money to pay her tuition. So it goes.

In recent years one sees signs in stores saying, SHOPLIFTING IS A CRIME. This is like being told that the Chrysler Building is a structure. What else would anyone suppose? Shoplifting is stealing. Stealing is a crime. Again, however, the rationalizations are at hand, used by many who have now convinced themselves that shoplifting comes in a special category—not really criminal. "The stores are insured for all this stuff." "I can't live in a decent way on my Social Security." "They rip the customers off with high prices. This is the only way to get back at them." Insurance rates for stores depend on the amount of thievery they experience. Who pays for the insurance? Ultimately, the customers—the *paying* customers. The people to deal with if Social Security payments are too small are Congressmen. If one considers that a store's prices are too high, one can shop somewhere else. This is not to say that we should lack all compassion for shoplifters. It is to say that they are behaving immorally and rationalizing it.

Are moral standards declining? Some statistics such as the crime rates suggest an affirmative answer. This is more than a statistical matter, however. It is a matter of daily experience. Many a man and woman who experienced prolonged poverty in youth but would never have dreamed of stealing or of cheating the government on taxes now hear comments such as: "Society has never given me a fair chance. I can only make it by ripping off society the way it has ripped me off." In some crisis such as an electrical power failure, throngs of people use the occasion to loot and pillage. (The other side of the coin, happily, is that many others voluntarily help to direct traffic, to stand guard, or whatever else they can do to serve the commonweal.)

Why are moral standards declining? Some patterns of social and economic change reviewed in earlier chapters may suggest some reasons. There may also be philosophical reasons at which we shall look later. The point, for now, is that such a change has been going on in a general way, although many millions of people have done all they could to resist such a trend and to set a better example in their own lives.

Incivility and Cyncisim

Politeness is observance of formal usages in conversation that have been adopted to help us all show respect and consideration for one another: "Please" . . . "Thank you" . . . "Could you help me?" rather than "Gimme a dime's worth of them candies" . . . "Whaddaya hafta do around here to get waited on?" . . . "What's the matter; you deaf or something?" Courtesy is not quite the same thing, although it overlaps. To be courteous is to show consideration and respect for others.

We shall deal with both kinds of behavior under the name of civility. Civility has also been taking a beating in recent years. This has happened in some places more than in others. Studies have shown that, as population density increases, courtesy and respect for strangers or casual acquaintances decrease, as a general tendency. We are somewhat like the animals who begin to snarl when other animals get too close. The cabbie who used to ask, "Where to, Madam?" now inquires, "Where's it gonna be, lady? You want I should drive in circles all day?" "Yeah" or "Gotcha" has largely replaced "Yes, sir" and "Yes, ma'am." The clerk who used to say "Please take a number and I'll be with you shortly" is now likelier to say, "Hey, lady, I got other customers. Take your turn!" This is not to suggest that all of the lapses are on the part of these humble functionaries. The customer who used to ask, "Can you take me to the airport, please?" may now say, "Airport, Mac, and step on it!" Instead of "Pardon me, but do you carry paper napkins?" he may now call out, "Hey, Jack, where ya keep the paper napkins? Are you hiding 'em?"

Some of the efforts to combat this decline of graciousness have a rather hollow ring. Among these is the studious, "Have a nice day!" Recently, the writer listened as a recording from the Weather Bureau told the caller of record-breaking blizzard conditions, followed by the inevitable exhortation to have a nice day. It is no great comfort to be told to have a nice day by an employee whose boss has told him that he will be fired if he doesn't express this wish to everyone.

Along with incivility has grown a pervasive cynicism about government. During the presidency of Franklin Roosevelt, few of us knew that he was crippled or remembered it very often if we did know it. Roosevelt shrewdly kept the fact out of public consciousness in various ways, one of which was that he was always photographed with no wheel chairs or crutches around. In dealing with reporters, Roosevelt had a standard rule: he could not be quoted verbatim. Thus, if anything that appeared in the news proved embarrassing, he could always say that he had been misunderstood or misquoted. The President's romantic involvement with Lucy Mercer was likewise kept out of the public eye by those who knew about it. It is unimaginable that such things could be now. The general supposition of the working press (once again, there are exceptions) is that anybody in government is involved in something improper, and the only question is what it is. "Fielding reporters' questions" used to be a phrase of derogation. Now it has become standard. One man said that his invariable rule at the voting booth was, "Vote against the incumbent. Chances are, he's been up to something." Alas, there are worse guides to voting behavior. Often, he *has* been up to something. In the Nixon administration a Vice President resigned under charges of financial misbehavior to which he pleaded *nolo contendere*. Later the President resigned in disgrace as an alternative to impeachment. He was the first President in American history to resign. His Attorney General, the chief officer in charge of enforcing the laws, went to prison. So did a considerable number of persons in the administration. Some of them subsequently began writing books about it all, showing that, in some circumstances, crime *does* pay. (We who buy the books make it pay.)

While crime and corruption in that administration were unprecedentedly flagrant, the man who wrote a book titled *It Didn't Start with Watergate* was basically correct. It didn't stop with Watergate, either. Many people were critical of President Ford's pardon of Nixon for "crimes he may have committed" and felt that the whole arrangement smacked of collusion. There have been questions about the propriety and legality of certain actions of members of the Ford, Carter, and Reagan administrations. There has been a rather silly pattern of praising those who are about to be cast to the lions. Carter said that he was "proud of Bert Lance." Nixon called Haldeman and Ehrlichman "two of the finest public servants I have ever known," which left unexplained why he was calling for their resignation and why they subsequently went to jail. President Reagan praised Richard Allen's character before replacing him as National Security Adviser. Does politics really require such double-speak?

A *touch* of cynicism about government is not amiss. As John Ingalls wrote, "The purification of politics is an iridescent dream." Still, we have ourselves to blame for much of what is wrong. The office-seeker who discusses issues strictly on their merits does not get elected. If we have peace and prosperity, it is because of the policies of the incumbent administration, according to its spokesmen. If we have war and poverty, it is a legacy from the previous administration. The rule is to take credit for whatever goes well and dodge blame for whatever goes poorly. Imagine what would happen to a Presidential candidate who stressed the need for a world government to avoid a drift toward nuclear war, say, or suggested that the Republican and

Democratic parties have had about equal shares of fools and sinners.

Most politicians, besides, are basically honest persons trying to serve the public. Some of them serve at far less pay than they could earn by doing something else. We live in a convoluted and dangerous world where many things must be kept secret for the welfare—perhaps even the survival—of the persons who complain about the secrecy. It is simplistic to blame the politicians for all of this.

New Forms of Religion

Religion, too, wears new faces these days. Religion and politics are mixing in ways that cause uneasiness in many people. To be sure, a loose coalition of Protestant, Catholic, and Jewish clergymen protested American military involvement in Vietnam and concerned themselves with other social issues of the decade from approximately 1965 to 1975. Now we are seeing sophisticated techniques of organizing and lobbying, studied exploitation of news media, effective fund-raising, cultivation of persons in high office. All of this is enlisted in the pursuit of making America a less secular nation. The groups who do this have their own ideas about what changes need to be made. The Moral Majority, Inc. refers to itself as a political group, but it is headed by the Rev. Jerry Falwell, pastor of a church where the organization is headquartered. The group grew out of the "Old Time Gospel Hour," a fundamentalist program on radio and television. The Moral Majority, which is tax-exempt, lobbies actively in Washington. It operates a Political Action Committee that contributes funds to candidates who support the organization's stands.

Other such organizations are also active. Religious

Roundtable is headed by Edward McAteer, who is also National Field Director for the Conservative Caucus. Christian Voice published a *Family Voting Issues Index* and takes the conservative side on such issues as abortion, women's rights, and the rights of homosexuals. The National Christian Action Coalition has a Christian Voters Victory Fund and publishes *Congressional Scoreboard.*

The ethical issues involved in what such groups do are hard to disentangle. One cannot say that religious beliefs have no political ramifications. If one believes that abortion is wrong, for example, it is certainly in order to convey that belief to the lawmakers. Doing so is even a duty. Problems arise if those with contrary beliefs do not get an equal chance to put them on the record and if any kind of coercion is used, such as boycotts of the sponsors of television programs that some organized group does not like.

Another sort of change in religion has been happening, dating roughly from the rise of the counterculture in the late 1960's. The writer dealt with this at length in *The Teenager and the New Mysticism* (see chapter bibliography). This broad trend is hard to characterize because it takes so many forms: astrology, psychedelic drugs (for which "drugs" has become synonymous in popular usage), Satanism, the Jesus Movement, transcendental meditation, Yoga, biofeedback, ESP, UFO-watching, seances. Certainly, there are major differences among these phenomena. Yet if we look closely, we can also see two important similarities: they all have religious elements, and they all involve some degree of repudiation of reason.

Clergymen in many religious denominations, seeing their flocks dwindle and their spiritual authority increasingly questioned, have responded by trying to make their approaches more rational and by turning the churches into social work agencies. The evidence strongly suggests that the opposite approach is what people generally wanted. Since the Catholic Church has relaxed some of its disciplines, has celebrated Mass in the vernacular, and has tried to encourage open dialogue in some areas once considered settled, conversions to Catholicism have decreased almost to the vanishing point, a large proportion of Catholics have stopped going to confession, attendance at Mass is far down, and many people engage in practices specifically forbidden by their Church, such as artificial birth control, while continuing to receive the sacraments. Many young people of various religious backgrounds who had abandoned organized religion are coming back, not to the conventional churches and synagogues, but to mystical cults. Mysticism is a direct experience of ultimate reality, independent of reason, observation, or any of the commonly recognized means of knowing. From a religious standpoint, this is direct experience of God. This is what the pill-poppers, meditators, and self-proclaimed psychics are seeking. Are they finding it?

Adjusting

All of us tend to assume, when someone does something, that he acts from about the same motives that we would have if we did the same thing. That is often a source of conflict between parents and children. Love, as the Bible says, seeketh not its own. That is, if we love someone in a mature way, we want this person to (in the current argot) self-actualize, not to become a carbon copy of ourselves. Yet within every parent there is that less mature urge that wants Johnny and Jane to turn out just like Mom and Pop. To the extent that you depart from the customs and values of your parents, they may feel it as a repudiation by you of themselves, perhaps without consciously realizing that they have this feeling. A man who changed his religion without any feeling that he was thereby rejecting his parents may feel that *he* is being rejected by his children if they exercise the same right to choose a religion for themselves.

Perhaps in subtle ways you can convey to your parents that one of the legacies from them that you value most is the capacity to make your own rational decisions and the feeling that they want you to do so. This will take much of the sting out of it for them when you do not choose as they would have done. Be sure, too, that you are not choosing X simply because Father or Mother chose Y. A young Jewish boy converted to Christianity, thereby causing great pain to his parents. Later he decided that all religion was nonsense and pronounced himself an agnostic. Still later he returned to Judaism and confessed that he now realized that his unconscious motivation in leaving Judaism had been precisely to inflict the pain that he did inflict.

We must try to maintain the same openness in judging the morality of others. First, we should try to make sure that we do not confuse the mores of a particular society at a particular time with basic morality. A century and a half ago millions of Americans saw nothing immoral about buying, selling, and owning slaves. Not so long ago, it would have aroused criticism if a woman were seen at the beach in a bathing costume without stockings and a skirt reaching to the knees. Many people remember when sports and shopping were out of the question on the Sabbath. As Sir James Jeans observed, burning witches was once considered a virtue, and lending money at interest was considered a vice.

Some behavior that we see around us is not simply the fruit of social change, to be sure. It is immoral. We need not condone such behavior, but we do well to remember that not everyone has a finely tuned moral sense, and we gain nothing by making ourselves miserable over that fact. Many people leave their doors unlocked and in other ways fail to safeguard their possessions because they would never steal from anyone and they cannot readily imagine that anyone would steal from them. Yet in an average day most of us probably see several persons who support themselves in that way.

If one believes something on a religious basis, a special effort should be made to remember that many highly moral people hold to different religions and therefore have divergent beliefs about the will of God. When Britain's Princess Margaret was seeing a divorced man, a priest said in a sermon that she would commit a mortal sin if she married him. Princess Margaret (who finally did give up the man because of her own faith) is not a Catholic, however. Even if she were, one cannot say from a Catholic standpoint that the hypothetical marriage would be a mortal sin for her without knowing a great deal about her state of mind and will at the time. This is an example of judging others as if they shared one's own faith. When we see sexual behavior other than what our own religious beliefs tell us is right, we must remember that some others have different religious beliefs.

Failures of politeness and manners in others need to be looked upon in the same benevolent light. A teacher mentioned that a young boy in his class said, "You know, Mr. ——, what you ought to be is a pimp." The teacher was about to send the youngster to the principal's office for whatever punishment that beleaguered functionary could think of, when he realized that he was being complimented. In this youngster's stratum of society, a man who controls a team of prostitutes is considered to have scaled the heights. Similarly, if the policeman on the corner is a bit rough and crude in his language, he does not necessarily mean disrespect, nor is he necessarily being unfriendly. He is not Talleyrand at the French court; he is just a simple man, probably, whose feet hurt and who is trying to get people to obey the traffic laws.

As regards corruptness in government, we do well not to feel too comfortably superior to the whole scene. Next time there is a public hearing to determine, say, next year's school budget, attend it. You will be astonished at how few citizens show up to express their views, compared to the number who will complain after the budget is established. Also, remember that whenever a political scandal breaks in the news it is one more solved, so to speak. Lest we forget, the Nixon administration did not survive the investigations. The system worked.

Much of what has been said here about adjusting amounts to learning to see life from points of view other than one's own. One should *have* a point of view and believe in it as much as evidence and logic seem to warrant. That does not change the fact that others will see the same fact in a very different light.

Swimming Upstream

Let us again suppose that, after due reflection, you have decided to resist the trends. What can reasonably be done? One suggestion made earlier was to talk with your parents or teachers and get it out on the table that you are acting from different basic beliefs. Another thing you need to do is take stock of what you owe these people. You may decide that, on balance, you owe them nothing, but it is better if that conclusion follows careful reflection. For example, if you are accepting money from your parents for your education or other support, or if you hasten home for consolation whenever trouble pops up, you should consider how ethically free that leaves you to adopt a life-style to which your family are vigorously opposed. The question is raised here, not answered. It is something to think about.

A degree of rebelliousness, to be sure, does seem to be a natural and healthy part of establishing identity. A child at about the age of threc tends to go through the same sort of thing. A youngster of about that age was told by her mother to go upstairs. She refused. Mother reissued the order. The little girl reissued the refusal. Matters escalated in this mode until Mother puts hands on hips, got a dangerous glint in her eye, and said rather loudly, "You march up those stairs right now!" "I'll *back* up," the little girl replied. And she did. By this compromise, she was able to placate her mother and still save face, still feel like a creature endowed with free choice.

Depending on how understanding your parents are in such matters, you may have to explain to them sometimes that you feel the need to do a little experimenting in order to know who you are. You may be pleasantly surprised by the response.

We can help to combat loose moral standards by the example of our own lives. Many years ago, the writer complained to a priest about what he saw as unprofessional conduct of a colleague, ending with the question, "What can I do?" The reply was instantaneous: "You can make sure that your own behavior is always better." As someone put it, "You treat the other fellow as a gentleman, not necessarily because he *is* a gentleman, but because you are." We need not stop with example. We have every right to point out other people's mistreatment of us to them, and, if they remain unmoved, to complain to their superiors. First, however, be sure that you are in the right. Did you give the other person some provocation to treat you rudely? Did he, in his own mind, treat you rudely? Second, *always start pleasantly*. If you begin with a sarcastic, snarling, hostile attitude, the other person will probably escalate the hostilities. Only rarely does a friendly approach fail to meet a friendly response. When it does, there is something wrong with the other person, not with the one who makes the friendly approach. It is especially important to remember the small courtesies to the folk of humble station with whom we deal: sales clerks, cashiers, porters, custodians, messengers. Don't forget "Please. . . . Thank you. . . . Sir. . . . Ma'am. . . . You're welcome. . . . You've been very helpful." If you watch a sales clerk for an hour, for instance, you can see how few customers practice these graceful gestures.

Cynicism about government can be reduced by holders of public office if they do their business as openly as prudence permits. Some things do need to be kept secret—locations of weapons systems, for example. The general nature of what is being done and why can usually be revealed even when some facts must be held back. Politicians do well to decline to answer a question if they feel secrecy to be necessary, rather than to talk their way around it. A mayor guesses that he will lose his bid for reelection. A reporter asks him, "Do you think you will be reelected?" One could say "No comment" or "I don't know. The election hasn't been held yet." Instead, we usually hear, "I would hope so." The mayor cannot even bring himself to say that he *does* hope so, merely that he *would* hope so should some occasion arise for him to entertain hope one way or the other.

Those outside of government can help to keep it honest by taking an active interest in its workings and speaking up when they feel that something is amiss. Much has been made of the duty of voting. It is, indeed, important to express formally one's will about a candidate or a proposal. That, however, is only the beginning of political duty. We need to keep abreast of the local, state, and national issues that are before legislative bodies, study and ponder those issues, and express our views to our elected representatives. If one does not know the candidates or the issues when election day has rolled around, however, *not* voting is probably a civic duty!

Those who wish to help others who are going through periods of religious confusion or reorientation face an extremely delicate task. It is so delicate that most of us are inclined to a "hands off" policy regarding others' religious beliefs. A friend or relative may need your help, however, may even ask for it. If your goal in such circumstances is simply to help the other person to sort out his present feelings and beliefs, you can do that best by listening carefully, expressing your support, and encouraging your friend or relative to talk it out. You might want to go further, however. You might want to help this person to evaluate the content of a belief-system. If someone adopts a religious creed that makes no use of reason and makes no claims of using reason, for example, you might ask the believer how this viewpoint squares with his approaches in other areas. If he feels that reason should be respected in some topics and flouted in others, on what basis does he believe that?

For those who wish to make their own evaluation of the new mysticisms, it is useful to differentiate two varieties: natural and supernatural. The latter is found in theistic religions: Christianity, Judaism, and Islam. The assumption here is that man proposes and God disposes. Perhaps we can do some things to make ourselves fitting candidates for divine illumination, such as prayer and good works.

Finally, however, God decides, for reasons no mortal can fathom, to which souls He will give this rare gift. When He does give it, the fruit is *union* with God, not *unity*. That is, the soul is fulfilled and perfected while remaining itself.

The other approach is naturalistic, even mechanical at times. It assumes that the individual has the power to produce mystical states in himself by something that he does, such as taking LSD, doing Yoga exercises, working with a biofeedback machine, or engaging in transcendental meditation. The aim here is usually not the fulfillment of the soul, but its dissolution. More precisely, one's individuality is seen as merging with a World-Soul, a pantheistic Deity of some kind, in most cases.

Use of psychedelic drugs is probably the most widespread of the naturalistic approaches to mystical experience. Nothing is left to God. Man proposes *and* disposes. You take the drug and have the experience. A supernaturalist would say that this is pseudomysticism. Kaspar von Ossic Schwenckfeld and Sebastian Franck were Protestant mystics in the supernaturalist framework. Although we hear little about these two men today, they were chiefly responsible for the influence of mysticism in the Protestant Reformation. St. Teresa of Àvila and St. John of the Cross are examples of Catholic mystics. Although all mystics agree that what they experience cannot be put into words, most of them never stop trying. Teresa was one of the more inspired writers on the subject, as was John of the Cross in his *Nocte Oscura* (*The Dark Night of the Soul*).

Jewish tradition has been more sympathetic to mysticism than Christian in some ways. The Jesus of the New Testament spoke much more like a Hebrew teacher than like a Scholastic philosopher. His discourse was never abstract, formal, and intellectual. The one metaphysical statement attributed to Jesus, perhaps, was, "Before Abraham was, I am." He taught through homilies, parables, proverbs, and example. The chief foundations for Jewish mysticism were laid in the Hekhalot, which drew upon visions of Old Testament prophets. The most profound part of this heritage is in the Cabala, especially in the *Sever-ha-Zohar*. This "Book of Splendor" describes the power of God and His inner life. It sets forth the principles through which the believer can regain *devequt,* or total adherence to God, which was destroyed by the fall of man from pristine purity. Martin Buber is a modern example of Jewish mysticism.

For Further Reading

Arbuthnot, Jack B., *Teaching Moral Reasoning: Theory and Practice* (New York: Harper and Row, 1981), pp. xiii, 289.

Duska, Ronald, *Moral Development: a Guide to Piaget and Kohlberg* (New York: Paulist Press, 1971), pp. v, 128.

Evans, Donald D., *Struggle and Fulfillment: the Inner Dynamics of Religion and Morality* (Philadelphia: Fortress Press, 1981), p. 238.

Joad, Cyril M., *The Present and Future of Religion* (Westport, Conn.: Greenwood Press, 1974), p. 310.

Nordberg, Robert B., *The Teenager and the New Mysticism* (New York: Richards Rosen Press, 1973), pp. xii, 126.

Schulte, Henry H., *Reporting Public Affairs* (New York: Macmillan, 1981), pp. xiii, 445.

Chapter VII

Problems or Progress?

We have seen that the changes in values and social patterns with which Americans are living can be seen as improvements or as degeneration. Which is which, and why? First efforts to answer that important question usually proceed from habit. Sigmund Freud equated superego with conscience. The two are alike in that they deal with right and wrong, but they do so in quite different ways. Conscience is mostly conscious and rational. Superego is mostly unconscious and irrational. Conscience is the turning of reason upon our actions. Superego is the primitive conditioning that we all undergo. No one raising a child invariably gives the child a rationale for every order or rule. A toddler would not understand our rationale as to why he should not play in the street, but he does understand that he will get a spanking if he does that. No parent, moreover, can be expected to have inexhaustible patience, to be always primed with an answer as to why one should not touch his lips to the public drinking fountain, should tell the truth, should not tell Mrs. Jones that she is ugly, and so forth.

The long years of habituation are not lightly thrown off. Someone who has been raised to think that public displays of affection are vulgar or that a man should never sit in a bus while any woman is obliged to stand will not easily cast off these reactions. Many people, indeed, never get beyond this sort of knee-jerk morality, judging their own behavior and that of others by what Mom and Dad said was right and wrong. The thoughtful person cannot remain forever content with this sort of unexamined life. The thinker asks what *makes* an action good or bad. Practical debates on that subject usually continue only until two who disagree can find common ground. Thus, Mr. X might tell you that lying is wrong. You ask him why. "It's against the Eighth Commandment," says X. If you regard the Ten Commandments as morally binding, and if you take the eighth one ("Thou shalt not bear false witness against thy neighbor") as ruling out all lying, the argument is settled for you. Suppose, however, that you do not regard the Ten Commandments as having divine sanction. "I see no reason for following those commandments," you tell X. "Very well," X replies, "forget the Ten Commandments. You should not lie because you mislead others when you do that." "Why should I not mislead others?" you demand. "Civilized living requires that people be able to trust one another," X replies. Now, if you agree that civilized living does pose this requirement, and if you see the maintenance of civilized living as the basis of morality, you will be convinced that you should not lie. You might be argumentative, alternatively, and reply along this line: "What you are calling morality is just a name for the actions that will keep society as it has been. I care nothing for that. I believe in a different set of social arrangements. If lying will help to bring them about, I shall lie without hesitation."

The example is not so farfetched. Communist leaders have said that whatever will advance communism is moral, and whatever retards it is immoral. It might be very difficult to find common ground with someone who held such a belief. In any case, the question that arises is, *What is the absolute good of man?* "Absolute" is used here in a technical sense, meaning that a thing is unconditioned by anything outside of itself. What is it, then, that is always and everywhere good, not because of anything it leads to nor for any other reason essentially outside itself, but purely and simply *good in itself?* A possible answer, of course, is that nothing is simply good in itself. Before settling upon that answer, one should be clear about its logical consequences. If nothing is good absolutely, then nothing is really good even relatively. There cannot be an infinite regression of goods justified by other goods. A series must have a beginning. A can be good relative to B, which can be good relative to C, and so on. Nevertheless, unless there is a Z, something good in itself, the whole house of cards collapses.

Most people do have a Z, or perhaps several of them, values that they take to be absolute and incontestable. We are not necessarily conscious of what Z is for us without some special efforts to find it. For some, this discovery comes when deeply held values are in conflict and one must make an ultimate choice. Suppose, for example, that a man who equates abortion with murder is told that an abortion is the only way to save his wife's life. Suppose that Gestapolike tactics against certain subversives are the only way to save a democratic government.

If more things than one are considered inherently good (and thus, more than one opposite thereto considered inherently bad), the problem of bad means to a good end can arise. Does the end justify the means? Most of us say that it does not, but most of us occasionally act as if it did. Is it ever justified to do evil to bring about good? If your mother is dying, are you justified in lying, telling her that she will get well, in order to ease her death? Is a man justified in stealing food for his starving family? Was it good for workers in Poland to defy the law by striking, and bad for air controllers in America to do the same thing? If so, why?

Confusion about what is good and what makes a thing good has always been near the surface of the life of any society. Now and then, such issues become conscious and public until more concrete considerations reassert their usual predominance. Justice Louis Brandeis was cursing big business as a step backward when Rexford Guy Tugwell was hailing it as progress, at the time of the New Deal. Half a century later, that debate still goes on. In early California, capital punishment for stealing cattle was considered a commendable practice.

Even those values that we tend to hail as universal have had their exceptions. Some Indian tribes that considered stealing a grave offense thought it meritorious to steal from an enemy tribe. We tell young men, "Thou shalt not kill," then thrust rifles in their hands to do exactly that in wartime. We place such value on human life that physicians feel obliged to prolong it as long as possible; yet the elderly are often unloved and neglected.

People habitually look to political leaders to sort out such problems. Oftener than not, the leader does not prove equal to the occasion. Most politicians are not very original in their thinking, and certainly not very speculative. Once asked for his philosophy, Franklin Roosevelt was startled: "Philosophy? Why, I'm a Christian and a Democrat, that's all!" Some political leaders are inclined to be passive and hope that things will sort themselves out. A politician must keep the next election in mind, moreover, or he will not be in office long. Thus, we usually get what we want, which is frequently not what we need. It has been said that a good leader is one who knows how to follow. When Dwight Eisenhower was President of Columbia University, an assistant approached him with the complaint that students were ruining the lawn by walking where there was no sidewalk. Eisenhower told the aide to find out where the students were walking and then to have sidewalks put in those places. There was a bit of wisdom in that, surely. Yet critics of Eisenhower's rather passive approach in the White House in later years might say that he was too inclined to limit himself to, as it were, putting sidewalks where people were already walking.

There is a paradox here. Leadership is certainly needed to direct social change, but the character and exercise of that leadership are limited by what exists already. The times make the leader and the leader makes the times. The wise leader, like the rest of us, does well to occupy himself with problems about which something can be done. The need to control and preserve the environment, for example, was little thought about until we began to see that dwindling resources could soon become a tunnel with no light at the end of it. Here, too, we are limited. Another Ice Age would find mankind largely at its mercy. For that matter, a healthy blizzard can still immobilize an American city.

Even if our value questions were all neatly sorted out and agreed upon, we could not, in the present state of human knowledge, predict the consequences of various social trends and inventions until those consequences had us trapped in their nets. Someone compared the human race to passengers in a bus with seats turned so that they look only backwards. The driver, too, can look only backwards, while the bus speeds forward to unknown places along unknown routes.

Values and Motives

We have talked about values thus far as current usage tends to do, referring to anything that is valued. That usage reflects subjectivism and individualism. In this framework, a value is a motive and vice versa. There is another way to look at the matter. Imagine a fictitious patient in psychotherapy, William. William is frequently in conflict between exercising his ability to manipulate and "con" people and his desire to be honest and open. Perhaps he learned one of those behavior patterns from his father and one from his mother. In the course of therapy, William comes to realize that what he cares about most deeply is manipulating and conning. He successfully rids himself of the urge to be honest and open. By all the standards of the "values clarification" movement, he has done what one is supposed to do: he has identified his conflict and resolved it. He has changed his habits accordingly. He is thus more integrated and, one supposes, more self-actualized. There is just one trouble: he was a better man before than he is now.

Values clarification as commonly practiced illustrates psychologism, a tendency to take psychological questions and answers as somehow more conclusive, fundamental, and reliable than other questions and answers. Values clarification completely begs the question as to what anyone's values *ought* to be. The leaders of the movement acknowledge this. They simply believe that there is no objective way to answer such a question. Therefore, as they see it, the only point at issue is what any individual wants most.

Value is spoken of both as a thing and as a process. In the second sense, it is to prize, to esteem, to appreciate. That is plainly a subjective event, quite aside from whether it has some objective basis. Viewed as a thing, a value may be abstract or concrete. In the first sense, it is a property that something may have. In the second sense, it is something tangible that has this property—a house, for instance. From another standpoint, a value may be either instrumental (a means to an end) or intrinsic (an end that is not also a means; therefore, absolute). If, for instance, the individual's absolute good is happiness, all other goods are instrumental and are to be judged on the basis of how well they promote being happy.

A debate has raged from antiquity until now as to whether values are subjective or objective. (We have noted that if the latter is the case they also have a subjective aspect, so we need not trip over that roadblock.) Whichever view one takes, the distinction between instrumental and intrinsic values is still legitimate. If values and motives are the same, values are subjective. If values are objective, they must be not only other than motives but in that respect contrasted to them. (Where a motive chances also to be a value, the distinction would be only formal.)

It is the writer's view that values are objective; that is, they exist independently of ourselves. That is a philosophical position. This is not a book on philosophy. Even if it were, this objectivist thesis would need to be developed at length within an objectivist system of thought, and the system of thought would also need to be defended. It would need to be shown, that is, that we can know things essentially as they are independently of ourselves. Luckily, there is a shorter, easier, but no less valid path that can be taken. If it can be shown that those who take values to be subjective are contradicting themselves in doing so, they must be mistaken. (If they are not contradicting themselves, they could still be wrong. An internally consistent system of thought can be wrong, but a self-contradictory system cannot be right.)

Within the more limited task identified, there are still alternative ways to proceed. We could demonstrate, for example, that those who function as scientists must presuppose a real, knowable world, in which case it is a self-negating position to revert to subjectivism in treating values. Some people would reply, however, that they are not scientists, do not trust science particularly, and do not wish to base their positions on any scientific grounds.

Therefore, we need another way. Fortunately, there is one. It is to show that nondirectivists in counseling (those who believe that a counselor should not give advice or interpret), "value clarifiers," and their ilk are sometimes objectivists about values and sometimes subjectivists, and that they fail to provide any rationale for the inconsistency. It is a cornerstone of client-centered counseling that the client is the best person to decide both what his goals should be and what are the best means of achieving them. It is reasonable to ask why, then, he needs counseling. The answer of Carl Rogers and others has been that the client is ego-involved and thus somewhat alienated from his deeper self. He needs a sympathetic ear, a sounding board. All that a therapist should do is listen and help the cient to clarify his own feelings. It is acknowledged that the counselor cannot avoid expressing something of his own beliefs, even in the way he dresses, for example. Nevertheless, he is admonished to minimize such influences.

Do you know anyone who counsels in that way? Even among those who call themselves nondirectivists, do you know anyone who counsels that way? There are many "hot lines" nowadays for persons who are contemplating suicide. If the nondirective philosophy were really followed, the purpose of such a hot line would be to help the caller to decide whether he wants to commit suicide or not and, if so, the best way to do it. Surely no hot line functions in that way. Problems of when, where, how, or even whether to take one's own life are not dealt with. The only question that arises is *how to prevent it*. Albert Camus said that the only philosophical question worth debating is whether to live or commit suicide. Those who staff these hot lines obviously have conducted the debate with themselves and living won. They have decided, further, that they ought to make the same decision for anyone else who is in doubt. These are major value judgments. The question now is not whether the judgments are correct, but whether they are made, and they plainly are. The situation is not resolved by pointing out that a client cannot make any choices unless he is alive to make them. That reasoning entails a tacit judgment by the therapist that making choices is a worthwhile activity, that it has value.

Again, there are centers for dealing with alcoholism and drug addiction. These clinics do not offer courses in how to become an alcoholic or a drug addict. They do not hesitate to label alcoholism a personality disorder. Drug addiction (which has come to be called "drug abuse," as if the drugs were taking the punishment) is always regarded as a problem, never as a goal. Clinicians and their clients do not discuss whether someone should become an alcoholic or a drug addict or whether he/she should remain one. The search is always for a cure. The same point can be made about some other phenomena. Psychotherapists do not discuss the pros and cons of stealing, murder, arson, rape, or child-beating. These things are taken to be wrong. A client who does not judge them to be wrong is taken to be confused. (The point at issue here is not the client's moral accountability. A rapist, for instance, might be mentally disturbed. Nevertheless, clinicians are as one in believing that rape should not happen.)

There are, of course, other areas where clinicians tend to be morally neutral, such as whether a client should get married, have children, go to college, change jobs, major in physics, give up a friendship, move to another city, sell his car, get up earlier, stop watching television. If asked for a reason, most clinicians would say something like "It's the client's business." Why aren't suicide, alcoholism, drug addiction, stealing, arson also the client's business? One common response is that it's the client's business when nobody else can be hurt. It does not take much analysis, however, to see that there is usually the good possibility that others will be hurt. Suicide seldom affects nobody but its victims. It takes two to marry. Even if it were true that a thing is all right if only the one whose chooses it can be hurt, that is still another value judgment made *by the therapist*.

In short, the concept of the subjectivity of values is one that no counselor or psychotherapist can or does hold consistently. Therefore, it cannot be correct. The value clarifiers and nondirectivists are really objectivists who, illogically, make certain exceptions and usually cannot tell us why.

Some schools of philosophy—Pragmatism and Existentialism, for example—have held that experience is the source of all values. In a way, it is. Yet everyone's experience is different. Does this mean that a particular standard of beauty or morality can be valid only for the individual? If that were true, why would people ever argue about value judgments? Yet they argue about them incessantly. Members of a family may benignly greet the news that Willie likes rhubarb while Mary cannot stand it. Yet they may argue passionately over whether *Ragtime* was a better movie than *Gone With the Wind*. What is the difference? It seems that two types of judgments are at issue. In judgments of the second type we do not create truth, beauty, and goodness. We *discover* them.

If value lies outside ourselves, what form does it take out there? Clearly, we cannot photograph or weigh it. We need not assume that it has an existence independent of particular persons, places, and situations, although that is a respectable possibility. It is enough to sustain the objectivist thesis if we say that value resides *in* particular persons, places, actions, situations. It is an aspect of reality, like truth. To be technical, value is a transcendental. That is, it can apply to any being whatsoever. (It *can;* this does not mean that it always *does.*) Other transcendentals are unity, truth, and "thing." Now, if something lies essentially outside ourselves, we cannot reach it by introspection or other such psychological exercises. Again, however, we must be at pains to be clear. We can reach it in the sense of *recognizing* it but not in the sense of *creating* it. Outside is not inside. Ultimate is not personal-subjective.

How, then, can the transcendental be reached? There are many answers to that, and you certainly have the right to conduct your own search for one. Here is one answer: If values are objective, essentially outside ourselves, they are rooted in being, not in experience. Whatever is rooted in being must be rooted ultimately in the Necessary Being—in God. Therefore, whatever means there are of knowing God can also be means of knowing values. These can include reason, revelation, intuition, mystical experience. Of course, there will always be a problem of translation to temporal situations, since we cannot grasp the infinite except in some finite, analogical way.

We know according to our natures. If what is known is above the nature of the knower, it can only be represented to his cognitive powers in some accommodated way. That is no particular problem in knowing, say, that the Number 30 bus does not stop on Broadway. It is a problem in trying to comprehend the Creator. In any case, it is always being that is intelligible. There is nothing to know but being under one aspect or another. Whether you think of a quantity, a quality, a material substance, a relationship, or an event, it in some sense *is*. You can think about something fictitious, of course, but then you are imagining, not knowing. Or you can think about an idea such as circularity or justice without predicating it on any particular circle or any particular just act, but then you do not have a complete judgment, merely one ingredient for a judgment. Again, one can believe anything, but one can know only what is the case, and what is the case is rooted in objective being. A thing is intelligible in proportion to its being.

All of this applies to instrumental as well as to intrinsic values. The instrumental, after all, is a means to the intrinsic. Because intrinsic values are objective, so are instrumental ones. Sometimes, of course, we have a choice among means that are not especially freighted with positive or negative values. Someone who is going to the movies may choose to walk or drive. Normally, the means of getting there makes little difference.

It might seem that we have brushed off "values clarification" as having no worth. Such a verdict was not intended. The point rather was to show its limits. Certainly, there can be great benefit in discovering more clearly what one's values (in the subjective sense), one's motives are. One may find, for instance, that one verbalizes one set of goals and lives by another. The writer likes to think of himself as devoting his life to certain religious goals; yet he often behaves as if his two great goals were comfort and convenience. The husband in Ibsen's play *A Doll's House* never doubted that he loved his wife deeply. Events showed that he loved her, not as precious in herself, but in relation to his own ends. When those ends were not being served, he could be unconsciously very cruel to her. If a politician tells you that he cares deeply about the have-nots of America, ask him how much he gave to charity last year.

The limitation of values clarification as it has developed

is that it cannot, in itself, go beyond psychology to ethics. No therapeutic technique can have dependable ethical ramifications except in relation to the question of the absolute good of man. There have been many answers, incidentally, as to what that absolute good is. Among them have been pleasure (Aristippus, Epicurus), utility (Bentham, Mill), the state (Hegel, some social scientists), humanity (Comte), progress (Spencer), pity (Schopenhauer), superman (Nietzsche), virtue (Spinoza), duty (Kant). The writer suggests that all of these answers treat something relative as absolute. If Absolute Being is God, then the absolute good of man can only be union with God. The end of a finite being, a creature, cannot be *identity* with the infinite being, the Creator. The same being cannot be finite and infinite, Creator and created. But *union* with the Creator can be a creaturely goal and attainment. If so, whatever brings one closer to such unity is good; whatever takes one further from it is bad. This idea is not greatly different from Plato's idea of the Good as the supreme value.

By now, the distinction between values and feelings has been all but lost in many quarters. People often speak today of "creating our own values." A distinction must be made if, as argued here, value is mainly objective and motive is mainly subjective. What values clarification places before the person is what *motives* he has. What *values* he *should* have is another question. Perhaps, if one is lucky, the one issue can prove a bridge to the other.

Good and Bad in Current Changes

How one will feel about the trends discussed in this book plainly depends—logically, at least—upon what answers one gives to the questions raised in this chapter. What is the absolute good of man? Why? *Is* there an absolute good?

Is value objective or subjective? Nevertheless, we can look at some of the changes and see what light the previous discussion throws upon them.

How shall we evaluate the attitude toward marriage that sees it as "a scrap of paper"? What merit was there in the old adage, "One life, one wife"? First, let's sort out the issues. It is one thing to ask whether fidelity between a man and woman is a virtue, another thing to ask whether the relationship in virtue of which this fidelity is usually expected should be sealed in some legal or ecclesiastical way. We have examined the psychological and social values of the marital relationship. It is not for everyone, of course. Nevertheless, for many people, going through life in this way is very helpful. It is also helpful for society. But, some ask, where's the harm in a little bit of sex on the side? We cannot answer that here from the perspective of any particular religious or philosophical system. Let us look at it psychologically and socially. A human being is an organism. This means that every part helps and is helped by every other part. A person does not say, "My arm raised itself." One says, "I raised my arm." What part of you does, all of you participates in doing. What happens to part of you, happens basically to all of you. The person is the proper subject for prediction of acts. Not "My finger bleeds," but "*I* bleed." Not "My cerebral cortex sorted out an incongruity," but "*I* was amused."

The sexual act is far from being an exception to this law of organic wholeness. Indeed, there is probably no other action that so involves our whole being. From a psychological standpoint, that is what is wrong with masturbation. It is like a bullet shot into empty air, or kissing a vacuum. Promiscuous people suppose that sex can be separated from the rest of existence. "If you're thirsty, drink," is an often-heard analogy. Like all analogies, it fits the situation imperfectly. Even so far as it does fit, it is its own undoing. Thirst as a drive is certainly related to other drives, needs, and actions. Sex and caring go together emotionally, not just logically. Have you ever known a sexually promiscuous person who did not show other signs of emotional instability?

From the standpoint of family endurance and happiness, too, the advantages of fidelity are obvious. There may be cases where a marital relationship is strengthened by adultery, but the usual consequence is the opposite. In cases where someone says, "Adultery saved our marriage," follow up for awhile and see how long the partners remain married.

Should the husband-wife relationship exist until the death of one or both? There is a joke about a couple in their nineties who applied for a divorce. "Why now, after almost 70 years together?", the judge asked. "We wanted to wait until the children were dead," the husband replied. In a Woody Allen comedy, the hapless hero recounts the miseries of his childhood home where a mention of the weather was sufficient to risk gunfire. "Didn't your parents ever consider divorce?" he is asked. "No," says the hero, "although I begged them to." We do need to question whether the permanence of marriage always works to the benefit of the offspring. Yet the effects of broken homes are familiar to every counselor and social worker. There are many benefits to husband and wife, moreover, in building their lives together. Each ought to maintain a distinct personality with its own interests, attitudes, mental sets, values. Yet with reasonable effort any two mature persons can adjust to one another and learn to appreciate one another's strong points. A husband who lives largely in his intellect may be helped to enjoy life and keep his feet on the ground by a wife who is strongly attuned to the world of the senses. A wife whose mental processes tend to be practical and prosaic may learn from an imaginative husband something of the joys of divergent thinking.

Must all of this be legalized or sanctioned by religious authority? Aside from whether or not it must be so sanctioned, *should* it be? There have been many ways of sealing marital contracts. How one feels about the roles of church and state in the matter will depend partly upon one's religious and philosophical views. In any case, our survey of the history of marriage suggested that those who believe they are defying the institution may be simply adding a footnote to that history. With courts beginning to grant "palimony," how is living together without a ceremony different in the practical order from going through the ceremony?

Do those who live together without benefit of clergy intend to stay together? For that matter, how many of those who promise a union of trust and fidelity "till death do us part" intend to keep the promise? A marriage ceremony certainly has the merit of making a commitment on the record. It is difficult to see why anyone who intends to keep the promise would object to having it on the record.

Whatever your views on all of this, you need to live in harmony with many people whose views diverge from yours. Perhaps one day you will find yourself married to someone who takes the institution more seriously, or less seriously, than you do. In the absence of contrary evidence, we must assume the other person's good faith in such matters, but it would help to have an explicit understanding in advance.

Much of what has been said here applies also to the decreasing reverence for and role of the family. A question that arises here is whether the family exists for its members or vice versa? In Western belief, the individual person tends to be the supreme finite value. John Jones does not exist for his family or for society or the state; those organizations exist for him. Paradoxically, though, Mr. Jones can fulfill his individual self properly only by some degree of subordination to the good of the whole.

Psychological studies of family life show that it produces harm as well as benefit, in varying proportions. Often, for example, the family has an unacknowledged scapegoat who is blamed for most things that go wrong. In some cases, the person is granted a few special privileges or exemptions as compensation for playing this role, although none of this is done consciously and certainly is never acknowledged. Still, for most of us, surely there should be a statute of limitations on how many years we are allowed to spend complaining to our psychotherapist or our friends about how Mom or Dad sinned against our psychological integrity. They were probably doing their best most of the time, and surely helped us on occasion. One must pick up a bit of broken crockery from an imperfect childhood and get on with the game.

How one feels about the drift away from the liberal arts will depend on how one feels about the life of the mind. We are rational creatures, though imperfectly so. Reflection differentiates us from the beasts. Literature, sciences, philosophy, the arts help us to develop our reflective powers, thus to have inner resources to take us through the difficult times with less pain and to add to our joy in the better times. There are those, of course, to whom deep reflection will never be congenial, people who viscerally prefer action. There are those whose capacity for academic thought is limited. There are also those, unfortunately, whose capacity and potential taste for the liberal arts are high enough but who have been persuaded that vocational training is all that matters beyond minimal literacy. Difficult decisions are posed here. Suppose, for example, that a student or his family can afford only four years of higher education, or that is about as much of it as the student has the capacity to profit from. Should those four years be spent in a general curriculum that will not prepare the student to earn a living at anything in particular?

It would be nice if educational institutions would do more to help students deal with this kind of quandary. Alas, they make the choice harder than it needs to be. New courses are constantly added in schools of engineering, business, and the like, with the result that the courses meant to liberalize generally cease to be required. It would be very helpful if a better balance could be found in curricula between the vocational and the educational. In the meantime, the student must simply make a difficult choice.

Attitudes of young people toward education mirror the attitudes of their parents in many cases. If both parents had four or more years of college, their children will probably take it for granted through their growing years that going to college is "where it's at." If Dad went to business college and Mom attended a two-year finishing school after high school, Willie and Susie will probably go to an undistinguished college that is nearby, show limited enthusiasm for it, and take about ten years to get through. If Mom and Dad didn't finish high school, the youngsters are not likely to enthuse for higher education. These are tendencies, of course, not universal laws. Sometimes, parents who would have liked to do certain things seek vicarious satisfaction by encouraging their children to do those things. Sometimes, the children really don't want to. It is a delicate balance in raising children to give them all needed encouragement for higher education without applying unhealthy pressure.

The whole trend against high academic expectations in

schools likewise raises a problem of ultimate values that has no easy solution. Some sort of case could be made for the virtue of verbal and mathematical illiteracy. Perhaps the thing to do is live on a mountain-top and eat wild berries. Reading and writing would be unnecessary because there is nobody to communicate with. Arithmetic would not be needed to balance the checkbook or pay the income tax. For those who hope to exist in society, however, there are things that need to be known.

On the industrial front, there are encouraging signs that leaders and members of labor unions are beginning to have a sophisticated awareness that they do not function in a vacuum, that the good of the whole must be thought about. As our discussion of productivity showed, the labor force eventually suffers when employers do not get an honest day's work for the wages they pay. Automobile workers generally understand the advantage of reduced salaries over no salaries. We are not far from the era when workers who tried to organize were sometimes beaten by goon squads. It is understandable if organized labor occasionally went too far in retaliation. Eventually, though, we must all look at the total economic operation.

The women's movement has tended to arouse emotions and prejudices as few other social phenomena of our time have done. Our earlier look at the historical roles of women might help to explain this. Many men feel that the pillars of society are crumbling if the familiar roles change. Many women agree with them. Life can go on much as usual when sexist discrimation is eliminated.

Granted that women and minorities have often been victims of discrimination, discrimination has sometimes been perceived where it did not exist. Coincidence is taken for causation. "I am a woman. I was denied a raise in salary this year. Therefore, I was denied a raise *because* I am a woman.'' Nowadays, when such complaints are filed with government agencies, the person or organization accused often seems to be taken to be guilty until proved innocent, an odd reversal of Anglo-Saxon tradition. How do you go about proving the nonexistence of discrimination? A recent incident in a large Midwestern city illustrates the problem. The city was having the worst storms in a century. Many people were on welfare. Someone conceived the idea of having ablebodied welfare recipients shovel snow to earn the welfare payments. Those who lived within a certain distance of a downtown government office were called and asked to do this if able. There were apparently no allegations that anyone was overworked or asked to do anything too physically difficult. Nevertheless, there was a subsequent charge that the action had been racist on the grounds that most of the people doing the shoveling were black. Was this a just accusation? Yes and no. Yes, in that the means of selecting the persons for this work was bound to result in a majority of blacks. No, in that there was no *intention* of recruiting blacks mainly or exclusively. If the majority of persons on welfare in that area had been white, a majority of those shoveling snow would have been white.

Another healthy sign of the times seems to be an increasing recognition that courtesy helps the wheels of life to turn smoothly. Perhaps there is something too unthinking, too automatic, too shallow, in wishing every customer a good day, and the like. Still, isn't that better than snarling at people? There is no great ethical issue in courtesy versus rudeness, but there is the *same* ethical issue that pops up in many other places: we should treat people as we like to be treated. Most of the value problems we have looked at do seem to come into adequate perspective, on the practical level, by that simple consideration: the Golden Rule.

For Further Reading

Cavarnos, Constantine, *A Dialogue on G. E. Moore's Ethical Philosophy* (Belmont, Mass.: Institute for Byzantine and Modern Greek Studies, 1979), pp. vii, 68.

Cooke, Alistaire, *The Americans* (New York: Penguin Books, 1980), p. 287.

Glickman, Jack, ed., *Moral Philosophy—an Introduction* (New York: St. Martin's Press, 1976), pp. viii, 692.

Lescoe, Francis J., *Existentialism With or Without God* (New York: Alba House, 1974), pp. xviii, 456.

Medved, Michael, and Wallechinsky, David, *What Really Happened to the Class of '65?* (New York: Random House, 1976), pp. xiii, 285.

Vonnegut, Mark, *The Eden Express* (New York: Praeger Publishers, 1975), pp. ix, 214.

Chapter **VIII**

How Did We Get Where We Are?

If we can see the folkways and mores of our time in historical perspective, coping with them intelligently becomes easier. The world did not begin yesterday, and it is not likely to end tomorrow. Nevertheless, anyone who attempts a historical view should recognize the perils that beset the effort. After all, we cannot study the past as we might study Arabia or Canada, by going there. We can only study what the present indicates about the past. We are bound to do this, moreover, from some viewpoint. The division of the past into ancient, medieval, and modern eras, for instance, is based upon a viewpoint. The identification of topics such as the history of women or of government reflects viewpoints. Some historians believe that perspective is bound to suffer when someone writes the history *of* something—women, blacks, education, industry, whatever—in isolation. Things do not exist nor events happen in a vacuum. The warp and woof of history is distorted when we pull out only what pertains to some special topic.

A perennial question is whether there is a design in history. We are more annoyed than satisfied by a descriptive narrative that simply presents a chronological sequence: In 1902 Britain signed a military alliance with Japan. In 1903 King Alexander I of Serbia was murdered. In 1904 the Russo-Japanese War began. Such an account gives us no sense of the flow of events, what is basically happening and how and why. Yet one ought to be suspicious when an Arnold Toynbee, say, finds every civilization neatly divisible into four stages, or a Hegel tells us that history marches forward in a dialectical pattern of thesis, antithesis, and synthesis. Our minds rightly seek some degree of order and sense in the parade of events, but we must beware of wanting too much order and sense.

So much for fair warnings! Now to the task. At the beginning of the seventeenth century, three nations—Britain, Spain, and France—were competing for dominion in North America. Britain, although last of the three to gain a foothold, finally became dominant. Within a century and a half there were thirteen colonies on the Atlantic Coast. Although they were British colonies, their populations were quite mixed: Dutch, Germans, Scandinavians, and so forth.

Many of us were told in school that the American colonists came here seeking religious freedom. That was part of the picture, but other considerations were at work, some of them economic and political. As time passed, the colonists wanted a greater measure of self-government. The colonies also developed plans for closer association among themselves. Independence from Britain was bound to come in time. When peace came after the Revolution, it found a new nation separated from Britain but internally divided in many ways. Some people wanted to continue living along British lines, including crowning George Washington as the first king. Others wanted elimination of all vestiges of privilege and inequality. Still others wanted gradual reforms. Even the most radical reformers, to be sure, did not suggest extending suffrage beyond white males.

America had an entrenched aristocracy at the time of the Revolution. Needless to say, most of those with a vested interest in this arrangement wished to continue it. Slavery was part of the class system. Advocates of American liberty were keeping 500,000 Negroes in bondage. If slavery was soon abolished in the North, it was probably because there were few slaves on that side of the Mason-Dixon line and they were not economically valuable.

Many factors figured in the rise of the American nation. One that was to have long-range significance was passage of the Bill of Rights. James Madison worked with 210 amendments to the Constitution that had been proposed by the ratifying conventions and boiled them down. The Congress finally passed 12 amendments, generally concerned with protecting individual citizens against possible excesses by the federal government. That was in 1789, less than two centuries ago. Yet opinion polls in recent years have indicated that most Americans would not support those items today.

The new nation pushed westward to the Pacific Ocean. North and South began to be divided by a complex set of issues, of which slavery was little more than the tip of the iceberg. The attack on Fort Sumter in 1861 amounted to a declaration that the South would not be allowed to secede from the Union. The end of the Civil War brought social and political changes to the South that changed the shape of American history. The treatment of the vanquished South by the victorious North was essentially benign, however. Despite the abolition of slavery, the Southern caste system continued.

After the Civil War, the greatest change in American life was the rise of industry, which we looked at in an earlier chapter. By the beginning of the twentieth century the United States was producing more iron and steel than Great Britain and had become more an industrial than an agrarian society.

In about two generations, the United States has passed

through two World Wars, the Korean War, and the Vietnam War. In the last two, we had no declaration of war and no declared intention to win. The goal was to contain aggression. Korea remains divided, with hostile troops staring at each other across the 38th Parallel. In Vietnam, to put it simply, we lost. The Communist North won. The "domino" theory of Dwight Eisenhower and John Foster Dulles would have it that all of Southeast Asia would then become a united force against America. Instead, the Communist nations in that part of the world have been busily fighting one another. Korea and Vietnam have been called the first major problems that America could not solve. Americans have had to adjust to a new concept: we are *not* invincible. We cannot do whatever we set our minds to. It is always a sad day for a child when he gives up magic and discovers causes and effects.

Many Americans remember the great depression, triggered by a stock market crash in 1929, which set off a deflationary spiral. President Hoover announced that prosperity was "just around the corner," but we did not seem to get to that corner. Factories closed, banks failed, mortgages were foreclosed, dividends were not paid, federal surpluses became deficits, prices plunged lower and lower. A nation was paralyzed. A charismatic leader, so forceful that we forgot he was in a wheelchair, was elected President. After Franklin Roosevelt's inaugural address, a mood of new confidence was already abroad. Roosevelt acted swiftly and decisively. He declared a bank holiday and worked out a system for protecting the banks and their depositors. In the "Hundred Days" program, his administration proposed much emergency legislation to the Congress.

Roosevelt remains a controversial figure. Only recently has it been easy to find any assessments of his thirteen years in power that look at both the good and bad of what he did and what he stood for. It is hard to imagine how a less activist President could have saved the country, including the capitalistic system, which many people said he was against. Yet Roosevelt turned the country in a new direction. America became a welfare state, one in which responsibility for the well-being of the individual is undertaken by government. The rhetoric of Democratic and Republican Presidents has contrasted upon this point, but the welfare state has grown under all of them. For instance, after campaigning on a platform of individual initiative, President Eisenhower promptly recommended an increase in Social Security payments. So it has gone.

In 1980 the election of Ronald Reagan as President was widely taken to be a mandate to turn the country around, to return to the days of rugged individualism. Yet within a year of Reagan's election opinion polls began to show that a majority of people did not like things the federal government was doing, although they liked its Chief Executive. The welfare state is all that most living Americans can remember. Its roots are very deep by now. Whether, in that respect, the country can or should be turned around is debatable.

Two of the systems pitted against each other in World War II were German, Japanese, and Italian fascism and Russian communism. From much of the wartime propaganda within the Western alliance, one might have thought that the Russian Soviet system was a model democracy, presided over by a genial, grandfatherly type named Josef Stalin. Beginning in about 1946, we were sharply reminded of the truth. President Harry Truman was quick to grasp the situation and to take action. Russia started violating her Yalta agreements almost immediately after the war's end. Whereas America did not annex an acre of ground from the war, Russia took over control of all of Eastern Europe. Demobilization of American armed forces had proceeded swiftly, as demanded by the public and the Congress. Winston Churchill, ever handy with a phrase, told the West it was engaged in a Cold War. So it was and is. Cooperative interludes on the Soviet side have been tactical. One hears that much of the malaise of contemporary youth stems from the prospect of nuclear annihilation. Watching a group of young people on a campus or at a drive-in, it is difficult to suppose that being blown up ranks high on their list of concerns, but one cannot be sure.

As various analysts constantly remind us, television has become a major force in American life, beginning in the late 1950's. One young man complained about how the Vietnam War had all but ruined his life. Inquiry revealed that he had not been fighting the war: he had been in his living room, watching it on Channel 7. There can be no serious doubt that television has, on the whole, been a deleterious agency. In its very nature, it emphasizes the concrete over the abstract, the ephemeral over the long-range, the sensational over the significant. Viewers are presented with an endless round of inane game shows, vulgar giveaways, and domestic comedies about—as one industry figure proudly put it—"happy people with happy problems."

Finally, the acceleration of cultural change has been a difficulty we have all had to cope with. Faster and faster come the changes: the computer age, the energy crisis, the women's movement, civil rights for minorities, human rights as a factor in international relations, exploration of outer space, increasing acceptance of homosexuality, incessant bombardment with news and information, atomic energy plants and attendant radiation hazards, endless inflation, organized religions in disarray—novelty seems to confront us everywhere. Some of the trends are in conflict with some of the others. The urge to return to a simpler life, for example, coexists with the computerization of the supermarkets. Our desire to deal with foreign governments according to how they deal with their own people coexists with our need to contain the aggressive designs of the Soviet Union. We can be pardoned for living in some degree of perpetual confusion. As even this brief glance at our national history suggests, that confusion is increased if we take the attitude, "To hell with yesterday! What's doing today?" There is another saying with an excellent caution: "Those who forget the past are condemned to repeat it."

For Further Reading

Agar, Herbert, *The Price of Union* (Boston: Houghton Mifflin, 1950), pp. xviii, 750.

Bailey, Thomas A., *Voices of America: the Nation's Story in Slogans, Sayings, and Songs* (New York: Free Press, 1976), pp. viii, 520.

Cooke, Alistaire, *Alistaire Cooke's America* (New York: Knopf, 1973), p. 400.

Hofstadter, Richard, and Wallace, Michael, eds., *American Violence: a Documentary History* (New York: Knopf, 1970), pp. xiv, 478.

Magill, Frank N., ed., *Great Events from History* (Englewood Cliffs, N.J.: Salem Press, 1975), 3 vols., pp. xlvii, 2,047.

Schutz, John A., *The Promise of America* (Belmont, Calif.: Dickinson Publishing Co., 1970), pp. xi, 360.

Chapter **IX**

Finding a Philosophy for the New Times

Almost any school child understands the meaning of "problem." If you can't get your galoshes on (or off), that's a problem. If your big sister teases you, that's a problem. If Mother won't give you the money to go to the movies, that's a problem. A problem is anything that perplexes or distresses you, or any question to which you want an answer but do not have one. It differs from a mystery in one important respect: a problem can be solved. It is like a crossword puzzle or Rubik's cube: there is one correct solution, and it can be found. If you cannot find it, someone else can; if not now, later.

Thoughtful people eventually begin to see that there are limits to what the "problem-solving" mentality can accomplish. For awhile "the problem" for American policy-planners was how to get into Vietnam. Then "the problem" was how to get out of Vietnam. In the 1930's the problem was to get government concerned with the plight of the little man. Lately we are told that the problem is to get the little man to look after himself. In short, "problems" are not metaphysical absolutes that fall from the sky. They depend upon a lot of assumptions. "Solving" a problem, too, can be a lot like what the beginner invariably does with Rubik's cube: get things lined up on one side at the expense of getting them out of line on other sides.

There is a philosophy, American in origin, geared to "problems." It is called Pragmatism. Its originators were Charles S. Peirce, William James, and John Dewey. Instead of looking backward for first principles, the Pragmatist tells us we should look ahead to consequences. Every idea should be judged by its practical results. If two ideas that seem to be different have the same consequences, they are really not different at all. The meaning of God, for example, is the effects that believing in God has in someone's life. James was more sympathetic to religion than Dewey or Peirce, but all religious doctrines were to be judged by how they affected believers' lives.

Whereas most people think of a true idea as one that mirrors some reality, Pragmatism sees truth as the quality in an idea of "working." Whereas some systems tell us to judge our practice by principles, Pragmatism turns the prescription around: judge principles by practice; judge ideas by their consequences. The Pragmatist, however, cannot answer this crucial question: *consequences for what?* To put it another way, how shall we judge the consequences? Pragmatists (also called Instrumentalists) in education talk about the student's "growth," but they cannot tell us: growth toward what? When a biologist talks about growth, he has a morphology in mind. He knows what the mature organism should be like. The impasse comes about because Pragmatism has the thing exactly backwards. Practice is to be judged by principles. Certain ideas "work" because they are true; they are not true because they "work."

The typical person, of course, has not read Peirce, James, or Dewey. He is "practical" because he has been raised to be practical and is living in a practical culture. In one way, this is good. Certainly, we need to consider how things work out in practice. We have seen, however, in looking at various contemporary muddles, that they reflect a kind of "practicality" that suffers from a deficiency of analytical thought.

Accordingly, in this last chapter, we shall look at how one can go from superficial "problem-solving" to building a systematic world view—a philosophy. Philosophy is knowledge of things by natural reason, according to their ultimate principles and causes. "Ultimate" here differentiates the subject from science, which essentially *describes* the world. What passes for explanation in science is simply a more refined description. Science deals with "how"; it does not concern itself with any ultimate "why." "Natural reason" emphasizes that philosophy does not deal with faith or divine revelation—although, as will be argued later, everyone needs a faith of some sort. The Big Bang theory in astronomy is an example of scientific "explanation." It is often said to tell us about the beginning of the universe. In order for a gigantic piece of matter to explode, however, it must be there. Somthing, moreover, must bring it from a nonexplosive to an explosive state. Thus, while the Big Bang theory may be a correct description of how the universe assumed its present form, it does nothing to tell us why there *is* a universe, why there is something rather than nothing. That is a philosophical question. Again, a scientist may say, correctly, that we now know what the far side of the moon looks like because men have traveled around it and photographed it. That is good science, but a philosopher could always ask, "Is reality what we can photograph?"

Pythagorus is said to have called himself a lover of wisdom, and "philosophy" is from the Greek *philein,* to love, + *sophia,* wisdom. Anyone acquainted with the history of the discipline in the twentieth century knows how lamentably distant that name is from what has been happening. Modern philosophy has become mostly a kind of parlor game, the players of which occupy themelves with such questions as, "Do we hear a real voice over the telephone?" Another favorite is, "If a barber in a certain town shaves all the men who do not shave themselves, who shaves the barber?" While such questions may help to beguile one in an idle hour, they do not come to grips with the urgent searches that arise in every soul: Where did I come from? Why am I here? Where am I going? What is worth doing? What is worth knowing?

You need not turn yourself into a technical philosopher in order to find answers to such questions that will help you to find your way intelligently and satisfyingly through the maze that is the second half of the twentieth century. It matters little where one jumps into the philosophical maze. Regardless of the starting place, you will soon find yourself in the same perennial questions that have troubled thoughtful people for at least twenty-five centuries.

Take, for instance, the matter of logical proofs. You tell a child that he will die someday. He wants to know how you are certain of this. After all, he hasn't died *yet*. The scientific approach would be to wait and see. "You will die because all people die," you tell him. In saying this, you are using logic. It is not technically complete logic, because you did not use a syllogism. This is a deductive method that uses a major premise and a minor premise to justify a conclusion. There are several kinds of syllogisms. There are also several kinds of enthymemes, the enthymeme being a partial syllogism in which the missing part can be supplied from what is given. (In the example above, for instance, the missing premise is "You are a person."). There are also sorites, chains of reasoning. There is also nonsyllogistic reasoning. If you know that Fred is older than Bill and Bill is older than Sam, you know that Fred is older than Sam.

This chapter is not about logic. Logic, nonetheless, is the philosopher's chief tool. It helps not only to be familiar with logic but to recognize the limits of problems of logical reasoning. One of the biggest ones is this: every conclusion must be supported by premises. These premises, if they are not to be taken on faith, must be supported by *other* premises. This cannot go on to infinity or nothing could be logically demonstrated. Therefore, either nothing can be logically demonstrated or there are some premises or principles that support themselves. These are called first principles. They could be the beginning of our chain. Note carefully: we wouldn't necessarily be able to reason forward *from* them, but we might be able to reason backward *to* them and reject any arguments that cannot withstand that treatment.

Aristotle recognized this problem and looked for a first principle. How, he asked, shall we recognize one if we find one? He laid down three conditions. First, it ought to be something about which it is impossible to be mistaken. It must be such that, when we understand what it means, we cannot deny it without falling into absurdity. Second, it must not be a supposition. Third, it must be naturally known. It cannot be derived from something prior, for there can be nothing prior to a first principle. This last point does not mean, incidentally, that we have some inborn knowledge of first principles. It is enough if we can recognize one when it comes along.

Consider, for example, how we know that a whole is greater than any of its parts. As soon as someone understands what the terms "whole" and "part" mean in relation to each other, he is bound to admit this. The statement about wholes and parts is self-evident, as a first principle must be, but it is not a first principle. Aristotle found three first principles. They are called the laws of identity, of noncontradiction, and of the excluded middle. They really all state varying facets of one truth. The first law is sometimes expressed as "A = A." Whatever is, is. The law of noncontradiction says that "A is B and A is not B cannot both be true." A thing cannot both be and not be at the same time and in the same respect. The law of the excluded middle may be expressed as "A is B or A is not B."

All three of these laws have been sometimes misunderstood and, it seems, deliberately distorted. The law of the excluded middle is sometimes said to mean, for instance, that only extremes are to be considered. Whatever is not white must be black. Whatever is not huge must be microscopic. This is a complete fairy story! Aristotle never said anything of the kind. There are, nonetheless, some technical difficulties about the law of the excluded middle. For instance, while it is true that it will either rain tomorrow or not rain tomorrow, it is not *now* true that it will rain tomorrow or that it will not.

Because of such technical difficulties, we can avoid confusing detours by sticking with the law of noncontradiction. It is a statement both about the way we think and about the world we think about. As a rule of thought, it tells us what *not* to do. We should avoid contradicting ourselves. We should not affirm and deny exactly the same statement. As a law about the world, it tells us that a thing cannot exist and not exist at the same time. Square circles are as impossible outside the mind as they are inside the mind.

Now let us take a step or two toward the practical order and see of what use this principal of noncontradiction can be. We have already seen that the biggest disagreement people have about values is whether the values are objective or subjective. That is, do they have some status independent of the mind of the individual? A way of thinking that reduces values to the personal and subjective is skepticism: the theory that we cannot know anything with certitude, that every belief must be doubted. If it can be shown that the skeptical position contradicts itself, then it must be wrong. But it *does* contradict itself. There are two ways to assert that knowledge is impossible. One is to make that statement without any supporting evidence or argument. Such a hollow assertion cannot be called a philosophical position, since anybody can assert anything. The other approach is to offer some logical demonstration for this skeptical conclusion. Whatever form this logical demonstration may take, this question arises: is it valid? If it is valid, the premises of the argument represent real knowledge, in which case we cannot say that real knowledge is impossible. If, on the other hand, the premises are not valid, the conclusion that follows from them has not been validly demonstrated. Thus, skepticism contradicts itself by requiring knowledge to be simultaneously possible and impossible: possible in order to support the skeptic's premises, impossible in order to support his conclusion.

Teleology and Mechanism

Taking knowledge to be attainable, let us look at two views of the world that have bearing on questions of values. Once again, we shall try to get at the heart of the matter without being unnecessarily technical. Mechanism is the theory that the universe is, in essence, a very big machine. All mental phenomena, all organic life, can be explained by the laws of physics and chemistry. If we cannot do this now, that is simply because we do not yet know enough about physicochemical laws. Nature is a whole whose parts serve its functioning as automatically as do the gears and pulleys of any man-made contrivance.

This view was advanced as long ago as the fourth century B.C. by Leucippus and Democritus, Greek philosophers. Mechanism is deeply entrenched in modern thought. We see it in most psychology, for example, especially the psychologies that explain behavior in terms of mechanical associations or in terms of an unconscious mind over which the rational part of us has no control. The supernatural is wholly excluded in mechanism. Its whole thrust is reductionistic. The reality of anything, that is, is seen as consisting of the smallest parts that can be found in it. One wag offered a reductionistic definition of violin music as the result of scraping horsehair over catgut. In the same vein, the secret of writing a great novel is to hit the right keys on the typewriter.

The opposed philosophy, teleology, takes its name from the Greek *telos,* meaning "end" or "completion." One instance of this world view is vitalism, the theory that living organisms have a vital force or *entelechy,* that their functions do not reduce to physical and chemical laws.

Teleology explains things in terms of purposes and goals rather than in terms of the workings of blind, mechanical forces. Where the mechanist sees the present as explained by the past, the teleologist looks to the future to explain what is happening now. In ethics, teleology leans to the view that some transcendent, objective good determines the standards for human behavior, rather than duty, law, or the like.

Some thinkers believe that neither of these theories applies to everything, so that it is not necessary or possible to choose between them. Some hold that teleology applies in the biological and psychological spheres, while mechanism applies to the physical universe. There are some difficulties about that sort of compromise. The reader is left to decide how it all may be. Consider, though: If you were to ask a runner to explain his behavior in a race, he/she might say, "I ate some Wheaties for breakfast this morning. My body turned that into energy. At the time of the race, habit took over and each leg reacted to what the other leg was doing." All of that would surely strike us as somehow beside the point. The runner would be more likely to say, "I wanted to win the race." This latter explanation works havoc with mechanical ideas of cause and effect. It points to a future event as the cause (the final cause, as Aristotle would say) of what is happening now. Suppose, again, that you find a student studying for an examination she is scheduled to take on the following day. You ask her, "Why are you studying?" The student might answer in terms of past stimuli: "'I saw my algebra book on the table this morning, and my roommate told me I should review it, and . . ." We would feel cheated by that kind of explanation. We would feel that something had been left out of account. A more likely answer would be, "We're having a test tomorrow." Once more, something that has not happened yet and may not happen is cited as the major cause of what is happening right now.

Mechanists and teleologists have contrasted ways of seeing the nature of anything. To the first, the nature of a thing, what it "really is," is whatever it started as. An oak tree is best understood as an acorn that a bunch of things happened to. An adult human being is best understood as a squawling baby after a lot of conditioning has set in. To the teleologist, the opposite of all this is the case. An acorn is best perceived as a potential oak tree. That is its *telos,* what it exists for, what it is trying to become. Human nature is best understood, not from studying an embryo or an infant or even a teen-ager, but from studying a mature person in the prime of life, when his/her physical, mental, and spiritual powers are at their peak.

Mechanism cannot really be reconciled with freedom of will and self-determination, though such reconciliations have been attempted. Teleology tends to fit these ideas quite comfortably. Does someone come to have a good character from performing good deeds or does he perform good deeds because he has a good character? Is personality pushed on from behind by what it has been or pulled on from ahead by what it is trying to become? The teleologist says that you cannot quite explain the self reductionalistically or by reference to past factors such as heredity and environment. These factors may predispose us, but they are not finally conclusive. Past sins, for example, make it harder to resist present temptations, but they do not completely rob us of volitional freedom.

In choosing among philosophical systems, there are some points of practical agreement that ought to be of help. To begin with, it seems that everyone, regardless of his choice of ethical systems, does differentiate in his everyday life between right and wrong. Wherever these ideas of right and wrong may come from, surely it is significant that we all have them. Except for sociopaths, moreover, we do not simply have detached *ideas* on these subjects; we have an active, constant *sense* that we ought to do the one and avoid the other. Again, regardless of theories, we all sense that we are free, within some limits, to choose what we shall do. Even Professor B. F. Skinner, in his famous book *Beyond Freedom and Dignity,* tells us in the last chapter to arise, as it were, cast off our chains, and build the kind of society he wants. Never mind that, through the rest of the book, he has been telling us that we have no power to transcend our conditioning and make such choices! When we *have* made a choice and have acted upon it, nearly all of us, it seems, feel a sense of moral responsibility. We also hold others responsible for *their* decisions, unless we recognize that someone decided under extraordinary conditions such as emotional upset, fatigue, or influence of drugs or alcohol. Most of us, too, occasionally experience that urge, not simply to do our duty, but to go beyond duty's call, to do more than anyone has any right to ask of us.

An ethical system ought to deal with these familiar facts of experience. We should be very cautious about embracing any theory that does not do them full justice. We shall not say more about ethical theories beyond noting the types into which they fall. The theories can be roughly grouped as cognitive and noncognitive. The cognitive systems hold that ethical principles can be conceptualized and put into propositions and that these propositions can have a bearing on our lives. Through most of history, all approaches to ethics were of this sort. In recent generations, noncognitive theories have been on the rise. These tend to reduce right and wrong to emotions and to deny that reason has any genuine connection with these emotions. A logical positivist would tend to say, for example, that the statement, "Stealing is wrong" can be paraphrased as "The idea of stealing fills me with loathing and repugnance."

From another standpoint, systems of ethics can be classified as metaphysical, naturalistic, and intuitivist. Metaphysical theories see the good as one aspect of being, which they try to put into its proper place in the scheme of things. Naturalistic systems rule out any transcendental values beyond our experience. Intuitivists, of whom the late G. E. Moore was an outstanding example, hold that we have a direct insight into good and evil that has no satisfactory explanation, scientific or metaphysical. The writer once asked a small boy how he knew a certain religious principle that the little boy had just enunciated. He rolled his eyes heavenward and said, "I just knowed it in the back of my head." That, roughly, is the position of the intuitivists.

The Need for a Faith

This book has argued for approaching problems of value by systematic reasoning. We all need more than that, though. Finally, we need a faith. Everyone needs some belief so deep and unshakable that he would face the firing squad for it. Science is itself such a faith. After all, the scientist *presupposes* a real world and order in that real world. He cannot demonstrate these things scientifically, because that would take for granted the very points in question. Philosophy is also a faith, this time in logic and reason. Aristotle said that you must philosophize, even if you are trying to prove that people should not philosophize. He was right, but the wise nonphilosopher will not get into that kind of trap. He/she will simply say, "I don't believe in philosophy." There is no answer to that! Even the person who believes you must get the other fellow before he can get you has faith, albeit not one that is likely to produce much happiness or contribute to social stability.

"Faith" here is not used in any of the technical senses proper to various religions. It simply means *firm belief without proof.* Most of our actions rest upon such a basis. If you are sitting in a chair as you read, you probably did not examine the chair first to see if it would hold you. If you switched on a lamp by the chair, you probably were confident that the gesture would produce light and that it would not give you a gigantic electric shock. As you hold the book, you are reasonably confident that there are no germs on the pages that will give you a fatal disease. Thus do we venture forth. Most of the time, we are right to do so.

Godspeed in *your* venturing, unseen reader!

For Further Reading

Anderson, Alan R., *Minds and Machines* (Englewood Cliffs, N.J.: Prentice-Hall, 1964), pp. viii, 114.

Donnelly, Dorothy B., *The Bone and the Star, Two Perspectives on the Scene of Time* (New York: Sheed and Ward, 1944), pp. x, 205.

Gewirth, Alan, *Reason and Morality* (Chicago: University of Chicago Press, 1978), pp. xii, 393.

Green, Ronald M., *Religious Reason: the Rational and Moral Basis of Religious Belief* (New York: Oxford University Press, 1978), pp. viii, 302.

Haught, John P., *Nature and Purpose* (Lanham, Md.: University Press of America, 1980), pp. ii, 127.

Kupperman, Joel J., *Ethical Knowledge* (London: Allen and Unwin, 1970), pp. iii, 157.

Coping With Changing Values

Robert B. Nordberg

HOME CARE FOR THE DYING CHILD

Professional and Family Perspectives

And now as a consolation they tell me that I am going to have more children. And where is Sonia? Where is that little personality for whom I honestly declare I should have accepted a martyr's death to bring her back to life?

Dostoevsky

HOME CARE FOR THE DYING CHILD
Professional and Family Perspectives

Edited by
Ida Marie Martinson, Ph.D., R.N.
Associate Professor of Nursing, School of Nursing
Lecturer in Physiology, School of Medicine
University of Minnesota
Minneapolis, Minnesota

ACC
APPLETON-CENTURY-CROFTS / New York

LIBRARY OF CONGRESS CATALOGING IN PUBLICATION DATA
Main entry under title:

Home care for the dying child.

Includes index.
1. Terminally ill children--Home care. 2. Terminally ill children--Family relationships.
3. Pediatric nursing. 4. Tumors in children.
I. Martinson, Ida Marie 1936-
RJ245.H63 649.8 76-29360
ISBN 0-8385-3824-X

76 77 78 79 80 / 10 9 8 7 6 5 4 3 2 1

Prentice-Hall International, Inc., London
Prentice-Hall of Australia, Pty. Ltd., Sydney
Prentice-Hall of India Private Limited, New Delhi
Prentice-Hall of Japan, Inc., Tokyo
Prentice-Hall of Southeast Asia (Pte.) Ltd., Singapore
Whitehall Books Ltd., Wellington, New Zealand

PRINTED IN THE UNITED STATES OF AMERICA

cover design: Karin Batten

DEDICATED TO
PARENTS

CONTRIBUTORS

Janice M. Anderson, M.S., R.N., Instructor, School of Nursing, Minneapolis, Minnesota

Joyce G. Anderson, M.A., R.N., Mental Health Clinician, Abbott-Northwestern Hospital Corporation, Minneapolis, Minnesota

Mary Ann Anglim, M.S., R.N., Assistant Professor of Nursing, School of Nursing, University of Minnesota, Minneapolis, Minnesota

Barbara Etzel, M.S., R.N., Instructor, School of Nursing, University of Minnesota, Minneapolis, Minnesota

Delphie Fredlund, M.P.H., R.N., Associate Professor of Public Health Nursing, School of Public Health, University of Minnesota, Minneapolis, Minnesota

Alice Graner, M.A., R.N., Instructor, School of Nursing, University of Minnesota, Minneapolis, Minnesota

Neil Hering, B.D., Chaplain, University of Minnesota Hospitals, Minneapolis, Minnesota

Carol Jorgens, M.S., R.N., Instructor, School of Nursing, University of Minnesota, Minneapolis, Minnesota

Karen R. Karni, M.Ed., M.T. (A.S.C.), Associate Professor of Medical Technology, School of Nursing, University of Minnesota, Minneapolis, Minnesota

John Kersey, M.D., Associate Professor of Medicine, School of Medicine, University of Minnesota, Minneapolis, Minnesota

Delores Krause, M.S. in Ed., Research Associate, School of Nursing, University of Minnesota, Minneapolis, Minnesota

Emily Kulenkamp, Roseville, Minnesota

Carolyn J. Levitt, M.D., Assistant Professor of Medicine, Director of Clinics, Children's Hospital, St. Paul, Minnesota

Michael C. Linder, M.S.W., Director of Social Services, Children's Hospital, St. Paul, Minnesota

Ida Marie Martinson, Associate Professor of Nursing, School of Nursing, Lecturer in Physiology, School of Medicine, University of Minnesota, Minneapolis, Minnesota

Paul V. Martinson, Ph.D., B.D., Associate Professor, Luther Theological Seminary, St. Paul, Minnesota

Mark Nesbit, M.D., Professor of Medicine, School of Medicine, University of Minnesota, Minneapolis, Minnesota

Sister Carol Neuberger, M.A., R.N., Assistant Professor of Nursing, School of Nursing, University of North Dakota, Grand Forks, North Dakota

Evelyn Peterson, D.N.S., R.N., Assistant Professor of Nursing, School of Nursing, University of Minnesota, Minneapolis, Minnesota

Shirley A. Pierce, B.S., Coordinator, Community Mental Health Center, St. Paul, Minnesota

Carol Reese, M.A., R.N., Instructor, School of Nursing, University of Minnesota, Minneapolis, Minnesota

Sue N. Sauer, R.N., Head Nurse, University of Minnesota Hospitals, Minneapolis, Minnesota

Romana Urueta, M.S., R.N., Assistant Professor of Nursing, School of Nursing, University of Minnesota, Minneapolis, Minnesota

Mary G. Wesensee, M.A., R.N., Assistant Professor of Nursing, School of Nursing, University of Minnesota, Minneapolis, Minnesota

David N. Wetzel, Minneapolis, Minnesota

Marilee Woehning, M.P.H., R.N., Instructor, School of Nursing, University of Minnesota, Minneapolis, Minnesota

PREFACE

This book grew out of the editor's three-year involvement in a study of the home as an alternative health care facility and of the parents as health personnel providing care for the dying child. It is based on today's increasing awareness that the child with a terminal illness, his parents and family, and the health professionals who work with the child, feel a need not only for adequate information pertaining to their situation but also for physical and emotional support. Specifically designed for health professionals, either actively engaged in or preparing for a career in the health field, the intent of this book is to share with them the knowledge and experience of a variety of concerned individuals involved in the care of children facing death.

Part I introduces the Home Care Project, and three parents who have lost a child relate their experience with it. Nurses who have been involved in home care of the dying child write of their experiences in Part II. In Part III several nurses, social workers, and a chaplain write of the effects on the family before, during and after death. Part IV discusses the medical, nursing, and technical aspect of care for the child with cancer. Part V, the final section, presents theoretical concepts for consideration by health professionals.

I wish to express deep appreciation to the contributing authors, all of whom, despite busy schedules, took the time to write because they recognized the need for this kind of book. I am especially grateful to the father of one of the families and the mothers of two others who have shared many of their experiences so that health professionals might understand their situation more clearly and, hopefully, improve our attempts to help.

I wish to express gratitude to the nonacademic helpers in this undertaking. My special thanks to Charlotte Gronseth for her editorial suggestions and her efforts in coordinating this project. My appreciation also to Helen McInnes, Coral Sampson, and Cindy Moews for their hours of service.

CONTENTS

PART III: THE FAMILY'S REACTION TO DEATH AND DYING

PART IV: THE HOSPITAL AND THE CLINIC: DIAGNOSIS, TREATMENT, AND NURSING CARE

PART V: THEORETICAL CONSIDERATIONS FOR HEALTH PROFESSIONALS

APPENDIXES

PART I

INTRODUCTION

In this chapter the author provides a general introduction to the Home Care for the Dying Child Project, and also describes the development of two nursing interventions for care of the dying child at home.

1

INTRODUCTION TO THE HOME CARE PROJECT*

Ida Marie Martinson

Several years ago when my father-in-law was dying of cancer, I experienced for the first time as an adult a death in my family. In the terminal stage of the disease my father-in-law had been hospitalized, but very soon he wished to return home to die. There were diverse reactions to his request. One family member felt that bringing him home would mean inadequate care for him. Three staff nurses thought he was too sick to bring home. Yet every day for seven days he requested that he be allowed to go home. Actually, since the first day of his request, I had been in communication with the public health nurse preparing for his return. Since there were three registered nurses in the family, I felt we would be able to care for him. The decision was made to bring him home.

In the beginning all three of us shared the responsibility for his care and things went well. However, one of the mem-

*The Appendix contains case records of two of the author's first involvements in the Home Care Project, "Recollections of a Nurse" and "A Nurse's Perspective."

bers of the family had to return to her home and the other, who was older, found it too exhausting. As a result, I became involved twenty-four hours a day. There was some pressure to hospitalize him again. Yet having his family around him meant a great deal to him. Even the grandchildren would bring him wildflowers they had picked or sing a song for him. He would respond with a smile—he had energy for nothing more than that—and this in turn pleased the children.

We succeeded in caring for him at home through the death event. One morning at about two-thirty family members wakened me when it was time for his shot. When I came in I found some changes in his condition—there was no sign of pain, his circulation was poor, and his legs had become mottled and cool to the touch. We called the others, and for the last five minutes he was surrounded by his entire family. For the first time, death was not frightening to me. In fact, it became a very positive family experience for all of us.

It was this personal experience that became the first major influence in my selection of "Home care for the dying child" as a research project. The second influence was closely related to it, namely, my growing concern regarding the limited availability of home care for the dying. Must this type of care be available only to those whose families include registered nurses or doctors? For many years we had heard about isolated instances of people who have died at home; but in most of these cases there has been either a health professional in the family or the financial capability of affording full-time professional care. The question to be answered, however, is: Is it not the responsibility of health professionals to make this alternative to hospitalization available to other segments of society as well?

Thirdly, I believe that this concern for home care of the dying clearly lies within the realm of nursing research. This belief has become especially strong because of my administrative position as director of research in a school of nursing, a position which carries with it a responsibility to develop pertinent studies in nursing. Just as the care of the dying child or the dying adult is considered one aspect of nursing practice, so too is health care delivery research a legitimate aspect of nursing research.

Moreover, I knew of no one at that time working with children dying at home. In fact, most literature on the dying patient—child or adult—assumes that the hospital is the appropriate place to die.

Finally, there was the shared interest of my neighbor, Dr. John Kersey, who felt a concern similar to mine. At the time we first expressed our mutual interest, I remarked that perhaps in five years' time I would consider a study in this area. However, on hearing about Eric, one of Dr. Kersey's patients, I became involved within a few days' time. Before sharing my experience with Eric and his family in some detail, I would like to give some of the background to my present and ongoing study.

The concept of home care as one segment in the continuum of progressive patient care has developed gradually. All persons concerned with health care—members of the professional team, consumers, and hospitals—have shown increased interest in developing home care service as an alternative to hospitalization. This interest has received impetus in part from increased awareness of the rights of patients, increased sensitivity to the total impact of hospitalization on the patient and his family, and marked concern for the sharply rising costs of traditional health care systems.

But the role of home care as an alternative health care delivery system needs to be extensively researched. While a single study probably cannot deal with all areas in need of research, in this article I will share some of the information and data regarding home care for the dying child with cancer and the cost of a program that would provide that care.

Although research studies on home care programs are few and do not speak directly to home care of the terminally ill child, the effect of hospitalization on children has been studied extensively. For the child under five years of age, the greatest fear is that of separation from the mother, and, secondarily, separation from things associated with her—other members of the family, home, and playthings. Hospitalization forces separation from the mother at the same time that it introduces the child to new people, places, and, frequently, painful routines. It is small wonder that hospitalization for the young child is often a traumatic experience. The child over five, in addition to the fear of separation, is preoccupied with the threat to his or her bodily integrity and functioning.[1] This preoccupation shows itself in fear of medical procedures and their possible outcomes.

The child's need for the mother increases markedly during serious illness but hospitalization reduces the child's access to her. The child comes to depend upon the hospital staff for care and relief from pain and may reject the parents because they do not take care of him and cannot bring the painful procedures and hospitalization to an end.

A recent study done at the City of Hope Hospital, Duarte, California, indicated that increased contact between the parents and the child tended to decrease the problems associated with hospitalization for both the parents and the child. Friedman states:

> Mothers, in particular, are helped in their own adjustment if they can participate in their child's care—not totally lose him to the physicians and nurses. Well intentioned ward personnel may urge a mother to spend less time with her ill child, . . . [but] a forced return home may add to her distress and guilt.[2]

The study I have been involved in, however, does not attempt to speak to the problem of the usual hospitalized child. Rather, it concerns itself with care of the child with terminal cancer. These children have the same problems and concerns as the child with a nonterminal illness. In addition, they have the added fears surrounding impending death. Recent studies have shown that even when a young child has not been told the seriousness of his illness,

> . . . he somehow picks up a sense that his illness is very serious and very threatening. The fatally ill child is aware that his is no ordinary illness . . . Even though the concern of the 6- to 10-year-old . . . child may not take the form of overt expression about death, the more subtle fears and anxieties are nonetheless real, painful, and very much related to the seriousness of the illness.[3]

At the present time there is no known medical treatment which can reverse the course of cancer in its final stage.

Therefore, children in the final stages of cancer who are admitted to hospitals are admitted to die. The hospital with all its technology and highly skilled personnel not only may not be essential in caring for the dying child, it may well be an obstacle to the provision of appropriate care for such a patient.

During the fall of 1972, I met with Dr. John Kersey and stated then my interest in identifying problems associated with home care and my willingness to work with a family utilizing home care if a family desired it. The parents of a ten-year-old leukemic boy indicated to Dr. Kersey their desire to keep their son, Eric, at home as long as possible. I became involved and worked with the family throughout the terminal stages of the illness. His mother later wrote:

> It was a very deep and meaningful experience to our family to have been able to personally take care of and be with him through the end when he needed us the most . . . We had not considered nor did we know it was possible to make it "all the way" until Dr. Martinson began her home visits with us . . . seventeen days before Eric died. Without her aid and reassurance, to both ourselves and Eric, I doubt that we could have succeeded in this venture.[4]

Some of the problems involved in home care of the dying child were identified in the course of working with this one family. In addition, Eric's mother agreed to serve as a consultant if a home care project were developed. Several faculty members at the University of Minnesota School of Nursing expressed an interest in working with other families who might want to care for their dying child at home.

As a result of the expressed interest of the faculty and myself to involve others in this study, a weekly seminar was organized in the fall of 1974 to investigate systematically the feasibility of home care for the dying child. This included developing a method for identification of the needs of the family and child, anticipating problems that might arise and possible solutions to them, and outlining the role(s) of health care personnel. In addition, some seminar members have also provided care to other families who elected to care for their dying child at home.

Since 1972, eight families have participated in the home care project. Five of the eight children died at home; the sixth child lived only two hours in the hospital. The seventh and eighth children were hospitalized and died there. The length of involvement with a family has averaged 45 days (range: 5 days to 6 months) and the estimated cost was $1,000 per child. The mean total hours of direct professional service (home visits, telephone calls, clinic visits) with the families was 20 (range: 15 to 40 hours). The number of home visits ranged from 3 to 10 per family and were supplemented with telephone calls (average number: 10; range: 2 to 20). A chart audit done in 1972 of ten leukemic children who died in the hospital showed that the mean final hospitalization was 28.5 days (range: 1 to 54 days) and the mean cost $4,480 (range: $595 to $8,906). Because of the sharp increase in hospital costs, the final hospitalization of these children today would average $6,612.[5]

The work done thus far has indicated an acceptance of home care of the dying child by parents. Preliminary analysis of data currently being collected also seems to indicate that registered nurses consider it an appropriate vehicle for the care of some patients and have expressed their willingness to assist in home care programs. Continued work needs to be done to identify the essential elements of home care for the dying child with the goal of determining which member(s) of the professional health care team can best provide the needed support and care, to assess the feasibility of institutionalizing the program, and to determine the cost to the family and community of this approach to health care.

In each of the cases thus far, the services of the home care nurse were offered to the parents verbally with the following contractual agreement:

1. The home care nurse would be available twenty-four hours a day.
2. The home care nurse would make arrangements for visits whenever and wherever the family deemed necessary.
3. The option of the child's returning to the hospital would always be open, and if this option was exercised, the home care nurse would continue the visits if desired.
4. The personal physican could be called at any time.

5. The home care nurse would attempt to help the family deal with any problems that might arise.

In return, the mother, or any other primary caretaker, would agree to share with the project staff their perceptions of their daily home care related needs and problems as well as their reactions to the nurse's contacts with the family and the child.

I have used primarily two interventions with the five families with whom I have worked. One is that of *parental control* and the other of *limiting the uncertainty*. Throughout my work with these families I have tried everything possible to leave the control of the situation in the hands of the parents, although I would obtain for the parents whatever they needed in order to handle the situation themselves. This is a difficult thing to do and I found it a challenge. It means in essence giving to the parents what we would like to keep for ourselves. Because of our knowledge based on both preparation and past experience, we, as health professionals, are more able to manage the situation, and by manipulation, to be in control. But being in control is something these parents need and have a right to, and, whether we are ready for it or not, will start demanding.

There are two aspects to parental control, the "perceived" and the "actual." Both must be considered at all times; control must be actual and be perceived by the parents as such. For example:

> Del and I were beginning to wonder if what we were doing was best for Eric. He had been a very creative child and there were a number of things he wanted to do but his arms and hands were getting more and more useless. We tried everything we could think of but the days were long and he would get despondent. We wondered if the hospital personnel would be better equipped to keep him satisfied; if occupational therapy would have better resources for him.
>
> Dr. Martinson would constantly reassure us that his care was as good, if not better, than he would receive in the hospital. And how I needed that reassurance—I knew Eric wanted to be at home but I was by no means all that confident that I was enterprising enough to handle it.[6]

In this illustration the parents' perception was that their care was not adequate, though in reality it was excellent.

The actual loss of control by one of the parents can be illustrated by the following:

> I had slept on the floor in Eric's room for the last two nights as he was afraid we wouldn't hear him if he called, as he was so weak, and he seemed to need the security of having me near.
>
> When I attempted to give him his medication in the morning, he was unable to swallow, hadn't the strength to sip water through a straw, could barely open his mouth, and began vomiting. I called Dr. Martinson and she gave me some suggestions on administering his medication, none of which worked.
>
> I called the doctor to see if we could get shots for the pain, explaining that Del had had some experience giving injections years ago while he was in the medics. I was sure Dr. Martinson would help so he said he would contact her and she called back, cancelling her appointments for the afternoon, and came out to the house.
>
> I was physically and mentally exhausted—I hadn't slept well for the past two nights and the day had started badly and certainly wasn't getting any better. Dr. Martinson arrived but Eric was resting so she spent most of the time with me, helping me work through my feelings and frustrations. She suggested hospitalization but I didn't want that. I didn't want to let Eric down—even though I wasn't even able to cope with him at the time and Del had spent the majority of the day with him except when it took the two of us for Eric's needs.[7]

In helping the parents to gain and maintain control, I would refrain from giving care to the child myself during home visits. If the child needed mouth care, for example, I explained how it should be done and then let the parents do it themselves. For me to be "the expert" and perform the care would undermine the parents' confidence in their ability to perform these basic skills.

To gain and maintain control, the parents also needed support in the affective domain. Crucial to this, I believe, was my encouragement for them to call me at any time, day or night, whenever they felt they needed help or advice, even if it meant a home visit. This freedom to call me at any time, twenty-four hours a day, was for each family, as they expressed afterwards, essential to their ability to manage home care for their child. They did make use of this opportunity and called me sometimes at three or four o'clock in the morning.

In the cognitive domain, I offered support by preparing

the parents for various complications that might occur, such as hemorrhage, infection or coma. At first I was not at all sure I ought to do this, fearing they would be frightened and suffer increased anxiety. In spite of my hesitation, I decided to explain the possibilities. "The child may hemorrhage," I said, "and therefore a good supply of towels should be on hand" (towels being the most readily available item to them).

Many of these complications never occurred, and I waited and worried over complaints about things that never happened. When there were no complaints, I decided to ask the parents directly. "Do you remember," I asked them, "when I told you there may be hemorrhaging? What are you feelings now that that never occurred? Would you have preferred that I had never mentioned it?" Each one replied that they were grateful for being prepared for these eventualities. In being made aware they had come to feel that they were important in the control of the situation, and that if these things had occurred they would not have become panic-stricken, knowing what to do until I would have been able to reach them.

The second intervention that I have used with these five families is what I call limiting the uncertainty. For example, one morning at three o'clock my phone rang. The parents of a child called to tell me that the child's leg had become cold. I thought to myself that the explanation was probably quite simple—leukemic cells causing a plug in the blood vessel, thus stopping circulation; this plug might move and circulation be reestablished. I explained to the parents the possibilities—that the leg might become even colder before returning to normal, or that the cold would continue, leading to complications, one sign of which would be color change. I asked them to keep in contact with me. In giving this information regarding the possibilities, I had thus somewhat limited their uncertainty.

Another time the phone rang at midnight. There was bleeding from the gums. What should the parents do? Again I said simply that the bleeding may increase and lead to hemorrhaging (and suggested what to do if it did) or that the situation may return to normal. Once a child's jaw became locked, and in their anxiety the parents called to ask me what might follow. Though I did not communicate my own anxious feelings, especially in light of possible hemorrhaging or vomiting, I explained the possibilities, including that the jaw might relax again very soon—which it did.

By informing the parents of all the possibilities, I was setting a limit to their uncertainty. When I was sure a situation would only get worse, that it would not improve, I told them so. I asked them afterwards if they had found it helpful for me to include the more frightening and discouraging possibilities as well as the more encouraging ones. With a sigh they answered, yes, it had been helpful, because even more frightening is complete uncertainty and ignorance of what might happen. Thus if lockjaw occurs, the parents have no mental limits to apply to the situation, especially if they have little or no understanding of anatomy and human physiology.

It has been quite a revelation to me to see how consistent and pervasive is this fear caused by uncertainty, and how much it can be alleviated by some understanding of the situation. The ramifications of the uncertainty surrounding the certainty of death must always be considered. Death is inevitable, and though the "who" and the "why" have been determined, the "how" and the "when" are uncertain. Into this situation we offer an alternative to the hospital as the "where."

When informing the parents of the possibilities which may occur, we have found it extremely important to choose words carefully, for the mental images our terminology may conjure in the mind of a lay person may be quite different from those in our minds. For example, one health professional, in attempting to reassure a mother, said, "Whenever you feel that you can no longer manage, we will bring your child to the hospital." But the mother asked, "When will I know when I'm no longer managing well enough?"

Although Eric's parents had not entered the experience of home care expecting to manage to the end, they did in fact care for their son through his death. This included communicating to Eric, although not as directly as planned, the fact of his approaching death.

When Eric's life finally slipped away, his parents were with him. His mother summarizes the experience as follows:

> This was by far the most difficult task of our lives—but also one of the most important. For us it also fulfilled a need. We were able to give Eric what he wanted—there had been so little we, or anyone else, could do for him—at least we could do that.
>
> Although we had the determination, once we knew what we wanted, it would have been impossible to have made it through the end without Dr. Martinson. Her only compensation was our eternal gratitude for her help.
>
> This may not be the answer for every family, but it was most definitely so for us and we feel it could be for a great many others if given the aid, means and support to carry it through.[9]

I find it significant that the parents of the five children who died at home have been enthusiastic in their response to home care. A common observation has been that the parents' grief over the loss of their child is eased somewhat by the knowledge that they themselves have done everything possible to help their dying child, and that they have been able by their presence to constantly assure the child of their support and love. One dying six-year-old boy asked his mother, "Will it be long now?" She replied, "No, it won't be long," and she carried him into her bed, where he lay between his mother and his father. When the parents awoke a couple hours later, their son had died—peacefully. This is another illustration of how a family can cope with this difficult experience in a way that conveys to the child the sense of security that he needs.

As I continue in this study, "Home Care for the Dying Child," my greatest encouragement comes from the parents themselves. As one wrote:

> No matter if it culminates a full life or a life shortened much too soon, does death have to be terrorizing? There are many to rejoice and aid in the event of birth, as with a patient that can be helped, but for those going through the frustration of "not getting better," when science and the masses, sometimes even family and friends who can no longer face them, have deserted; could there be a greater challenge or more considerable need for help?[10]

REFERENCES

1. Spinetta J J, Rigler D, Karon M: Anxiety in the dying child. Pediatric 52:841, 1973
2. Friedman S B: Management of fatal illness in children. In Green M: Ambulatory Pediatric. Philadelphia, Saunders, 1968, pp 753–759
3. Spinetta, Rigler, Karon: *loc cit*
4. Kulenkamp E, Martinson I M: Eric. Minneapolis, University of Minnesota School of Nursing 1974, pp 2–28
5. Larson N: Personal communication, 1975
6. Kulenkamp, Martinson: *op cit*, pp 21–22
7. Kulenkamp, Martinson: *op cit*, pp 25–26
8. Kulenkamp, Martinson: *op cit*, pp 20–28
9. Kulenkamp, Martinson: *op cit*, p 31

This chapter relates the experiences of a mother in caring for her son who died at home from leukemia. The writer includes the family's perception of the health professionals involved.

2

ERIC

A Mother's Recollection

Emily Kulenkamp

I never thought the day would come when we would pray for the death of our beloved son. But we did, at the same time not wanting to let him go. We loved Eric deeply, and it was an agonizing experience seeing our child die, little by little each day.

There were moments when I considered euthanasia and later discovered my husband, Del, had too. But there were so many deterrents—my lack of know-how for it to be painless and quick; our desire for an autopsy with hopes it could help other children with the same disease; the "shame" on the family, if discovered; and our daughter's need for me which I felt would increase after Eric's death. Maybe these weren't valid excuses; maybe they were just my way of rationalizing away a deed I hadn't the courage to do—although I had the conviction. But those extenuating circumstances were also important to me, valid or not.

Had we followed that course, we would neither have seen

nor felt the true peace that can come with death. Perhaps what we discovered in the last seventeen days of Eric's life made his continuing struggle worthwile, if not for him, for others.

Eric had been diagnosed as having acute lymphoblastic leukemia two years and three months before his death. He had been through the full scope of radiation and chemotherapy treatments prescribed for his disease and there was no longer any reason to expect remission from another course of drugs. He was bedridden due to paralysis brought about by the leukemia infiltrating the central nervous system for the third time in his illness, a rare occurence.

We had wanted to keep him home as long as we could physically and mentally carry on, especially since we had always been a close family and saw no reason for letting Eric's impending death interfere with that relationship until absolutely necessary. We had told Eric he could choose to be hospitalized if he felt we weren't caring for him adequately. There had been times in the past when he had been willing to be readmitted to the hospital, realizing he needed the help that could be given to him there. However, inadequate as we felt we were, Eric preferred "home."

We contacted the doctor regularly, usually about once a week, and made occasional clinic visits. But Eric was well aware of his obvious physical decline, the questions that were being evaded, the treatments that were refused. He came to feel that "the doctors aren't doing anything for me anyhow, so I don't want to see them."

About this time Dr. John Kersey of the University of Minnesota, Eric's doctor at the time, mentioned during a telephone conversation that a nurse was attempting to set up a home nursing service for families in situations similar to ours. He asked me to consider the problems involved in giving Eric care at home. I agreed to meet with the two of them the next week.

Accordingly, Dr. Kersey contacted Ida Martinson, and it developed that our family initiated the project, "Home Care for the Dying Child."

Dr. Martinson stayed an hour and a half on her first home

visit. She visited with Eric for a few minutes, explaining to him the purpose of her call. He responded, "Just make me better." Though he was having pain at the time, he didn't want any medication, as he many times did not, determined to make it without. He was finally convinced to take a Tylenol.

Dr. Martinson and I sat and talked during most of her visit. I found it very comforting to converse with her as she seemed to understand all the aspects of our problem, not only in her professional capacity but through having undergone a similar experience with her father-in-law.

We discussed the idea of "guidelines" for parents regarding when to call the doctor and drug management. Though I had been dispensing potent drugs for over two years, I never lost my fear of them as I had seen what their toxicity could do. At the time, Eric was taking prednisone for symptomatic relief, valium as a relaxer at bedtime, and Tylenol to ease the pain. We had been told we could get codeine when Eric needed it. There was no doubt it would be needed soon. Because of the difficulties involved in obtaining narcotics, Dr. Martinson strongly encouraged us to have codeine on hand so that we would have it when needed.

She mentioned that terminal patients go through a stage of wanting to be alone more toward the end—their way of subconsciously separating themselves from loved ones. I was relieved to hear this as Eric had been displaying such tendencies, and I was beginning to feel rejected. This behavior was unlike Eric because he had formerly wanted me with him whenever possible; now there were times when he wanted to be alone.

During one of the initial visits, Dr. Martinson brought up the possibility of our "making it all the way," something we had not even considered. At first we were rather repelled by the notion. We had heard that the manner of death in leukemics was never predictable and that sometimes their deaths were violent. How could we be prepared? Would we be continually plagued with the thought of a nightmarish happening? What if Betsy, Eric's six-year-old sister, whom we didn't feel could be forewarned, were around to witness such an event? Those close to us who knew what we were considering felt it would be too difficult for us physically and emotionally. Del wondered how much more I could take; Eric and I had been especially close and Del felt I wouldn't be able to bear his death, much less be an active participant helping Eric through it. The doctors had said, "When you can no longer manage caring for Eric at home, bring him to the hospital." From this we assumed there would be a time when we would no longer be able to handle the situation. We considered it seriously, but tried not to think about what tomorrow would bring.

Although Dr. Martinson had mentioned the possibility of getting a public health nurse to come in to help, I never gave it much thought, if any. I really had no desire for "outside help" and doubt I would ever have sought it. Nor did I believe Eric would want someone else to care for him. We had been able to accommodate his needs and assumed he would be hospitalized when we could no longer manage.

I was at ease with Dr. Martinson. She had a quiet and unassuming manner, yet her inner strength and capabilities were evident. I felt she had something worthwhile to offer and was pleased when she told me that we would be her home visit family.

Dr. Martinson wondered whether I should be taught to give injections. However, the doctor did not think they would be needed at that time. I felt the doctors didn't believe we would make it through until the end, but neither did we at that point.

One of our most "up-and-down" days was Eric's tenth birthday, ironically the same birth date as Dr. Martinson's. It hadn't been expected that Eric would live that long. When he had asked if he would be better by his birthday, the doctor had replied, "I hope so." Eric interpreted this as he wished. "The doctor said I'd be better by my birthday but I'm worse off. I have a feeling I'm never going to get better, it's been so long already!"

He had wanted to walk for his birthday but was bedridden. He was unhappy we had wrapped his gifts since he couldn't unwrap them. He was pleased with his presents, displeased we had "spent so much." He made us promise not to spend much for him at Christmas; but in the next breath he said he wanted an expensive microscope.

The management of Eric's favorite restaurant remembered him and agreed to prepare their specialty as a "take-out," a seven-course Sicilian dinner. A half hour before the meal, Eric could "no longer stand the pain" and had his first taste of codeine. I was so relieved we had it on hand. Del carried Eric downstairs for our candlelight dinner. Eric proposed a toast: "To the happiest but most miserable birthday of my life." He was grumpy at first, but as the dinner progressed his spirits rose. He stuffed himself, explaining he had been dieting for a week looking forward to the occasion. We had thought he hadn't felt well enough to eat.

On Dr. Martinson's third visit, Eric requested us both to stay and talk with him for a longer period of time. He had begun to have confidence in her and looked forward to her visits, as did I.

It wasn't a matter of her being company for him; he could have had plenty. But he had become intolerant of most visitors, even those he normally loved dearly, because their bedside manners were more tiresome to him than pleasing.

I, too, did not always appreciate visitors. I didn't have the time to sit around and chat and was extremely vulnerable to their words and sometimes to their obvious avoidance of certain subjects, which would set my mind in turmoil.

Dr. Martinson told me she would come more often the next week as she thought we were getting closer to the end.

The following Sunday several relatives came over for Eric's usual birthday celebration. Once the party had begun the tension Eric had exhibited earlier in the day seemed to disappear, although he didn't want candles on his cake as "wishes don't come true." Afterwards he became moody again.

For some time I had been considering telling Eric that he was going to die, in fact ever since that day over a month earlier when he had confronted me with the statement, "I want to go to heaven." I was in no way prepared with an answer for him then, but now felt the time had come to tell him. I hoped to relieve his deep frustration of "not getting better"; to tell him that he wouldn't be like he was for the next 65 to

70 years, a normal life span, and that soon peace would be his.

Reminding him of what he had said, I asked, "Eric, do you really believe in a better life to come?" "Yes," he replied, "but I've spent four to five years working on my collections—stamps, rocks, shells, butterflies, flowers, leaves. If I went to heaven, I'd have to start all over again!" I was crushed that he hadn't mentioned leaving me. We talked and talked for 45 minutes, but he wasn't being receptive to the big announcement I was going to make, and so I let it go. He really didn't want to die; yet sometimes life seemed so hopeless for him.

Subsequently, there was a marked change in his mood; he was more relaxed and compatible. Del also noticed this even though he wasn't aware of what our conversation had been at the time.

By Dr. Martinson's fourth home visit Eric had seen the "spots" on his feet. He asked me, "What are those black things stuck to my feet?" Although the capillary leakage had been noticeable for over a week by then, I had been careful to prevent him seeing his feet. However, in my haste to ready him for school that day, I was less careful and he saw the disfigurement. I told him it was a little bruising, and he then was distracted by the arrival of his homebound teacher. Eric later told me he felt like a monster: "All the monsters in the horror movies have spots."

Dr. Martinson and I again talked about drug management, the possibility of Eric's death at home, and what might happen in that event.

Del and I had begun to wonder if what we were doing was really best for Eric. He had been a very creative child and there were a number of things he wanted to do but his arms and hands were becoming increasingly useless. A perfectionist by nature, he would spend hours trying to get one stamp in his stampbook. We were not allowed to help; he hated being so dependent on us, and wanted to do it himself. However, frustration was getting the best of him.

He had seen again and again the reruns of his favorite television programs. He had spent hours listening to the talking-book records received from the Minnesota State School for the Blind and Handicapped. He loved school, even if it had to be at home, but his active mind was exasperated with that incapacitated body. We tried everything we could think of, but the days seemed so long and he would get despondent. We wondered whether the hospital personnel would be better equipped to keep him satisfied, whether occupational therapy would have better resources for him.

Dr. Martinson would constantly reassure us that the care we gave him was as good, if not better, than what he would receive in the hospital. How I needed that reassurance. I knew Eric wanted to be at home but had not been at all confident that we were enterprising enough to handle it.

The next day, Eric's coloring seemed to have changed markedly and his vision was deteriorating. He was concerned that we hadn't been continuing the physical therapy sessions and wanted me to exercise his legs. Shortly after that he needed codeine for the pain. For the first time he wasn't sure whether he wanted school the next day. He didn't want to be too tired when Dr. Martinson came because "I like to talk to her about my problems."

The next morning Eric changed his mind, which we had become accustomed to, and decided to have school in spite of his confused speech. His speech had become markedly worse, which he asked me to explain to his teacher so that she would wait for him to give the correct responses. After the math class his teacher remarked that he had some of the answers even before she had the problems completely written out. He was as mentally alert as ever and remained so until the end.

Eric now wanted me with him more. He said no one else understood what he was trying to say. Unless we had a general idea of the subject matter, it was very difficult even for us to understand some of his words. The advantages of his being at home were reinforced by our comprehension of his speech. How could complete strangers understand his utterances in order to care for his needs?

By then Eric's pain had increased and the codeine dosage was doubled. He had also become so weak that he was afraid we wouldn't hear him if he called during the night. So for two nights I had slept on the floor in his room. He seemed to need the security of having me near.

When I attempted to give Eric his medication in the morning, he was unable to swallow, hadn't the strength to sip water through a straw, could barely open his mouth, and began vomiting. I called Dr. Martinson. She gave me some suggestions on administering his medication, none of which helped.

In the midst of all this, Eric decided he wasn't up to having school. How he even knew it was Monday amazed me; all the days seemed alike. But he had forgotten that his teacher would be out of town for Thanksgiving and would be unable to come.

I called the physician to see if we could get injections for Eric's pain as he was unable to take anything orally. I explained that Del had had experience giving injections years ago while he was in the medical corps. I was sure Dr. Martinson would help, so he said he would contact her. She called back, cancelling her appointments for the afternoon, and came to the house.

In the meantime, school had been let out early and Betsy arrived home with big plans for a Thanksgiving party at our house for ten of her neighborhood friends. I explained that Eric was very sick and the party would have to be postponed.

Betsy then asked, "Is Eric going to die?" It wasn't a question that took me by surprise. She had also asked her father two days earlier and her conversations and expressions had more and more centered around dying. I answered, "I think Eric will die quite soon, but then he will go to heaven and be able to use his hands, walk, and run and play and do all the things he has been unable to do for so long." She cried, and we cried together. After thinking about it for awhile, she asked, "Can Eric come back then, after he's fixed in heaven?"

The day had started badly and certainly wasn't getting any better. I hadn't slept well in Eric's room and felt exhaustion closing in on me. My sister had come to help with Betsy and she decided to stay the night.

Dr. Martinson arrived. Since Eric was resting she spent most of the time with me, helping me work through my feelings and frustrations. She suggested hospitalization but I didn't want that. I didn't want to let Eric down even though I felt I was unable to cope with him at the time. Del had spent the major part of the day with Eric except when it took the two of us to care for his needs. As her home was within a short drive, Dr. Martinson left after about two hours, leaving word to call her when Eric needed an injection.

A short while later I called Dr. Kersey to inquire about getting suppositories for nausea and vomiting. He also asked if I wanted to hospitalize Eric. I replied, "I can't do that to him."

Dr. Martinson returned to help administer the Demerol. When Eric saw her in the doorway of his room he thought she had come to take him to the hospital and said, "No, no, I can't go with you. Mommy, mommy!" This was the most clearly understood group of words he had said in the past few days—that he wanted to stay home.

We reassured him that he wouldn't have to go. Those deeply appealing words made it clear that we couldn't betray him and were given the needed impetus to keep trying. Dr. Martinson felt then that because of the traumatic changes that had taken place in his body over the last twenty-four hours, Eric knew he was dying.

Dr. Martinson showed Del how to give the injection. He did it then with her watching and encouraging him, which he appreciated, fearing to add to his son's pain.

With Dr. Martinson's help, I was feeling better and once again was able to resume my place beside Eric. He asked me to stay and sleep in his room again. I stayed with him until midnight, but was unable to fall asleep, so Del took over. For some reason, at 4:00 A.M. I awoke from a sound sleep. I relieved Del.

When I entered Eric's room, I had the distinct feeling that he would die very soon as his breathing was labored. Dr. Martinson had said she thought his breathing might get very erratic near the end.

I sat by Eric's bed and he held my hand. I asked if he needed anything and he replied, "No." How I longed to be able to talk with him, to find out how he really felt, to tell him more of my own feelings. But conversation was very limited; except for simple words he wasn't able to communicate.

An hour later, I thought he was finally resting more peacefully as the difficult breathing was no longer evident. I lay on the floor to get some rest. Lying there, I automatically listened for his breathing but heard nothing. I got up to check. There was no more breathing or heartbeat. Eric had died while holding my hand, at peace at last.

For the last time I held my son, told him how very much I had loved him, and that "Jesus will take care of you now." I spent several minutes alone with him before wakening Del. We returned to Eric's room. I gently wiped the side of Eric's mouth, which led Del to comment, "Thank God he no longer hurts when he's touched."

I had never seen anyone die nor had I ever experienced the loss of someone I had dearly loved. It was extremely important to me to have been with Eric during the actual transition from life to death, to really know firsthand that it went smoothly for him. The dreaded fear, death, wasn't ugly as I had thought it would be—Eric was at peace.

We, too, had a feeling of peace. Eric's problems were over and we did not have to bear the guilt of not having done all we could for our son. To bear his loss was in itself a great enough burden.

Dr. Kersey came, after arranging for an ambulance, and Eric's body was taken from home. "Our Eric" didn't ever have to leave.

We have our regrets. The principal regret pertaining to this particular time is that we had Eric's body taken from home, for Betsy's sake, before she awoke in the morning. She too wanted to touch and see her brother for the last time, and how much better it would have been, for her also, at home.

As I listened to the silence during those long nights following Eric's death, I longed to hear him call me. How I wanted to be with him, hold him, just one more time. But I knew once more would not be enough and I realized he was the only one who had found peace.

I no longer fear death itself. But I'll never be able to accept human suffering. I've seen more than I ever want to see again, and most of it was emotional pain, not physical.

During the years of Eric's illness, my heart was torn seeing him go through difficulties of the disease and side effects of therapy treatments that gave us a little more time.

There comes a time when there is a fine line between whether continued therapy is for the sake of research for future leukemics or whether it is truly best for the child at hand. Del and I felt much sooner than the physicians that the time had come, but it was more a feeling from the heart than from professional objectivity. Eric, unaware of the full circumstances and that the odds were against him no matter what, had wanted to go on with treatment for a longer period than we felt necessary. Maybe we should have been more open with him; that is something we will never know.

When precious time was gained, interludes free of pain and problems, how grateful we would be for those good days. The conflict of whether to go on or to quit is something that can probably never be easily resolved. In retrospect, the point at which to suspend treatment is easily seen. When one is in the midst of the situation, however, not knowing exactly what the future will bring, it is an entirely different question.

I am thankful, at least, that there was a point at which we and the physicians could agree. There was a risk factor involved, for all of us, especially with Eric at home. But once the decision was made, we received full support, more than we ever expected. We deeply appreciated this.

Paul Tournier in his book, *The Meaning of Persons*, writes: "We think that by being cautious we are protecting life, whereas we are slowly smothering it." He was not writing of leukemics or terminal patients, but it struck me as being even more appropriate for them. The life that they live, short as it may be, must not be smothered. Risks must be taken, life lived to the fullest when possible, and the rest will take care of itself.

Dr. Martinson made eight home visits during this short period of Eric's home care. We had five conversations by phone, and one joint meeting at the clinic. Two of the home visits and three of the phone calls were on the last day. I was astonished when I found she had been coming over a period of only seventeen days. Being such a crucial period for us, it had seemed much longer.

By the time Eric died, I had come to depend on and feel very close to this woman who had helped us through a difficult, but very deep and meaningful experience. She seemed truly involved in our situation, and this made it possible to freely discuss feelings and issues: Eric's feelings, the family's feelings, what was going on, and what could happen. She made sure we felt free to call her at any time; she would be available and would come if needed. Acting as a liaison between ourselves and the doctor, she was much better able to explain situations to him than we were.

It had been our initial impression that Dr. Martinson was coming specifically for the care of Eric. But as Del remarked, her home visits were certainly doing a lot for me mentally, and we wondered if this was her main purpose. Whichever it was, she handled both more than adequately.

She sensed my need to take care of Eric personally and allowed me to do so. I'm sure there were times she observed that we weren't doing things professionally, but she didn't let her professional self interfere with her constant reassurance to us. There was nothing we could do that would be detrimental. It was no longer a matter of striving for life, but making existence as desirable as possible for all of us.

The specific help that Dr. Martinson gave in nursing care is probably elementary for a trained nurse. However, as lay people we knew little of technical procedures and it was in these that her experience was invaluable.

We felt the disadvantages of hospitalization outweighed the advantages. There was no longer a need for the inevitable institutional procedures. Though our family life was hardly normal, it was not nearly as disrupted as when Eric had been hospitalized. Even if we had been able to help Eric physically in the hospital, our inadequacies would have been more conspicuous in the company of professionals. In some ways it was easier to screen visitors at home; yet Eric was able to have the visitors he wanted when he wanted them, including his young friends and even his pets.

Though not always with complete success, we felt we were more able to handle Eric's mental frustrations at home. No one could give him the answers that he wanted to hear, but at least we were always available and our love was there to help soothe those frustrations—and love can overcome many obstacles otherwise unsurmountable.

We tried to maintain our life style, restricted as it was. Del would usually carry Eric down for supper, sometimes for breakfast, and on an occasional excursion to a favorite place. He was apprehensive about carrying him, especially after Eric developed large bruises on his back and sides. But, as Dr. Martinson said, the pleasure Eric experienced from going places surpassed the pain in getting there, and was worth it.

In many ways we had a lot going for us: We were within a 20 minute drive to the University, Betsy was in school, Del's work was only three minutes away, and help was available from my sister and Del's dad. There were also some disadvantages, the major one being Eric's paralysis, the inconveniences of a two-story home for a handicapped person, and Del's working hours.

We would like to have spared Betsy this ordeal. There is no benefit to be derived from losing a brother, especially when he is the only sibling. Eric's going away to die would not have eased the great pain of losing the older brother she worshipped and depended upon. I think she was able to relate to our having him at home and wouldn't have wanted any less for him. Betsy also needed the security of our being home and of her not having to be "farmed out."

There were times when her exuberance was wearing on Eric. She tried to subdue her abundance of zest in his presence and we tried to explain to her the meaning of his sometimes negative reactions. She treasured the times she could be with him or do something for him.

In the memorial service for Eric, the minister concluded with, "A little child shall lead them." It was so true: Eric did lead us with his great courage, love and faith. And now another child has taken over the role. Betsy, more than anyone, keeps us going. Her openness keeps our heads on straight. She knows her feelings and expresses them, bringing out those we tend to suppress, making us the better for it.

We still have our bad days and moments. There is still an emptiness. A great part of our life has been taken from us. How we miss that beautiful smile that could brighten up our world like sunshine; that inquisitive, searching mind and wit that we were hard pressed to compete with; and that love that only a child can give so fully. Some day, by God's grace, we'll all be together again.

A father shares his feelings about his daughter's terminal illness and his experiences with the hospital personnel. He describes his own response to the child's last days as he and his wife cared for her through her death at home.

3

MERI

Recollections of a Father

David Wetzel

When Jodi and I decided on home care for our daughter, Meredith, she had lived eight years with leukemia and we felt that she was suffering as much from her treatment as from the disease. We did not ask to bring her home; in fact, until the last few months of her life, we refused to think beyond the facts of her relapses, treatments, and remissions. However, we were forced to do so in her last year, since her relapses now came more often and seemed more acute. She was also in pain more frequently than before from the bone pain that we learned was associated with the accelerated production of leukocytes in the marrow, and in three months she had progressed from over-the-counter drugs to codeine to Demerol I.M. for relief.

We were informed by Dr. Peter Coccia, her regular clinic specialist, that the drug program and radiation therapy had been exhausted, and we agreed to try one or two recent drugs which had, he said, no guarantee of effectiveness. It was during this time that we read of Emily Kulenkamp's experience caring for her son, Eric, at home. We were interested, but did not think seriously of doing the same thing with Meri. However, it was not long before Dr. John Kersey, an assistant professor of pathology, suggested the program to us as an alternative to what was becoming an intolerable course of hospitalization for Meri, ourselves, and her doctors as well. He introduced us to Ida Martinson, a professor of nursing with a Ph.D. in physiology, who had originated the home care program with him a year earlier.

Since I had not worked for a year and Jodi's job allowed her some flexibility to be with Meri during her relapses, we were in a favorable position to care for Meri. Ida Martinson told us what to expect and discussed the preparations we would need to make before and after Meri's discharge from the hospital. She and John Kersey would be available to give us advice, and she would make regular visits as well as emergency calls if the need arose.

During the days which followed, as Meri's condition improved slightly, the station staff gathered medical supplies for us—alcohol wipes, cotton balls, Band Aids, hospital incontinent pads, and an emesis basin. They also supplied us with syringes and told us to practice injections on each other until we developed some assurance and skill; we also studied a well-illustrated medical guide which discussed procedures and sites for injection in detail.

Meri was ready for discharge sooner then we expected, only four days after we had talked to John Kersey and Ida Martinson. She was able to walk, itself a good sign, and her spirits were up even though her general apathy made this hard to detect. She said goodbye to all the people on the staff who had cared for her, and a student nurse helped carry her things down to the car. The process seemed rushed and incomplete, but that feeling probably came from leaving the security of the hospital and its familiar routines.

Once Meri was home, it was like any other time following her return from the hospital. We felt renewed and full of energy. We read to her from a favorite book, *Little Women*, and she seemed fairly comfortable if not cheerful. When she began to have pain, we massaged her back and legs and hoped that this might be all that was necessary for the time.

Her first severe pain came as a shock that night. We tried to allay it as we had earlier, but it did no good. I got my courage up and gave her a shot as quickly and confidently as I knew how, though it was much harder than the practice injections with Jodi. Meri cried a bit but did not resist, and I was surprised that the process took so little time. The real difficulty was initially finding the correct place of injection; after that the previous needle marks could guide us.

The next day Meri was definitely worse. She had gotten little sleep and complained of pain often. While Jodi was at work, I stayed with Meri and tried reading to her or playing the games she liked while in the hospital, but she either refused or paid no attention. I began to feel truly helpless and quickly went through a variety of ad hoc approaches—cheerful, firm, sympathetic, unheeding—afraid to let her know that I was doubting my ability to comfort her. It was hard to believe that her emotional state could change so radically overnight. Perhaps too easily discounting the obvious—that she was suffering a resurgence of cell blasts which could no longer be halted—I suspected that it was due to her coming home, that she might actually rather be back in the hospital and was expressing her insecurity with us.

I called Jodi about this, and she got in touch with Dr. Malka Goodman, a child and adolescent psychiatrist who had seen Meri some months earlier. At that time, Meri would get nearly hysterical over a cut or a bruise, and she was so afraid of hurting herself or being hurt by other children that she rarely went out of the house. She never talked about death, and never asked if she might die herself. This year, for the first time, she wanted to know what leukemia was, but she didn't ask too much about it. Our approach was passive; we answered whatever questions she had but did not volunteer information. It was clear that death was a central issue which we would soon have to face with her, if, ironically, she lived long enough. She was certainly aware and resentful of being sick more often than well, of the increasing trips to the emergency room, the clinic, and the hospital stations, and the time she spent at home recovering. At Christmas she had said, "Goodbye 1973—you were my worst year."

The problem for Jodi and me, which went back to Meri's second relapse five years earlier, was that we did not know how to deal with her pain. It was the most difficult and frustrating condition of her disease and a singular cause of the anger and bitterness that accompanied her treatment. What we did not understand at the time—and what Malka Goodman tried to show us—was that it was not Meri's pain alone. Everyone who had anything to do with her shared it. The medical staff was obligated to find the cause instead of treating the symptoms, but this usually meant delays and tests and countless examinations by different specialists. Jodi, who most visibly responded to it, regarded much of the testing as a useless aggravation of the pain itself. I did not question the medical procedures but tried to somehow alleviate Meri's suffering by being with her during the bone marrows, spinal taps, and special I.V. treatments.

Every time Meri went into the hospital or through a new course of tests, we would get locked into an almost predictable set of roles and feelings which led to arguments with the doctors and staff and between ourselves, and the general tension and depression would not let up until Meri was home again. How much of this affected Meri and influenced her own sense of pain and anxiety about it is impossible to say—certainly it did. By the time we saw Malka Goodman it was too late to do much about our relationship with Meri—she was becoming more closed to us and we were growing farther apart and more mutually resentful. The counseling we did receive, however, opened up the possibility of breaking down our personal barriers. During the last months of Meri's life, she was able more freely to show anger without guilt. Once she said, "Why can't you have leukemia instead of me" Why, indeed?

We regarded the chance to care for Meri at home, to take more responsibility for sharing her suffering, as a big step toward relieving the frustration, depression, and impotence we had felt. From the time we spoke to John Kersey, all the energy that had been wasted and blocked could go into our determination to see that Meri would be as comfortable and secure as possible. We were almost convinced that we could accomplish this simply by bringing her home. But now that she was expressing more pain and anxiety than before, it was a serious blow to our mutual spirit and confidence. We needed help and asked Malka if she would see Meri again; she agreed to come on Thursday.

On Wednesday, because Meri was having so much continued trouble, Jodi stayed home from work. We bathed Meri and rearranged her room to allow for the hospital bed that John Kersey had ordered through the American Cancer Society. She seemed a little better this morning, and with the two of us there, we each had some time to be with her and by ourselves. As time went on, we found that it was absolutely necessary to have a break from the demands of her care, either by doing other kinds of duties to keep our day-to-day lives going or simply to sit outside on the lawn and play with our son, Richard, or talk to friends. Before the week was over, Jodi had been granted leave from her work for the duration of Meri's home care.

Malka Goodman saw Meri alone Thursday afternoon. In an effort to find ways for Meri to ease her pain, Malka encouraged her to imagine things she liked to do or had done in fantasy or real life—flying away by herself or visiting Disneyland or thinking up new stories that she liked to write and illustrate. Meri had already written several "books" about animals, shapes, and creatures which, like the "Huging Huger, Who Hugs You To Death," reflected her recent thoughts. Over our concern about drugs, a major one during the three weeks of home care, Malka advised that we not try to delay medication at Meri's expense and least of all worry about addiction. We agreed with this, but it was still hard for me to accept Meri's frequent need for Demerol and the implication that Jodi and I could not substitute for it.

That day something happened which seemed to bring Meri to the low point of her stay at home. At noon she developed a nosebleed which revived every time the cold packs and pressure were removed. At first it looked like a bad sign that might turn into an emergency, but she sometimes had nosebleeds before when her platelet count dropped to a dangerously low level, and this stopped after about two hours. Aside from minor bleeding that resulted from softening of her gums later on, this was the only occurrence of bleeding throughout her home care.

That evening some friends brought in dinner and took Richard out so that Jodi and I could be together with Meri. Since Wednesday we had begun taking turns staying with her at night, sleeping on couch cushions beside her bed. We had also taken Richard out of the room which they had shared for two years, and put his crib in ours. Though it was now crowded with furniture, her room was fairly bright and pleasant. She had a shelf of Madame Alexander Little Women dolls that her mother and grandmothers had helped her collect, several mobiles, and a large braided octopus (made for her by a nurse) that she used to hang on her I.V. stands. There were also stuffed figures of all sorts around the room and several on the bed above her pillow. She had already begun getting cards for her birthday next week, when she would be 10 years old, and these we pinned to her curtains.

Late that night I drove to the airport to pick up her grandparents, who had flown from our home town, Salt Lake City, on a visit planned in advance of our decision about home care. I was surprised and especially happy to see Jodi's sister, Mitzi, whom we had not expected. She was an LPN who had worked with terminally ill children, and was very close to Meri. Though I was doubtful that Meri's listlessness and lack of affect would change much, Jodi and I were glad they had come.

As soon as we got home, I saw that I was wrong about Meri's reaction. She brightened up immediately on seeing them and was soon more animated than she had been in a week. After a relatively good night, she sat up in her bed and spent the morning cutting paper dolls, singing with her Grandma Peg, and coloring. It might have been my imagination, but I thought it was the brightest morning since her return home. For her birthday, she said, she wanted a dog. It hurt not to grant her request, especially since she had pleaded so urgently, "Daddy, I want a dog, right now." Looking back, I wish we had gotten her one, but at the time we were so overextended that a dog would have been an impossible burden. Her grandparents compromised with her on a pair of hamsters, which she could handle better than a dog and watch from her bed as they played in their cage. She was satisfied, on the surface at least, and seemed satisfied with everything that day. In the afternoon two of her neighborhood friends watched TV with her, and that evening she ate better than she had before, in spite of her low-fat diet.

We then noticed a constant lengthening of intervals between shots, and the feeling we had as she complained less and less of pain was one of release, joy, and gratefulness for Meri and ourselves. The experience was almost heady; we found ourselves doing everything enthusiastically. When she was in pain we could assist her to a certain degree, by propping pillows between her legs or changing her position in bed, by giving her rubdowns or placing hotpacks on her arms, legs, and chest—but in this we could get little of the satisfaction that we had when she was more responsive. Through no choice of our own, we became unusually attuned to changes in her mood, even when they were slight and transient.

Physically she showed as yet no significant symptoms. Petechiae, the rashlike pinpricks that indicated a falling platelet count, had appeared in various places; her legs were slightly atrophied from lack of solid food and exercise; and she was bruising at injection sites. She preferred to have shots on the sides and backs of her hips, and a couple of sites were beginning to show it. We rotated these four areas with her thighs, but she refused to let us use her arms. I personally hoped that we would not have to do so either, because I had struck her shoulder bone once and was more sickened by it than she was hurt.

Her bone pain centered on her thighs, arms, and sternum, and she was getting sensitive to touch everywhere. Usually she asked someone to help her turn in bed and only occasionally tried to do it herself. She could no longer tolerate getting up to go to the bathroom; often she even refused the bedpan, which forced her to raise her hips, and we simply spread incontinent pads beneath her. We gave her a tub bath only when she felt particularly well; even so, she was frightened and rigid during the whole process. To make it easier, we used Richard's old plastic baby carrier as a backrest. This could be slanted to any angle and would allow Jodi or me to use both hands for washing. However, Meri preferred the bed bath, and this was the common procedure.

Her grandparents and Aunt Mitzi stayed the weekend and gave Meri a lot of attention. We borrowed a projector from a friend and made several trips to the public library for 8-mm films and cartoons, and her teachers brought us a slide projector from the school's audiovisual department. Twice Meri got up in the wheelchair that had been donated with the hospital bed, and it was a delight to take her around the house or wheel her to the front window to look outside.

With additional help from Jodi's family, we were able to keep Richard at home most of the time. Earlier in the week we sent him to his sitter part of the day. Emil and Marie had looked after him for over a year and had become his surrogate grandparents. Later, when we had to concentrate solely on her care, they kept Richard with them for a few days. We did not intend to prevent him from seeing her, but we also wanted him to get the attention he needed. At home he did not spend a lot of time with Meri. He would play in the bedroom, sometimes telling her he was sorry that she was sick and reaching up barely to touch her on the high bed. She needed this affection from time to time, but did not appear to miss him when he was away.

On Monday, a week from the day we brought her home, we took Meri to the clinic for a checkup. As well as she had been doing, it was a struggle to get her there and back. She cried more often whenever we lifted her and hated leaving her bed. After the examination, we talked privately with John Kersey and Dr. Rolf Simonson, the resident physician. They said that her hemoglobin had fallen and her platelets were so low that she might require a transfusion. We could do this now or wait until she began to bleed, showed an oxygen shortage, or became infected. Since any of these possibilities could add to her discomfort, we agreed to bring her into the emergency room for transfusion if necessary; but as she had no complications, we decided to wait until they developed. For the first time we felt like partners in her medical care.

Outside in the car, while Jodi got a supply of Demerol from the outpatient pharmacy, Meri had a resurgence of leg and back pain. It could have been a minor crisis; there was nothing that I could give her. However, I recalled the childbirth education techniques Jodi had used when in labor with Richard, and told Meri to stare at a single object and pace her breathing. After a few minutes' silence, I asked her how she was doing. Still staring intently at the dashboard, she said, "Quiet! Can't you see I'm concentrating?" After a while Jodi returned, angry that the prescription had taken so long to fill, but Meri's determination did not break down until we were nearly home.

That method did not work again, nor had we expected it to. Half our effort during this early period was devoted to thinking of new ways to keep her going or getting her involved in something. When reading to her lost its effectiveness, we showed movies and slides on the wall of her room, and she regularly asked to see them twice. During the better moments she liked to do simple, homemade crossword puzzles or draw pictures. The picture that we cherish the most was her last, a drawing with the names of all her family brightly circled in rings of color.

By Wednesday, Meri's grandparents and aunt had gone home. Though she was without their direct stimulation and encouragement, she continued to do well. Jodi and I integrated her care as much as possible into the normal pattern of our homelife. Since I went to bed late and Jodi rose early, we simply extended this time for ourselves into shifts which changed about 3 A.M. Richard went to Emil and Marie's in the morning, when we got most of the housework done, and returned in the afternoon. We traded off fixing meals and doing dishes, and several times our friends brought us food or helped with various tasks.

Ida Martinson visited on Thursday and brought Meri a

beautiful hand-painted Chinese spoon which would not irritate her gums and mouth. She was now going without pain 8 to 10 hours at a time, though a pattern had developed of alternately long and short intervals. Ida's examination revealed nothing new since our clinic visit on Monday. She recommended, however, that we brace Meri's feet against a pillow to prevent slackness in her ankles, which could contribute to her leg pain. During the visit, Meri asked for a shot, and Jodi's skill was put to the test as Ida watched. But this went well since Meri, though she cried and begged us to hurry, was always cooperative. In the past year she had become very proud of being "tough," and we assured her that she was, after so many shots, spinal taps, and bone marrow aspirations. Afterward, she even became playful, and was delighted when Ida fell for her snake-in-the-peanut-can trick. Later we spoke to Ida alone about Meri's condition. She was concerned that we get as much help as possible during what might be a long period of decline. We were beginning to feel quite worn, yet Meri's symptomatic improvement over the past week kept our spirits up. Our confidence was growing; by this time we knew that bringing her home had been the right decision.

Later that day my mother arrived on her customary visit from "Europe-Switzerland," as Meri called it. As with Jodi's family, we believed that my mother's presence would help, though I was concerned about her because she had only recently gone through a series of postoperative tests for cancer. I did not want to put her through another emotional strain but needed to have her there, and she very much wanted to see her adopted granddaughter. We could not have realized that Meri would degenerate so quickly in the next week.

Friday Meri's fourth-grade teacher called and asked if he could bring her class over from the school, which was two blocks away. We had discussed this before, tentatively agreeing on a time when she would be up to it. It appeared that she was quite ready now. But we were in no way prepared for the birthday cake, the cards, and the tape-recorded message they had spent the morning making. As they arrived, I tried to send them into the house in small groups; but seeing their enthusiasm and impatience, I let caution go and sent them all in. Meri held up well, though she told one of her classmates "I'm too sick to smile." She was probably grateful for the protection of the side rails and height of the bed against this sea of friends. It did not matter that it was not her birthday yet; it was no time to wait on such a small formality.

Afterward, Meri played the tape and listened to a mixture of birthday greetings, songs, and general horseplay. The kids asked her to make a tape for them in return, but it did not appear that she would do it. Naturally, it took every ounce of strength to extend herself.

Following a remarkably good weekend, during which her high and variable temperature dropped to nearly normal, she went once again to the clinic. It turned out to be an inauspicious event—she was seized by severe pain while waiting in the examining room—this only two-and-a-half hours after her last dose of Demerol. Respecting the spirit of the home care program, Dr. Mark Nesbit, her attending physician in John Kersey's absence, allowed Jodi to give Meri the injection in spite of all the medically trained people there. The examination showed only a slight advance of petechiae and further bruising, but Meri had become so sensitive that it was difficult to palpate her abdomen. In fact, the entire clinic visit was extremely trying for her. We sensed that something had changed, even if it didn't show. She would not be able to come to the clinic again, we suspected. For me, it was strange to see the other parents and children as we passed through the waiting room, knowing that Meri had been there as an outpatient only a month before, and that we were now distinguished from the others only because we no longer had any hope.

Mark Nesbit told us that we could give Meri shots more frequently as needed, every three hours instead of four, but no more often than that. We could also use Seconal to help her sleep. When he found out that her birthday was coming up soon, he made a birthday card out of a prescription slip, and this pleased her. Hearing that Meri was in the clinic, Ida Martinson also came to see her and to wish her a happy birthday.

At home that day and during the following days, Meri began asking more frequently for small things to make her comfortable. We were constantly changing pillows, adjusting the angle of her bed, and replacing hotpacks. These attentions were easy to give, even if she wanted to shift positions five or six times an hour, but they were becoming more ritualized. She soon lost interest in films, records, stories, or anything that had formerly served to draw her out. She would lie for long periods of time and pick nervously at her face and chest.

By the middle of the week, she was getting shots as often as prescribed, and there were times when she wanted medication sooner than that. She complained of pain in other parts of her body, usually fleeting, and she no longer had the use of her arms. At night we took more frequent turns sleeping with her. I learned to doze on my back, ready to get up in a moment, and Jodi did the same. These were the most difficult times, when Meri would ask every 15 or 20 minutes if she could have another shot. Once, however, I woke up to hear her singing to herself, and for the next hour we sang to each other until she could get her medication and sleep for a while.

Before long, it seemed as if the Demerol and Seconal were doing nothing for her—and later we found this to be true. When Ida came again on Thursday, we asked about using something stronger, either larger doses of Demerol or shifting to morphine, Ida called John Kersey about this and gave him a description of Meri's symptoms and of her experience since the last clinic visit. He thought that we should wait a little longer, most likely because none of the more apparent signs of terminal leukemia had been evident.

My mother had been spending more and more time with Meri, unable to do anything for her constant crying and pleading. She saw no reason to keep Meri conscious in her present state, and it was perhaps only because I could express my feelings in so many activities that I had not been aware of the degree to which Meri was in pain. By then I did realize it, and we were all upset that afternoon. Ida was in a particularly difficult position, knowing what Meri was going through. Yet she explained that if Meri was drugged too heavily, she would not be able to express her needs to us.

By morning, however, there was no question that Meri needed morphine. It was obvious that the Demerol was having no effect, not even giving her the usual hour's respite. She had had no sleep and was frantic. This was the last day of Mother's visit, and though she was unhappy about leaving us at such a time, there was little point in her staying longer. In spite of everything, I thought she had grown closer to Meri than ever before, but Meri was so distracted that none of us could do much for her.

When I returned from the airport, Jodi had already called John Kersey about the morphine, and he agreed it was now necessary. I waited with Meri for what seemed an interminable time while Jodi was at the hospital pharmacy. Since Meri had been given a shot of Demerol three hours before with no symptomatic relief, another one would probably have done no good, and she would have to wait three more hours for the morphine. Realizing this, I could only hold her hand and try to comfort her. I encouraged her to send the pain out of her own body and into mine, while I concentrated earnestly on drawing it away from her. Though this attempt failed, it did keep her, for a time, from pleading desperately with me to take her life.

Jodi was very upset when she returned. She had been told that the prescription would be waiting at the pharmacy and it was not there. After waiting an hour and unable to find John Kersey, she grabbed another doctor, who wrote a prescription; otherwise we might not have gotten emergency help and Meri would have agonized longer.

It was the most unfortunate crisis of Meri's home care. While in itself a circumstance that did not reflect John Kersey's attitude, we were sensitive to the general opinion about narcotics expressed by a number of physicians who had treated Meri. We understood the masking effect of pain killers, but we also got the impression that symptomatic relief was regarded as a last recourse instead of a primary need. The incident raised many old feelings we had had during the turmoil of Meri's hospitalization, particularly now when her comfort was the only consideration. But it was thankfully a short-lived crisis; Meri at last got the morphine and slept for the first time in twenty-four hours, her first solid sleep in two days.

Later that afternoon, euphoric from the drug and the relief, she talked with an animation we had not seen for a long time. Despite all that she had been through, she still had the presence of mind and memory to repeat in minute detail a story she had learned in school. It amazed me that she could rebound so quickly and readily from the grip of her symptoms—not only then but during the course of her former relapses—as though nothing at all had happened. In response to her mood, we found ourselves relaxing, too. Once again we could touch her, and after a rubdown she slept all night long.

So far as her external symptoms were concerned, however, this was to be only a lull. Though she had taken morphine the previous summer in the hospital with few undesirable side effects, she now developed several. Shortly she began to get restless, sensitive to touch again, and subject to a constant itch. We had John Kersey's assurance that she was definitely not in pain or discomfort, and the freedom with which she moved, despite her outward signs, led us to agree.

But the morphine began to affect her speech and thought processes. First, she was impatient when we could not understand her; then she simply gave up all effort to communicate, and finally she entered a kind of delerium marked by regular, almost mechanical moans. Clearly she wanted to sleep, but something resisted it; whenever she dropped off, something would pull her back again and she would cry out. Though she could not tell us what her needs were, we continued to treat her as though she were conscious and alert. We developed a double and opposing mentality; relief that she was no longer in pain and frustration that outwardly she seemed to be in so much. Since we had lost her now—there was no question about that—it was, strangely, easier to care for her but impossible to comfort her.

On Monday, we suspected that she was falling into a coma or semicoma. As her usual two or three minutes of sleep stretched to ten and twenty, a half-hour, an hour, two hours and longer, we gradually and gratefully accepted the peace that had finally come to her. She woke up a few times, but easily went back to sleep again.

Over the weekend several of our friends came to help now that our relatives had gone home, and some volunteered to stay the entire night with Meri. Having delayed funeral arrangements longer than we should have, I asked one of our good friends if he could make an appointment someplace. In the afternoon he and I talked to a mortician and returned to find several people with Jodi. With Meri sleeping soundly, our mood became literally carefree. Jodi and I both sensed that Meri was close to death; we knew that she was in no pain, and for the first time in many days we could relax. We were surprised when Ida arrived; in fact, we had forgotten that she was coming that day, so filled had it been with our happiness that finally Meri could rest.

Though Ida agreed with us that Meri might be comatose, she cautioned again that we needed to be prepared to care for her several more days, possibly a week or two. That morning John Kersey had said that Meri would probably not live more than forty-eight hours, and we had the feeling he was right.

In the evening Meri continued to sleep, though from time to time she moaned as before. At eleven o'clock Jodi and I went to bed and left Becky Kroll, a friend, to sit with her, planning as usual to stagger the shifts. We had been asleep about two hours, apparently very lightly, when a change in the sound of Meri's breathing woke us up. It was hard to tell exactly what was different, but it was obvious that her condition had changed. As we watched, her respiration quickened and her teeth became clenched; but even as we called Ida for advice, Meri seemed to relax. Ida told us to make sure that she had a clear air passage; otherwise, if there were oral bleeding or vomiting, she would suffocate. Though it was now about 2 A.M., Ida said she would come over if we needed her. Since Meri seemed stable, we said we would call if anything happened.

After sending our friend to bed, Jodi and I sat with Meri

and opened the last of her birthday gifts, which had been ignored during the hectic days of the past week. Ida had told us that hearing was thought to be the last body sense to fail, so even though Meri did not respond to us and stared inquiringly at nothing, we spoke to her and described the gifts she had gotten and read the birthday cards. Periodically we checked her vital signs, particularly her respiration. Though her breathing was shallow, it remained steady. The momentary air hunger that she suffered earlier had apparently passed; she was unalarmed, relaxed, and motionless.

Then her breathing changed again, so slightly as to be undetectable any other time. We listened carefully and noticed that while her respiration rate was steady, she seemed to be taking in less air with each breath. Jodi went immediately to the phone and called Ida, who said she would be over right away. Now Meri was dropping fast. Her eyes were fixed and calm and still faintly quizzical, but she was not gasping for air. By the time Jodi entered the room and came to her side, Meri was dead.

Together we held her for the last time and cried over her. Soon Ida arrived and sat with us while we talked about Meri, about what had suddenly seemed like a distant life, and shared the grief we had for her. When the mortician came, he thoughtfully waited for us to say goodbye a last time to Meri and accepted my offer to help him remove the body. This was important to me—it seemed to make our participation in her dying and death a finished one. Then, after informing our relatives and friends of her death, we walked to Emil and Marie's to bring Richard home and tell him, too.

Meri's funeral and burial were in Salt Lake City, after which we had a memorial service at her favorite park, Wirth Park, in Minneapolis. Ida attended the service and continued to stay in touch with us, not only to offer help and share our experience but to discuss our feelings about Meri's home care. After a month or so, we also talked to John Kersey, who explained the probable direct cause of her death, central nervous system failure, and answered questions we had about it.

Our experience could easily have been different—it might

have been more difficult or traumatic or lonely, or it might have been easier for Meri. When we decided on home care treatment, we did not know whether we could handle all the problems that might arise, but we were certain it was our only recourse. We have since found that it was the most significant and healing moment of the life we shared with Meri.

Death need not defeat the human spirit. A mother recalls how the dying process of her fifteen-year-old daughter reaffirmed her own faith in life and its meaning. The creative result of her personal emotional struggle is a poem composed to her daughter.

4

LISA

Joyce G. Anderson

We who know the loss of a child through death share a common emptiness. But each of us has unique memories and feelings because each experience living with a child is individual to that special relationship.

Lisa was a beautiful, bright, healthy and vivacious fifteen. Her fifteenth year caused me to take note and often watch her in wonder. She was determined and difficult in pressing for independence; but at the same time she sparkled with wit and intelligence, and began to exhibit a charming poise that made me somewhat amazed at this delicate transformation taking place from a child to a woman. So many times my watching her gave me a private glow inside. What a neat person she was!

Lisa's dying was different from that of most dying children, because for the last six months of her illness she was in a sense already dead, or so medical opinions revealed. Following a bicycle-automobile collision, Lisa lay unconscious for seven-and-one-half months. The many unknowns that those months of unconsciousness held were for me my major dilemma.

I was at Lisa's bedside daily. During the first months my primary concerns were those of staying near her, showing her love, affection, and encouragement, seeing that she was well cared for and as comfortable as possible, exercising her body and stimulating her mind for a future of living again.

Initially shock took the form of stoicism. Later came hours of painful thinking, required in order to transform the tragedy from the unbelievable to the terrible reality that it was. All of those months of her illness were jammed with conflicting, changing thoughts and feelings—hope, despair, acceptance, denial, anger, determination—the whole gamut of human emotions.

I believe my coping with Lisa's situation was both eased and complicated by the fact that I am a nurse. I needed to attempt to understand every possibility of her diagnosis, prognosis, and care. Because of my background, the medical and nursing people involved seemed more willing to give me those details and I was able to comprehend most of them.

My knowledge, however, complicated my dealing with the situation as I tended to become unnecessarily obsessed with details of her condition and needed to know of any slight changes from day to day. I insisted on my involvement in decisions concerning her care to the point of acting to make certain that my decisions were carried out.

My behavior as a nurse-mother was a problem for a part of the staff and was seen as inappropriate by some. Nevertheless, it was inevitable. I was a parent whose child's life was hanging in a delicate balance. As any parent, I would reach out for anything that might save or help her. I was both Lisa's mother and a nurse. The two roles were integrated within me and inseparable.

In retrospect, I am sure I did indeed cause the staff problems. Many health professionals are parents. Some will be parents of critically ill children and will be emotionally distraught and frightened. At such a time we may lose the sense of professional boundaries; then we need help from the staff as any other grieving or frightened parent does.

The realization finally came that Lisa had no meaningful life ahead, regardless of any and all attempts at rehabilitation. With this came a desperate struggle for meaning and resolution of the hard reality that was Lisa's fate.

Earlier I had written a song expressive of my love for her. I wrote the words to "Lisa, My Lovely One," as a poem and hung it over her bed with her picture. I wanted the staff in some small way to know Lisa as she was when still a normal child. That picture was a great comfort to me. At the same time, as I grieved the loss, I was proud and thankful for her. Somehow that picture bound the beautiful healthy vivacious child with the diminished, quiet, "rag doll-like" little body in the bed. I spent hours pondering the two, trying to integrate them as one. The contrast was difficult to believe and reconcile.

A long-time faith in God's love and care supported a new, growing faith and belief in God's ability to act even in the face of tragedy such as this. I began to pray for Lisa's death, believing that death would release her from this meaningless existence into wholeness again in God's love and care.

Lisa seemed close to death four times during her illness but the strength of her youth persisted. I needed to come to terms with her death and after much soul searching found comfort in writing a second verse to "Lisa, My Lovely One," which expressed a completeness in my caring for her and a resolution to her death in God's care. The song was later sung at her memorial service.

When death finally came, I was with her. I had wanted—almost needed—to experience this with her and so felt that a prayer had been answered. Lisa's life ended without struggle—only two soft melodic sighs which I treasure, as during the previous months I had heard her voice only in cries of pain and discomfort.

As Lisa died, I was loving her, caressing her as I had done for months, in hopes that she might recognize my touch as loving and caring for her. This night was not so different from all the others, except for a feeling of expectancy and the fleeting way that her entire lifetime seemed to pass through my mind. I recalled needing to hold and caress her following her birth. Strangely, my feelings now were similar. Our life together had begun in a hospital room, just as it now was ending—but her birth had been ecstasy. This was grief. Yet both events were profound and deeply meaningful.

Since Lisa's death it has become very clear to me that those painful months following her accident are not to be forgotten, as many well-meaning friends would suggest and hope for me. Rather, those months are as significant to me as any of her fifteen healthy years. Lisa's entire lifetime has left me with memories of what we shared as mother and child. Death brought an end to them. I will cherish them all.

Much more, the tragedy of Lisa's illness and death leaves me with a new and richer appreciation of life and the relationships it brings. Each day since this experience I look at each of my other children with a greater awareness of how special each one is—how valuable and unique. Each day with them is a gift, watching them grow and hoping for their future. Experiencing death has taught the profound beauty of life.

Lisa, my lovely one, now you are gone.
Oh, how I cared for you. To our love I belonged.
I can still see you smiling, see your laughing eyes.
Beautiful my happiness then, close to you.
Lisa, my lovely one, I care for you now.
Lisa, my lovely one, I still care for you now.

Oh, to awaken now, how it would seem
To find you near to me if it were but a dream.
Eager I'd run to you, sing to you, cling to you,
Tenderly bring to you all my thoughts of love.
Lisa, my lovely one, I care for you now.
Lisa, my lovely one, I still care for you now.

Now God has come for you, freed you from harm.
Worries no longer dwell as you're safe in His arms.
I will still see you smiling, see your laughing eyes.
Beautiful my happiness then, close to you.
Lisa, my lovely one, I care for you now.
Lisa, my lovely one, I still care for you now.

Oh, to imagine now, God's special plan
To receive you His child, as only He can.
Eager He runs to you, sings to you, clings to you,
Tenderly brings to you all His thoughts of love.
Lisa, my lovely one, God cares for you now.
Lisa, my lovely one, God does care for you now.

Your Mom*

PART II

THE NURSING EXPERIENCE OF HOME CARE

A nurse who serves as advocate for the dying child documents her interventions and describes the child's development of a rite of passage.

5

THE ROLE OF ADVOCACY IN THE RITE OF PASSAGE*

Barbara Etzel

Death is an awesome experience, one which many of us avoid contemplating until we are compelled to do so by life itself. I was fortunate to share in this experience with the Nelson family during the last three months of their son's life.

Marty Nelson was six years old and dying of leukemia when I was referred to him as part of a project to assist families in caring for their dying children at home. My experience with Marty and his family reinforced the fact that there is little *rite de passage* attached to the experience of dying in our society. In the broadest sense, rites of passage are societal rituals surrounding major life changes. In the absence of such rituals, the rite of passage evolves from the needs and wishes of the person involved and becomes a highly individualized process. Thus Marty forged his own

*Supported in part by Faculty Research Facilitation Grant (USPHS IR02-NU 00475-01)

rite of passage as his condition deteriorated from that of a sick child to a dying child.

The process was difficult, not only for Marty but for all those who cared for him because Marty's experience of dying and our society's expectations of that experience were in great contrast. Our society assumes that dying takes place in old age, without pain or consciousness of what is happening, and that it occurs within the confines of a hospital. In contrast to these expectations, Marty was young, he was in pain much of the time, and he wanted to die at home. Thus, Marty and his family needed someone to support them through this process and to intervene or mediate when they encountered problems either with the institution where he received his care or with their own feelings and apprehensions about what was happening.

When I first met the Nelson family, they were coming to terms with the fact that Marty was dying. He had been through three remissions in a span of two-and-one-half years, and the medical staff had exhausted most of the alternatives for treatment with the exception of experimental, highly toxic drugs. The Nelsons now faced the decision of whether to terminate treatment. It was at this point that I became involved and served essentially as advocate and supporter in Marty's passage through the final stages of his life.

Marty was a very determined little boy who had probably accepted the reality of his death better than those of us who cared for him; as a result of this acceptance, he knew at least how he wanted to spend the final days of his life and was able to evolve a rite of passage that provided both him and his family with the most comfort possible.

It seems to me there were three distinct stages in the development of Marty's rite of passage. In *Passage Through Crisis*, Davis[1] has described the passage of children and their families through the crisis of polio. Much of what he identified is similar to Marty's rite of passage through the dying process. Davis identified four stages: prelude, warning, impact, and inventory. Marty's experience appeared to include the first three stages: prelude, warning, and impact (death).

The prelude includes the period of time from the initial

diagnosis to the last exacerbation of the disease, lasting approximately two-and-one-half years for Marty. At the time of diagnosis, Marty and his family were faced with the fact that his illness could conceivably result in death. During the time that followed, they were able to accept the fact of his serious illness, although they knew he was being treated with all that was medically available in hopes of preventing death. As Marty's illness progressed, it became clear that such hopes were unjustified.

About three months before his death, Marty entered what I term the warning stage. Medically, Marty had received all the treatment his family was willing to allow without further pain and discomfort and there were no signs of a remission. Death, it was clear, was imminent. Physically, Marty's condition had begun to deteriorate—he had developed petechiae over his body, he was eating less and vomiting more of what he did eat, he had begun to bleed from his nose and rectum. Psychosocially, he had begun to withdraw—he had stopped going to school, he did not dress but lay on the couch in only his undershorts, he had become compulsive about keeping clean and was very particular about everything around his body, and the doctors were finally able to say that his death was imminent.

It soon became apparent that Marty and his family had differing, though compatible, objectives for this stage. Marty's main objective was to remain in his own home; his family's main objective was to keep him comfortable. Thus, Marty's rite of passage evolved from his wish to be at home and his behavior there. He developed a daily ritual which included eating breakfast at the table, even though he had little appetite and usually vomited afterwards. He would then move to the couch where he would spend the whole day, sometimes only semiconscious, in the midst of family activities and with the TV on. His routine also included daily bathing and preventing irritation to his skin. Thus, this stage in his rite of passage was basically an egocentric one, and part of that egocentricity included having his family nearby at all times.

My role as an advocate was determined by the objectives of both Marty and his family during this stage. Advocacy with the medical staff became necessary to fulfill Marty's desire to remain at home. Some of the medical staff, legitimately concerned about Marty's worsening condition, felt that he could be more closely observed and be kept more comfortable in the hospital. During several conferences in which we discussed the ramifications of a decision to have him remain at home, I supported the suggestion of home care and Marty's wish to remain at home. After the decision to attempt home care had been made, I maintained contact with the staff and made visits to the family, thus continuing my role as mediator and interpreter for both staff and family.

My role as an advocate with the medical staff included other dimensions focused on the family's objective to keep Marty comfortable during this stage. Since his pain was increasing, the university hospital pharmacy supplied us with Demerol and disposable syringes. The family learned how to give injections should they become necessary. Through project funds, equipment was provided to facilitate Marty's care at home—a bed tray and a stethoscope.

The final stage in Marty's rite of passage through the dying process was his actual death, when all of the symptoms he had experienced in the warning stage became intensified. On the last day he began vomiting more and his general discomfort increased. Late that night the Nelsons took him to bed with them. He seemed more comfortable and indicated that he knew he was dying. "This is it, isn't it, Mom?" he asked. "Yes," she replied, "but we're here with you and we love you." Then Marty fell asleep. When the Nelsons awakened several hours later, he had died. Soon afterwards Mrs. Nelson called me and I shared her grief. It seemed to me Marty had had the best death possible—he knew he was loved, and this knowledge comforted both him and his family.

My advocacy during this final stage consisted primarily of arranging with the medical staff and the family for an autopsy and for transportation of the body to the hospital. Much of this the family was able to handle on its own.

My home care experience with the Nelson family and Marty during the final stages of his illness and death provided a unique opportunity to observe the evolution of a rite of passage which provided substantial comfort and support to everyone. Marty was able to die with a minimum of discomfort in the place he wanted most to be and with those in whose love he felt most secure. Marty's own acceptance of his death and his family's ability to share their concerns and grief somehow helped to make the whole experience more acceptable.

REFERENCE

1. Davis F: Passage Through Crisis. New York, Bobbs-Merrill, 1963

The control of pain in dying children is one of the vital concerns of the Home Care Project. This chapter suggests several approaches to pain control.

6

THE EFFECTS OF PAIN ON CHILD, PARENT, AND HEALTH PROFESSIONAL*

Alice Graner

In working with families of dying children, one of the most problematic and persistent factors identified in our Home Care Project was the control and effects of pain on the child and his family and its implications for the health professionals actively supporting the family. Pain and the fear of pain in these families seemed to consistently rank above the fear of death itself. It appeared that most families had come to acknowledge the inevitability and nearness of death, but most were fearful of the pain and suffering. Pain was not a new element for the child or family, as all of the children had long-term progressive disease processes which resulted at times in at least brief periods of pain, either from debilitating aspects of the disease process or as a result of diagnostic and therapeutic medical interventions. These past experiences and the anticipation of pain were significant factors iden-

*Supported in part by Faculty Research Facilitation Grant (USPHS IR02-NU 00475-01)

tified by the nurses working with these families in the Home Care Project.

This chapter is an attempt to look at some of the effects of and responses to pain in the eight families who participated in the Home Care Project. Descriptive data were compiled by nurses working with these families, and were analyzed specifically to look at pain responses and the effects of pain on the parents, the child, and the nurse working with the family. Some data were also obtained through group discussions with the nurses working with these families. It is my intent to explore the commonalities found from the perspective of the parents in particular, but also of the child and the nurse. By describing some of the currently recognized pain concepts and theories, some implications for more direct interventions can be identified for the health professional supporting similar families.

The most direct and frequent responses by parents to their child's pain were feelings of helplessness, anger, gulit, and powerlessness in their ability to sufficiently relieve, control, or prevent pain. These feelings were often directed to their concern over insufficient prescription for pain medication and its availability, or their own inability to eliminate the pain. The resulting frustration precipitated expressions of anger toward physicians who, they felt, were reluctant to prescribe more potent medication in anticipation of more intense pain, or who had not observed the child during an episode of severe pain. Parents also felt the physician had less insight into the additive and stressful effects of pain over a prolonged period of time. Some families had difficulty in procuring certain narcotics from community pharmacies which were not prepared to dispense those narcotics, and this increased their aggravation. Thus, in several instances, control of pain was seen as a precipitating factor in rehospitalization. As one mother stated, "They don't trust us with treating pain." Pain was also the most frequent reason for the family to seek immediate assistance from the nurse, particularly at night when pain is generally more frequently noted. Parents acknowledged anger in having to demand additional medication, which then resulted in feelings of guilt over their anger and in venting anger to those around them. There was the persistent fear of addiction or tolerance, a fear seemingly reinforced by some health professionals as well as social attitudes. One child believed he would become immune to the medication if he took too much. Prescriptions were sometimes given only after the need was retrospectively acknowledged by a frightening episode of intense pain. Situations like this also reinforced strong feelings of anger and powerlessness in the parents.

On the other hand, home care was seen by some parents as a means for preventing and controlling the pain too frequently associated with hospitalization and medical procedures. Some families had actively participated in the decision to stop additional therapy because of the pain and suffering it relentlessly evoked. In their own home, parents expressed feelings that they could have more control of the environment and could eliminate some factors identified as precipitators of pain. They were extremely adept in recognizing degrees or types of pain; however, they were not always aware of the significance of their perceptions. Likewise all parents were able to recognize and initiate some unique comfort measures to reduce the perception of pain and thus provide a means for minimization of pain other than drug administration. These included such things as distraction, fantasy, sensory stimulation, and control of environmental variables that had increased or decreased the pain response. The use of some of these methods of pain control, however, was sometimes seen as diversionary tactics with but temporary effectiveness and so unacceptable.

In the descriptive data analysis the children's responses to pain were described primarily by the degree of pain and its location. The pain was generally described as mild, aching, moderate, severe, or intense. Duration appeared to be intermittent, varying from short episodes to as much as eight hours of incessant pain. Bone pain, as it was described, appeared to be most intense and occurred primarily in the back, legs, or around the joints. Abdominal pain was also a complaint, usually described as aching in quality, unless there was marked distension or some suspected abdominal bleeding. There were also complaints of extreme sensitivity to touch and pressure. Wearing clothes bothered some children and they preferred few or none. Behavioral responses included general irritability, inactivity, use of rhythmic or rocking movements, acute withdrawal, decreased response or stoic adaptation to pain. Some children even faked pain relief. There were several situations in which the pain appeared uncontrollable; the child was described as hysterical and actually demanded a knife to stop the pain. If pain was severe, the child would sometimes request hospitalization to relieve the pain, even though pain was frequently associated with hospitalization.

The nurses who are working with these families directed considerable effort to minimization of pain. On early visits they taught parents to administer injectable drugs, most frequently at the parents' request. It appeared that they saw this as a primary means of control of pain, or it may possibly have been a learned response from earlier treatment or alleviation of pain by health professionals. The nurse also responded to pain by becoming a patient advocate in negotiating for alteration or procurement of drugs. She became an empathizer and supporter, primarily of the mother, in searching for comfort measures that would minimize or alleviate the pain. The nurses in group discussion also expressed feelings of frustration, powerlessness, guilt, and anger when confronted with some aspects of pain.

Since pain appears to have such a poignant effect, it seems apparent that health professionals could provide more support to terminally ill children. This may be possible by integrating a concept of pain with the child's experience of it. This would then give specific direction to their total assessment of pain and some additional means of pain control and management. It could also decrease the interruption and stress the child's pain normally imposes on family situations. There are several current theories that can give some basis for understanding some reactions to pain; namely, the specificity pattern theory and the gate control theory.[1] The gate control theory by Melzack and Wall provides explanations of how psychological, social, and cultural factors can influence pain. The basic concept of this theory suggests that pain, which is transmitted from nerve receptors through the spinal cord to the brain, can be altered or regulated at either the spinal cord, brain stem, or cerebral cortex. This is described physiologically by Dorothy Siegele:

> Small diameter fibers of the peripheral nerve conduct excitatory pain signals to the cord. If nothing blocks them these excitatory impulses travel to the transmission cells in the dorsal horn and from there via the anterolateral tract to the thalmus and cerebral cortex. Melzack and Wall propose that substantia gelatinose or function unit of densely packed cells which extends the length of the spinal cord is the site of a transmission blocking action which "closes a gate" to impulses entering the spinal cord on their way to the transmission cells in the dorsal horn of the spinal tract. When the gate is open the pain signals proceed through. The gate can be closed by stimulation of large diameter cutaneous afferent nerves on the surface of the skin or stimulation of nerve fibers descending from the portions of the reticular formation in the brain stem and from the thalmus and cerebral cortex which are responsible for pain perception and response.[2]

The thalmus and cortex control cognitive discriminatory and affective processes which can alter the perception of pain as well as the response. The theory is important because it gives insight into the numerous variables to be considered, such as past experiences, the meaning of pain, and cultural aspects. It also reinforces a nurse's working definition of pain: "Pain is whatever the experiencing person says it is and exists whenever he says it does."[3] Less emphasis can then be placed on determining whether or not the child has pain. The disease pathology and the course of pain should be looked at less intently since in these situations the source of pain rarely can be eliminated. A consideration of the perspective of chronic pain, "pain that persists despite treatment" can provide health professionals with some additional ways of looking at different attitudes and approaches to pain.

Health professionals who are active in the primary care of terminally-ill children should consciously and deliberately explore and make continued assessments of the meaning of pain not only to the child but also to the families of these children. Discussions should be directed toward facilitating the family's awareness of the significance of pain to the child and the resulting effects on family relationships. Pain may be seen initially as an indicator of a deteriorating state and a relentless reminder of increasing pathology or death. It may also, however, symbolize more subtle changes, particularly those involving loss, which may be highly personalized and covert, and unique to that particular family structure. When pain occurs to such a degree that it prohibits relating with the outside world, it can result in the termination of a close relationship. Pain may also be a reflection of more overt losses, such as the inability to carry out some routine daily patterns of activity for a number of family members. It can represent a loss of privacy if the child's bedroom is moved to the living room for closer observation and if activities there must be curtailed when the child can not tolerate increased noise or activity levels. Loss of sleep, especially if prolonged, can be increasingly stressful to most family members and can be cumulative in many family groups. Group discussions with family members can facilitate the expression of feelings among those who may not have shared their fears and concerns about the meaning of pain for the child and its effect on family members. Through discussion their reactions and responses to pain may be explored. Verbalization can effectively reduce the loneliness and uncertainty that frequently accompanies pain, both in the individual experiencing the pain and in those who are attempting to provide support or minimization of it.

If a family must face pain with a child over an extended period of time, it may be helpful to discuss with them the concept of pain. Done at an appropriate level of understanding, they may better integrate the numerous variables that are influencing the perceptions and responses to pain. Parents should be shown that one can deliberately alter or block pain sensations through providing methods to "close the gate," as described in the gate control theory. They should be shown that many of the practical approaches they have used to minimize pain are very acceptable and can be explained by physiologic rationale. Too often parents, and even nurses, experience guilt feelings when using distraction and household remedies of heat and massage. Because these are only temporary diversional tactics, they are primary stopgaps only until more sophisticated methods of pain management are available. Medication is frequently considered the most assured method of pain relief, and health professionals can also utilize it as quick remedial measure.

Sensory and tactile stimulation should be advocated more directly as a means to decrease the perception of pain. The use of massage, vibration, and motion as sensory stimulation can also provide relief. The child, depending on developmental age, and his parents may explore sensitive body areas unrelated to the pain which may provide some pain relief if stimulated.

It may also be beneficial for the parents of the child to keep a log of the pain experiences, a technique sometimes recommended in chronic pain programs. A person is encouraged to look especially at patterns of the pain experience. Frequently it serves several purposes. It may determine whether there is a pattern to the pain response in terms of time of onset, duration, type, and location of pain. It may be used in exploring variables which might provide clues to pain alleviation or actual prevention. A log may also give the older child a sense of responsibility and be helpful in discovering ways to control his own pain. It gives parents a directly purposeful activity and provides an element of objectivity over a period of time. The physician and other health professionals, who can be more accurate and directive in their assessment of the pain over a period of time, may also find it useful.

Anticipation of pain increases anxiety, and anxiety then increases the perception of pain. Therefore, the family should be helped to prepare in advance for managing more intense pain, which is always one of their major concerns. Instruction in the administration of injections should be made available to help the family feel that they have some control over the pain even if the child may not require it. The dosages and side effects of the drugs prescribed should also be carefully explained, and opportunity given for clarifying and exploring attitudes and values surrounding the drug being used. The fear of drug addiction should be assessed, and consistent and frequent reassurance given by all health professionals involved in the support of these families. Other approaches that may be utilized, particularly with children, are the use of fantasy as a method of distraction or the deliberate use of such techniques as Waking Imagined Anesthesia (WIA). Similar to distraction, WIA is an attempt to have the person think deliberately and consciously about reliving some very pleasurable bodily experiences. If the child has an active imagination he may be able to think of a pleasurable feeling and allow the painful experience to lessen or to be overcome. Parents could actively encourage this pleasurable experience by supporting the fantasy, and helping to describe it. Pictures, music, and recollections of family fun can facilitate these experiences.

The use of relaxation techniques is another approach to be considered in the support of certain children. Generally this involves concentrating on comfort measures and attempting to consciously relax and contract alternate groups of muscles, thus providing some pain relief. The Lamaze method of preparation for childbirth is an example of such a conditioning technique. This requires some specific instruction, practice, and experience in the control of respiration and powers of deep concentration. A study of relaxation techniques may provide a means of helping control long-term pain, and in some cases patients might attempt to cope with pain by use of deliberate concentration.

The Home Care Project with dying children reveals the need to conscientiously pursue and explore the multiple effects of pain and suffering accompanying the process of dying. Every health professional working with a dying child who has pain should give particular consideration to the complexity of pain, its unique and diverse effects, and then engage the entire family and health team in planning interventions and providing support to the child and to each family member.

REFERENCES

1. Jacox A, Stewart M: Psychosocial Contingencies of the Pain Experience. University of Iowa, 1973, pp 11–13
2. Siegele D: The Gate Control Theory. AJN 74:498, 1974
3. McCaffrey M: Nursing Management of the Patient with Pain. New York, Lippincott, 1972

The author of this chapter details the complexities of family interactions during the course of one teenager's fight with cancer. The important relationship between the hospital's health professionals and the child is identified.

7

A MYRIAD OF RELATIONSHIPS*

Mary Weisensee

The death of a teenager—what could be a more devastating and untimely conclusion for parents who have hopes, dreams, and ambitions for their creation? The focus of this chapter is a recount of the author's experiences with a teenage boy and his family during the last two-and-one-half months of his life and her follow-up discussions with the parents several months after the death. Included also are suggestions for health care personnel regarding possible changes in interventions.

At the time of the author's entry into the Peterson family's myriad of relationships, the situation was one of bitterness, game playing, and at times a conspiracy of silence. The family had been referred, by the pediatric oncology department of a large, midwestern medical center, to a nursing group which was providing home care services to families who had

*Supported in part by Faculty Research Facilitation Grant (USPHS IR02-NU 00475-01)

leukemic children in their terminal stages (when chemotherapy and other forms of treatment were no longer effective). The physician and social worker had described the family as having multiple "needs," being a rather fragmented and separated family who could benefit from any assistance with the forthcoming crises. Therefore, the goals of this author were to provide supportive care in whatever form needed by the various family members during the approaching situational crises and to help maintain as nearly as possible their normal, desired functioning roles.

JOHN'S FAMILY BACKGROUND

The author was introduced to the Peterson family two-and-a-half months prior to John's death. The original nuclear family consisted of Ann and Arnold and their four children. In 1970, when the diagnosis of John's leukemia was initially made, the parental relationship was weak and communication was ineffective. The additional stress of John's illness magnified the previously existing weaknesses and their relationship rapidly deteriorated. Conflict in the family was manifested in destructive comments and actions, and within a few months following John's diagnosis of leukemia his parents were divorced.

Ann Peterson obtained legal custody of the four children and they lived with her for some time. She found a job and became financially independent. Through this position she was able to receive health insurance coverage for herself and the children.

Arnold Peterson was a self-employed contractor whose work was sporadic and fluctuated with changes in the economic situation. He had remarried and, at the time the author met the family, John was living with him and his wife, Lynn.

The original nuclear family was from a semirural suburb of a large metropolitan area. The family was Protestant and had been quite active in the church until shortly after the diagnosis of John's leukemia. Within a few months following this crisis, the family's attendance and participation in the church diminished and eventually ceased altogether. According to their minister, Reverend O'Grady, the church members had made special efforts to be of help to the family in their crisis situation. Since Reverend O'Grady had performed Arnold and Ann's marriage ceremony and the church held memories of more pleasant times, these two members—now separated—found it uncomfortable to interact with the congregation or to meet each other at church functions while maintaining their former roles as active members.

The trauma of chronic illness with fatal prognosis, increased medical expenses, divorce, and alimony payments resulted in deep animosity between Ann and Arnold. Arnold characterized Ann as weak and unable to tolerate stress, and blamed her for keeping the boys until "they got in her way and then she kicked them out." He stated that it was irresponsible of Ann to send John to his appointments at the clinic or hospital either with a relative or alone on the bus. The boys were living with him now, he said, because she couldn't stand the stress. Ironically, Ann described Arnold as unable to tolerate stress: "He's just like his mother; he can't sit and talk about anything." According to Ann, the boys were sent to live with their father because when they became teenagers they needed the "father image" that she could not provide; and it is true that John and his father enjoyed outdoor sports together and had a mutual interest in guns and bows and arrows.

Since the original family was not intact, Ann and Arnold had assumed independent roles as parents; this was not modified a great deal during John's terminal phase of illness, hospitalization, and death. Arnold could arrange to be absent from work in order to take John for clinic appointments or, during John's hospitalization, to visit him in the hospital in the early afternoon. Ann visited on weekends or during the evening and would thus avoid the risk of meeting Arnold.

Both Ann and Arnold knew persons upon whom they could rely for support. Since Arnold was remarried, he had new, additional family members; Ann had a close male friend. Both had living parents, siblings, and friends who lived within convenient driving distances. Other resource persons available to both were the physicians, the nursing staff, and the minister, who functioned as coordinators, mediators, and catalysts at certain critical points in the terminal phase of John's illness.

In retrospect it seems that much of the family interaction that occurred was because of John and the arrangements that had to be made for him, such as where he should live and with whom he should spend his holidays. He existed in a state of limbo between home and the hospital family that he had acquired over the four-year duration of his illness.

The family dynamics described above were highly influential in planning interventions to offer support for numerous significant tensions and conflicts.

NO SINGLE DECISION MAKER

Much of the confusion, indecision, and negative feeling resulted from the lack of a single decision maker and of unity within the group.

LEGAL AND FINANCIAL CONSIDERATIONS

Since Ann had legal custody of the children, she had ultimate control in many matters whether she wanted it or not. Though Arnold attempted some decisions, such as bequesting John's body to a medical school, he was thwarted by Ann, who did not concur with this decision and used her legal power against it. It seemed, in fact, that decisions were made independently and without regard for others or for the consequences which might result. Ann vetoed the decision to donate John's body to the medical school partially because she was not consulted beforehand and partially because of family tradition and personal beliefs.

Ann's legal custody of John also brought her the financial responsibility for his care, even though he had been living with his father. Thus she held the health insurance plan which covered John through her employment. However, at the time of John's last admission, Arnold did agree to pay the hospital expenses which exceeded the insurance coverage. When informed of available county financial assistance, Arnold had wanted to apply for it, but Ann had refused to sign the appropriate papers. Her explanation was that she had not known exactly what she was supposed to sign nor understood to what she would be held accountable after signing.

PERSONAL AND SOCIAL RELATIONSHIPS

Prior to John's death, Ann expressed concern about how the two factions of the family would interact during the memorial service and wondered whether there would be merely physical separation and nonverbal communication (which was the case) or whether there would be verbal attacks from Arnold or his mother. The only decision mutually agreed upon by Ann and Arnold concerned the cremation and the memorial service following John's death, the arrangements for which were made by Reverend O'Grady. In a conversation two months following the memorial service, Ann stated that the entire service went better than she could have ever hoped. The person who gave her the most support during this loss and bereavement was her friend, Deah. She felt that her own mother was depending upon her for support which she in her own grief was not able to give. Her daughter, Ruth, with whom she had earlier discussed John's approaching death, seemed to comprehend and to be able to deal realistically with the loss of her brother. Ann had felt especially concerned about preparing Ruth for this death, since she wanted to spare Ruth what she herself had suffered as a child when her brother had met an accidental death. Fulton has said:[1]

> Families are not only sources of gratification and affection and love; they can also be the origin of frustration, hostility and hate. The cultural emphasis on the idea of loss at the time of death tends to ignore the full panoply of emotions that may be expressed by the bereaved person.

John's family situation precluded the formulation and implementation of a mutual contract between the parents and the home care nurses which would have made home care and death at home possible. The factors which did not promote the option of home care are discussed below.

Separation of John's parents. When John was feeling well enough to be discharged from the hospital, yet not strong enough to attend school, he was home alone during the day. This was satisfactory until he became too weak to manage alone, and he needed assistance for ambulating to the bathroom and for administering the injectable medication now necessary for pain control. This assistance would, of course, have been available in the hospital. In the hospital John would also have been able to see both parents during their usual visiting times. At home, John would see only the parents with whom he was living, since neither parent ever visited the other's home.

Prior to John's last hospitalization, the family had received home visits from the nurses for approximately one week. With the steady progression of John's weakness, Arnold decided that it was time for John to be admitted to the hospital for full-time care, because "it was too much for them" at home. After talking with Arnold and Lynn (stepmother), the author informed Ann of Arnold's plan to admit John to the hospital the following morning. Ann then spoke at great length about the whole experience of John's illness, the divorce, the inability to communicate with either Arnold or his mother, and her concern about the funeral arrangements. At that time she was not certain if she wanted Reverend O'Grady or some "neutral" minister, such as the hospital chaplain, to conduct the service. The author's primary goal at this time was to ascertain the type of support system available to Ann during the forthcoming crisis. It became apparent that she had more resources than were previously known and was probably able to deal with the stress as successfully as anyone could under the circumstances.

John's hospital "home." When Ann or Arnold wished to shift the responsibility for care to someone else, they knew the hospital would always welcome John back. Although he enjoyed going home, the pediatric ward was also "home" for him.

Absence of parents from home. Since Ann and Lynn were employed during the day, there would be no one home for several hours. The author and nurses from the pediatric staff did make home visits. However, because of the added responsibility for other family members, Arnold's family felt home care was too difficult.

Lack of sufficient motivation. After coping with the chronic illness for four years, the physical and psychological energy levels of the family members were not sufficient to motivate them to accept the responsibility for home care. If the family had been a closely knit one, perhaps there would have been enough support from various members to share the responsibilities and to have made complete terminal home care possible. There was also a fear of the "last events," expressed especially by Arnold. He was concerned that should extensive hemorrhaging occur, it would have a traumatic effect on the other children in the home. Furthermore, the various family members were unwilling to communicate and to make compromises, for instance, trading off care for John or alternating the assistance of the two grandmothers.

Traditional social values. It is traditionally held in this country that the hospital is the proper place for the very sick, especially for those who are about to die. Only recently have reports been written of successfully coping with the death of one's child at home.

Influence of the lack of a single decision maker. As John's illness progressed, the physicians and nurses in the hospital and clinic absorbed many of the parental roles John's parents would normally have filled. He seemed to find the relationships within the pediatric ward very meaningful, and the ward almost became for him a third home. During one clinic visit when the author was present, the physician asked John whether they should plan for his admission for chemotherapy (it was to be his last) before or after the approaching holiday. "Oh, it doesn't matter," said John, "I have a ball over there" (on the pediatric station). Since hospitalizations had been occuring over a four-year period, most of the nursing staff, station secretaries, and physicians knew and were fond of John. He was truly a part of their hospital family and he enjoyed the patient-centered, informal atmosphere on the station. For John the hospital environment provided security and substitutes for the personal relationships lacking at home. For him the hospital did not suggest loneliness, deprivation, and subordination, as it does for many, but rather their opposite. John was fond of the nursing staff and they had a mutual feeling for him. He would frequently ask his mother to bring cookies or candy for the staff. John was quite mature for his age in his attitude toward his illness and approaching death. Once, however, he displayed some anger—a unit of blood ran longer than he had calculated at a time when he was eagerly looking forward to going out on pass for a weekend hunting trip with his father. Normally he was cooperative and patient during treatment, diagnostic tests, and pain; he was possibly even stoical, and only occasionally would he cry when joint pain became severe.

IMPLICATIONS FOR THE HEALTH PROFESSIONALS

Reflection on the events and interactions of those involved in this situation has had much meaning for the author. Written from the point of view of one entering the situation during a crisis and functioning as a researcher, clinician, and educator, this section will deal with some of the author's reactions to the situation and the implications for health care personnel for improving care in the future.

The author's observations and experiences during these critical days underscored the importance of recognizing the uniqueness of each individual. Authors often discuss the adolescent, the dying person, or the separated family as though one could approach all adolescents, all the dying, or all separated families in the same way.

Many of the usual assumptions about a child's death did not apply in this family situation. Possibly this separated family, that underwent much internal stress in addition to John's four years of illness, had had time to accomplish tasks and do anticipatory grieving, with the result that they exhibited less shock at the time of actual death. If the impact of death depends upon the quality of life an individual has experienced, then the time of death may not be the time of greatest stress for the survivor. In fact, death may come as a relief to the stress that the significant others have been experiencing. The times of greatest stress may be those of the initial diagnosis and of the first remission when the reality of the poor prognosis is confirmed. From Ann's point of view, the evening that the hospital called her to say that John was dying was her most stressful time. This may result from the contrast between the immediacy and finality of death and the stress at the time of initial diagnosis. Arnold, on the other hand, felt that the most stressful times were each of John's repeated hospitalizations when Arnold did not know if "he would make it." Arnold mentioned that although the four-year duration of chronic illness really "got to be a drag," it did give the parents time to prepare for the death and loss of their child, which parents of a child who is suddenly killed do not have.

These differing perceptions of which is the most stressful time for the parents were studied by Lascari and Stehbens:

> Opinion was divided as to what part of the course had been most difficult for the parents. A third felt that the most difficult period had been at the time of diagnosis, another third viewed the time of death as the most difficult and a third considered the time of diagnosis and the time of death equally difficult.[2]

No mention is made in this study of any of the parents experiencing divorce or how the difficulty of adjustment after the child's death compares with the stress at the time of diagnosis and at the time of death. Neither does it differentiate between the husband's perception and the wife's perception as to which is the most stressful time for each of them. Statistics vary as to the major problems of parents and when they occur, whether before the terminal stages, during the terminal phase, or in the postdeath adjustment period. But it seems that there is agreement regarding the immense stress put on parental communications and relationships. Some studies state that because of this stress up to 80 percent of parents of a leukemic child will eventually divorce. In a study by Kaplan,[3] families of 50 leukemic children were interviewed before the child's death and 39 were reinterviewed within three months following the child's death. Of these 39,

> . . . 18 had divorced or separated after the child became ill, and marital problems became exacerbated for 11 others. In 14 families the surviving children had difficulty, and four of them were placed outside the home. Preoccupation with the surviving children's health was noted in 12 families. Unresolved grief, reflected in such behavior as going to the cemetery daily, preoccupation with the deceased child in conversation, complete avoidance of the subject, or 'shrine building' was admitted by 27 parents. Drinking problems surfaced in 14 families, eight parents sought psychotherapy for the first time, and six had psychosomatic complaints such as ulcers. Problems at work were encountered by 14 parents, and six children had serious difficulties in school.

Four months following John's death, Arnold felt that his family had adjusted. They were making plans for a camping trip, he had lost almost 40 pounds (since he was not nervous anymore, he did not have to nibble), and his business was flourishing even though the economy was not at its best. His perception was that the members of his family were the happiest they had been in a long time. Positive adjustment of John's brother was confirmed in conversation with the school nurse and teachers, who had noted no dysfunctional changes in his behavior or academic performance.

Ann commented that although she had some "down days" she generally felt good. Her relationship with her daughter was satisfying. They would occasionally discuss the past and both seemed able to communicate quite openly and honestly. Ann had a favorable relationship with her friend, Dean. Though he was divorced and wished to remarry, Ann stated she did not desire to remarry even though it would be financially advantageous. She spent her time visiting with friends, and sometimes with her parents and siblings, all living within an hour's drive from her home. Still employed full time, she found her work rewarding and became bored with too much time off.

DIVORCE AND SOME IMPLICATIONS FOR HEALTH PROFESSIONALS

There are special problems created for the health care professional when there has been a divorce, especially when it is accompanied by the refusal of either party to communicate in any meaningful manner. At no time did John's parents confer with the staff at the same time.

Today there is a high divorce and remarriage rate. Although there seems to be a trend toward greater acceptance of divorce with less stigma attached to it, Goode[4] states: "The kinship institutions do not make provision for the consequences of divorce within its structure." He also states that of all the situations in which a mother may find herself, the ambiguity of the status and role of the divorcée-mother is the greatest.

In communicating with the Peterson family, many mistook Lynn, the second Mrs. Peterson, to be John's biological mother. This increased the friction between the two families. The first time that I met Ann, I greeted her as Mrs. Peterson, to which she emphatically replied that she was Ann, *not* Mrs. Peterson! Communication of appropriate information did not always reach Mrs. Peterson.

Arrangements and behaviors that may appear to be maladaptive to health care professionals at first glance may actually preserve the remaining family solidarity and the mental health of its members. For instance, the seemingly premature withdrawal of Arnold from interaction with John during his last hospitalization and the lack of involvement of Arnold's second wife were examples of interactions which seemed incongruent for parental roles at the time.

Other modifications in relationships which occured during John's last hospitalization are of interest. John progressively regained his closeness to his mother. This was probably due to several factors: (1) Ann's recognition of John's approaching death and the finality of it; (2) John's increasing physical dependence because of his decreasing energy level (the result of more frequent epistaxis, joint pain with further invasion of the leukemic cells throughout the body, and the appearance of numerous petechiae); and (3) Arnold's disengagement from the situation. Prior to John's last hospitalization Arnold had asked Reverend O'Grady to come to their house to meet with them and pray for John. However, after the last admission Arnold essentially severed his relationship with his son, his visits becoming fewer and briefer. He told John that he could spend both Christmas Eve and Christmas Day with his mother and that they would have a big celebration at home when John was discharged from the hospital. (No one, however, expected this to happen.) Arnold had "given up" and had effectively abandoned him, thus psychologically and sociologically burying John two weeks prior to death, while Ann was becoming increasingly involved. John went out on pass during weekends and in the evenings, spending time with Ann, his sister, Ruth, and Dean whenever they had time off from work. In fact, he returned from his last overnight pass, less than thirty-six hours before his death, having attended communion at church on Christmas Eve and slept beside the Christmas tree at home.

Arnold's family was disengaging and pursuing new goals at a time when the focus of the health team and Ann was centered on John. This was rather difficult for the nursing staff to cope with, since it seemed that Arnold should have been more interested in John. Perhaps this was an illustration of the phenomenon, observed by Singher,[5] that fathers "find ways to absent themselves from the painful involvement . . . which does not reflect a lack of concern or interest." Thus the meaning of behavior is different for each individual and subtle variations carry different messages.

One implication for the nursing staff is the need for resensitization to the types of family arrangements with which we as health care professionals will be working in increasing numbers. Toffler calls this the "aggregate family," resulting from divorce and remarriage and involving "my kids, your kids, our kids." Such a situation increases the complexity of the communication system and requires extreme caution in determining "with whom to share which information."

IMPLICATIONS FOR COMMUNICATION

The assistance of the minister, Reverend O'Grady, was of utmost importance in this situation. He had performed both of Arnold's marriages and obviously knew a great deal about the history, strengths, and weaknesses of the family. We found it to be mutually beneficial to share information. For example, he would share past events of social and behavioral significance and in turn was informed by the author of the health status and progression of John's illness. Having the current information about the prognosis he was better able to counsel the family about the memorial service, cremation, and burial. He came frequently to visit at the hospital and assisted in making arrangements for John to attend the Christmas Eve communion service at church rather than having special communion brought to him at the hospital. Mrs. O'Grady led the choir in caroling outside Ann's house. In John's case, the minister, along with the health professionals, functioned as integrator, catalyst, and surrogate parent during the process of changing relationships and deteriorating health. Reverend O'Grady, with his past experiences with Ann and Arnold and his understanding of their situation, proved an invaluable asset to both the author and the family. It was of special interest to the author that in the 20 years of his ministry, Reverend O'Grady had not once been contacted by a nurse involved with the care of a family in his congregation.

IMPLICATIONS FOR RESEARCH.

Although the Peterson family deviated from many of the original goals concerned with family preservation as part of the Home Care Project, and although they did not initially request the service (as had the parents of Eric and Meri), it was considered valuable to study various types of families. Situations change so rapidly in a crisis situation and no one solution (eg, home care of the dying child) is optimal for all family situations. This type of action research has been recommended by Parsons and Fox[6]:

> It is our belief, however, that most important and far-reaching of all is the fact that both theoretically and empirically, the social and psychological sciences are now highly enough evolved to make "illness, therapy, and the family" a fruitful field of action research.

Vanden Bergh[7] also recommends that the universal experience of dying and its problems should be studied "even though there are no charity drives to raise money for this study."

Since home care was not a totally serviceable option for the Peterson family, it is important to examine some of the factors contributing to or favoring hospital care for the terminal phase. In some countries "where to die" is a topic of more consideration than it has been in this country. Singher[8] cites a survey which shows that up to 90 percent of people in the United States desire to die in the hospital. He also states that the minority of parents who decide that their child should die at home usually report pleasant experiences in their familial setting prior to the death. Parsons and Fox[9] state three reasons why extrafamilial care of the sick is positively functional.

> The first is protection of the family against the disruptive effects of the illness of its members. The second is the preservation of some of the positive functions of the sick role. . . . The third is facilitation of the therapeutic process—not only technologically, but in a motivational sense as well.

Hospital care has been more prevalent than home care largely because of the many technological changes in this country that have advanced the scientific aspect of care of the individual afflicted with an incurable disease, while the other aspects related to the human art of caring have been lost somewhat in the chaotic struggle for continuing technological advances. Therefore, after the need for surgery, chemotherapy, and radiation has ceased, the individual patient and those that are significant to him still remain with their numerous psychological as well as physiological needs. There is still a good deal of research and reporting needed regarding the controversy of hospital versus home care for the various age groups. This research should be approached from perspectives of the consumer and the professional, and include the economic, sociologic, psychologic, and technologic aspects.

Even though the the Peterson family was not able to complete the cycle by caring for John at home until his death, it is probable that he was able to remain at home at least one week longer than he would have if the assistance of nurses by home visits or telephone calls had been unavailable. As Murphy and Dineen[10] state, the telephone can provide an invaluable tool in providing nursing care. Telephone calls were made by the author to Ann, Arnold, Reverend O'Grady, the physician, the nursing staff, and John on days when he was home alone. It seemed on some occasions that conversations were more productive in the evening when both parents were in the comfort and privacy of their own homes.

The situation described above in the family structure and John's very positive experiences in the pediatric ward were criteria which were of utmost importance in selecting the hospital setting for John's death.

REFERENCES

1. Fulton R: Death, grief and social recuperation. Omega 1:26, 1970
2. Lascari A, Stehbens J: The reactions of families to childhood leukemia. Clin Pediatr 12:213, 1973
3. Leukemia strains emotional ties. Medical World News, April 6, 1973, p 23
4. Goode W: Pressures to remarry; institutionalized patterns affecting the divorced. In Bell W, Vogel EF (eds): A Modern Introduction to the Family. Free Press of Glencoe, 1960, p 326
5. Singher LJ: The slowly dying child. Clin Pediatr 13:865, 1974
6. Parsons T, Fox C: Illness, theraphy and the modern urban American family. In Bell W, Vogel EF (eds): A Modern Introduction to the Family. Free Press of Glencoe, 1960, p 360. Reprinted from J Soc Issues 13:31, 1952
7. Vanden Bergh L: Let's talk about death. Am J Nurs 69:71, 1968
8. Singher: *op cit,* p 866
9. Parsons, Fox: *op cit,* p 359
10. Murphy D, Dineen E: Nursing by telephone. Am J Nurs 75:1137 1975

Those health professionals who work with the dying recognize the need for a support system for themselves. The writer focuses on ways whereby such a system could facilitate the grief work in which the staff must engage.

8

SUPPORT SYSTEMS: A NECESSITY FOR PROFESSIONALS IN HEALTH CARE*

Carol A. Reese

"Support the patient!"
"The patient's family needs the support of the staff."
"The dying patient must be supported."
"Fellow staff members also need support."
"Support must be provided for the patient's friends as well as their families."

How often have you read or heard statements such as the above? Not only are those of us in the health care field familiar with the concept of support, but we also discuss its importance with others. The provision of support is seen as the responsibility of health care givers, perhaps even more so when we are working with dying patients and their families.

Even though statements like the above can be read in literature[1] and research reports,[2] heard in discussions, and seen

*Supported in part by Faculty Research Facilitation Grant (USPHS IR 02-NO 00 475-01

in care plans, there are a number of questions related to the concept of support. For example, the term "support" is frequently used without clear definition, and its meaning in a given situation may be doubtful. It is also unclear how this support[3] is to be translated into behaviors which demonstrate the concept, and how these behaviors can then be duplicated to provide consistency of care.

Despite the ambiguity of both the definition and the practical application of "support" or of "being supportive," the concept behind these words is an important aspect of health care. Given this assumption, I would like to ask what happens to the health care personnel who provide such support. Do they find receptivity to it? And if so, how is this evidenced? How great is the need for support?

It would seem that if health care professionals are required to provide support, they in turn need to be supported. In this chapter I would like to suggest and discuss behaviors which may indicate the need of a staff or a staff member to give support, and some mechanisms for providing this. The focus here will be on health professionals who give care to the dying and to their families. With the help of Webster's New World Dictionary,[4] a "support system" is defined in this discussion as an established, orderly way of receiving encouragement and help, being maintained, and having an established advocacy procedure, especially when one is involved in working with the dying. In such a situation demands for support are greatest, and a staff person may be unable to continue functioning without reinforcement.

In the professional and lay literature of the last 10 to 15 years, health care officials have been asked to examine the quality of care that is available to dying patients and their families. Nurses and physicians, in particular, have been accused of absenting themselves from involvement with the dying, even to the point of not acknowledging the presense of a "dying patient" in a hospital unit.[5–7] This expression of professional and public concern has resulted in many changes. The most obvious, perhaps, is the number of discussions and seminars on ways to alter existing conditions. There has also begun a trend toward enabling people to die in their own homes. [89] Moreover, topics on death and dying are increasingly being included in curriculums, and open discussions abouth death and the care of the dying are more frequent. In spite of these changes, health care professionals still find working with dying patients stressful.[10] Shneidman identifies three types of hospital units[11]: The first type is the benign, where death occurs only rarely and the staff reaction is one of shock at administrative and professional failure. The second is the emergency unit, where patient contact is short-term and death is an expectation; here the staff becomes inured to the constant stress of death. Finally there is the "dire" unit, where patients with poor prognoses remain for long periods and the development of close staff-patient relationships is possible, especially between nurses and patients. Here, because of personal involvement, death evokes a loss response. According to Shneidman, the stress on health personnel in the third type of unit is great enough to make supportive interventions necessary for the staff.

There have been many attempts to explain the reluctance of professionals to become involved with dying patients. This reluctance may be based partly on the lack of encouragement and reinforcement from peers and from the lack of mechanisms available to assist the staff person with his grief following a patient's death. Certainly it is not a reluctance based on the lack of positive response from the patient himself or his family.[12] This lack of support may become even more crucial if more patients elect to die at home where those involved in the care are fewer than in an institutional setting.*

Whenever a patient dies after a significant staff-patient relationship has developed, the staff suffers a loss. Without mechanisms built into the institutional structure to work through feelings of loss, the staff may cope by withdrawing from patient contact, becoming afraid of involvement with patients, and changing jobs. Anger or cynicism may be the final result. These behaviors, which seem to evidence unresolved grief, may give rise to fears in the dying person, who may plead, "Don't leave me—I don't want to be alone."[13,14]

*As was pointed out in J. Quint's study, the coping mechanism used in institutions is the rotation of "difficult patients" from staff nurse to staff nurse.

Using a grief model,[15–17] we may compare behaviors caused by unresolved grief and staff behaviors which I believe indicate a need for support.

One very common complaint about staff members is that they become immune to the suffering of others; they become "hard and calloused" and "just don't care any more." Difficult as it may be to admit, this may well be true, because caring is often followed by hurt. Just as in grief some people shut themselves off from both old and new relationships, so do some staff members avoid involvement with patients. Just as the patient and his family in their grief often find it difficult to acknowledge the reality of the situation, so do staff members at times refuse to admit that "their patient is going to die." There may be times when the nurse, for example, although away from the hospital setting, thinks about "his/her" patient and feels an overwhelming sadness—maybe even anger—that this "awful thing" is happening. Sometimes, whether in the presence of the patient or not, tears must be shed. At such a point it becomes very uncomfortable if other staff members remain unsympathetic and expect stoical acceptance.

There is a reluctance among staff members to enter the room where a person is dying. For family, staff, and even the patient there are many reasons for the discomfort. One may worry, for example, "What do I say?" or "I don't want to upset them. They already have enough to cope with." Another may feel, "They're so depressed and I can't stand it." There are times when it is much easier to avoid that room than to be subjected to such discomfort.

These feelings, behaviors, and statements are not infrequently heard from staff members and evidence a need for help from within the work environment. If the grief resulting from a patient's death is not resolved, the need for help increases with each patient-staff relationship. The responses to the most recent loss must be dealt with in addition to those from the preceding losses. Otherwise, there is a danger that the primary coping behavior will become repression of feelings and an unwillingness to "become involved." The directive, "Don't become attached to patients," is a protective measure communicated to staff people both overtly and covertly. In order to provide the quality of professional care requested by both professionals and lay people one cannot advocate noninvolvement. This does not mean, however, that the professional person loses sight of the purpose of the involvement or is unable to define the boundaries of the relationship. Health care settings must provide an environment in which it is safe to become involved with dying patients. These patients must be acknowledged as unique individuals, who are capable of involving themselves with the staff. The fear of being left alone must not be allowed to materialize.

How then are the staff needs for support to be provided?[18,19] What follows are some suggestions for support that could be made available. The model of grief work has again been used.

Of primary importance to the staff member is the assurance that there are individuals available who can help in defining his/her needs and in identifying ways to meet those needs.

Just as the bereaved need to be able to discuss the relationship with the one lost, so do the staff members when the patient has died. They need to express what meaning their relationship with the patient had for them, whether from a professional or a personal standpoint. They need to consider with others what inner resources they may have to help them cope. Both the positive and negative aspects of the patient and his/her care must be acknowledged, for there may well be very unpleasant memories as well as delightful ones.

The importance of evaluation in order to insure high quality health care is generally recognized. But in working with dying patients, evaluation of both the care needed and the care given is essential. This must be done not only from the viewpoint of the recipient, but also from that of other professionals. When there is sharing both in assessment and in planning, staff members may benefit in many ways and the quality of care may improve. One may learn additional skills and may feel comfort in the knowledge that others are actively concerned with both the individual staff member and his/her patient. It may also become apparent that someone else on the staff or in the community is better able to provide certain aspects of care and arrangements may be made accordingly. In this way not only will the quality of care be improved, but the staff will also become more aware of resources available to them.

Just as the family needs relief during a period of stress, so also does a nurse, for example, who is closely involved with a dying person. Such relief could be provided by other staff members volunteering to continue specific interventions during his/her absence. If this nurse shows signs of stress, they may need to discuss the possibilities for relaxation when off duty. This is particularly important if there are only a few staff members involved in any given situation.

A very important aspect of support is verbal reinforcement between staff members. All too often we in health care do not give such reinforcement for the effective care, both physical and interpersonal, that has been given. This is unfortunate, for such encouragement may provide strong motivation for future responsibilities.

During one case of a dying patient, I personally experienced such support. Other staff members notified me of changes occurring during my absence. One staff member called me at home when the patient was dying and another assumed some of my morning responsibilities on the unit so that I could be with the family. Later, a group of us from the unit attended the funeral together, which for me was very meaningful. Generally I felt my suggestions and plans were accepted and valued by the other staff. I discovered that being able to talk with others who are concerned for the dying person and for you as a staff member may indeed be the most significant aspect of support.

Finally, because each new loss is in some way reminiscent of earlier losses, the group may need to specifically discuss the similarities with the previous cases. Specific suggestions derived from the current situation may also be useful later on. In this way none of the losses exist in isolation; each can be viewed as a learning experience.

How then may such a support system be put into practice? I would like to suggest the following for consideration:

1. During the report session, whether with the entire staff or with a portion of it, discuss the patients who are dying,

the reactions of the staff, and the care plans. Discussing specifics will aid others to also implement effective means of care.

2. During staff meetings identify those staff members who have, or will have, the greatest amount of involvement, thus alerting the remaining staff to those who may be most in need of reinforcement.
3. During interactions with other staff members, give both verbal and nonverbal reinforcement whenever interpersonal or physical care has been done well. The two seconds this would cost would be worthwhile.
4. Because care plans are not always written or followed through and care conferences on patients are not often held, set aside some time that could be used for sharing knowledge, ideas, and plans and for evaluating goal achievement. In this way the staff may come to feel a real sense of accomplishment.
5. In order to evaluate each experience against the standard, the purposes for the care measures need to be defined and evaluated.
6. Time is probably a major concern for most staff. However, it takes very little time to give a word of encouragement and maybe only five to ten minutes to let someone cry with you or to discuss a patient. This will influence the quality of care as well as the well-being of the staff.
7. If each staff member can find one other person with whom to share his/her experiences, it will be an enrichment and a support to both staff and patient.

The grief felt by health care personnel in their loss of a patient may be resolved through a personal clarification of the meaning of the loss, and through an attempt to replace that loss in their lives. The existence of any behavior indicating unresolved grief should underscore the need for a support system. In the area of health care, personnel may aid each other in defining the meaning of their losses. Moreover, new significant relationships with patients are always available to replace that which was lost. Not all grievers are so fortunate.

REFERENCES

1. Shneidman ES: Postvention and the Survivor-Victim. In Death: Current Perspectives. Palo Alto, Calif, Mayfield, 1976, pp 347–356
2. Hampe SO: Needs of the Grieving Spouse in a Hospital Setting. Nurs Res 24:113, 1975
3. Quint J: The Nurse and the Dying Patient. New York, Macmillan, 1967, p 176
4. Webster's New World Dictionary. New York, Popular Library, 1973, pp 573, 579
5. Quint J: *op cit*
6. Glaser BG, Strauss AL: Awareness of Dying. Chicago, Aldine, 1965
7. Sudnow D: Passing On: The Social Organization of Dying. Englewood Cliffs, NJ, Prentice Hall, 1967
8. Martinson I, Kulenkamp E, Fredlund D: Eric. Minneapolis, Minn, University of Minnesota, 1973
9. Wetzel DN, Martinson I: Meri. Minneapolis, Minn., University of Minnesota, 1975
10. Epstein D: Nursing the Dying Patients. Reston, Va, Reston Publishing, 1975, pp 181–182
11. Shneidman ES: *op cit*
12. Kübler-Ross E: On Death and Dying. New York, Macmillan, 1969
13. Kübler-Ross E: What is it like to be dying? Am J Nurs 71:54, 1971
14. Hoffman E: Don't Give Up On Me! Am J Nurs 71:60, 1971
15. Parkes CM: Seeking and Finding a Lost Object. Soc Sci Med 4:187, 1970
16. Morris S: Grief and how to live with it. New York, Grosset and Dunlap, 1972
17. Kries B, Pattie A: Up from Grief. New York, Seabury, 1969
18. Epstein C: *op cit,* pp 181–189
19. Shneidman ES: *op cit,* pp 354–355

The writer of this chapter shares the effects on her child of a death in the family. She discusses important considerations regarding the reticence of parents to talk about death and the child's development of an understanding of death.

9

THE REMAINING CHILD

Delphie Fredlund

The basic goals of public health are the promotion of a high level of well-being and the prevention of disease and disability. Because I am a public health nurse my concentration is not on the dying person, but rather on the survivors, particularly the children. I care very much about the dying person; however, I have so often seen the aftermath of unresolved grief and the very painful feelings of rejection and guilt experienced by some children, in spite of their families' best intentions, that I must devote my major efforts to the living.

I also have a personal reason for my concern about surviving children. My own children experienced three deaths in our home during a four-year period when they were very young. The first was my husband who died when they were ten, five, and one. A year-and-a-half later his mother, who had always lived with us and who was very close to the children, died suddenly from a heart attack. Two-and-a-half years after that, we came home one day to find my father dead. He had also been living with us at the time and had also died suddenly from a heart attack. When we were preparing for the third funeral, my middle child, a boy who was nine at the time, said, "You know, we are the only family in the neighborhood that has funerals and we have them all the time. How come?" I can remember my cliché answers about not being punished by God, about the neighbors not being better than we were, about it being "just one of those things." Many years elapsed before I realized that I hadn't answered his question. I actually hadn't heard them. The words of his question were, "Why do we have funerals when our neighbors don't?" But the intent of his question was something quite different. He was asking, "Who's next around here? What about you? What about me? My brother? My sister?" I think he was trying to tell me, "Man, it's scarey around here," and I didn't even hear him. If I had it to do over again, I wouldn't talk so much myself. I'd say, "Paul, tell me what you are thinking," and then I'd listen. I'd *really* listen and I'd take my cues from what he told me.

Kastenbaum reports that the loss of a parent has the greatest of effects on children and that their bereavement has been correlated with suicide attempts and depression occuring many years later.[1] Certainly not all parental deaths in childhood lead to such a drastic aftermath, and many other factors in the individual's life must also be considered. But it is an extremely important childhood crisis to lose a parent, and how the event is handled may be crucial to the child's emotional development.

So too the death of a sibling is an extremely profound crisis. Kastenbaum reports on a study done by Cain and associates at the University of Michigan.[2] Cain found that children often experienced behavior disturbances after a family death and sometimes a child's personality was permanently altered. When the death was that of a sibling, a sense of guilt often manifested itself, the surviving children feeling that they had caused the death and that they "should have died instead." Some children still felt guilty five years after the death.

IMPORTANT CONSIDERATIONS

THE PARENTS' RELUCTANCE TO TALK ABOUT DEATH

Modern parents try very hard to shield and protect their children from life's unpleasant experiences, particularly from knowledge about and contact with terminal illness and death. They often find these topics extremely hard to talk about because they themselves have not resolved their own conflicts about death and dying. Yet children do find out in various ways, with or without their parents' help, that death exists. Very often they have a hard time getting their questions answered, with the result that they quit asking. Thus the cycle is repeated—the children grow up to be parents who find it difficult to be open and accepting of their own children's questions. For example, a young boy wrote this letter to God:[3]

> Dear God:
> What is it like when you die? Nobody will tell me. I just want to know—I don't want to do it.
>
> Your friend,
> Mike

This letter suggests two of the most important points to keep in mind when we are dealing with the subject of children and death. First, "Nobody will tell me" indicates unsatisfied curiosity, the knowledge that questions are being avoided and left unanswered. Secondly, "I don't want to do it" implies a fear of death already forming at age seven or eight.

THE CHILD'S DEVELOPMENT OF AN UNDERSTANDING ABOUT DEATH

A number of writers have described the sequential process by which a child develops an understanding about death. It used to be far easier to acquaint children with the phenomenon of death because it occurred so frequently in the home.

Only few decades ago most people died in their own homes, services were conducted there, and children were expected to help with the responsibilities after death. A century ago the books written for children, filled with poems and stories about children's deaths, reflected the actualities of life at the time. In 1900, 53 percent of the deaths were children under 15 years old. Now an entirely different population is dying. In 1974 only 7 percent were children under 15 years of age, whereas 70 percent were persons over the age of 65.

How do children develop an understanding about death? Of course, it neither emerges full blown into their consciousness at any particular age, nor is it understood in the same way by different children. It varies according to their life experiences and how these were handled.

There is general agreement among researchers that the understanding of death develops through several stages beginning in very early childhood and continuing into adolescence.

Children Under Three. Prior to the age of three, children rarely understand anything at all about death. They may experience grief because of the loss of a significant person, but it is the separation they react to rather than death per se.

From Three to Five. Sometime about the age of three or four, children begin to realize that there is some kind of power beyond human control and that they have to adjust to it.[4] They look upon death as a departure, a change of housing, but they do not comprehend it. For them, immobility is the identifying feature, but it is a reversible immobility.

Preschool children have great confidence in their parents' ability to fix anything, even a dead bird or animal, and they often make such requests. They also have considerable faith in their own power and their ability to make things happen simply by wishing. By five, children think that dead people and *things* still somehow eat, breathe, and feel at a time when nobody is looking. They do not yet conceive of death as occurring to themselves or to other children.[5]

From Six to Nine. At about the age of six when the time sense begins to develop, children realize that death is not casual or reversible and many of them become exceedingly anxious. Children are naturally violent in their play and so believe that death happens only by violence. Six-and-seven-year-olds usually still consider themselves immune from death, but as they get closer to eight most of them realize that everyone will die—including themselves. As they approach nine they become very interested in cemeteries and caskets, and seem almost morbid at times. They tend to personify death as a skeleton, a reaper, a death man, or a bogey man which could come and carry them away.[6] They connect death with darkness and are very concerned about what happens to the dead body.

From Ten into the Teens. When children are around ten years of age, they think about death as a stopping of all bodily functions, "the termination of life on earth," "destiny," or "simply the end."[7] They are ready to face up to the reality of death. But they are often troubled and fearful about their own deaths, since they are now sure that this event is not only inevitable but unpredictable, which is worse. They need a great deal of reassurance, particularly in regard to their fears of being somehow responsible if a death has occurred in their family. If this time they have outgrown most of their belief in magic, they are still frightened of the possibility that something they may or may not have done has brought about such disastrous results. To cover up their anxieties, children in this age group often assume airs of bravado. They tell each other gruesome stories about worms crawling in and out of the casket and the body, and imaginary tales (which they swear are true) about ghosts and skeletons. They sometimes sound unfeeling and insensitive. Arnstein, however, has said that this is a period of "necessary whistling in the dark," because they are actually very concerned about what will happen to them and are coping with the idea of being buried in the earth.[8] It is at this age that they make up jokes about death (a practice which continues far into adulthood) and sing over and over again in a compulsive way such songs as, "When I die, don't bury me at all; just pickle my bones in alcohol."[9]

Adolescents continue to make fun of death, but a new element of defiance has been added. Many of them go through a period of ridiculous risk-taking behavior, as though they are trying to prove again and again that death cannot "get" them.

When a child loses a family member by death it is extremely important to consider what his understanding of death is, both intellectually and emotionally.

THE CHILD'S RELATIONSHIP TO THE DEAD SIBLING

To understand a child's relationship to his dead sibling, one must consider the difference in age between the two children, the sex of the children, the relationship they had before and during the terminal illness.

The parents' attitude toward both children is also important, and how open and honest they are able to be with both of them. Healthy children often can tolerate and accept limited parental attention and anxiety if they know what's happening and if they feel free to ask questions which they believe are honestly answered. Even when parents try to protect their children from sorrow by attempting to be cheerful and by giving them evasive answers, they will know in a hundred ways that something is terribly wrong. Because young children are notorious "magical thinkers," they may assume that they are at fault for whatever is going on, and because they don't or can't even talk about it, they are at a loss to find out what they have done—that they must be really bad people. Judged by adult standards, children often do not think logically and realistically. What may seem to be the absolute truth to children may be so far from the parents' thinking that they are unable to give reassurance. Keeping communication open in a household where there is a dying child or where a sudden death has occurred is essential. What child of five or older has not said to his sibling, "Drop dead," or "I wish" this or that? Children need very much to be absolved from their feelings of guilt about what they may have said, thought, or done. So often children get lost in the whole experience and have to figure things out for themselves through a long, painful process; or worse yet, they may never get things satisfactorily resolved and may carry the scars for life.

DEATH AND THE PARENTS' RELATIONSHIP TO THE REMAINING CHILD.

I cannot imagine what it would be like to lose a child, but I think it must be devastating. I have experienced the deaths of many significant persons but not of a child. To receive a diagnosis of incurable illness and then to watch a beloved child die, must take all the strength one has, particularly today when the medical world keeps hope alternating with despair, and remissions are followed by exacerbations. With the heavy demands on parents' energy for care of the ailing child, not to mention that expended in mere self-survival, the overwhelming grief, and the sense of guilt, it is understandable that the other childrens' needs are of lower priority for most of the time.

I think it is very sad for families with dying children that it is no longer customary in our culture to have live-in grandparents, aunts, uncles, or even long-term servants, who could help tend the hurts and fears of the other children as well as support the grieving parents and the dying child. Lacking the extended family as a resource in most situations, doctors, nurses, clergy, school personnel, and neighbors must become involved with the bereaved children until the parents have coped with their own grief and have emerged from mourning, ready again to shoulder their responsibility to the remaining children.

REFERENCES

1. Kastenbaum R: The kingdom where nobody dies. Saturday Review 56:36, Dec 23, 1972
2. Kastenbaum: *loc cit*

3. Marshall E, Hample S: Children's Letters to God. New York, Essandess Special Edition, 1967
4. Plant JS: The Envelope. New York, Commonwealth Fund, 1950, p 41
5. Ilg F, Ames L: Child Behavior. New York, Harper & Row, 1955, p 310
6. Rosenblum, J: How To Explain Death to a Child, Order of the Golden Rule, 1963, pp 10—12
7. Nagy, M: The Child's Theories Concerning Death. *J. Gen Psych* (Sept.1948) pp 24–26
8. Arnstein, H: What to Tell your Child. New York, Bobbs-Merrill, 1960, p 160
9. Talbot T (ed): The World of the Child. Garden City, N. Y. Doubleday, 1967, pp 325–350

PART III

THE FAMILY'S REACTION TO DEATH AND DYING

In the first article in this section on the effects of a dying member on the family before, during, and after death, this writer focuses on the reintegration of the family after the death of a the death of a child.

10

REINTEGRATION OF THE FAMILY AFTER THE DEATH OF A CHILD*

Mary Ann Anglim

Reintegration of the family after the death of a child is facilitated by home care programs, thus enabling a greater number of families to come through such stress as stronger, healthier families. Such reintegration is directly linked to the attitudes developed, and activities engaged in, prior to the death of the child. While the death of a child is one of the greatest of stresses placed on individuals and families,[1] it can also serve as a stimulus for growth. Both individuals and the community can benefit from the family that has been strengthened through a successful coping with crisis.

One of the most important factors affecting the reintegration of the family is the preparation for this process prior to the actual death of the child. Home care of the child appears to aid in developing the basis from which the rehabilitation

*Supported in part by Faculty Research Facilitation Grant (USPHS IR02-NU 00475-01).

of the family can be accomplished. Simply, what the family does and feels about what it does during the last weeks or days of the child's life will significantly affect the family's future.

One study has cited a 50 percent breakup of families that had a child with leukemia.[2] While family dissolutions may be on the increase in the United States in general, this high a rate is most significant and is indicative of the stress to which these families are subjected. Therefore, home care for the dying child should be considered a viable alternative to hospitalization, not only to facilitate a less traumatic death for the child, but also to help the family remain healthy rather than have them handicapped by its experience. Moreover, long-range benefits will also be felt by society.[3]

At present there is no particular health professional who assumes the responsibility for assisting the family to resolve its grief. With the death of the child, the doctor and hospital staff, who have focused their efforts on curing disease, or palliating its effects, frequently have no identified purpose for maintaining their relationship with the child's family. The tendency of family members to linger at a hospital after the death of a child there, suggests that the family has grown accustomed to the support of the hospital staff and is reluctant to give up this protecting relationship. With the home care nurse the objective is continuing support of the parents. This does not change after the child's death, although the means to accomplish this goal may change.

Looking at the concepts inherent in home care programs, it becomes apparent that the role of the nurse in maintaining parental control (ie, responsibility) is a crucial one. Health professionals often set goals that are unknown to the family, and sometimes even at odds with the family's goals.[4] Parents need to be able to make decisions concerning their child, whether in the hospital or at home, since this is consistent with their parental role. For families that normally use problem-solving approaches to deal with crises, it is especially important to reinforce this healthy coping mechanism.[5] Problem solving, however, cannot be successfully utilized if parents are given insufficient information on which to base their decisions. Parents need to know what complications might occur while caring for their dying children whether at home or in the hospital, ie, hemorrhage, infection, pain. They must know what to do if these problems occur. Families have demonstrated very creative ways of dealing with difficulities. For example, with the extreme itching associated with leukemia, parents have given their children soft bath brushes for gentle scratching in difficult-to-reach areas. Bleeding needle tracks following injections for pain were covered with cotton and pink pin-curl tape instead of bandaids which damage the skin. Between bouts of nausea and vomiting at home, one child happily munched sunflower seeds; or, with sores in the mouth, ate spaghetti.

Families that remain actively involved in the child's care and its decision-making process seem to be greatly facilitated in resolving their grief after the death. This involvement should not be superficial, but rather similar to the care and involvement parents normally expect of their relation to their children. They should decide whether the child needs more pain medication or oxygen to assist breathing. Health professionals need to give their support to parents; to let them know what is available, what the various possibilities are. When decisions have been made by parents, health professionals need to support the family in those decisions.

Maintaining their role as parents throughout the crisis of dying makes resolution after death more possible. These parents never have to reproach themselves for having abandoned their child to others' care during this final crisis. Direct responsibility, heavy as it may be, has not been surrendered to professionals. Maintenance of their normal nurturing role throughout the dying process strengthens their view of themselves as parents and as individuals.

Fulfilling their role expectations appears to strengthen the appreciation of husband and wife for each other. In one family, the husband told his wife after the child's death that he had never realized she could be such a strong person. The wife also had come to an acute realization that her husband was the one and only person able to help her with decisions and to support her active involvement with the child's care.

Even if the child is in the hospital, role expectations can be fulfilled, provided health professionals value this concept.

However, this is more difficult since parents tend to compare their efforts to those of the doctor and nurse, with the result that they tend to feel quite inept. However, if supported and encouraged to maintain their activities with the child, they can function in an extremely effective manner, especially in the eyes of the child.

Good assessment of any anxieties the family may have is necessary, regardless of whether the child is hospitalized or at home. Fear of the loss of self-control was mentioned by mothers in all the families of our Home Care Project. Most mothers were concerned about how they would respond to death, since most deaths occur in hospitals out of public view. Their active role in the care of the child and discussions about what might happen seemed to lessen their fears of the unknown and eventually every parent met the crisis of the death with behaviors acceptable to them. The fact that none of the parents "lost control" further strengthened their self images and their admiration for each other. Therefore the verbalization of these fears is important, and interventions to diminish the fears prior to death are essential for the eventual reintegration of the family.

Protecting the parents from the painful events surrounding death is not helpful for the final reconstruction of the family. Parents realize the death will be a most terrible event for them—separation from their child. But in trying to spare them from reality we often do them a disservice. They, as father and mother, need to know what their child is experiencing and to continue to protect and help their child through this difficult time. Well-meaning doctors and nurses often withhold information considered too painful and ask parents to leave the room during procedures. One child, for example, was asked to go to sleep so that her parents could get some rest. The mother then suggested to her child that she pretend to sleep to satisfy the nurse. The nurse's intent was to spare the mother—in fact, it accomplished the opposite. In another case, when the child was experiencing difficult respirations, the mother asked for some oxygen to ease the child's breathing. Reminding the mother of her decision for "no further treatment," the doctor cautioned her that oxygen was a treatment. The mother insisted, however, and the child was allowed to have the oxygen. This "treatment" may or may not have comforted the child, but it was an important intervention in the mother's perception.

Parents are consistently more aware of the changes in their child's behavior resulting from pain medications than are the staff members, who are not so well acquainted with the child's normal actions. Parents of one child on morphine were very tolerant of her demands and continued to reassure her when she was distrubed by her own uncontrolled behavior. This same girl's mother patiently watched as the child painstakingly counted out miniature chocolate bars to send home for the family of the home care nurse. Her mother was quite aware that the child needed to do this herself, no matter how long or how hard it was to do. Playing a central part in fulfilling the child's wishes during his or her last days is important to parents even though the stress is great. They can be prepared for the fact that things will be hard, which is also what they usually expect. Being able to have that last close involvement with their child, while still maintaining their role as parents, is worth whatever stress accompanies it.

After the child dies the family is suddenly faced with a new identity and the members of the family with some new roles. The father and mother are no longer the parents of a sick, handicapped, or dying child, and the siblings no longer have a "sick" brother or sister. They have one less family member to plan for and there is a dramatic difference in the mobility and flexibility of the family without the sick child. Suddenly, the family can take trips without worrying about pain; they can go places with much less planning and anxiety. Mothers can just go out for coffee or the family out for a pizza. Parents have more time for different activities with their other children, such as working puzzles and going skating. The family goes unnoticed in public places. Dining in a restaurant, for example, the family is no longer stared at because the little child on crutches or the one with puffed, cushinoid features or the one with thinning hair is no longer with them. It becomes necessary now for the family to adapt to a new identity—one of a normal, healthy family.

Frequently the household, as well as family activities, has been organized around the needs of the sick child. Putting away the linen in the linen closet can be difficult when the mother suddenly realizes that the closet is organized for the convenience of getting linen for the sick child. That organization has no meaning or purpose anymore, and new ways of organizing a household and family life must be found.

There appears to be a time lag between the need for changes in identity and roles and the awareness of this need. Helping the family realize that they will experience these changes in role prior to the death of the child seems to help. The home care nurse needs to assist the family in interpreting what they are feeling and experiencing; it is she who serves as a facilitator for the change that must take place.

The families in our program found that few friends or relatives were willing to listen or talk about the child who had died. The nurse must help parents to understand our societal avoidance of the subject of death and in turn give families a chance to talk with her about the dead child. Establishing a trusting, open relationship prior to the death will facilitate the family's willingness to ask questions and share their feelings after the death. Support groups that have been established prior to the child's death seem to serve as an excellent source of comfort. Groups started after the death, however, appear to some parents as "therapy" and are rejected, therefore, unless things get "really bad."

Families had many concerns after the death of their child, at a time when the relationship with the doctor and hospital or clinic has lost its focus. Most families experienced what would be considered normal grieving responses,[6] but these were usually tempered with the relief of knowing that the child will no longer suffer. Although greatly saddened, most parents were realistic and objective, their hopes having been directed not to cure usually, but to comfort. One mother's expressed hope and prayer had been that her child would not hemorrhage. She was grateful and felt her prayer had been answered when there was not frank bleeding when the child died.

In some of the families with whom we worked, funerals were planned before death; in others they were not. Health professionals sometimes believe that preplanning the funeral is inappropriate behavior, but these families feared the difficulty of planning it after the death. The literature indicates that such planning is indicative of anticipatory grieving, and presents a risk of withdrawing support from the sick child.[6] This withdrawal, however, did not occur among our families despite preplanning of funerals by some parents. Responsibility and active involvement were maintained by parents throughout the dying process. Similarly, health team members seemed to consider it inappropriate to consider autopsy before a child had actually died, whereas it was found that the parents did actually think about such matters. It might be hypothesized that most parents do think about this aspect of the death but are reluctant to verbalize these thoughts. Without being judgmental, the nurse must encourage parents to share these thoughts. Keeping communication open between nurse and parents is essential, and discouraging their planning ahead may discourage them from sharing thoughts and feelings. In a study[7] of a group of parents with leukemic children it was discovered that a long time elapsed before parents asked about the death event, although all had been thinking about it. It is difficult to understand why health professionals avoid such subjects, which are obviously very important to the parents.

Religious beliefs helped in reintegrating many of the families. In some instances the family's faith made it easier to explain to siblings what happened to the deceased child; for example, it could be said, "She is home with Jesus." In one family without religious ties the parents told the siblings that the dead child was now a star, that others could see. Sharing with the nurse what they planned to tell the children, or had already told them, was helpful to the parents since the nurse could reinforce their decisions and consider with them the expected outcomes of their plans.

Talking with the nurse about what responses the siblings were demonstrating was also helpful. For instance, some parents indicated that the other children had a tendency to want to wear things belonging to the deceased child and to "borrow" his or her things. This was especially true of the younger children under five who seemed to think that if they didn't take what they wanted, the deceased child would return and they would lose their chance. The nurse then explained the normal, small child's concept of death and reassured the family that the responses of their children were quite normal. Overprotection of remaining children was discussed, as well as the tendency to check the siblings for the disease symptoms of the dead child. In one situation a mother expressed disgust with herself for yelling at her surviving children, even for small things. Yelling at the children seemed highly inappropriate behavior to this mother, since in reality she was, she stated, grateful for them and loved them deeply. Encouraging her to recognize that her responses to this stressful situation were quite normal helped her a great deal. Such sharing and reassurances are very important in the process of reintegrating the family. The nurse also reinforced the positive ways in which parents were dealing with the children. One mother, for example, would not go away from home for several weeks before the death without taking the two remaining siblings with her, thus decreasing the likelihood of the children's developing fears that she too would leave them. It was surprising and gratifying to note the depth of understanding and sensitivity many parents demonstrated in dealing with the remaining children.

The bereaved families discovered that certain neighbors were extremely helpful after the death of the child. Other neighbors and relatives seemed to avoid the subject of the deceased child or were embarrassed if it did arise during conversation. Support sometimes came from unexpected sources, such as another parent from the grade school who would write to say that he cared or that the child had been very special in some way. The "Avon lady" was more supportive of one mother than some of her neighbors. It was important for the nurse to help these families understand why people responded as they did and to help the parents feel free to express their feelings rather than repress their grief.

Society's expectations posed certain problems for these families. One friend told a mother that she did not understand how this mother could talk about what had happened. She herself had once lost a child and had been unable to talk about her loss for a whole year. It was explained to our families that discussing what had happened and how they felt was healthy and normal behavior, especially since they had already established a pattern of open communication with the home care nurse prior to the child's death. Similarly, crying, or lack of it, gave rise to questions. People asked parents whether they were crying all the time. The parents, mothers especially, began to wonder whether they were abnormal if they could talk about the death of their child without being constantly in tears. When talking with the nurse they received continual reassurance that these were normal responses for them, even though not necessarily for all others.

Review and reconstruction of what had happened seemed tremendously important to these parents after the death of their child. Essentially they were judging their own performance as parents. They needed someone with whom they could share these reflections, some of which were pleasant and some not. Painful memories needed to be talked about, such as things the parents felt they had not handled well. Feelings of guilt remained for one mother who had refused to let her child stay overnight with a friend, fearing that pain would ensue and terminate the stay. The teasing at school, the pushing, pinching, and pulling off of wigs were remembered. Although the common response of the community was that the child was now gone and the parents should forget the past and move on to other things, the parents themselves did not want to forget and, indeed, seemed fearful that they would forget. They needed to feel that they had fulfilled their role as a parent. Having actually participated in their child's care and having made decisions about this care, the role fulfillment helped normalize the experience. It was important for them to remember, to judge themselves as competent, and to verbalize both good and bad events, thereby putting the past into perspective. They concluded, in time, that their child brought something special to the world and that they as parents "must have done something right."

During the reconstruction of events, families can come to a realization that they have tremendous strengths, strengths never tapped before and, until then, often unrecognized. Thus while they review what has happened, vent their feelings, and seek clarification, they are also developing a new awareness of themselves as individuals and as a family.

Not only does the nurse serve as listener, clarifier, and reassurer to the parents when they recollect events and feelings, but also when they consider the future. Some of the families imagined what the future would have been had the child survived. They perceived the period of adolescence as the most threatening, a time when differences are most noticeable and sensitivities heightened.[8] Parents considered the possibilities for their child if he or she had not died; for example, in winter sports, school, dating, the effects of drugs, and radiation. This projection into the future seemed as necessary as the review of the past in helping families to reconcile their loss. By providing a perspective from which to evaluate, it helps the families in the process of reintegration.

Comparison of siblings is an area that is quite nicely avoided by doctors and nurses. Yet in families with a dying child, such comparisons are frequently alluded to. Seldom is direct reference made to the dying or dead child as more valuable or "better" than a sibling, yet this child becomes increasingly valued and difficult to part with. Our society dictates that we do not overtly compare our children and that they be treated equally. Inevitably, however, parents will note qualities of the dying or dead child which none of the other children has. If they are permitted to express these particular feelings of loss, they can then more easily move on after the death crisis to recognizing the qualities of the remaining children. Several mothers mentioned that the dying or dead child was the brightest of all the children. Yet one of these mothers admitted to becoming consciously aware of how really intelligent her remaining little boy was only after his older sister's death. Telling bereaved parents that they should be happy to have their remaining children serves no purpose, because the lost child became irreplaceable, endowed with an extremely high value through the threat of separation.

One very important function of the home care nurse is to inform the parents of the dying child of the many resources available to them in their community.[9] The significance of this role becomes more obvious when one considers that insurance policies do not provide for the maintenance of dying children at home, that health professionals find it less convenient to call at the home than to call at the hospital, and that provision must be made for a substantial amount of drugs and equipment. Without resources provided by the community in these areas the toll taken on a family physically, emotionally, socially, and economically will decrease its ability to reintegrate itself after the child dies, and the home care program will not have benefitted either the family or, indirectly, the society of which it is a part.

Some families felt that the most difficult time was after the death. Others felt that prior to death, when the child was in pain, was the most difficult. Generally, families who had had the benefit of a home care nurse seemed to find the process of reintegration smoother than those who had not. The fathers found that after the death their business picked up, and mothers found that they had time to do things with the other children they had never done before. Families took trips. The parents could justifiably feel that they had collaborated successfully to help their dying child through this last experience in life, and not abandoned that task to others. The families in our program seemed to be a more cohesive, adaptable group after weathering this crisis together and developed greater appreciation for each other.

When the child is in the hospital for his terminal care, parents frequently comment on how "helpless" they feel, especially when they compare their own attempts to help with the skill of the professionals. It is no wonder the professionals claim that parents become immobilized, deny the situation, withdraw from it.[10] While it is devastating to see one's own child in pain, under home care the child remains dependent on the parents and they can maintain their normal relationship with the child and much of their own autonomy as well. If we can learn to expect that the family can manage, and convey this confidence to the family, many more families will wish to keep their relatives at home through the dying process—and they will be able to do so.

Nurses, then, must function in a supportive role and maintain this role past the time of death. The parents need to be directly involved, not left in the periphery. The nurse serves as a facilitator, communicator, confidante, interpretor, advocate, evaluator, and mediator. The role is not a disappointing one, since families who adapt well have gained in strength through their experience of loss. It is from this growth of the family, that the nurse derives her rewards and satisfactions. The nurse must begin her role early; at the time of diagnosis would be, of course, the most satisfactory. She must begin at that time to lay the foundations for reintegration of the family by setting patterns for talking about feelings, clarifying and gaining information, making decisions, and so on. These are behaviors that will be carried over into the period following death. It seems most appropriate at present that the nurse, who is already well accepted by families, fill this role, rather than that a new health profession be established for this purpose.[12]

The role of the hospital at present is not geared to help in the reintegration of families.[11] This is not to say that the hospital cannot be expanded to include this role if it continues as the most common source of support for the dying and their families. Decisions about living are different from the decisions made during dying; the family is probably best able to provide the latter. We need, then, to utilize the family in ways that will not only help the dying, but which will also facilitate growth in the living.

The question may arise of how to recognize which families can handle the type of crises involved in home care. The answer probably is that we don't yet know; but despite this, every family should have the opportunity to try, if they wish, to keep their child—or any family member—at home. Parents need not be health professionals to do this since they will tend to continue functioning primarily as parents. Families must be reassured that they will get the help that they need and that they will be able to accomplish what they set out to do. Families seem to be very resourceful in what they do to comfort their dying member, frequently more so than health professionals. What better place could a child be than where an angora bunny can munch his apple while sitting on the child's stomach; where the child can get the food he wants, although it is not necessarily what is considered most suitable; where with his eyes shut or vision failing he knows exactly where everything is—and where everything is both familiar and safe.

Caring for a dying child at home is not the best alternative for every family and every child. It's not even the best for every nurse. But it can serve as a tremendous growth experience for individuals and families, and can help the families to reintegrate and to reach for their optimal function as a loving, giving, growing group of people.

REFERENCES

1. Kübler-Ross E: Questions and Answers on Death and Dying. New York, Macmillan, 1974
2. Strauss A: Chronic Illness and the Quality of Life. St. Louis, Mosby, 1975
3. Kraut M: Dying and Dignity. Springfield, Ill, Thomas, 1974
4. Olsen E: The impact of serious illness on the family system. Postgrad Med, February 1971
5. Williams F: The crisis of hospitalization. Nurs Clin North Am 9:37, 1974
6. Heffron W, Bommelaere K, Maslers R: Group discussions with the parents of leukemic children. Pediatrics 52:831, 1973
7. Schoenberg B et al: Loss and Grief Psychological Management in Medical Practice. New York, Columbia Univ Press, 1970
8. Davis Fred: Passage Through Crisis. Indianapolis, Bobbs-Merrill, 1963
9. Kübler-Ross E: Death: The Final Stage of Growth. Englewood Cliffs, NJ, Prentice-Hall, 1975
10. Gyulay J, Miles M: The family with a terminally ill child. In Hymovich D, Barnard M (eds): Family Health Care. New York, McGraw-Hill, 1973, pp 438–457
11. Schusterman Lisa: Death and dying. A critical review of the literature. Nursing Outlook 21:465, 1973
12. Kraut, M: *op cit*

Although most of this book centers on the child who is dying, this writer shares her observations of children in the family with an adult who is dying. She identifies four major areas of concern.

11

CHILDREN IN THE FAMILY WITH A DYING MEMBER

Marilee Woehning

Everyone thinks seriously about death at some point in his life. Some are faced with the reality of death much earlier in life than others because of their own impending death or that of a friend or a family member. A child may have his first experience with death while still very young, most frequently when a pet dies, though perhaps also at the death of a grandparent or even a parent. For the elderly, concern about death can be quite normal and preparation for dying an anticipated task. Regardless of age or attitude, death brings loss and separation.

Death continues to pose unanswerable questions and to challenge our understanding because it is so illusive and its finality so incomprehensible. Dying is a phenomenon that cannot be completely explored or totally grasped because for each person and each family the experience is unique. However, four basic areas of concern have been identified in families with an adult member facing death.

Although these four areas of concern are not all necessarily experienced by each family, the frequency of occurrence is significant. These concerns are: first, the difficulty of coping with the unknown and the need for information; secondly, the emotional conflict resulting from a change in status from personal independence in the past to an enforced dependence in the present; thirdly, the adjustment to feelings of impatience in situations normally responded to with a relative degree of patience; and finally, a need for honest and direct dealing with problems and questions while still maintaining hope. To illustrate these four areas of concern, examples specifically related to families with children have been chosen.

A question frequently posed by a family, "How much longer?" expresses the uncertainty that many experience when trying to cope with the unknown, the "when" of death. In one family, Mr. B. was concerned that his wife was getting weaker, not stronger, each day and seemed to have progressively less energy and desire to fight the disease. One of the questions he struggled with was whether to ask the children who lived out of state to come home to see their mother while she was still alive. "How much longer will she live?" Mr. B. asked. In another family, a wife and mother of three children found it difficult to answer the question, "Should we tell the children? And if so, how and when?" Although both of these families knew that there were no definitive answers to their questions, they felt a degree of comfort in being able to talk about them with someone who would listen and who could discuss the present condition and possible changes on which their decisions and plans depended. Most families are relieved and grateful when they can remain in as much control as possible in their decision-making. This is possible only if they have sufficient information on which to base a judgment, even when this involves the unknown and unfamiliar question of death.

The second area of concern relates to the struggle between the desire to remain independent and the knowledge that this is becoming less and less possible. This struggle often becomes evident in the woman who feels her responsibility as mother and wife for raising her children and sharing in the marriage relationship. It can also be threatening for a husband who is or who views himself as the mainstay in the family. A role change is frequently necessitated because of illness and death in a family.

A mother in one family said very emphatically, "I don't want to impose on the children." Even as Mrs. J. said this, she knew that she was becoming less able to do things for herself and needed to rely on others even for basic physical care. Another mother, dying of cancer, said that she could not cry in front of her children because they had never seen her cry. She had always cried behind the locked bathroom door, but now she could not even get out of bed.

The feelings of frustration accompanying unaccustomed dependence on others are expressed at different times in different ways. When these frustrations are verbalized, it is important to recognize them and to listen with patience. In another family the husband was forced to leave his job and remain at home because of debilitating metastatic cancer. The role reversal was very difficult for Mr. L., because very soon he had to depend entirely on his wife and two sons for all of his needs. It was particularly upsetting when he realized that his wife would have to return to work, and that his sons would be taking his place in caring for her. Initially he found it demeaning to talk about these feelings of dependence and the role change in the family. However, having someone who would listen nonjudgmentally and accept whatever feelings were expressed made the transition from independence to dependence more tolerable. It must also be recognized that these feelings are not just a one-time occurrence but recur frequently and must be heard and responded to with patience each time.

The third area concerns the feelings of impatience experienced by the dying person, as well as by family members. Most individuals can relate numerous, if not daily, instances of feeling impatient with themselves, children, spouse, and friends. However, these feelings are magnified when someone is sick or dying. Feeling less and less in charge of his behavior, the patient must remain passive as family roles change and can only look on as everyone else carries on everyday activities with little effort. Mrs. F. clearly expressed the frustration of feeling impatient during a visit to the clinic. A 46-year-old mother of four children, she was diagnosed with disseminated cancer. She said, "I just don't have the energy to tolerate the childrens' demands . . . it bothers me that I am so short-tempered because they are just normal, growing children."

The children may also feel impatient. In another family, John, one of the teenage sons, said, "I just can't bear to watch Dad suffer any longer." Although he felt guilty for saying this, he was somewhat reassured when told that it was not uncommon to have feelings of impatience. He was also relieved to hear that many others have expressed similar feelings when living with long-term suffering in their family. Another teenager, knowing her mother was slowly dying, questioned, "If she has to die, why can't she just die? What is keeping her alive?" Beth was not expecting an answer, rather she was asking for someone who could listen to her with understanding and respond to her feelings of impatience and frustration.

The fourth area of concern is the family's need for an honest and direct approach to their questions and problems, but one which does not eliminate an element of hope. It is becoming recognized that although these families want their questions answered directly and honestly, they do not want to be told continually that death is close. Some have expressed that since they themselves could see that their mother, father, or spouse was dying they did not need to be told. As death approached, they continued to want information about vital signs, response to treatment, significant communication, and various changes whether good or bad. At the same time, they needed to hold on to even the slightest hope until death became a reality. Most had expected earlier in the course of the disease that the facts would be presented to them in an understandable way and that someone would be available to listen and to care until death occurred.

Following the diagnosis of Mrs. B.'s leukemia, the four children were told by their parents that their mother had leukemia and would receive medicine for the disease.

Though she responded well to treatment for approximately two years, the disease was progressing and Mrs. B. knew that she would not live much longer. Throughout the course of her disease, Mr. and Mrs. B. had been faced with many difficult situations, including an incident related to their six-year-old son. Once when one of his friends said to him, "Your mom has cancer and is going to die," he answered, "My mom doesn't have cancer, she has leukemia." The parents wondered whether they should explain the situation more clearly to their son. They finally decided against it, not wanting him at such a young age to live the next months in fear of her death.

In another family, Grandmother T. was dying and it was in question whether or not the five-year-old granddaughter, who was close to her grandmother, should visit the nursing home "one more time." In spite of opposition from members of the family who thought she should remember Grandma T. as she had been when she was still well, the parents decided to take Carrie. Because Mr. and Mrs. T. had talked openly about Grandma being sick and Carrie had previously visited at the nursing home, she responded well. Upon leaving the room Carrie touched her grandmother's hand, and although she was unresponsive, Carrie said, "Goodbye, Grandma, I'll see you." The next day Carrie came to her mother and said, "Mother, if you love the Lord, it's okay to die." This brought tears to Mrs. T.'s eyes and a reassurance that hope had been maintained in a beautiful way by a small five-year-old.

In each of these four areas of concern the families pointed out that their greatest help had come through understanding, listening, and a nonjudgmental but direct attitude. This approach remains a challenge to us as health care professionals committed to the care of those who need it in the many stages of life from birth to death.

> Death is the last phase of the miracle of life, beautiful and strange as birth, and as much a part of the whole inexplicable human experience.
>
> *King's Good Servant,* Olive B. White

Having worked with several families with a dying child, Sister Carol shares her perceptions of the family's need for someone who can listen to them and who understands the cultural attitudes toward disease and dying.

12

DYING—A WAY OF FAMILY LIVING

Sister Carol Neuburger

> I am not afraid of tomorrow, for I have seen yesterday and I live for today.
>
> White

Dying is a process that may take only a few seconds, days, or weeks—or perhaps even years. Yet it is a process which takes place while we are still living. During this time the dying person is living in a new way, preparing for death, making last-minute arrangements, preparing others for his absence. All life leads to this point, and yet it is seldom considered as part of life itself.

Recently I have been working with children who are dying and with their parents, trying to help both during this process of their lives. In each of these cases, the child had been discharged from the hospital so that the whole family might live reunited and provide mutual support during a period of deep stress and grief. Although the child had returned home, the option of readmission to the hospital at any time was been made very clear to the parents.

During my visits to these families, I have helped the parents with any nursing care that was required for the child and taught them ways to improvise necessary supplies from materials they already had on hand. My main function, however, has been to be a good listener. Many questions are asked by the parents, such as, "Is he in pain?" "How will I know when he is dying?" "How will he die?" "What do we do when he does die?" These and many other concerns plague the minds of the parents and just having someone to listen as they verbalize their feelings and problems can be very helpful.

Similarly, when the child has died I try to be with the family very soon afterwards, to offer any help or support that I can give. These visits continue for some time in order to help the family cope with the death of the family member, to adjust to it, and to integrate it into the family life.

During these experiences I have observed the progress of grief in face of death. On initially learning of impending death—one's own or one's child's—the sense of isolation can be overwhelming. Sometimes death is denied altogether. When parents have been given a fatal diagnosis for their child, I have often seen the father angrily leave the hospital, not returning to see his child for a long while. Seemingly unable to accept the diagnosis, he is denying the truth of it. Only gradually will such parents be ready to talk and to share their loneliness and grief, either in words or by nonverbal communication. If there has been a previous death of a loved one which has not been successfully coped with, the second time of grief will be even more stressful. In one case, a mother's hospitalized child was dying of a very rare disease. This was not to be her first loss—five years earlier another child had succumbed to the same disease. One might expect her grief to be the greater for her double loss and for the normal feelings of anger to be deeper, but since she had not "worked through" the previous death, she expressed her anger with unexpected intensity, venting her fury mainly on the students caring for her child.

In time, grief in the face of impending death usually leads to an acceptance of it, when neither depression nor anger are any longer present. In accepting his death, a patient finds a peace that is almost void of feelings. His circle of interest diminishes and, frequently wishing to be left alone, he begins to cut himself off from others. This has often been misinterpreted as rejection. Physically, the individual becomes progressively weaker and with an increasing need for sleep frequently dozes off. The mother in one of the families I was visiting told me of her young son, Tom, who was dying of leukemia. Little Tom was spending more and more of his time sleeping. Until this time, he had often asked his mother to hold his foot which gave him a feeling of security and the assurance that someone was close at hand. When he stopped making this request, his mother offered to hold his foot, he quite harshly stated "No." Then quite softly he added, ."O.K., if you want to." He seemed to regret his harshness and so agreed, thinking it would be a favor to his mother. Having already begun his emotional separation from others, he no longer felt his former strong need for his mother's presence.

It is very important not only that the patient reach the point of acceptance, but that the family reach it also. A friend of mine, while she was still in her twenties, was dying of a brain aneurysm. Her parents found this very difficult to accept, particularly her father. After surgery, the doctors informed them that there was nothing more they could do and that she would die. Not able to accept this, her parents kept saying in her presence, "Sue is not going to die, I won't let her die." Sue remained unconscious, continuing to merely exist. After about a week her father was finally able to accept the prognosis and was willing to let her go. Very shortly afterwards, she died. It seemed as though her father's acceptance of her inevitable death had given Sue the freedom to die. This contrasts vividly to the case of a little boy for whom I cared, diagnosed to have a bilateral Wilm's tumor. His parents, though they experienced the usual progress of grief, coped exceptionally well and soon came to an acceptance of the child's illness and prognosis. The child's condition gradually deteriorated, but with no struggle on his part to remain alive for the sake of his family, he finally died peacefully with his parents close by.

It has been suggested that children respond much better when they are told the truth of their expected death and are then given the support that they need. Although many are not told, they nevertheless frequently sense that something is very wrong and are able to guess the truth. From my experiences with dying children I feel that they are in most instances capable of accepting the truth and, in fact, prefer open communication rather than the "protection" afforded by secrecy.

Ten-year-old Bobby had been diagnosed with leukemia, but this fact was kept from him. As usual for a leukemic patient, he was frequently in and out of the hospital and needed frequent blood transfusions. During this time the parents were gradually adjusting to their grief. Finally, on his last admission, Bobby, who had long known he was critically ill and sensed that he was dying, asked his mother if this was so. She admitted that it was and finally explained his situation to him. The child became very quiet and remained silent for a long time. Later, when he too had had a chance to adjust to this confirmation of his suspicions, he was able to accept it and began to talk about going to God and about how wonderful that would be. Shortly after this, Bobby's condition became critical—he hemorrhaged severely, became very bloated, and frequently went into coma. It was at this time that the parents through their own spiritual strength as well as Bobby's decided to take him home to die, close to his brothers and sisters. On the day of discharge, despite his critical condition, Bobby smiled broadly, glad to be returning home again before he died. A week later he died at home, surrounded by all those he loved most dearly. During this last period, the open and honest communication within the whole family had freed Bobby from fears he had previously carried alone and relieved the family of the burden of secrecy—Bobby was able to die in peace.

Recently I have helped with the home care of two other children who knew they were dying. One was a ten-year-old girl who for some time remained very quiet, avoiding any talk about death. Whenever I visited with her mother, she insisted on being present, not wanting us to talk about her when she was not also present. In time, however, she was able to accept the fact that she was dying. Out shopping once with her mother, they bought her a dress which she loved very much and was able to wear once or twice. This was the dress, she stated, that she wanted to wear when she died.

Jim had also been told by his parents of his prognosis. By nature a very active boy, he continued enjoying much activity and frequently asked his dad to take him on rides around town. He loved guns and asked to be taken with his dad to the gun club; even though he could not participate, he was at least close to the activity. He was home only one-and-a-half weeks before he died, but maintained his eagerness for an active life as long as he was able to enjoy it.

Working with home care for the dying child I have also been able to observe the reactions of siblings to the death of a child in the family. This has varied, of course, with the age of the child, the family situation, and the amount of support given during this time. Shirley, who was ten years old when she died, had seven brothers and sisters. During my first visits to Shirley's home, her mother seemed reluctant to have me meet the other children in the family. When I asked her about the effect of her illness and impending death on the siblings, she seemed assured that there would not be any problems, explaining that all of the children understood the situation and were prepared for Shirley's death. The youngest child was a four year-old boy. During Shirley's illness he seemed to show no reaction to the situation. But just after she died he came into the room, and as the rest of us knelt and prayed for her, he simply stood beside her and looked at her with a very puzzled expression. When we all stood up again, he walked over to his father and said, "Daddy, does this mean Shirley will never play games with me again?" When his father responded positively, he again stood looking at her, incomprehension clearly written on his face. His puzzlement continued as he asked repeatedly, "Is she not going to wake up any more? Is she going to sleep like this forever?" When his parents explained to him how his sister had gone to heaven and would be there always and that he could pray to her whenever he needed some help, he seemed satisfied. But the impression of her death was deep, and now, two years later, he still talks about her.

The child who had had the closest relationship to Shirley was her eleven-year-old sister. During Shirley's illness she had spent many long hours with her. At her death, she broke down and cried, standing beside her sister's body for some time. All at once she stopped crying, knelt down and kissed Shirley, then rose and walked away. Though others of the children also cried, they did not show the same closeness. One of them, the oldest sister, who was a student in practical nursing, cried immediately on seeing Shirley, but also had many questions which I tried to answer for her.

When the mortician arrived, the children all went to the kitchen to watch as they entered. Although there was some remark about stepping aside, the children followed into the front room and watched as Shirley was lifted onto the stretcher and covered. They followed the stretcher out of the house and silently watched as it was placed in the hearse, the door was closed, and the hearse finally drove off.

The oldest boy, who was sixteen, didn't show much emotion until the day of the wake when he broke down for the first time. At the funeral home others of the children who had not expressed their feelings much before did so more freely, particularly the older boys. The oldest sister again asked me questions and sat for quite some time talking about Shirley, and about death in general, stating that she really wanted to read more about it in order to understand it better. As I talked with the mother she stated that during that final illness, "all of the children wanted to do everything they could for Shirley. They wanted to tell her that they loved her."

In aiding a family to adjust to the death of one of their members, it is very important to be aware of the significance of religious beliefs and practices which they may have. In Shirley's family their religious faith aided them greatly. However, one may unwittingly deprive the bereaved of such comfort. When I was a very young nurse on the pediatric ward a woman of the Moslem religion was brought into the emergency room where she delivered a premature infant weighing three pounds. The child was about a week old when it became evident that nothing more could be done and the child was dying. When the physician talked to the parents, they seemed to accept this diagnosis quite well. Somewhat later, the father came out and asked me if they could give the child some milk. The physician overheard this and said absolutely not—it would cause more problems for the infant. Accepting this, the father returned to the room. After the doctor had left he came out again and asked if they could give the child just a drop of water. Again he received a negative answer and again he returned to the room. Shortly after the baby died, the mother became inconsolable. I had sat with the parents for a long time before they finally informed me that in their religion it is believed that food of some form must be given to the dying person to sustain him on his journey and they had not done this for their baby. Had this been understood earlier, we could have aided them much in their grief.

> In grief, let us put our arms around each other. In joy let us sing and dance together. In life let us celebrate our health. In death let us celebrate our hope.
>
> Robert A. Raines

The writer summarizes the function of the chaplain's role as mediator, enabler, intercessor, and teacher. He shares his experiences with children, parents, and staff.

13

A CHAPLAIN'S PERSPECTIVE

Neil Hering

I am going to share with you from my perspective as a chaplain some reflections on experiences with children and their families who are facing life-threatening situations. I am grateful to the other members of the chaplaincy department at the University of Minnesota Hospitals for the time spent talking together about our experiences and I am thankful for the time spent with the group of parents of leukemic children. They have given much by sharing what it is they face and what they have gone through.

My basic assumption is that the chaplain within the hospital is both priest and pastor. His identity is determined not primarily from being within a medical institution; rather his role is an extension of the work of the priest or pastor within the local parish. As the pastor in the local parish represents the concern of the Christian community, so the hospital chaplain represents the care of both the pastor and of the worshipping community. In this way the tragedy of illness does not totally isolate the child and his family from their meaningful human and faith relationships.

The function of the chaplain can be described in various ways. First, there is his role as mediator and/or healer. Traumatic experiences so paralyze the child and family that communication within both the marriage and the family becomes obscured. Emotionally and physically fatigued, the family members have no energy left to sit down and talk. Even though exhausted, the need for communication remains because tension arises between child and parent, husband and wife, family and staff, family and God. Conflicts are brought out into the open and communication is facilitated by bringing together those who are involved.

Another function of the chaplain is that of enabler. He is the one who encourages the expression of the love that is felt within. There are times when tension makes one afraid to love. Parents fear they will say the wrong thing and upset the children. This creates an atmosphere in which the children, too, may become inhibited, fearing to hurt their parents. These feelings gradually rise to the surface as the chaplain enables communication to develop. He also provides the opportunity for both the child and family to give expression to their convictions of faith, or to share their questions and concerns in this area.

Another function of the chaplain is that of intercessor. There is a close connection between emotions and faith. The faith and trust that a person has in his God comes from the very depth of one's being. Prayers often bring forth tears. In return, many prayers flow as an expression of a person's joy or sadness. Often children and their family want to pray. This has been and does become an important part of their lives. But because the heaviness of their illness makes it difficult for them to pray, they will often ask the chaplains to pray for them. This does not mean that they have given up in their faith, but rather that they need help in giving expression to it. They need the chaplain to do for them that which they feel incapable of doing for themselves. At the same time, the chaplain prays with the family to deepen and enlarge their love by having others join together with them in prayer. A mother told me how five hundred people had gathered together on a week night to pray for her daughter and their whole family. At that moment she received the greatest possible gift of love and faith.

The chaplain also functions as teacher. A priest from our chaplaincy department visited a young child. They went to the meditation room together. There the child turned to the priest and asked, "What is heaven like?" In answering that question, he was giving hope to that child as he fought against the fear of the unknown and the inexplainable. The child in trusting the authority of the priest found courage. The authority of the chaplain is thus to give faith and trust in the face of the mysterious. He is there to bring love and closeness so that the power of the unknown cannot destroy our love for each other or God's love for us. It is this close connection between authority and trust that develops a sense of security and hope for the child and the family in relationship to what they are experiencing.

The chaplain who works in the hospital brings a dimension to his care that is different from that of most other helping professionals. Most other hospital personnel are oriented to the deliveries of medical care, which has as its final goal either the cure or control of physical illness; though the chaplain's concern must also encompass this, his primary goal is to interact with the family members so that they might experience by his presence a personal relationship of concern. His main interest is not that of therapist or even of counsclor. He is there to be a pastor. The greatest asset we have to give is our time. This is a prerequisite for involvement. In giving our time we give our our undivided attention to hear, to pick up, and to respond to what is going on around us and within other people.

One of the tragic results of illness is that it pushes out of a person's mind beautiful memories and comforting thoughts. This contributes greatly to the feelings of loneliness. The hospital chaplain taps the resources of faith which may have been forgotten under stress. The affirmation is that faith is real even then. The comfort the chaplain brings need not be in words. Rather it is his presence, which is a visible symbol of God's love and presence. The pastor represents Jesus to many children who have been brought up in the Christian faith. For the child, trust is simple—"Jesus loves me, this I know!" That is all there is to know. The chaplain comes to bring these thoughts to mind.

There are times when parents are fearful of a chaplain's visit to their child, afraid that with his visit the child will think that he or she is close to death. Children associate a doctor or nurse with pain, and frequently a child will cry upon their entering the room. I cannot remember one incident when a child broke into tears on seeing me. An incident with one of our priests illustrates this. He came to see a young child of around two years of age. After the priest's blessing, this child offered him his little toy. The next time the priest came the child was in total isolation. When the chaplain entered the room with gown, gloves and mask, the child began to cry. Realizing that the child did not recognize him, he pulled the gown down enough for the child to see his clerical collar. The tears changed into a smile as the priest slowly moved his hand in blessing over the child's head.

The chaplain functions as priest and pastor by integrating these two roles together within himself. As priest, he brings the blessing of God and the prayers of the Church, as God's caring people, to the child and the family. He brings to them, through sacraments and devotions, the comfort and the assurance of their faith.

As pastor, he bears the love of Christ in himself through his listening to and acceptance of their hurts and fears. Comfort and hope come through the blending of these two functions within the identity of the chaplain.

In working with the child who has a life-threatening illness, we cannot focus on the child apart from the dynamics of the marriage and the family unit. The feelings of the child affect the emotions of the parents; the emotions of the parents, in turn, have a great effect upon the child. For example, when a mother feels anxious, she may become overprotective of her child, especially in the face of illness. This may affect the child by causing him to become a discipline problem or to become more passive and resigned.

One example of this interconnection is the following instance of a breakdown in communication. We had at our hospital a six-year-old child who was being treated for an illness that could not be diagnosed. After several weeks the mother's nerves were very much on edge. She was spending a disproportionate amount of time with her daughter. I found it difficult to visit the mother because of her constant complaining. She began by saying that she had waited all afternoon to talk with the doctor, that he had promised to stop by and still had not shown up, and that now she was planning to go home and get some rest. She said she could not take this any more and would not leave until she had gotten some answers from the doctor. What was happening for this mother was that her already agitated emotional state was intensified by the anger building up within her. She felt that she was being ignored and forgotten by the medical staff. But because of her excessive demands, she was driving the medical staff away, with the result that her needs were not being met. A vicious circle had been set up. In the meantime, the child was becoming impossible to handle. The key to breaking this destructive pattern was to give whatever time was necessary for lessening the mother's anxieties. For me this consisted of listening and responding to her complaints and alerting the medical staff to the dynamics involved. For the physician, this meant spending time letting her know which questions could be answered and which could not. The result was that the mother felt freer to leave her daughter, and in her absence the staff could consistently follow through with the limits and controls upon the behavior of the child.

At times the significance of the chaplain's visit with the child is felt more by the parents than the child, because the parents feel relieved that the responsibility for care of their child does not totally rest on them. At times this responsibility is more than they can bear, since they feel so helpless to meet all the needs. This feeling of helplessness which often leads to feelings of guilt and inadequacy may become overpowering for the parents. I often hear the exclamations, "If only I could do more!" or "If only it was me instead!" We cannot ever adequately explain why a child has to suffer or die. Even our best attempts sound shallow and empty. Yet there is a strong urge to aid in lessening the parent's feelings of helplessness. To stand totally stripped of all strength is a most difficult task. Feelings of guilt seem to attend mortality. This is intensified when parents live continuously with the expectations that they are to care for their child. Not only can parents no longer meet the physical needs of their child; there also comes the time when the emotional needs are too much to bear. Matters are complicated when the parents want to give the strength of their faith, while at the same time they are struggling to find that resource for themselves. They are caught in a dilemma. Such feelings of guilt are not easy to rid oneself of. There is no greater need than for grace, mercy, and the peace which passes all human understanding.

Even as parents feel relieved in knowing that others are involved with their child, they may also find themselves more frustrated as the medical care of their child progresses. This frustration develops mainly because others are increasing their involvement at the expense of their own. The parents feel more and more pushed out of the picture as medical care intensifies and the hospital stay lengthens. This frustration may gradually develop into anger. The irony is that the parents actually do want the involvement of others with their child to help them bear their burden of responsibility. The chaplain becomes important simply because he is not one of the medical professionals directly involved in the child's care. For this reason parents feel freer to express to the chaplain their tension and anger. This could not easily be done toward the medical staff directly because it is too threatening to be angry with the persons directly involved in the care of your child. Behind this frustration and anger is a sense of powerlessness and loss of control. The parents lose their position as mother and father. Others seemingly become more important to the child. The parents can only stand by and sit and watch. For this reason it is vital that we do everything possible to affirm the importance of the parents, not as substitute doctors or nurses, but as loving parents. The unique contribution of their love to the child is that it can come only from them.

An area of growing concern is the effect the breakdown of marriage and the family has upon children, especially those with life-threatening illnesses. Already there is added tension and stress upon the marriage and the family with the occurrence of an illness. When there has been strife in the family before the illness, the tension is greatly intensified. Support for the child comes from within the stability and security of the home. Good medical care includes sensitivity to the child's total person. The emotional state of the child is determined, to a large extent, by those significant relationships or the lack of them. In one instance I was involved with the parents of a child who was dying of leukemia. The parents had been divorced for several years. What happened was that all the resentment between them was expressed in their fighting over the funeral arrangements before the child died. The boy was being torn between the parents. His main concern was that he would be able to love both parents. As helping professionals, we cannot salvage marriages. We can, however, point out the emotional needs of the children for their parents' love in a way that places the responsibility upon them for their relationships; we also need to convey our willingness to be available to support and strengthen their love for each other under stress. Thus, it becomes important at times to have an outside person present when separated parents work on their mutual problems, both to facilitate understanding and to set protective limits.

Children do not hide their feelings. This is what makes a child such a beautiful person. The fears that rise within a child usually focus around pain and that which is hidden or unknown. In one sense, there is conflict between a child and an adult over how to deal with fears. There is a strong urge within adults to run away from that which frightens us, because they cannot be in control. This in turn sets them going in a different direction from that of a child who becomes afraid of that which adults want to keep hidden. Parents and helping professionals alike face the struggle of trying to deal with that which is unpredictable and frightening because of the potential for destruction.

Paul, a retarded six-year-old, has taught me much in this respect. He was a patient in a four-bed room. The night before I met him, one of his roommates had become very seriously ill and died early the next morning. As I was with the parents of the dead child, I noticed Paul, huddled up, almost in the fetal position, on a litter in the hallway; his mother stood by his side with a frightened look on her face. The mother told me what had happened in the room and said that she didn't know how to help her son. She couldn't stop him from mumbling. I asked her permission to bring Paul in to see this roommate who had died. She hesitated. She asked if I would check with the head nurse to see if it would be all right. After doing this, both the head nurse and myself, together with the mother, brought Paul back into the room to the bedside of the child who had died. No one said a word. Paul saw the child lying there quietly; his mumblings then changed into sobs. The mother sat down and tightly held her child to her breast while the tears poured down. When the sobbing had subsided, I had a short prayer of blessing, placing the child in the care of God and praying His peace upon the dead child's family and upon Paul. We brought Paul back to his bed and quietly held him. Soon thereafter he fell asleep.

I have many different thoughts in remembering that moment with Paul. We all were afraid. A child had just died. Another child was retreating further and further into himself. The mother felt helpless. What should we do? We were all busy; yet we were afraid not to be busy. Fear is man's worst enemy, because it blocks the giving and receiving of love. What made this experience with Paul precious to us all was not that everything worked out well, but rather that in facing this tragic death directly, Paul was able to cry and his mother was able to love. Love is given and received through the expression of emotions.

The child especially looks to adults for reassurance. This plea for reassurance may first take the form of "Tell me everything will be all right!" Soon, under the stress of strange places, strange people and strange treatments, it may take the form of "Don't leave me alone." Just as the child needs continuous reassurance of the presence of parents, the most significant persons to them, so also they look for the reassurance that others too are with them, from their friends to their

God. Comfort is given through presence rather than through words. Words are spoken and feelings are shared to enhance that moment of meeting. To touch and to hug is important, for children need to feel our presence rather than to hear of it. For approximately three months I visited an eight-year-old boy who had received a bone marrow transplant. Very few words were spoken between us. At first, I tried to interest him in playing games like checkers, but that never really worked. As time went on, what he came to enjoy most was this little game between us. I would come in, and he would hide himself under the sheet. I would put gloves on to reach through the plastic shield between himself and me. Then I would try to find him under the sheet. First he would be quiet; then he would start to giggle; finally he would throw the sheet back, and we would look at each other and smile. The important thing for him was not that I was trying to get at his feelings or have him talk to me. He wanted me to touch and to hug him. In reality he was saying to me, "I know how important I am by how hard I make it for you to come and find me." This same boy, at the end of our visit, would, as a matter of ritual, turn to me and ask, "When will you come back?"

The significance of our visit as chaplains is that we give of ourselves through our presence. We come. The knock on the door, the meeting of our eyes, the touch, the embrace, the sharing of what we genuinely feel for the other person all give reassurance and warmth. Even though little may be said, there is still the experience of our care by our coming.

The chaplain comes to bring the love of Christ to children and their families at a particular moment in their lives. Each situation determines the form and function of that specific relationship. Our task is bringing hope in the face of despair, faith in the face of doubt, love in the face of evil, and the victory of life in the face of death in the name of our God and Lord.

Ida Martinson has been involved in a group developed for parents of terminally ill children organized in Minnesota, beginning in December of 1974. Carol Jorgens is committed to carrying on with support groups for other parents. These authors combine what they have learned from the review of literature and from first-hand experiences, in the hope that other groups so organized can benefit from this information.

14

REPORT OF A PARENT SUPPORT GROUP

Ida Marie Martinson and Carol Lundeen Jorgens

". . . And after a day at work, I would just sit for five or ten minutes . . . trying to pull myself together so I could go home and maintain some normalcy in our lives. . . ."

The listeners were deeply moved, for they had all experienced a variation of this pain. This self-disclosure came from the father of a child with cancer, and nearly all of the listeners were themselves parents of dying children. It occurred in the context of a parent support group, a group that existed because the members had directly or indirectly contacted one of the authors in search of support services for themselves. They were all finding their previous support systems inadequate for helping them to cope with their present situation. This author's interest in providing support to parents of terminally ill children was known to them via personal or published reports of the Home Care Project which this author initiated.

It was this author's belief that the support they needed could best be offered via the formation of a parent support group. This belief grew out of several observations. Parents of dying children are often seen to seek out each other, formally or informally, and many report that their best source of comfort is these contacts. The bonds they form are often strong and enduring and grow from their discovery that only someone who has experienced what they have experienced can comprehend the depths of its meaning.

Group therapy in the health professions is not a new phenomenon. As long ago as the early 1700s Anton Mesmer used mass hypnosis in medical treatment. In the mid-twentieth century psychiatry provided a great impetus to the use of group therapy. Today the group process is a major focus in most health fields, including medicine, social work, and nursing. The public has responded well. The informal gatherings of patients attempting to cope with their colostomies has led to the colostomy-ileostomy club; those experiencing mastectomies have formed a group called "Reach for Recovery." The list of such groups is increasing. In *Pediatrics* in 1971 Heffron, Bommelaere, and Masters reported their use of group discussions with parents of leukemic children. Although they may not have taken the same form, other such groups have been attempted.[1] Dr. Mark Nesbit, Professor of Medicine at the University of Minnesota, states that he is aware of several attempts at the University but that these groups have usually had a short life span. Parents would come once or perhaps twice, but the group deteriorated into sessions of complaining. Because of reports such as this, it was with caution that this author approached the establishment of yet another group. In doing this, the main question became: How can we as health professionals help the parents? The first step must be to learn from the parents themselves, to determine what, in the immense uncertainties implicit in their situation, we can do to support and encourage them. Where do they feel their greatest needs lie?

The family has long been recognized as the primary social unit with responsibility for nurturing and protecting the child. Yet, in our culture, most parents confront the parental role with more insecurity and hesitancy than comfort; formal preparation and adequate role models are often all but lacking. Their problem is intensified by the reality that the nuclear family is not able to provide by itself the support systems needed to meet all the demands placed on it. As Hill states, "Compared with other associations in the society, the average family is badly handicapped organizationally. . . . This group is not ideally manned to withstand stress, yet society has assigned to it the heaviest of all responsibilities. . . ."[2]

It is no wonder, then, that "The impact of a diagnosis of fatal illness on a family is devastating, but the threat to a family of the loss of a child presents a crisis which may disrupt family functioning entirely."[3] The parent–child relationship is generally regarded as the most intense of all relationships. "For the parents, [the loss of a child] means the loss of cherished hopes and values and affirms that their aspirations and strivings for their child were in vain. It represents an assault on the parents' self-image, particularly an assault on their role of omnipotent protector."[4]

When the child's diagnosis is cancer, the course of the disease may be such that parents must watch and care for their terminally ill child for a period of months, even years. Most of these parents experience trauma and disruption at a level that exceeds their ability to cope effectively; and it is increasingly apparent that support systems are not readily available to such parents in our society.

"These stresses—chronic and severe—can activate old family conflicts, exacerbate existing tensions, and bring about long-term detrimental consequences for the integrity of the family unit and for the emotional well-being of its individual members."[5] In a retrospective study of 20 "leukemic families" Binger et al reported that in "half of the families at least one member reacted so strongly to the crisis as to need psychiatric help . . . none had required such help before. Divorce, illness, and children's behavioral and school problems are also common."[6]

Crises are generally defined as experiences where the usual pattern of action is blocked and new actions are demanded. "[What] a man has known and counted on ceases to be. From such a realization comes despair and disillusion. A search begins, a search for order and harmony in a universe that now appears to be flighty, unstable, and capricious . . . 'Who am I? What do I want?' "[7]

Crisis is essentially self-limiting in the temporal sense, and the person who emerges from crisis may be dramatically changed. Many people seem to assume that this change, if it occurs, will be "negative" and that if an individual is fortunate enough to "hold up well" under crisis, he will emerge "status quo." This belief appears to us to be clearly too narrow.

Most serious observers of crisis experiences would agree that crisis has growth-promoting potential. A threat to—or loss of—what one values and a confrontation with the inadequacies of one's manner of functioning ordinarily precipitates the exploration, and perhaps a "trying on," of new values and behaviors. Latent strengths may surface and be mobilized when tensions rise as the crisis peaks, eliciting a "turning point" in the crisis experience. The risk and the potential is illuminated by one mother when she says, "We lived those memorable moments in the shadow of death which can petrify parents, or generate 'the internal energy which strengthens and extends.' "[8] It is at this time that people may be more amenable to "help" than they may ever be again.

Thus, the author undertook the organizing of a parent support group to offer and evaluate "help." She arranged for an informal get-together for the parents who had expressed interest, and sought to determine whether or not these parents would choose to organize for a continuing support group. At this meeting the mother who led the group, as well as the other parents present, shared descriptions of difficulties in relationships between spouses, between siblings, and with grandparents, neighbors, teachers, and friends. The group expressed interest in another meeting and the author invited them to meet at her home the following month. Ann (as we shall call her), the mother who had led the group, agreed to contact all the parents of leukemic children that she knew of; the author offered to invite two additional parents who had contacted her earlier but who were not present at this meeting. The group elected to invite two physicians as well, Dr. Mark Nesbit and Dr. Carolyn Levitt from Children's Hospital in St. Paul. Dr. Levitt has organized a support group for parents following the death of a child.

At this next meeting several additional couples with leukemic children were present. One couple had a nine-and-a-half year old girl, Jane, diagnosed three years earlier as having leukemia. Jane, the parents told the group, had a very strong religious faith. When one of her friends died some time before she had spoken of her as having gone to heaven to be with Jesus. She had also talked with her mother about death, stating that after death you will live in heaven forever. Jane's mother mentioned that she herself frequently converses over the phone with another mother of a leukemic child. Though this friend did not want to attend these meetings, she was able to share her concerns and feelings over the phone.

The parents of Joan, a little six-year-old diagnosed the previous year, also attended. Though her father was rather quiet during the meeting, he mentioned over refreshments that all the children in their neighborhood seemed to have heard from their parents that Joan was going to die. He was deeply worried that Joan would one day hear of this from the children. How much can a six-year-old understand about death and dying, he wondered, and how should he answer if Joan should one day ask him, "Am I going to die?" or "What is it like to die?" For parents of terminally ill children, the issue of how to psychologically prepare their child for his or her own death is probably one of the most painful issues they will ever confront. Some parents elect to attempt the virtually impossible, they attempt to shield their child from awareness of impending death. Others assume this position more by default than by plan—they simply cannot find the courage needed to bring the subject out in the open with their child. Many parents attempt to avoid at all costs the "horror" of "going to pieces" or otherwise exhibiting emotional distress in front of their child; this behavior would be totally incompatible with their concept of the successful—or even OK—parent, a self-expectation of adjustment to their child's diagnosis.

A third set of parents had a daughter named Susan. Susan

had been diagnosed only six months previously and had consequently had a hysterectomy with both ovaries removed. She now had essentially the same medical treatment as the leukemic children. Some of the other parents expressed at this time the preference that the group exist mainly for informational purposes, ie, educating the parents about leukemia and related needs. However, Susan's parents felt that the group should also give emotional support when morale was low and provide the opportunity for a sharing of concerns not possible elsewhere.

During this meeting much significant sharing took place. Joan's father expressed the deep need to understand the course of the disease and all the phases of the treatment. Others agreed on the importance of the need to know, of not remaining "in the dark." The use of information to gain a sense of control is a common behavior pattern in our culture. This is especially true in high stress or crisis periods. Answers and reasons probably help persons preserve some sense of rationality in a situation that seems basically irrational. Parents of terminally ill children often seek "the whole picture," the "whys ," the "whats to expect." When answers are not forthcoming, parents may construct their own. For some, it seems, almost any answer is better than uncertainty. Parents are often uncertain about whether their past actions—or nonactions—contributed to their child's illness; they are likewise uncertain about what is to come, and how—and if—they will be able to cope with that. Answers limit this uncertainty and allow them to better focus their energies. Within limits, then, this search for data as a means to feeling some control may be healthy. Occasionally, however, the process of intellectualizing is extreme and suggests a state of great fear and fragility.

One parent suggested that the group meet at the American Cancer Society where many facilities are available; there the first half-hour could feature a special speaker, followed by open discussion. Some objected to this rather formal approach, feeling their greatest need was mutual support among the parents themselves. For example, Jane's mother mentioned that one of her greatest difficulties was all the unsolicited advice she received from well-intentioned friends, who pressured her to take Jane to Mexico for the Latrille treatment, or to try the Kathryn Kuhlman cures or numerous folk cures. For others, the grandparents presented difficulties in not understanding the disease and in consistently denying that the child was indeed fatally ill. Parents of terminally ill children commonly find that friends and relatives are more of a burden than a help when the parents are attempting to confront the reality of the events around them. One author concluded that:

> Typically, the children's grandparents tended to be less accepting of the diagnosis than the parents, with more distant relatives and friends challenging reality even more frequently. . . . [This] almost made it appear that some of the parents were surrounded by "concentric circles of disbelief."[9]

According to these authors, many parents find themselves feeling the uncomfortable need to "defend the diagnosis," support would-be-supporters, or, at best, repeat details over and over again to the large number of friends and relatives that beseiged them with requests for information. At the same time that most of these well-meaning persons refused to allow parents an expression of hopelessness, they paradoxically expected them to appear grief-stricken.[10]

Most parents of terminally ill children do not have the energy to meet such unrealistic expectations. Upholding phoninesses is too costly a strain for some, and they drop off this behavior little by little. Often there is a concomitant dropping away of friends, partly in response to the parent's behavior, we expect, but probably in part because these people are so uncertain regarding what they "should say" or do to help the parents that they find it easier to say nothing and do nothing.

The parents also expressed concern regarding the time when treatment would no longer be feasible: With whom does the decision lie regarding cessation of treatments? When treatments have ceased, will medical help still be available? Ann, who had a seven-year-old boy diagnosed a year earlier, was particularly convinced of the value of a parent support group and suggested that this group become organized and meet on a regular basis. With this goal in mind, another meeting was set for the following month.

Later on in the evening of this second meeting, when the parents had all left, Dr. Levitt and the author discussed the meeting. Dr. Levitt stated that in the parents' group at Children's Hospital the concerns and objectives were more clearly focused. However, that is to be expected, we believe, for the circumstances are quite different. Because the parents in that group have already been through the experience of their child's death, the uncertainties surrounding impending death have all been removed; the situation for them is more clearly defined. The difficulties they must cope with are more easily recognized. The parents of children approaching death experience an uncertainty that permeates all of life and quite naturally prevents clarity of objectives in organizing such a parent group.

Dr. Richard Lansdown, an English pediatrician, spoke recently in a radio interview regarding this uncertainty[11]:

> Life was much easier when one could predict what was going to happen to a child. I've interviewed a number of parents in London recently just before I came here; my last question was always: "What has been the most difficult aspect of the child's illness?" I've stopped asking the question now because I always get the same answer in some form or another: "It's uncertainty; it's not knowing what is going to happen."

He continued to say that this kind of uncertainty can be on several levels. First, there is the uncertainty over a particular kind of treatment. For example, some of the drugs used with children today make them vomit. Occasionally a doctor or a nurse will forget to tell the parents of this side effect. Consequently, when the child returns home and soon begins to vomit violently, the mother becomes very distressed, wondering what she's doing wrong, whether the hospital is helping her child after all, and so on. At another level there is the question of when the child will die: Will it be within six months, or two years, or five years? Another problem with leukemia which is not common to many illnesses is the stage of remission, when the symptoms have apparently abated and the child seems quite normal. He can go to school; he can eat well; he can run around; he can join in games. "It's at this time," Dr. Lansdown said, "that other people, and particularly grandparents, it seems, come in to say that there's nothing wrong with the child, really." "What's all the fuss about?" they say. "Why do you want to keep taking him up to that hospital? He's really fine. Look at him—he's running around like a two-year-old. I think there's been a mistake somewhere. I think those doctors don't know what they're doing." When that period of remission ends, it's extremely difficult, for the child is readmitted to the hospital and is again very sick. "It's a period of uncertainty," said Dr. Lansdown, "because there is no assurance as to how long the period of remission will last. It may be six weeks, it may be two or three years."

The following month the parents met as planned. One mother told the group that her daughter, who had had leukemia for three years, had now developed complications—she was becoming blind and her kidneys were functioning very poorly. She also stated that the tension caused by their child's illness had brought a decided strain in the marital relationship of her and her husband. Because her husband was gone much of the time, she had assumed more and more of the responsibility for the care of the child. Arguments began regarding her care of both the sick child and the remaining well child. Tension came to a critical point and finally her husband decided they needed outside help. Binger found in a study on parents of children with leukemia that the fathers found many ways to absent themselves from painful involvement with their troubled families. This type of behavior is a coping mechanism, and often indicates the father's need for additional support. Although others may look upon such behavior as expressing a lack of interest or concern, it is a way of avoiding the pain of an ongoing involvement with the dying child. Such avoidance, however, often leaves the mother bereft of much needed support. Fathers who manifest this type of behavior should be helped to express their painful feelings and to look at the effect on their families of this method of coping.[12] Mothers generally find that direct giving of care is more compatible with their self-concept and experience. When the mother who described this problem in the group meeting was asked what one could do to prevent this type of difficulty, she answered that the parent's awareness of the possibility of this tension arising can help much, as might efforts to have both parents share equally in the responsibility for the child. One father mentioned several unfortunate occurrences at the hospital in the care of children. One nurse was heard to say, "If you don't swallow this medicine, I'll give you a shot." How tragic that this should be said to a child who was diagnosed with a disease requiring innumerable shots. He stressed also the need for honesty and openness, and the desire of parents to know what is happening. Another parent, who was enthusiastic about the outcome of the meeting, took home the pamphlet "Childhood Leukemia," offering to make suggestions for corrections and improvements. He seemed to feel that the group now really had a purpose for meeting.

At the next meeting the mother of a boy who had died a year-and-a-half earlier shared some of her experiences. The other parents were eager and persistent in their questions, particularly regarding John's death. "When did he die?" "Was the mother there?" "Was he alert?" Questions such as these generally arise from an intense concern, a concern which may be focal for virtually all parents of terminally ill children. It is our impression that for some parents the intensity of this concern is so great that it is never formulated into words. Group members also asked this mother what the most difficult period was for the parents? Her answer to the last question was that their greatest marital difficulties came after their son's death. Until that time they had been able to work together for their son. After his death there was for her a sense of emptiness and meaninglessness, and a deep need to do something of long-range value. The writing of a monograph about their experience had been a great help in filling this void. When she was asked about her husband's experience, she suggested that at a future meeting he describe for himself his experience during this crucial period.

Accordingly, her husband came to the next meeting. In answering the many questions which the other parents directed to him, he told of some of his meaningful experiences during their son's illness. These all included doing with their son something the boy had most wanted to do. He valued these experiences greatly, in spite of the difficulties which had been involved. He stated that his work had suffered during this time. His output had decreased markedly and he had not been as helpful or as creative as usual; and yet, he said, none of those things really mattered. Of prime importance to him was that he be with his son and help him as much as possible. He agreed with his wife that the period following his son's death was even more difficult. As was true for her, much in life seemed to have lost its value and there was little that truly held meaning for him. The group members seemed to be moved by what he said and indicated that they appreciated his openness with them.

The group met again the following month and once more there was mutual sharing among the parents. One of the fathers told of a frightening experience he had just recently had. On coming home one afternoon, a child had stopped him and said, "Your daughter is dead." Going around the corner of the house, he saw his daughter on the ground with a second girl leaning over her. Again the child said, "She's dead." He realized then that the children were just playing, and that it was a mock death. He was deeply shaken by the experience because this was a brutal reminder of what he knew was to come. Learning to live with impending death is difficult.

At the next meeting the parents prepared a written evaluation of the Parents' Support Group up to that time. They listed first the advantages.

1. The small group atmosphere allows for open communication among the parents regarding their children's and their own personal problems relating to their special situation.
2. The basic need to feel that one is not alone in this situation can be met by informal sharing and mutual caring.
3. Because the group is small it is possible for resource people to focus on individual problems and situations.
4. Informational materials on cancer provided for the parents can aid them in facing the various stages of their children's condition.

Then the group identified the disadvantages:

1. Clear direction for the future course of the meetings is lacking.
2. It is often difficult to schedule resource people to meet with a group as small as this.

The following suggestions were made by the parents regarding the future of the group:

1. Prepare for laymen literature describing cancer, its various phases, and special problems related to the disease, etc.; make this available to parents of children diagnosed with cancer.
2. Compile a list of sources for available information on cancer, including knowledgeable resource persons, programs and activities sponsored by the American Cancer Society, for instance.
3. Educate and influence various professionals regarding the needs and concerns of parents with leukemic children.
4. Influence local, state, and federal governments to pass necessary laws relating to health care of children suffering from fatal illnesses.
5. Provide greater parent support during the last weeks or months of a child's life.
6. Expand from the present single group into perhaps three groups which could then profit from comparison of achievements and goals.

It is our impression that the Parent Support Group was a growth-producing experience for its members. As Moustakas believes:

> All people need love, safety, belongingness, acceptance, and respect as conditions basic to their growth. When these conditions are provided by the human environment, growth occurs naturally through actualization of one's potential. . . . Relations must be such that the individual is free to affirm, express, actualize, and experience his own uniqueness.[13]

Our assessment is that these positive conditions were generally present in this group. Group members appeared to engage in a relatively high degree of self-exploration and self-disclosure; nearly all of the group members indicated in some way that they felt safe to do this. There were a variety of behaviors that suggested growing self acceptance, something we value highly. Moustakas speaks to the importance of this when he says, "The individual, to keep on growing as a self, must continue to believe in himself, regardless of what anyone else may think of him. When he does not accept and value himself, much of his energies will be used to defend rather than to explore and to actualize himself."[14]

We valued their ability to share their feelings in the group setting, and agree with Moustakas when he states his belief that unless "the person is free to express his own uniqueness and distinctiveness, his capacity for growth is stifled and denied. Self-expression is the individual's way of asserting his own yes-feeling."[15]

Interaction is acting and reacting; as we act and react, we tell the other person both something about ourselves and our view of him. Many believe that through this feedback process it is possible to come to know ourselves as well as others. The person who values the opinion of others highly will—if he is ready—grow in trust and confidence if he can discover that that which he perceives to be the worst in himself is accepted by others. "Full disclosure of the self to at least one other significant human being," according to Jourard, "appears to be one means by which a person discovers not only the breadth and depth of his needs and feelings, but also the nature of his self-affirmed values."[16] Another writer put it more simply: "Express your feelings and you control them. Repress your feelings and they will control you."[17]

Would-be-helpers too often lack respect for strengths and rights of the person they seek to "help." They see them as fragile and avoid opening "touchy subjects" for fear of unleashing a "Pandora's box" that they believe neither they nor the person they wish to help can handle. The following statement by a nurse seems fairly typical of this approach. "In fact, they looked so frightened and uncomfortable that I was almost afraid to ask them what was troubling them, fearing the situation would become too difficult to handle." Gendlin states, "We should never avoid what an individual *implicitly* feels because we fear he cannot take it. He is already taking it! The question is: 'Will you enable him to live it with you or only alone (two entirely different sorts of experiential processes)?' "[18]

In facilitating parent support groups, a central policy we have maintained is to attempt the reduction of barriers to self-exploration. Evidence demonstrates repeatedly that people vary considerably in their willingness to allow themselves to be open to their own feelings and experiencing. One of the big obstacles for many seems to be their belief that "submerging" their feelings will aid them in postponing, or even avoiding, "intense distress." Many seem to fear the consequences of "letting go of control" of their feelings and their behavior. There is danger in generalizing regarding the basis for these fears, for they are as individual as other elements of a person's perceptual worlds; yet it seems that for a significant number of people the value they put on the opinions of others is a real factor. Our culture tends to label this loss of control as "weakness," and "weakness" is generally deemed very undesirable.

To reduce barriers to self-exploration, we selected a physical setting free from nongroup members and relatively free from other distractors. The continued use of that site minimized the introduction of new distractors. We encouraged participative decision making regarding the objectives of the group and avoided an excess of structure.

A second policy was to facilitate the sharing of feelings and experiences as a means of self-exploration. We believe that one person can aid another in carrying forward his experiential process—perhaps in ways that he alone cannot. To this end we attempted to avoid directing the focus away from any aspect of themselves on which they chose to focus. We listened. We tried to avoid behavior that might be perceived by group members as meaning that we were judging them, that we wanted them to act in any way that they did not value, that we were stereotyping them, or that we saw them as something other than persons.

We tried, above all, to demonstrate our acceptance of them—something we felt. We sought to create the type of "safe" environment that the person in crisis may need before he is able to express what he is feeling. As Moustakas says, "Under threat, the self is less open to spontaneous expression—that is, more passive and controlled." He believes that significant learning is promoted if "the threat to the self is at a minimum while at the same time the uniqueness of the individual is regarded as worthwhile and is deeply respected."[19]

We made a great effort to avoid suggesting there were standards to which one must conform. If we gain access to the person's perceptions—from him, of course—we may well find that he is already dealing with alterations in his own expectations, and the pressure of expectations imposed on him by outsiders can be highly detrimental. The individual wishing to be "helpful" must avoid the pitfall of leading the person in crisis to believe that there is any role or model to which he must conform (ie, "be strong," and the like). The person in crisis may waste precious energy in role playing, and this is hardly an impetus to resolution and growth.

We sought to exhibit our own humanity and to become actively engaged in the process of exploring ourselves. In our relationship with the group, we tried to be "ourselves" and to avoid any role playing.

We hoped to expose the group to a demonstration rather than an exhortation; to express feelings as well as thoughts. We do not want the person in crisis to merely intellectualize. Is it not then important that if we are to aid the person in crisis we also must avoid the pitfall of merely intellectualizing? Many would-be-helpers function with much artificiality and much limitation of their involvement as persons, as if to avoid the error of betraying their own weaknesses. One wonders to what extent they can possibly be "therapeutic" in helping persons explore their experiential world when they are so out of touch with their own. Is it surprising that many (or most?) of them equate "control of emotions" with "prevention or resolution of crisis?"

We tried to be sensitive to the negative effects of any action which might hinder the parent in their attempt to verbalize their experiences. Gendlin points out how often the person struggles for exactly the right way of saying something. "That exactly right statement has a powerful experiential effect. The person may visibly relax, exhale deeply, and feel released and deeply relieved, often despite the fact that the statement asserts something awful."[20] This is particularly important to remember when we are asked questions by persons in crisis. Answering some questions prematurely may mean that we are cutting off important exploration/expression of feelings. It is important to explore with the person just what it is he asking and why.

We avoided trying to tell them what to do in order to facilitate their exploring the alternatives that existed for them. We offered descriptions of things we or others had tried and found helpful, with an emphasis on our belief that these approaches could be helpful to some persons but are not answers for all. We pointed out and/or demonstrated our own consideration of alternatives. We encouraged each group member to discuss approaches that worked for them.

At times when particularly painful experiences were described in the group, we were apprehensive about the impact of that disclosure on the listeners. The listening parents, however, volunteered statements indicating they appreciated such sharing. In all likelihood this sharing allowed opportunity for vicarious learning. This probably offered parents an opportunity to predict how they would respond if or when similar situations might arise for them and, therefore, a chance to begin accepting or modifying these responses. One author states that, "Reflective thought (including fantasy) is a kind of 'trial action.' It proceeds with low quantities of psychological energy as compared to the energy required in action. It is one of man's most useful adaptive instruments."[21] Furthermore, awareness of the behavior of other parents may help parents to recognize better the "normalcy" and/or uniqueness of their own behavior. Exposure to a wide variety of coping measures found effective by other parents may improve the quantity and quality of their own alternatives. An important additional benefit, which may arise from hearing other parents describe their experiences, is the recognition that these parents survived. They had confronted the experience and survived.

Another of our policies was to provide honest information when parents sought it. Usually nothing which these parents would have to cope with would be as bad as the things imagined from ignorance. Information sets limits to their uncertainty and fear. An important basis for trust is the sharing of information truthfully. Many parents have experienced necessary or unnecessary contradictions in the information given to them, and an important factor in their ability to trust health care professionals is their perception of a willingness on the part of such individuals to be open. Often a frank discussion does much to prevent or relieve months of anxiety. For many parents the information allows them to help significantly in the care of their child and may help them to work through guilt feelings. Friedman's "impression was that this direct approach gave parents confidence in their ability to master subsequent developments."[22]

A final policy we employed in helping the parents was to support them in their decision-making process. When their choices were based on self-awareness, realistic data, and consideration of alternatives we supported their choices. Parents often had excellent ideas but were sometimes reluctant to act on them until an "expert" gave his/her "stamp of approval," whether a "parent expert," or a "health care professional expert."

The two underlying needs reflected in the parent's evaluation of the support group are the need for support through sharing and mutual caring and the need for knowledge and a clearer understanding of the situation of the leukemic child. Lascari and Stehbens in "The Reactions of Families to Childhood Leukemia" underscore the latter point. After interviewing parents of 20 deceased leukemic children they report:

> The appraisal shows a central theme, expressed by virtually all the parents. They appreciated honesty and wanted "the facts" about their child's illness and did not want to be misled with overly optimistic or unrealistic hopes.[23]

Earlier in the report they had stated it even more strongly:

> The universal response was "we want the facts," with unanimous agreement that they be told the whole truth and not be misled.[24]

The parents in the support group initiated by the author originally made a six-month commitment to the program. At the end of that period, however, they clearly wished to continue; the group is still active more than a year-and-a-half after its inception. Parents are eager to publicize the benefits of their experience and are seeking ways to extend similar services to other parents of terminally ill children. Perhaps this is the best indicator of program success.

REFERENCES

1. Heffron W, Bommelaere K, Masters R: Group discussions with the parents of leukemic children. Pediatrics 52:8, 1973
2. Reuben H: Generic features in families under stress. In Parad HJ (ed): Crisis Intervention: Selected Readings. New York, N Y Fam Serv Assoc of Am, 1971
3. Hopkins, LJ: A basis for nursing care of the terminally ill child and his family. Maternal-Child Nurs J 2:93, 1973
4. Share L: Family communication in the crisis of a child's fatal illness, A literature review and analysis. Omega 3:187, 1972
5. *Ibid,* p 187
6. *Ibid,* p 187
7. Moustakas C: Creativity and Conformity. New York, Van Nostrand Reinhold, 1967, pp 108–109
8. Craig Y: The care of our dying child—a parent offers some personal observations based on recollection. In Burton L (ed): Care of the Child Facing Death. London, Routledge and Kegan, 1974, p 87
9. Friedman SB et al: Behavioral observations on parents anticipating the death of a child. Pediatrics 32:618, 1963
10. *Ibid,* pp 618–19
11. Landsdown R: How parents cope with a dying child. Aired on All Things Considered. Radio station KSJM, 25 November 1974
12. Binger CM et al: Childhood leukemia. New Engl J Med 280:416, 1969
13. Moustakas C: *op cit,* p 9
14. *Ibid,* p 10
15. *Ibid,* p 7
16. Gordon C, Gergen K: The Self in Social Interaction. New York, Wiley, 1968

17. Miller W: When going to pieces may hold you together. Lutheran Brotherhood Bond 52:7, 1975
18. Gendlin EY: Existentialism and experiential psychotherapy. In Moustakas C (ed): Existential Child Therapy: The Child's Discovery of Himself. New York, Basic, 1966, p 243
19. Moustakas: Creativity and Conformity, p 11
20. Gendlin: *op cit,* p 222
21. Kliman G: Psychological Emergencies of Childhood. Grune & Stratton, 1968
22. Friedman: *op cit* p 610
23. Lascari AD, Stehbens JA: The reactions of families to childhood leukemia. Pediatrics 12:213, 1973
24. *Ibid,* p 212

The observations of four professionals involved in establishing a parent support group are reported. Parents in this group have already experienced the death of a child.

15

PARENT SUPPORT GROUPS FOR THE GRIEVING PARENT

Carolyn J. Levitt, Michael C. Linder, Sue N. Sauer, Shirley A. Pierce

A parent can suffer no greater loss than the death of a child. When their child has died parents often ask, "How can I go on living? Will there ever be joy in living again?" On the death of a child from cancer or other chronic illness, a family suffers greater emotional trauma and family upheaval than was ever evident throughout the prolonged illness. Many parents suffer acute, incapacitating anxiety and depression with suicidal tendencies. Communication within the family unit breaks down, often leading to separation and divorce. After years of medical treatment and support for their chronically-ill child, the family is left devastated, alone, and without help.

We have observed repeatedly how, after years of caring for her leukemic child, a mother cannot adjust to life without her child, and to the family disruptions which have developed.

Deeply frustrated by this, we recognized the need to develop a program for parent support following a child's death. Discovering that the standard methods for dealing with depression were ineffective, we developed a group therapy program to aid parents in their struggle to return to a more normal lifestyle. Listening for many hours as parents described their hidden feelings, we gained some understanding of the unique emotional problems they suffer and consequently developed a successful treatment program for them.

Doctors, nurses, and social workers are repeatedly exposed to death and grief. They have been taught the "stages of death and dying" and some have learned how best to help the dying patient and the grieving family, both during the illness and at the time of death. However, medical professionals in general are unaware of the scope of grief beyond the hospital walls after the child's death. Help for the grieving family is usually left to the clergy, relatives, and friends. The clergy will admit that they have no ready answers, and that the problem of suffering and pain remains a mystery. This cannot fill the void the parents feel. Relationships with relatives and friends, which seemed perfectly normal before the child's death, afterwards seem distorted. After the funeral, friends seem to avoid the grieving family, and those who still try to help, avoid talking about the dead child for fear of hurting the parents more. Friends and relatives advise them to get busy in order to forget their sorrow. This is generally impossible, for the parents are depressed, lack energy, have no strength to overcome the inertia they feel, and literally cannot cope with everyday life.

The physician caring for the child with a terminal illness becomes central in the parents' lives. For years during the protracted illness he or she provides emotional support for both the child and the family. When the child has died it is natural for the parents to turn to the physician for help. During the repeated hospitalizations often a particular nurse has cared for the child and has been supportive to him and his parents through many necessary but unwanted procedures. She too can help in the family's bereavement. If the physician and the nurse have allowed themselves to become emotionally involved with the child, their help will be greater in that they naturally share the parents' grief.

Our involvement with this program began in 1972 with a series of requests from various parents. Over the years, as our experience has grown, our ideas and approaches have been continually modified. Following the death of her child, one mother sought to convince her child's pediatrician that something must be done to prevent others from going through what she had experienced all alone. Shortly after, another mother whose child had died two months earlier, also sought help from the pediatrician—she could not sleep nights and was talking in a strange, high-pitched voice. Some time later she attempted suicide and was referred for therapy. After a few unsuccessful sessions, the therapist enlisted the help of the first mother mentioned above. It soon became obvious that the best source of help was another parent who had experienced the same loss, the same devastation and pain.

At present our program consists of bimonthly group therapy sessions attended by four to six couples, the physician or nurse closest to the parents during the child's illness, and two social workers. At the time of the child's death, the physician or nurse explains to the parents that the time ahead may be very difficult but that help is available. Anticipating the parents' difficulty, the professionals must be alert to subtle "calls for help." One mother called her doctor to ask whether the death certificate had yet been signed. This was her call for help. If the parents themselves do not seek help, a follow-up phone call is made a few weeks after the funeral to invite the parents to the meetings. When a new couple attend the group, they are asked to tell about their child, and each parent is encouraged to support the other in relating the events leading up to their child's death and the problems thereafter. In most cases the group is composed of relatively "new" parents, who are still early in their grieving process, and "old" parents, who have already been attending for several months and have to some degree learned to deal with their loss. Usually after six to twelve months they begin to drop out of the sessions.

Parents who have lost children have a natural bond with one another. Grieving for any loss is painful, but the loss of a child carries new dimensions. Over and over again parents state that a part of themselves has died along with the child.

Mothers, especially, feel this "death," and even state that, at times, their healthy children and their husbands seem to matter very little to them. Parents report that their hopes for the future of that child and their total investment of love was greater than any other committment in their lives. Because this extension of themselves is so hard to give up, they find it more difficult to adjust to their loss.

Parents within the group develop a sense of mutual trust and are able to share feelings about their unique relationship with their child. They do not tire of hearing each other's stories as do many friends and relatives. They feel comfort in the freedom to open up raw areas. The sense of risk in baring feelings to the group is lessened by the promise of understanding and support. The realization that the others are going through the same things forms a bond between them. This enlightenment and assurance of understanding and acceptance leads to further sharing, including feelings about such things as suicide. They begin to understand that it is alright to hurt and alright to feel as badly as they do. Guilt associated with these feelings can be lessened by understanding that this devastation is shared by others.

Frustration in being unable to help their own child and in the futility of trying to prevent their child's death lingers with them long afterwards. This frustration often leads parents to feel a strong need for fulfillment by helping others because they were unable to help their child. Thus in helping each other in the group sessions, they are also helping themselves.

The actual helping process seems to come through the parents' sharing of ways to handle the daily trials until time can take over and heal. There seems to be both a fear to talk about the child with siblings and relatives and also a fear not to talk about the child, a fear of forgetting the child. One mother, sobbing, told of how relatives tried to prevent her from seeing the movies of her dead child's last birthday party, thinking they could help her in this way. Parents in the group encourage one another to take these risks, to talk freely about their loss with siblings, friends, and relatives, who wish to help but who are unprepared and lacking in the knowledge of ways to help. Parents will tell each other how to struggle through those days spent in agony, crying, and hiding in bed under the blanket of sickness.

During the group sessions, the parents frequently speak of signs of approaching insanity. It is often with great surprise that they realize that nearly all the parents have experienced this. One mother was relieved to know that she was not alone in feeling an overwhelming anxiety while waiting in line at the grocery store or riding the bus. Others also reported the feelings of sudden needs for the security and comfort of their homes. Mothers often relate how they see and hear their dead child in daily activities. As other children go off to school in the fall, they tend for a moment to see their dead child in the group. As a blonde boy of ten rides by on a bicycle, the mother at the window realizes after a moment that it is not her dead son, but only a boy who resembles him. As the group therapy progresses, and parents learn to cope with their loss, they often come to feel guilty about their lessening grief; they feel that somehow they are betraying their dead child in regaining happiness.

Holiday and birthdays need special preparation. Parents describe a feeling of depression, a deep foreboding as these celebrations approach. They are preoccupied with what happened last year at this time, haunted by both the good memories and the bad. One mother tearfully described how it took her several days to gather the strength to unpack the Christmas decorations, knowing that she would find the Christmas stocking which she had so lovingly made for her dead daughter the year before. Sometimes, the only comfort seems to be that someone else has made it through the same thing. Parents feel secure in knowing that they can call on any group member at any time, day or night, when the going gets rough.

Understandably, the new parents have many questions regarding the handling of the surviving children. Recovering parents reveal the subtle ways by which children will later show how they were affected by their parents' silence. The siblings of the families in our group, varying in age from infancy to adulthood, suffer grief, but of a different kind from their parents. An 18-year-old boy reported that one could not expect him to care as much about his dead five-year-old sister as did his mother. To him she was a "kid sister," not a part of his entire life and future. Children take clues from their parents as to how they should react. By causing Mom to cry again when they ask painful questions, they soon learn to withhold them and thus lose the opportunities for what could be therapeutic discussions. Moreover, they are often isolated. When separated from their parents into a group of their own, children from different families also share with and support each other in working through their problems of being the surviving siblings. Frequently they have fears regarding their own health. While the sick child is still living, the mother tends to underplay their other children's illnesses. After death, however, it is common for these mothers to overprotect their remaining children, having lost their ability to judge the severity of their illnesses.

In cases of leukemia or other chronic illnesses which require regular outpatient visits with periods of remission and exacerbations, the care of the child is quite commonly restricted to the mother. In many cases, she alone hears the bad news from the doctor regarding the blood work. She spends endless days in the hospital during exacerbations. Meanwhile, the father continues working and must hear information at second hand. Because of the mother's need to care for the sick child, the father becomes more actively involved with the rest of the children. This seems necessary in order to assure the mother that she did everything she could for the child and to relieve her of possible guilt after the child's death. However, following her child's death, the mother's life is left with a huge void. She no longer needs to plan for the clinic visits or to watch continually for signs of returning illness. This problem can sometimes be minimized by insisting that the father be present for some of the clinic visits or at least present for major decisions relating to the child's condition. After a short time, the mother must gain reentrance into the family constellation. This is not always easy as the family has learned to function with only her partial involvement. This in turn leads to an increasing feeling of emptiness on the part of the mother.

Cultural values teach that men are to give emotional stability to their families. The father is expected to be the stoic, unchanging "pillar of strength." However, the father in an effort to avoid the anxiety-provoking situation may dodge all communication with his wife. If not recognized and dealt with this chasm grows and may soon encompass nearly all areas of family life. In general, men feel that they must grieve alone, that society must not see them behaving in an "unmanly" way. Many fathers have admitted to becoming more involved at work, working longer hours, in an effort to escape facing the unhappiness at home.

Therapy consists of reestablishing communication between the parents, particularly regarding their feelings and memories about their child. One couple described lying in bed at night turned away from each other, unable to sleep, but unwilling to share their problems for fear of hurting each other more. The goal of therapy is to help the couples learn how to comfort one another. It has been found that it is therapeutic for both parents to confess their grief and feel bad together. Generally speaking, however, those who have experienced marital dissatisfaction prior to the death of their child find their problem magnified.

The roles of the professionals within the group vary. Doctors and nurses may find themselves working out their own grief along with the parents. Social workers may find themselves facilitating the group dynamics—clarifying and reflecting words and feelings back to the group. Support is given in many ways and is conveyed by the personalities involved. Parents select those who seem able to help the most. The professionals must be able to share with the parents in their grief and to have a deep feeling for what they are going through; conveying warmth is essential.

Therapists have found this group process different from the usual group therapy situation. They find themselves experiencing the feelings and emotions of the group and the pain of each member. In fact, the therapists find they also have a need to share and support each other. They need to validate their own gut reactions about what is going on among the parents. Occasionally, they recognize that additional individual therapy for one of the parents is required.

Since the onset of the group therapy program, we have dealt with a total of 44 parents, who have lost a total of 27 children. Two families each lost two children. Twenty-two couples, or sets of parents, were living together at the time of their child's death and three mothers lost their children as single or divorced parents. Of the 22 couples, 3 couples divorced following the death of their child and one couple separated temporarily. Many parents in the group readily admitted to having seriously considered suicide. One mother reported fantasizing all the stages of dying and wanting to die with her child. Another mother reported a strong urge to escape her grief by driving her car, carrying her and her dying child, in front of an oncoming truck. Three mothers were hospitalized for treatment following suicide attempts and one later actually did commit suicide. Another mother required psychiatric hospitalization for inability to cope with her everyday life after the death of her child.

We learned that the single parent had to be dealt with separately. The group therapy sessions were not as successful for them as they were for the other parents. Couples in the group were taught to turn to each other for help. They reported that following the therapy sessions, they communicated and shared more than at any other time during the rest of the week. Single parents, however, had no one to continue the therapy process with at home. They returned to their troubled, empty lives and had to be helped in developing new supportive relationships with other people.

The professionals involved in the program have benefited from the insights they gained about the problems of the dying child and his family. We do not know if our group of parents is representative of all parents who lose children. We can only report the feelings of one group of parents, at varying stages in the recognition of their needs. We hope that what we have learned from these parents will help us and other professionals in dealing with the dying child and his family and with their grief after his death.

PART IV

THE HOSPITAL AND THE CLINIC: DIAGNOSIS, TREATMENT, AND NURSING CARE

These two physicians report the latest medical advances and treatment of acute leukemia of children, and give an overview of the diagnosis and drug management as well as covering the results of bone marrow transplantation. A very informative and compact chapter with a detailed bibliography, it will serve as a useful reference for health professionals.

16

ACUTE LEUKEMIA OF CHILDHOOD

Mark Nesbit and John Kersey

INTRODUCTION

Acute leukemia is a primary malignant disease of the bone marrow cells characterized by abnormal proliferation and lack of cellular differentiation. This process is associated with the suppression of normal hematopoiesis, through unknown causes, which leads to infections, pallor, and bleeding. There can be further symptoms and signs caused by infiltration of these leukemic cells into normal extramedullary tissue as manifested by hepatosplenomegaly and lymphadenopathy. It is not surprising, when looking at the varied clinical picture that is associated with the initial presentations of leukemia, that it is difficult to make the diagnosis. There are some signs and symptoms that have special emphasis for the physician dealing with children. The combination of bone pain, fever, and pallor often suggests rheumatic fever and rheumatoid arthritis and are often used alone to diagnose the disease. The fact that in leukemia the same symptoms complex is common makes it imperative that all new patients labeled with the diagnosis of acute rheumatic fever or acute juvenile rheumatoid arthritis should have a bone marrow aspiration as part of their initial work-up. Besides the confusion with the collagen vascular diseases, the similarities of the hematologic finding associated with iron deficiency anemia to leukemia is not stressed enough in children. Many of the physical findings such as hepatosplenomegaly and pallor can be seen in both diseases. Furthermore, the occurrence in the bone marrow of increased numbers of mature and immature lymphocytes in iron deficiency anemia can present a real challenge to the physician.

ESTABLISHING THE DIAGNOSIS

The only way the diagnosis of leukemia can be established is by morphologic examination of the peripheral blood and bone marrow. Examination of stained smears of blood and bone marrow aspiration can usually differentiate at least four main types of leukemia: *lymphoblastic, myeloblastic, monocytic,* and *undifferentiated.* The morphologic similarities of the premature cells and the marked resemblance of the clinical and morbid anatomic appearance makes it simple to refer to all acute leukemias as undifferentiated. With the realization that the morphologic types respond to different treatment regimens, efforts have intensified to differentiate the lymphoblastic from the undifferentiated, myeloblastic, and monocytic types of leukemia. In a study of 1,770 children with acute leukemia from Children's Cancer Study Group,[1] a morphologic delineation along these lines revealed that 78 percent of the children were classified as lymphoblastic and undifferentiated, 8.5 percent myeloblastic, 8.2 percent monocytic, and 5.3 percent not classifiable.

The cytologic classification that we have used at the University of Minnesota originated in 1946 and was proposed by

Sundberg.[2] It differs from those used in many other laboratories in that a subclass of subacute forms of both myeloid and lymphoblastic leukemia are included.

ACUTE AND SUBACUTE LYMPHOBLASTIC LEUKEMIA

In acute lymphoblastic leukemia, the malignant cell can be classified into two major cytologic subtypes: (1) lymphoblasts and (2) the immature lymphocyte. The lymphoblast has a fine nucleus and prominent nucleoli with a very slight rim of light blue cytoplasm, which is sometimes vaculated. The immature lymphocyte is different from the lymphoblast in that it is smaller, has a coarser nuclear chromatin pattern, and the nucleoli are less apparent. The designation of acute lymphoblastic leukemia is made when more than 60 percent of the nucleated cells in the bone marrow are lymphoblasts. The designation of subacute lymphoblastic leukemia is made when the malignant cell population is composed primarily of immature lymphocytes. In children, the majority of lymphoblastic leukemias are diagnosed as subacute lymphoblastic leukemia, while in adults it is more common to see acute lymphoblastic leukemia. The cytochemical stains are usually not helpful in the lymphoblastic varieties since the leukocyte alkaline phosphatase, Sudan black B, and myeloperoxidase stains are normal. The PAS (periodic acid-Schiff) stain in the lymphoblast can show some coarse granules or blocks of positivity but this is very variable.[3]

ACUTE AND SUBACUTE NONLYMPHOBLASTIC

For the nonlymphoblastic types of leukemia, there are five major subtypes: *myelocytic, myelomonocytic, promyelocytic, erythroleukemia,* and *monocytic.*

Myelocytic. The designation of acute myelocytic leukemia is used when the percent of myeloblastic cells in the bone marrow exceeds 60 percent of the nucleated cell population. Subacute myelocytic is used when there are less than 60 percent blasts in the bone marrow and there is more evidence of myeloid differentiation in the blast cells. The blast cells are usually quite uniform in nature. Azurophilic granulocytes plus Auer rods are often present in the cytoplasm. Besides the above morphologic criteria, the cytochemical staining characteristics are extremely helpful. Usually one or more of the myeloperoxidase, Sudan black B, and naphthol ASD chloroacetate esterase stains will be positive and identify the myeloid differentiation of the blast cells.

Myelomonocytic. This subtype is designated when there is a definite population of myeloblasts in the bone marrow that are differentiating morphologically into both monocytic and granulocytic lines.

Promyelocytic. This designation is used when the overwhelming percentage of leukemic cells are abnormal promyelocytes. Most of these cases have a large number of Auer rods in each cell.

Erythroleukemia. This form of myeloid leukemia is designated when there is predominance of red cell involvement in the leukemic process. These erythroid precursors show a wide variety of abnormalities such as multinucleation and megaloblastic changes. PAS staining reveals blocks of PAS positively in the cytoplasmic vacuoles.

Monocytic. This group of myeloid leukemias is characterized by a predominance of blast cells that appear morphologically as differentiating monocytes. There is a newly reported variety of acute monocytic leukemia that is referred to as acute monoblastic leukemia.[4] The blasts show no clear evidence of differentiation, but cytochemically the blasts exhibit strongly positive, nonspecific esterase activity which is inhibited by incubation with sodium fluoride. Both the myeloperoxidase and Sudan black B stains, which are usually positive in the myeloid subtypes, are negative in this type.

FUNCTIONAL STUDIES

Since morphologic classification has its limitations, there recently has been an attempt to classify the leukemias by functional characteristics. This has been especially true in the case of the lymphoid malignancies.

Two well-established subpopulations of normal human lymphocytes have been shown to be characterized by different cell surface markers. This is based on functional differences that take place at the membrane surface. Thymus-derived lymphocytes (T-cells) bind sheep erythrocytes (E) and also react with heterologous antisera produced against human thymus lymphocyte antigen (HTLA).[5] T-lymphocytes are largely responsible for cell-mediated immune defense against fungal, viral, and bacterial pathogens. They also appear to participate with thymus-independent lymphocytes (B-cells) as "helper" cells in antibody response.[6] With these methods, we find that 50 to 78 percent of normal peripheral blood lymphocytes bind sheep erythrocytes (E) and HTLA.[7]

Thymus-independent lymphocytes (B-lymphocytes) are derived from bone marrow and other sites and are predominately involved in humoral immune responses. B-cells bind fluorescein-conjugated antisera directed against surface immunoglobulin (SIg). The vast majority of normal peripheral lymphocytes carry one heavy-chain class μ, γ, or α and one light-chain class κ or λ. In addition, B-lymphocytes carry receptors for complement components, especially C3b and C3d.[8] Complement receptors are generally detected in a rosette assay in which a marker red cell (eg, chicken, pigeon, or human) is incubated with antibody and complement. About 7 to 25 percent of peripheral lymphocytes appear to be B-lymphocytes depending on the method employed in the individual laboratory.[7]

The procedures described above can be used to demonstrate the surface characteristics of human malignant lymphocyte populations especially leukemic ones. This method of immunodiagnosis already has provided a better understanding of pathogenesis and also can be used in the more effective treatment for the different subgroups. Previous experience has shown that the morphologic and cytochemical differentiation of the lymphocytic leukemias from the myeloid leukemias has important therapeutic and prognostic implications. Unfortunately, there are little helpful morphologic or cytochemical differences in the lymphocytic malignancies.

In children using surface markers on blast cells, it is possible to differentiate at least three distinct groups of patients with lymphoproliferative malignancies. The first group is E-negative lymphoma and leukemia, which makes up the largest number of patients. Characteristically, these patients have bone marrow and peripheral blood involvement. Though these patients have no E receptors, about 40 to 50 percent are positive for the HTLA antigen and therefore share characteristics of normal T-cells.[9] The second group of patients has receptors for sheep erythrocytes (E-positive lymphoma and leukemia); they may also have complement receptors on their blast cells. Clinically, this group has a high incidence of mediastinal or nodal masses and their bone marrow and peripheral blood are often not initially involved.[10] The third group, B-cell lymphoma and leukemia, morphologically has the appearance of non-African Burkitt's lymphoma; these patients have monoclonal immunoglobulins with either $\mu\lambda$ or $\mu\kappa$ on their cell surfaces but are negative for E-rosettes or complement receptors.[11]

In contrast to the high incidence of T-cell malignancies seen in children, the majority of adult lymphoreticular malignancies involve cells with markers for B-lymphocytes. Solid tissue malignant lymphoma in adults as well as a majority of the cases of CLL represent B-cell proliferation.[12] In a study done at the University of Minnesota, a B-cell origin was found in 17 adults classified as nodular (N) or diffuse (D) poorly differentiated lymphocytic lymphoma (PDLL).[13] We recently reported an adult with acute lymphocytic leukemia of B-cell type.[14]

TREATMENT

Treatment of a child with the recent diagnosis of acute leukemia presents a complex problem. Successful care of such a child requires that the physician have a basic understanding of the disease and its complications, be skilled in the principles of chemotherapy, and be cognizant of the emotional impact of the disease on the child and family. Although the ultimate goal in therapy is cure, successful management cannot be measured by control of the disease alone, but must consider the total care of the patient, the quality of life provided, and the emotional needs of the patient and his family. Present treatment has established a median survival of greater than five years for children with lymphoblastic leukemia.[15] An estimated 30 to 40 percent five-year, disease-free survival appears to have been achieved from analysis of studies now ongoing.[16] Childhood leukemia of the lymphoblastic variety can no longer be considered a hopeless disease, and everyone must reconsider their pessimistic view of the treatment of this disease. If a physician has not had experience with present methods of treatment for this disease, the initial treatment should begin at a large treatment center. Such centers provide experienced laboratory and supportive care facilities which are absolutely essential as a part of the present treatment schedules for acute leukemia. This does not exclude the personal physician; quite the contrary, for increasing effective survival allows most of a patient's ongoing treatment to be undertaken by the patient's private physician close to home. In order to provide some mutual understanding of the present modalities of therapy for acute leukemia, the following treatment guidelines are presented.

CHEMOTHERAPY

Chemotherapy has played the most important role in the improved survival of children with acute leukemia. In order to familiarize the reader with drugs used most commonly in the treatment of acute leukemia, a brief discussion of each drug is given below to include mixing instructions, methods of administration, reported mechanism of action, and type of acute and chronic toxicities that one might expect.

Adriamycin. The drug is stored in 10 and 50 mg vials at room temperature and given intravenously. When mixing, dissolve the red powder in 5 ml of normal saline without preservative. The drug should be discarded after mixing. If the total dose of Adriamycin is over 30 mg, then mix with 50 cc of normal saline and drip intravenously, over one-half hour. If the total dose is less than 30 mg, mix with 10 ml instead of 5 ml of saline without preservative, and give by slow intravenous push.

Adriamycin (14-hydroxydaunomycin) is in the anthracycline class of antibiotics and was isolated in 1967 from *Streptomyces peucetuis coesuis.* It exerts its antileukemic effect by intercalcating with DNA and prevents transcription of RNA and replication of DNA.[17] The drug's principal acute toxicity is nausea and vomiting that occurs after administration, and stomatitis and myelosuppression that occurs 10 to 14 days after administration. Alopecia is frequently seen and can include both eyebrows and eyelashes. The most serious toxicity is a cardiomyopathy. It generally does not occur, however, until a total dose of 500 mgM^2 is exceeded. If the patient receives concomitant radiation therapy to the chest, possible enhancement of the Adriamycin cardiomyopathy can occur.

L-Asparaginase. This drug is stored in a 10,000 IU vial in the refrigerator and can be given either intravenously or intramuscularly. When mixing to administer intramuscularly, use 1.1 ml of saline without preservative. Dilute slowly to avoid denaturation and use only clear solution. Use zephiran only to clean the skin prior to I.M. administration. With I.V. administration, mix with saline without preservative. Though unstable, unless it is frozen, the mixture should be discarded after mixing.

L-Asparaginase catalyzes the hydrolysis of L-asparagine, a nonessential amino acid, to L-aspartic acid, thereby depleting L-asparagine in the body fluids.[18] Some leukemic cells cannot synthesize L-asparagine in adequate amounts, which often affects protein, DNA, and RNA synthesis. The spectrum of toxicities is related to asparagine-induced deficiency of normal tissues. The most common are disturbances of liver function, as manifested by hypoalbuminemia and decreased clotting factors, and of the pancreas, as manifested by hypoinsulinism.

Hypersensitivity reactions are the most serious side effects.

They vary from skin rashes and abdominal pains to anaphylaxis and death. Most of these occur after rapid intravenous administration and can be greatly decreased if the L-asparaginase is given by the intramuscular method.[19]

5-Azacytidine. Store in the refrigerator in 100 mg vials and give intravenously. The white lyophilized powder is to be reconstituted with 10 ml of sterile water which may be added to 30 ml of D5W for I.V. fast drip (15 to 20 minutes). The solution should be used within 15 minutes after mixing since the drug is rapidly decomposed in solution.

5-Azacytidine is a pyrimidine analogue of cytidine. Its pharmacologic mode of action is thought to be related to its incorporation into DNA and RNA polynucleotides in place of cytidine.[20] The major toxicity seen is bone marrow suppression. Recovery usually occurs by day 14 following a five-day course of therapy. Nausea, vomiting, and diarrhea are also a frequent occurrence. The other major toxicity occurs in the liver. It is recommended that 5-azacytidine be used with caution in patients with impaired liver function.

Cyclophosphamide. Both the 25- and 50-mg tablets and the 100, 200, and 500 mg vials should be stored at room temperature. The drug is given intravenously, intramuscularly, and orally. When mixing the 100 mg vials, use 5 cc of water without preservative. For the larger vials, use 10 to 20 cc of water without preservative. It is sometimes difficult to get the powder into solution and it helps to warm the diluted powder to facilitate its disbursement. Though it is stable for 24 hours after mixing, it is usually best to discard the unused portions.

Cyclophosphamide is an alkylating agent and causes cell death by alkylating DNA. Several events may occur such as strand separation and inhibition of DNA repair, breakage of DNA chain ring cleavage, and finally cross-linking between DNA and its associated proteins.[21] Toxicity with the intravenous administration can cause immediate nausea and vomiting that may require antiemetics. The major toxicities are myelosuppression, gastrointestinal, and urinary. The latter is the most serious. It causes a hemorrhagic cystitis that can lead to chronic bladder fibrosis and even ureteral reflux. In order to prevent this toxicity, fluid intake should be liberal after administration of cytoxan. At least a minimum of 3,000 cc/M^2 of fluids should be given the day of cytoxan administration. To avoid prolonged bladder contact it is further advised to give the drug in the morning so that high concentrations of drug are not excreted during the night. If hematuria does occur, cyclophosphamide should be immediately discontinued and not reinstituted until the urine clears of red blood cells.

Cyclophosphamide has also been reported to produce pulmonary disease.[22] Common to most of these cases is an interstitial pneumonitis with the production of atypical pulmonary and bronchial epithelial cells and varying degrees of interstitial fibrosis. The real possibility exists of significant chronic pulmonary changes and insufficiency.

Cytosine arabinoside. Store the 100 and 500 mg vials in the refrigerator. The drug can be administered intravenously, intramuscularly, intrathecally, and subcutaneously. When mixing to give intramuscularly or subcutaneously, use 2 ml of diluting solution provided. If to be given intravenously, mix with 10 ml of the diluting solution. When the drug is to be given intrathecally, it should be buffered because of its low pH, preferably with Elliot's B solution. The solution is stable for two weeks if kept in the refrigerator.

Cytosine arabinoside is an analogue of deoxycytidine. It inhibits RNA, protein, and especially DNA synthesis by inhibition of DNA polymerase.[23] The major toxicity is hematologic. When large doses are given intravenously, nausea and vomiting can be observed. With intrathecal administration, meningeal irritation as manifested by pleocytosis and meningismus is common.

Daunomycin. This drug is stored in 20 mg vials at room temperature. The drug is given intravenously. As with Adriamycin, when mixing, dissolve with 5 ml of normal saline without preservative. If the total dose to be given at one time is over 30 mg, then mix with 50 ml of normal saline and drip intravenously, over one-half hour. If under 30 mg, mix with 10 ml, and give by slow intravenous push. The drug will cause tissue reaction if there is tissue extravasation of the drug.

Daunomycin is an anthracycline antibiotic like Adriamycin. Its antileukemic effect is thought to be due to intercalcation between base pairs of DNA and inhibition of DNA dependent RNA synthesis.[24] The predominant toxicities are bone marrow depression, stomatitis, nausea and vomiting, and alopecia. Cardiac toxicity consists of a syndrome including tachycardia, arrhythmia, and congestive heart failure. The incidence of cardiac toxicity increases when a total dose of 600 to 750 mg/M^2 are given.

6-Mercaptopurine (6-MP). Store the 50 mg tablets at room temperature. The drug is most commonly given orally, but there is an intravenous preparation which is used mostly as an investigational drug. The tablets are stable for long periods of time.

6-Mercaptopurine is a purine analogue that was synthesized as a hypoxanthine analogue. It is converted in vivo to the active form (6-MP ribonucleotide) which interferes in the metabolic pathway of inosenic acid to xanthylic acid. By further competition, it further interferes with conversion of inosenic acid that eventually inhibits DNA synthesis.[25] The dose-limiting toxicity of 6-mercaptopurine is marrow suppression. When allopurinol, a xanthine oxidase inhibitor, is given along with the 6-MP, the 6-MP's activity is enhanced because it is not as rapidly detoxified. If the two drugs are administered together, the dosage of 6-MP should be 25 percent of the normally calculated dose. Occasionally, dermatitis, obstructive jaundice, and mouth ulcerations are noted. There are two other toxicities associated with the chronic administration of 6-MP that is not as often mentioned in drug brochures: the first is recurrent abdominal pain and nausea, and the second is a dramatic increase in the incidence of warts. Though both are not life threatening, they can become difficult clinical problems to handle.

Methotrexate. This drug occurs in 2.5 mg tablets and 5 mg and 50 mg vials, which should be stored at room temperature. The drug can be administered intravenously, intramuscularly, intrathecally, and orally. For intrathecal administration, the parenteral methotrexate should be diluted using Elliot's B solution without preservative to a concentration of

1 mg of methotrexate to 1 cc of dilutant. It is important to try to avoid using preservative containing vehicles for intrathecal use. For intravenous use, dilute the parenteral preparation in 20 to 100 ml of D5W or normal saline, depending on the total amount to be given. The mixed drug should be discarded after 24 hours.

Methotrexate is a folate antagonist which inhibits DNA synthesis and cellular replication as a consequence of its combination with the enzyme dihydrofolate reduction and interference with the formation of tetrahydrofolate.[26] Inhibition of DNA synthesis is dependent on levels of intracellular free methotrexate above a specific threshold for each tissue. Methotrexate, when given in relatively large doses over a short period of time, can be associated with a number of acute toxic reactions. These consist mostly of cellular necrosis and death of vaginal, pleural, pulmonary, and bladder epithelium, as well as skin and conjunctival and gastrointestinal surfaces. As with cyclophosphamide, pulmonary episodes are the most serious acute toxicity. Both acute and chronic pneumonitis has been reported in patients associated with methotrexate administration.[27] When methotrexate is administered intrathecally, it can be associated with evidence of inflammation of the leptomeninges. The signs and symptoms most associated with this toxicity are headache, fever, meningismus, and spinal fluid pleocytosis. Seizures, paresis, and death have occasionally been reported.

The type of methotrexate toxicity in normal tissue with chronic administration appears to effect mostly the liver and bone. The liver damage is of enough serious consequence that all patients who receive methotrexate for extended periods of time should be carefully evaluated with liver function tests. Those patients with consistent liver function abnormalities should have liver biopsies to determine the extent of damage.

Prednisone. Prednisone is packaged in 5, 10, and 20 mg tablets and stored at room temperature. The drug is given orally. Though this steroid compound cannot be given parenterally or intrathecally, there are other steroid compounds which are available to be given intrathecally as well as parenterally.

Prednisone has a profound lympholytic effect, but the mode of action is unknown. It is known that steroids can inhibit both RNA and protein synthesis and therefore result in cell death.[28] The toxic effects are quite serious though they do not have the myelosuppressive toxicity with which most of the other chemotherapeutic agents are associated. A list of the adverse reactions are:

1. metabolic
   a. sodium retention and potassium loss
   b. hyperglycemia
2. myopathy
3. osteoperosis
4. cataracts
5. immunosuppression
6. depression of granulocyte and macrophage function
7. peptic ulceration

In children, the propensity to peptic ulceration is not as great as it is in adults and we do not try to reduce stomach acidity.

6-Thioguanine. Store the 40-mg vials in the refrigerator. The drug is given orally and is stable for a long time.

Though similar to 6-MP, the drug inhibits DNA synthesis by being incorporated into DNA rather than inhibit purine biosynthesis.[29] Since detoxification and excretion does not involve xanthine oxidase, allopurinol can be used to prevent hyperuricemia without altering the dose. The major toxicity is myelosuppression though there are often some gastrointestinal symptoms.

Vincristine sulfate. Store in 1- and 5-mg vials in the refrigerator. The drug is given intravenously. The drug comes with its own diluting fluid and should be mixed with 10 cc per vial. It is stable for two weeks in the refrigerator after reconstitution. The drug will cause extensive ulceration secondary to local tissue extravasation.

Vincristine sulfate (Oncovin) is a plant alkaloid that comes from the *Vinca rosea,* a periwinkle plant. It produces metaphase arrest in most cell systems, but its major mode of action as an antitumor agent is really unknown.[30] Its dose-limiting toxicity is neurologic; peripheral neuropathies, nerve palsies, and obstipation. After the first one or two injections, jaw pain often occurs. It usually is not seen after subsequent injections. Another toxicity rarely mentioned is that of vincristine-induced inappropriate antidiuretic secretion (IADH).[31] The symptomatic hyponatremia can be prevented by fluid restriction and does not mean that the drug must be discontinued.

INDUCTION

The initial goal of treatment is to induce complete disappearance of all clinical and pathologic evidence of the leukemia. When the bone marrow and peripheral blood has returned to normal, and physical examination reveals no evidence of leukemia, the child is considered to be in complete remission (Table 1). In children with the lymphoblastic variety of acute leukemia, the induction rate has been quite successful. With the use of the combination of Prednisone and vincristine, a remission rate of 83 to 87 percent has been achieved.[32—35] Recently, a study of 823 children reported that

TABLE 1.
Criteria for Complete Remission in Acute Leukemia in Childhood

---

I. Pheripheral blood
   A. Hemoglobin (g/100 ml)
      1. Less than two-years old: >10
      2. More than two-years old: >11
   B. Neutrophils granulocytes (per mm^3): >1500
   C. Blast cells (%): 0
   D. Platelets (per mm^3): 100,000
II. Physical findings: No evidence of organ involvement
III. Bone marrow*
   A. Lymphocytic
      1. Blasts: 0 to 5%
      2. Lymphocytes and blast cells: 0 to 40%
   B. Nonlymphocytic: Blasts: 0 to 5%

---

*The bone marrow must also contain qualitative and quantitative normal erythropoiesis, granulopoiesis, and megakaryopoiesis.

using the combination of Prednisone, vincristine, and L-asparaginase produced a remission rate of 93 percent.[36] This combination of drugs has little or no serious myelosuppressive toxicity and avoids some of the marrow toxicity seen with earlier drug combination.

For the nonlymphoblastic subtypes the success has not been as good. Using the same drugs, the response rate has been lower than 40 percent.[37] With the introduction of some newer drugs, the induction rate has risen to 40 to 60 percent. Using a combination of cytosine arabinoside, cyclophosphamide, and vincristine, a 57 percent complete and good partial remission rate was seen in 71 children with nonlymphocytic leukemia.[38]

BONE MARROW TRANSPLANTATION

As an alternative to chemotherapy as the sole means of inducing a remission, other forms of multimodal therapy have been considered for this type of leukemia, such as the combination of chemotherapy and immunotherapy and the combination of chemotherapy and bone marrow transplantation. This latter form of therapy is still in the early stages of development but does offer considerable promise. Because of its possible future use, a discussion of its present role as a treatment modality for various forms of hematologic disorder seems appropriate to discuss here.

UNDERPRODUCTION OF MARROW: APLASTIC ANEMIA

Marrow underproduction results from decreased production of red cells, platelets, and neutrophils, a condition known as aplastic anemia. It results from any number of insults including certain chemicals such as benzene derivatives, certain drugs like chloramphenicol, and viruses. However, despite a long list of marrow toxic agents, the majority of causes of marrow underproduction remains unknown. Mortality is very high, approaching 60 percent by four months.[39] Death generally results from bleeding or infection despite support with blood products and antibiotics.

Attempts have been made to induce marrow formation in patients with aplastic anemia using a number of pharmacologic compounds, the most widely used are the androgens and the corticosteroids.[40] Currently, the use of these agents continues in many centers despite the fact that there is little if any data supporting their beneficial effect.

Transplantation of bone marrow has been suggested for a number of years as a treatment for aplastic anemia. Early attempts at marrow transplantation were frustrated by early deaths from infection or bleeding before evidence of engraftment was attained. Recently, results of marrow transplantation in aplastic anemia are much improved with some cases showing long-term marrow engraftment and complete reconstitution of marrow function. Most dramatic are cases of identical twins. In these cases, marrow is given without immunosuppression and in five of eight cases full recovery has followed with only minor hematologic depression up to 12 years postgrafting.[41]

The largest reported series of successful grafts in nonidentical twin combinations is from Seattle. This group of investigators has concentrated on sibling pairs matched at the major histocompatibility (HLA) complex. By the end of February 1974, a total of 37 patients had received marrow grafts. Pregrafting conditioning in most cases has been with cyclophosphamide, and in some instances also in combination with procarbazine and antithymocytic globulin. Fifty percent of the patients were alive four months after transplantation and only one death has occurred after this four-month period. Several patients are alive and in remission for more that three years.[42] A significant difference was observed between children and adults, the former having been successfully grafted more often than the latter.

At the University of Minnesota, several patients with aplastic anemia have received marrow transplants. Five patients have been transplanted; all are alive. The first patient rejected an initial transplant and was retransplanted 17 months ago. He has a successful and well-functioning graft but suffers from a chronic skin problem due to the reaction of the graft against his own cells. This reaction, known as the graft versus host reaction, is a frequent and sometimes fatal reaction associated with marrow transplantation. Our second Minnesota patient is now 10 months postgrafting and is in complete remission. The third patient has a successful graft which was rejected after six months and is currently in the process of being retransplanted. The fourth patient has had a successful graft but developed graft versus host reaction two months postgrafting. The fifth patient, an adult, has a successful graft two months postgrafting.

Recently, an International Aplastic Anemia Study Group was formed to study among other questions, the question of whether marrow transplantation is the treatment of choice for aplastic anemia. Preliminary results from the members of the group indicate that mortality in the transplanted group is about 30 percent, while that in the nontransplanted group is more than double that figure (68 percent). Fifty-four patients have been entered into the study, including patients from the University of Minnesota.[43]

OVERPRODUCTION OF MARROW: ACUTE LEUKEMIA

Acute leukemia remains as the most common malignancy of childhood. This group of disorders, which appears to have origin in the marrow, is generally of lymphoid or myeloid (granulocytic) origin. As discussed elsewhere in this chapter, major progress has been made in producing prolonged remissions in acute lymphatic leukemia of childhood. Acute myelogenous and refractory cases of lymphatic leukemia remain as major challenges, however. One approach to the treatment of acute leukemia refractory to conventional chemotherapy is the use of extremely high doses of chemotherapy combined with total body irradiation and "rescue" using marrow transplantation.

This combination of intensive chemotherapy irradiation and marrow transplantation as an approach has been used on a limited scale in a number of centers. The series are generally too small to provide meaningful data. The largest series of patients have been treated in Seattle.[44] Their results, summarized in a recent review, report a one-year survival rate of 26 percent (6/23). Patients in this series have generally been prepared with a combination of high dose cyclophosphamide (120 mg/kilo) and total body irradiation (1000 rads). In most instances, patients received allogeneic marrow grafts from matched siblings. The Seattle group has further transplanted a total of 20 patients with acute leukemia who had identical twins as donors. In the identical twin series, results are approximately equal to those in the matched sibling group. These results, while preliminary, are important as they suggest that no major immunotherapeutic or graft versus leukemia effect is observed when alogeneic marrow is transplanted.

In the past year, we at Minnesota have had some experience in marrow transplantation for refractory acute leukemia. Three patients have been treated. The first patient with acute lymphoblastic leukemia went into remission following cyclophosphamide and total body irradiation but died of graft versus host disease and toxoplasmosis. The second patient, with acute myelomonocytic leukemia (AMML), was treated with cyclophosphamide, total body irradiation, cytosine arabinoside, and BCNU, followed by a marrow transplantation from an HLA matched sibling. He is currently at home and in remission eight months following his transplant. The third patient with acute lymphoblastic leukemia developed intracranial bleeding and sepsis and died two weeks following the transplant.

UNSOLVED PROBLEMS IN MARROW TRANSPLANTATION

Despite some success in marrow transplantation, a number of major problems must be solved before it can be used as a practical treatment modality. First, the incidence of graft versus host (GVH) reactions remains at about 60 to 70 percent. GVH disease is currently fatal about 20 percent of the time. The nonfatal GVH reactions may be quite chronic and extremely debilitating. Such cases are a major psychological problem for both patient and family, requiring extensive nursing care, and physical and occupational therapy.

Second, the complexity of the marrow transplantation procedure, including a prolonged period of immunosuppression with high risk of infection, requires that patients remain hospitalized for two- to three-month periods. During this period, patients remain in protective isolation and generally receive oral, nonabsorbable, and topical antibiotics in an attempt to reduce the incidence of bacterial and fungal infections.

Of equal importance is graft rejection. In patients with aplastic anemia, the incidence of graft rejection still remains at about 20 percent. While we and others have had some success in retransplantation for patients rejecting an initial graft, the majority of patients who have rejected a graft have died of infection before they could be regrafted.

Lastly, for patients with leukemia who are transplanted, there remains the risk of exacerbation of the original disease. In the Seattle series, 15 of 70 patients (21 percent) have had recurrence of their leukemia process. This includes 4 patients with acute myeloblastic leukemia (AML) and 11 with acute lymphoblastic leukemia (ALL) who recurred as early as seven weeks and as late as 800 days after transplantation. The early recurrences tended to be marrow relapses and the later relapses tended to occur in the central nervous system. In two of the patients prepared for transplantation with total body irradiation alone, the leukemic relapse occurred in the donor cells. In recent years with the addition of chemotherapy to total body irradiation, all the relapses have been in recipient cells.[45]

MAINTENANCE THERAPY

The objective of this phase of treatment is to maintain the status of complete remission, hopefully without serious toxicity. Previous studies have well documented that the use of maintenance chemotherapy significantly prolongs a successfully induced initial remission. The chemotherapeutic drugs which have been shown to be the most successful in this period of treatment for the lymphoblastic leukemias have been methotrexate, 6-mercaptopurine, and cyclophosphamide. Using these agents, the median duration of remission has exceeded 52 months.[46] For nonlymphoblastic leukemia, maintenance results have not been as encouraging as reported with lymphoblastic leukemia. The chemotherapeutic agents which have resulted in the best results in the nonlymphoblastic leukemias are cyclophosphamide, cytosine arabinoside, 6-thioguanine, and adriamycin. In a study where cytosine arabinoside was used with or without cyclophosphamide, the median duration of remission was 195 days.[38] Recently Haghbin[37] reported a median survival of 19 months for children using cytosine arabinoside, 6-thioguanine, and adriamycin. For the reader who wants a more detailed discussion of treatment protocols, they should refer to the latest articles which outline the most recent treatment regimens. The progress in this field is so rapid that any detailed protocol here would be outdated by the time this is in print.

EXTRAMEDULLARY RELAPSE

One of the major obstacles to the cure of acute leukemia in childhood has been extramedullary relapse. The most common form seen is that involving the central nervous system (CNS). Evans analyzed 209 children with acute leukemia who were treated with the same chemotherapeutic agents from 1963 to 1964 by Childrens Cancer Study Group and reported an overall CNS leukemia incidence of 51 percent.[47] The incidence was 56 percent in patients with acute lymphoblastic leukemia. The increasing incidence of CNS leukemia was thought to be due to a prolongation of survival time and increasing awareness of the disease. In many instances, 25 of 46 episodes (56 percent), the CNS leukemia occurred during bone marrow remission. This means that a high percentage of patients treated only with chemotherapy for the induction of remission and maintenance would develop CNS leukemia during bone marrow remission.

Actually, many authors have noted persistent leukemic cells in extramedullary tissues even after the "complete" eradication of leukemic cells from bone marrow and peripheral blood. Nies, in 1964, reviewed autopsy results on 15 patients with acute leukemia who had no evidence of leukemia infiltration of the bone marrow at the time of death.[48] Of these, 10 patients had evidence of leukemia elsewhere, including the kidney, liver, testes, lung, intestine, and brain. In 1966, Mathé did an extensive histologic and cytologic survey of 31 patients with acute leukemia in "complete remission" and found nests of leukemic cells in 12 patients.[49] In 1967, Sharp and Nesbit studied 10 children with leukemia in initial bone marrow remission for remaining leukemic cells in the liver, kidney, or central nervous system. Two patients had hepatic infiltrates, and two others had kidney infiltrates.[50]

The presence of "hidden cells" in extramedullary tissues is considered to be attributed to various extracellular factors such as anatomic site, vascular distribution, or in the case of the nervous system, a blood–brain barrier that prevents effective drugs from entering the central nervous system. As early as 1965, presymptomative treatment of the central nervous system was investigated at the University of Minnesota. Twenty-five patients who achieved an initial remission with chemotherapy were treated with 1200 rads of cranial-spinal irradiation.[51] The incidence of development of craniospinal leukemia, prior to bone marrow recurrence in these two groups treated with 1200 rads presymptomatically, was four percent (1 out of 25 patients evaluated). This result is equivalent to the results reported by the other groups treated with 2400 rads. But there is increasing evidence that CNS leukemia may be prevented equally well with intrathecal Methotrexate alone or in combination with cranial irradiation.[52] It is fair to say, however, that some form of central nervous system prophylaxis will be necessary for all children treated with acute lymphoblastic leukemia. Though there is less experience in nonlymphoblastic leukemia, I am sure it will also be an integral part of their treatment in the future.

Recently, two other areas of extramedullary involvement

have become more of a clinical management problem. Renal involvement in leukemia has variable manifestations. Enlargement of the kidneys due to leukemic infiltration is said to occur in 30 to 50 percent of patients with leukemia of any variety. Massive enlargement (2 to 10 times normal size) is less frequent and occurs only in 10 percent. In one child seen at the University of Minnesota, the kidneys were more than 10 times normal size, but the child had normal urinalysis and BUN. Since the leukemic infiltrate is primarily interstitial, the glomeruli and tubules, though compressed, can still function. These children usually have a normal urinalysis and BUN, though rare instances of azotemia have been described. Of more serious consequences is the so-called "uric acid nephropathy," that is, urate deposits in the lumen of the collecting tubules, particularly at the tips of the renal pyramids, causing obstruction resulting in increased BUN. Uric acid, being an end product of purine metabolism, may rise rapidly in leukemic patients with a high white count who are receiving cytotoxic drugs. Over 50 percent of the urinary uric acid is an un-ionized state and is less soluble in acid urine. The collecting tubules where urine has its maximum acidity are the sites of uric acid precipitation. These precipitates appear grossly as linear yellow-orange/opaque streaks in the pyramids and amorphous pink staining material histologically. Function is limited by the high intraluminal pressure. This condition is reversible with the advent of allopurinol therapy. The last drug is a xanthine oxidase inhibitor which inhibits uric acid production. Besides the resulting renal failure associated with hyperuricemia, gouty arthritis has also been described but is much less common than the renal complications, both of which frequently occur following initiation of treatment.

We have recently evaluated our results at the University of Minnesota in the treatment of symptomatic extramedullary involvement of the kidneys in acute childhood leukemia.[53] Of 489 children seen between 1964 and 1974 with acute leukemia, 21 were treated in the renal area for the following symptoms: hypertension—2, renal oliguria—5, mass-related symptoms—5 and as an adjuvant to allopurinol to prevent renal failure—9. All but two of the patients were in bone marrow exacerbation.

Twelve had acute lymphoblastic leukemia, two had acute myelogenous leukemia, and seven had the leukemic phase of non-Hodgkin's lymphoma. Using 1200 rads irradiation to renal fossa, we were able to improve the clinical situation in 8 of 12 children who had symptomatic involvement. Nine patients were treated with radiation to the kidneys prior to the institution of chemotherapy because they were thought to have a high risk of developing renal failure. All had enlarged kidneys, and elevation of BUNs, Creatinines, and uric acids. These patients were treated with doses of 300 to 1100 rads (median of 600 rads) plus supportive therapy. No patients developed renal failure and seven of the nine had no further renal problem. From previous experience, this group of patients would be at high risk for developing symptomatic renal disease.

Our experience with gonadal involvement has been similar to that seen in the other extramedullary areas. Of 163 male patients with acute leukemia seen between January 1963 and December 1972 at the University of Minnesota, 13, or 8 percent, developed clinical evidence of testicular involvement. One hundred and forty of the total group of patients had acute lymphoblastic or undifferentiated leukemia, 18 nonlymphoblastic leukemia, and 5 had had leukemic transformation of non-Hodgkin's lymphoma. The diagnoses were made clinically in 11 cases and in 2 cases by biopsy. Of the thirteen patients with testicular involvement, the testicular relapse preceded any other evidence of disease in eight patients. However, relapse became evident in other areas in all patients shortly thereafter (a median of five weeks).

All but one of the patients were treated with irradiation alone, one patient received surgery followed by irradiation. In all but two cases, both testicles were irradiated. The total dose delivered varied from 300 to 2800 rads at d_{max} and ranged from 100 to 400 rads per treatment with a median of 250 rads. Our findings of complete remission in six of six episodes treated with doses from 1000 to 2800 rads suggests that the minimum effective dose of irradiation may be just above 1000 rads. We are now recommending 1200 rads d_{max} (given dose) in six treatments over 6 to 8 days. Both testes should be included in the treatment field.

DURATION OF MAINTENANCE THERAPY

The question of duration of maintenance therapy has lately become very relevant, especially in lymphoblastic leukemia. The importance of this question is portrayed by an increasing incidence of fatalities reported during prolonged remission. In a study at St. Jude's Childrens Hospital, their frequency of fatalities in remission was 16 percent.[54] This frequency is not surprising considering the addition of more aggressive radiotherapy to combination chemotherapy. Immunosuppressive cytotoxic therapy is the most important predisposing factor. Our present day maintenance therapy must be considered as a possible threat as well as potential advantage in maintaining remission. In 1967, Childrens Cancer undertook a study to help answer this question. Fifteen patients in complete remission for two to three years were paired as well as possible according to age, initial white blood cell count, disease status at onset, and therapy. Therapy was discontinued for eight patients and continued for seven.

Now 10 years after initial induction, and 7½ years after secondary randomization, there have been three relapses in each group. They occurred in the group with continued chemotherapy at 3½, 6½, and 7¼ years, and in the no treatment group at 3½, 3¾, and 7½ years after initial induction. Five of the six children had marrow relapse, two having simultaneous central nervous system leukemia. All five have died. The sixth (no treatment) had testicular leukemia, underwent orchiectomy and is alive two years later. A semilog plot survival curve for all patients still reveals a continuing fall-off at eight years (Fig. 1). Although these patients are surviving longer than eight years after their original diagnosis, the impression that all children free of disease at five years are cured of their disease is not necessarily true.

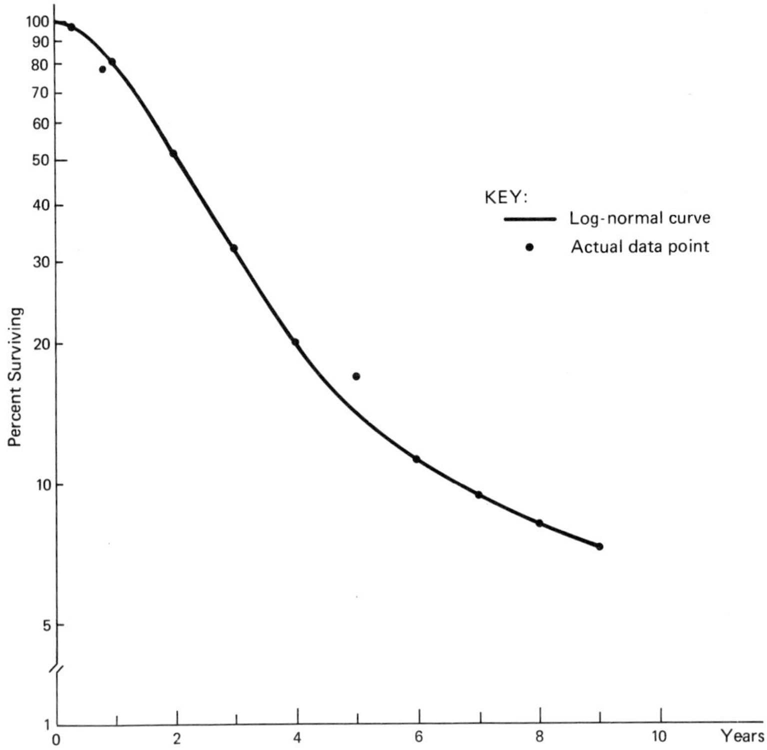

FIG. 1. Semilog plot showing the survival rate in acute leukemia of childhood. Children's Cancer Study Group A (CCSGA), cyclic–sequential study, 1963–73, data based on 165 patients.

If you plot this data along with survival data presented by studies undertaken by Acute Leukemia Group B and compare them to the expected survival of normal children, you can see we have a long way to go (Fig. 2). I expect survival of patients treated with today's treatment program will continue to fall probably at a somewhat different slope but still no where approaching the normal survival for children. We could consider the task of curing leukemia in childhood as still in its induction phase. The use of combination chemotherapy and some form of presymptomatic CNS and sanctuary therapy is just the beginning. Continuation therapy probably should consist of new approaches such as

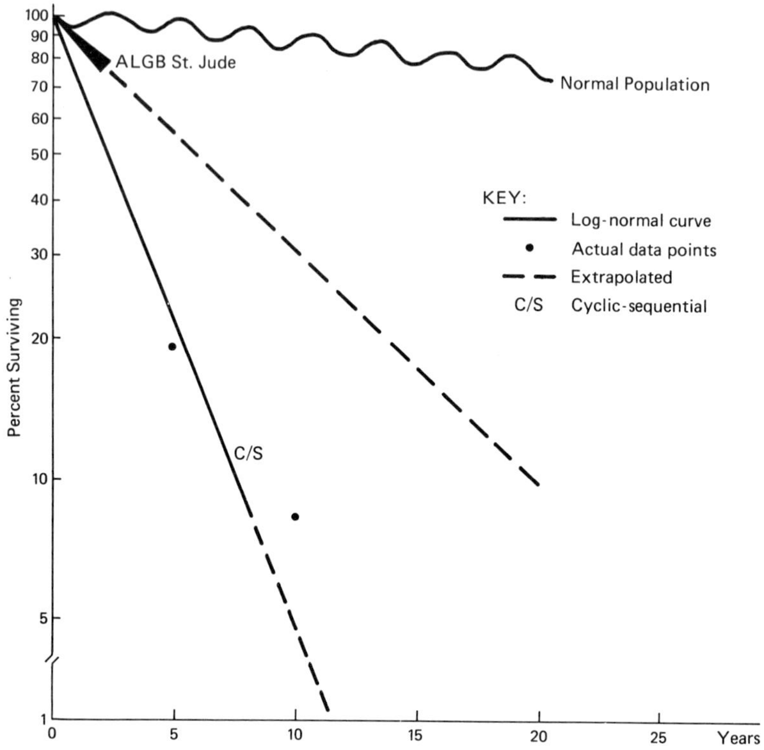

FIG. 2. Semilog plots comparing survival rates based on data from (1) cyclic–sequential study (CCSGA), (2) Acute Leukemia Group B (ALGB), St. Jude's Childrens Hospital, and (3) normal populations.

immunotherapy or specific therapy against the etiology factors when they are discovered (Fig. 3).

SUPPORTIVE THERAPY

BLEEDING

Active hemorrhage is most often primarily due to thrombocytopenia. But if the platelet count is greater than 30,000/ mm^3, other contributing causes such as disseminated in-

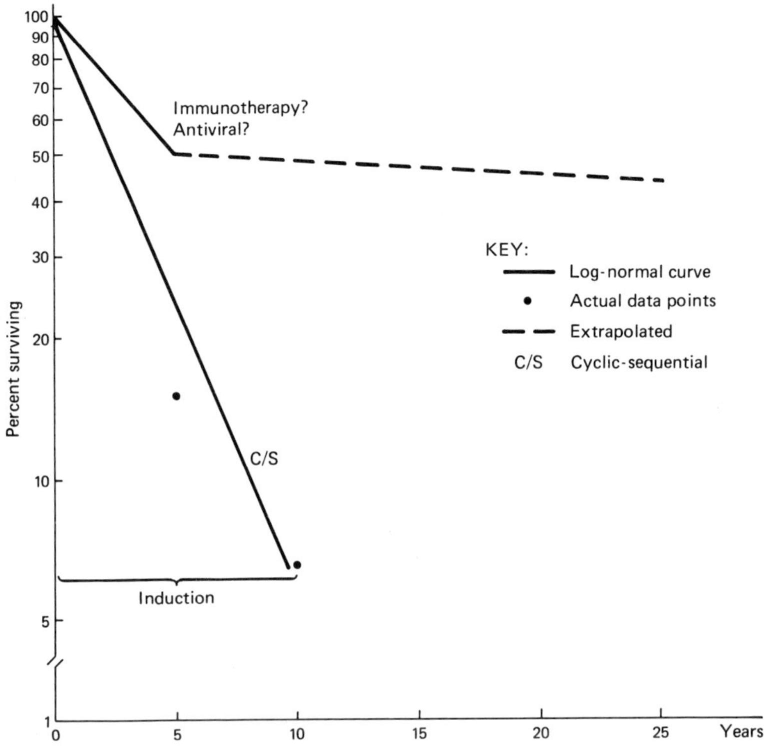

FIG. 3. Semilog plots of survival rates comparing data from cyclic–sequential study (CCSGA) and prospective results of immuno- and antiviral therapies.

travascular coagulopathy of platelet defects induced by agents such as aspirin should be investigated. Blood loss may be replaced by careful transfusion of fresh whole blood or packed cells. When active bleeding is not present and a transfusion is required, it is best to transfuse with small increments of blood, especially at lower hemoglobin levels. Platelet transfusions are indicated when patients are having serious bleeding associated with thrombocytopenia. Thrombocytopenia alone without bleeding is not an indication for platelet transfusion. When a platelet pack is indicated, the usual dose required to stop severe bleeding is 6 units per m^2. If facilities are available, type-specific platelets (HLA matching) are most efficient. Fresh whole blood, given as soon as possible after collection, is also a source of platelets if platelet packs are not available.

INFECTION

Treatment of infections is not as difficult as adequately diagnosing them. In many instances, fever in a patient can be a result of the primary disease, not an infection. It is important, however, to search for an infection in all patients with fever. Blood cultures (at least three), along with urine, nose, throat, and stool cultures, should be obtained after a careful physical examination. It must be remembered that the usual signs of infection, such as inflammation and exudate, are often not present because of the inadequacy of a normal polymorphonuclear response or steroid suppression. Antibiotic therapy should be withheld until a specific microbiological diagnosis is obtained, unless the child's clinical condition is deteriorating so that waiting 24 to 48 hours would be life-threatening. The hazards of antibiotic-resistant organisms are themselves a reason for not instituting the shotgun approach to fever and a suspected infection. White cell transfusions obtained from either patients with chronic myelogenous leukemia or normal donors, by means of a cell-separator, are useful in treatment of infections associated with severe granulocytopenia.

PSYCHOLOGIC SUPPORT

The emotional impact on the patient and family is variable, but most often they are overwhelmed and in a state of acute panic. During the care of a child with leukemia there are several important areas of communication that should be emphasized. The initial interview is crucial and it is at this point where a great deal of the foundation for further communication is built. It is a good opportunity to explain the disease process of leukemia to the parents. As many of the adult family members who will have contact with the child should attend. A special effort should be made to include grandparents. They often are a source of significant problems if they are not also informed of the situation and treatment planned. In most cases, they have a real medical gap in their awareness of present treatment modalities. The initial reactions of the parents to the diagnosis usually contains strong persistence of guilt feelings as well as hostility and anger. They fear having a nervous breakdown.

It is best to begin by establishing the diagnosis. There has often been some ambivalance about the certainty of the diagnosis, and it "clears the air" if you establish your agreement on the diagnosis of leukemia. I then try to explain in medical terms what normal blood cells are, where they are from, and something about the function of each one. After a discussion of the general concepts of cancer as it relates to leukemia, I mention the different morphological subtypes of leukemia and an explanation of the type the child in question has been diagnosed. In most cases the family is reluctant to bring up many questions except the most superficial ones. It is best to anticipate some general concerns:

1. Of what long-term significance is the fact that the diagnosis was not made earlier?
2. Does previous illness or lack thereof make any difference in the success of the child's treatment?
3. Will my child be able to go to school or continue normal activity?
4. What do I tell my other children, friends, and distant relatives?
5. What should I tell the child?
6. How long will the child be in the hospital?

If the physician is at a large referral center, the parents often question the competency of the referring physician. This doubt is often a part of the general anger of the parents at the diagnosis and since they do not want to express their hostility directly at you, they often transfer it to their own physician. It is very important to support the referring physician, since he will become such an important part of the child's continuing care. After this initial phase of the discussion, I outline the planned therapy. It is helpful if you provide some paper so the parents can write down some of the information. Though these notes are often very superficial, it does give the parents some tangible evidence of the meeting. When they discuss the problems among themselves, they can refer to their notes and use them as the basis for future questions.

But the anger and frustration is not all with the patient. The physicians who treat children with cancer find that a conflict arises, which is often more easily perceived by the parents than by the physician handling the child's care. It arises because there are two powerful and normal responses when one is involved in the care of a child with leukemia. First of all, there is the response of compassion which produces an impulse to move toward the child with aid and comfort. On the other hand, there is the repulsion by the threat of death, which produces the impulse to move away from the child in order to protect himself (the physician) from any loss or realization of failure. It is necessary, in my own mind, to constantly reexamine my own reactions, both toward the patient and the parents, throughout the course of treatment. Though it is important to achieve an honest relationship, I have found that too close an attachment is more detrimental than beneficial.

SUMMARY

This chapter has been presented as an interim discussion of some of the treatment aspects of childhood acute leukemia. The dramatic improvement in the control and number of long-term survivors has opened up a whole set of new challenges. The significance of late effects of our treatment on normal tissue, will make it necessary for us to reevaluate our present treatment and delineate those aspects of our present treatment which may be more harmful than curative.

REFERENCES

1. Pierce MI, Borges WH, Heyn R, Wolff JA, and Shield SMA: Epidemiological factors and survival experience in 1770 children with acute leukemia treated by members of Children's Cancer Study Group A between 1957 and 1964. Cancer 23:1296, 1969
2. Sundberg RD: Aspiration biopsy of bone marrow: Bull Univ Minn Hospitals, 21:471, 1950
3. Humphrey GB, Nesbit ME, Brunning RD: Prognostic value of the periodic acid-Schiff (PAS) reaction in acute lymphoblastic leukemia. Am J Clin Path 61:393, 1974
4. McKenna RW, Bloomfield CD, Dick F, et al.: Acute monoblastic leukemia: Diagnosis and treatment of ten cases. Blood 46:481, 1975
5. Kersey JH, Gajl-Peczalska KJ, Nesbit ME: The lymphoid system: Abnormalities in immunodeficiency and malignancy. 84:789, 1974
6. Claman NH, Mosier DE: Cell-cell interaction in antibody production. Progr. Allergy 16:40, 1972
7. Fleisher T, Luckasen J, Sabad A, Kersey, J.: T and B lymphoid subpopulations in children. Pediatr 55:162, 1975
8. Ross GD, Polley MH, Rabellino EM, Grey HM: Two different complement receptors on human lymphocytes. One specific for C3b and one specific for C3b inactivator cleaved C3b. J Exp Med 138:789, 1973
9. Kersey J, Nesbit M, Hallgren H et al: Evidence of origin of childhood acute lymphoblastic leukemias and lymphomas in thymus-derived lymphocytes. Cancer (in press)
10. Coccia PF, Kersey J, Gajl-Peczalska K et al: Positive correlation of surface markers with morphology and clinical presentation in childhood non Hodgkin's lymphoma (NHL). Am Soc Clin Oncol 16:1138, 1975
11. Flandrin G, Brouet JC, Daniel MT, Preud'homme JL: Acute leukemia with Burkitt's tumor cells: A study of six cases with special reference to lymphocyte surface markers. Blood 45:183, 1975
12. Ross GD, Rabellino EM, Polley MJ, and Grey HM: Combined studies of complement receptor and surface immunoglobulin-bearing cells and sheep erythrocyte rosette-forming cells in normal and leukemic human lymphocytes. J Clin Invest 52:377, 1973
13. Gajl-Peczalska KJ, Bloomfield CD, Coccia PF, et al: B and T cell lymphomas: Analysis of blood and lymph nodes in 87 patients. Am J Med (in press)
14. Gajl-Peczalska, KJ, Bloomfield CD, Nesbit ME, and Kersey JH: B cell markers on lymphoblasts in acute lymphoblastic leukemia. Clin Exp Immunol, 17:561, 1974

15. Borella L, Green AA, Aur, RJA et al: Clinical and immunological recovery of children with acute lymphocytic leukemia to "total therapy" studies. In Mathé G, Pouillart, Schwarzenberg L (eds): New York, Springer, 1973, pp 145-50
16. Dowling, Jr, MD, Hagheben M, Gee TS et al: Comparative results obtained in the treatment of acute leukemia. In Mathe' G, Pouillart P, Schwarzenberg (eds): New York, Springer, 1973, pp 133-144
17. DiMarco A, Gaetani M, Scarpinato B: Adriamycin (NSC-123127): A new antibiotic with antitumor activity. Cancer Chemother Rep 53:33, 1969
18. Oettgen HF, Tallal H, Tan CC et al: Clinical experience with L-asparaginase. In Grundmann E, Oettgen HF (eds):Experimental and Clinical Effects of L-Asparaginase. New York, Springer, 1970
19. Nesbit M, Chard R, Evans A, Karon M: Evaluation of intramuscular versus intravenous administration of L-asparaginase in childhood leukemia. Blood (in press)
20. Jouvovick M, Raska K, Sovmova F, Sorm F: Anabolic transformation of a novel antimetabolite, 5-azacytidine and evidence of its incorporation into ribonucleic acid. Collection Czeck Chem Commun 30:3370, 1965
21. Livingston RB, Carter SK: Single Agents in Cancer chemotherapy. New York, Plenum, 1970, p. 27
22. Rodin AE, Haggard ME, Travis LB: Lung changes and chemotherapeutic agents in childhood. Am J Dis Chil 120:337, 1970
23. Livingston R, Carter S: Cytosine arabinoside (NSC-63878)—a clinical brochure. Cancer Chemother Rep 1:179, 1968
24. Calendi E, DiMarco A, Rigiani B, Scarpinato B, Valentine L: On physico-chemical interaction between daunomycin and nucleic acid. Biochem Biophys Acta 103:25, 1965
25. Livingston RB, Carter SK: Single Agents in Cancer Chemotherapy. New York Plenum, 1970, pp 173–194
26. Werkheiser WC: Specific binding of four amino folic acid analogues by folic acid reductase. J. Biol. Chem. 236:888, 1961
27. Nesbit M, Krivit W, Heyn R, Sharp H: Acute and chronic effects of methotrexate on hepatic; pulmonary and skeletal systems. Cancer (in press)
28. Werlhamer S, Hicko C, Arnarol L: Protein synthesis in human leukocytes and lymphocytes: 1. Effect of steroid and sterols. Blood 34:348, 1969
29. LePage GA: Basic biochemical effects and mechanisms of action of 6-thioguanine. Cancer Res 23:1202, 1963
30. Nesbit ME, Yarbo J, Krivit W: Mechanism of action of vincristine sulfate. Am Assoc Cancer Res 54, 1968
31. Cutting HO: Inappropriate secretion of antidiurectic hormone secondary to vincristine therapy. Am J Med 51:269, 1971

32. Selawry OS: New treatment schedule with improved survival in childhood leukemia: Intermittent parenteral vs. daily oral administration of methotrexate for maintenance of induced remission. JAMA 194:75, 1965
33. Storrs RC, Wolman IJ, Gussoff BD, Hananian J: Remission maintenance in acute lymphocytic leukemia with hydroxyurea. Cancer Res 26:241, 1966
34. Holland JF, Glidewell O: Induction, consolidation, intensification, reinduction and maintenance chemotherapy of acute lymphocytic leukemia. Proc XII Congress Int Soc Hematol, 1968, p. 9.
35. George P, Hernandez K, Hustu O et al: A study of "total therapy" of acute lymphocytic leukemia in children. J. Pediatr. 72:399, 1968
36. Ortega JA, Nesbit ME, Donaldson MH et al: L-asparaginase, vincristine and prednisone for induction of first remission in acute lymphocytic leukemia. Am Assoc Cancer Res Abst 26, 1975
37. Haghbin M: Acute non-lymphocytic leukemia: Clinical and morphological considerations. In Pochedly (ed): Acute Childhood Leukemia. Basel, Karges, 1975, pp. 39–58
38. Sonley MJ, Nesbit ME, Pierce M et al: Cytosine arabinoside, cyclophophamide and vincristine in children with acute myelogenous leukemia. Proc. Am. Assoc. Cancer Res 12:87, 1971
39. Williams, DM, Lynch RE, Cartwright GE: Drug induced aplastic anemia. Semin Hematol 10:195, 1973
40. Davis S, Rubin AD: Treatment and prognosis in aplastic anemia. Lancet 1:871, 1972
41. Buckner CD, Clift RA, Fefer A et al: Human marrow transplantation. Semin Hematol 12:299, 1974
42. Storb R, Thomas CD, Buckner CD et al: Allogeneic marrow grafting for treatment of aplastic anemia. Blood 43: 157, 1974
43. Cametta B, Thomas ED, Nathan G et al: Severe aplastic anemia: An indication for marrow transplantation. Am Soc Hematol Abstr 47, 1975
44. Thomas ED, Storb R, Clift RA et al: Bone marrow transplantation N Eng J Med 292:832, 895, 1975
45. Thomas, ED: Personal communication, 1975
46. Hustu HO, Aur RJA, Verzosa MS et al: Prevention of central nervous system leukemia by irradiation. Cancer 32:585, 1973
47. Evans AE, Gilbert ES, Zandstra R: The increasing incidence of central nervous system leukemia in children. Cancer 26:404, 1970
48. Nies BA, Bodey GP, Thomas ED: The persistence of extramedullary leukemic infiltrates during bone marrow remissions of acute leukemia. Blood 26:133, 1965
49. Mathé G, Schwarzenberg L, Mery AM: Extensive histological survey of patients with acute leukemia in complete remission. Br Med J 1: 640, 1966

50. Sharp HL, Nesbit ME, White JG, Krivit W: Renal and hepatic pathology following initial remission of acute leukemia induced by prednisone Cancer 20:1395, 1967

51. Kim T, Nesbit M, D'Angio G, Levitt S: The role of central nervous system irradiation in children with lymphoblastic leukemia. Radiol 104: 635, 1972

52. Jones B: Prophylactic central nervous system-therapy of leukemia. In Pochedly (ed): Acute Childhood Leukemia Basel, Karges 1975, pp 99–112

53. Stoffel TJ, Nesbit ME, Levitt SH: The role of radiotherapy in renal involvement in acute childhood leukemia. Radiol (in press)

54. Simone JV, Holland F, Johnson W: Fatalities during remission of childhood leukemia. Blood 39:759, 1972

The role of the laboratory in the care of children with leukemia is introduced in the following chapter. The writer has analyzed the laboratory records of Eric and Meri, summarizing for us the number and variety of tests performed.

17

THE VIEW FROM THE LABORATORY

Karen R. Karni

How is the laboratory involved in the diagnosis and treatment of leukemia? First, the diagnosis is primarily determined from laboratory data, especially data from the hematology section of the laboratory. Second, laboratory values are used to monitor the status of the disease. Laboratory tests can show whether an individual with leukemia is in relapse or in remission. This chapter will attempt to explain the role and function of the laboratory in the diagnosis and treatment of leukemia, especially as it relates to the two children, Eric and Meredith, described in Chapters 2 and 3.

Generally, if an individual has such symptoms as pallor, fatigue, easy bruising, fever, or bone pain, a CBC (complete blood count) is ordered from the laboratory. A CBC includes the following basic tests:

Table 1
Normal Values of the Cellular Components of Blood

Elements	*Children (5–10 years)*	*Adults*
Red cells	$4.0–5.3 \times 10^6$ /mm³	Male: $4.4–6.0 \times 10^6$/mm³ Female: $4.2–5.0 \times 10^6$/mm³
Hemoglobin	11.5–15.5 g/100 ml	Male: 13.5–18.0 g/100 ml Female: 12.0–16.0 g/100 ml
White cells	4,500–10,000/mm³	4,500–10,000/mm³
White cell differential (%)		
Neutrophils	45	60
Lymphocytes	48	32
Monocytes	3	4
Eosinophils	3	3
Basophils	1	1
Platelets	150,000–400,000/mm³	150,000–400,000/mm³

Table 2
Blood Findings for Eric and Meredith Compared With Normal Values

Elements	*Eric*	*Meredith*	*Normal Values for Children*
Hemoglobin	7.9 g/100 ml	5.7 g/100 ml	11.5–15.5 g/100 ml
WBC count	18,000/mm³	00/mm³	4,500–10,000/mm³
White cell differential (%)			
Neutrophils	2	4	45
Lymphocytes	18	56	48
Monocytes	0	0	3
Eosinophils	0	2	3
Basophils	0	0	1
Lymphocytes and immature lymphocytes	80	38	None
Platelets	13,000/mm³	16,000/mm³	150,000–400,000/mm³

1. Hemoglobin
2. White Cell Count
3. White Cell Differential

The first determination, hemoglobin (grams of hemoglobin per 100 ml of blood), is usually done to determine whether an anemia is present. The others, white cell count (number of white cells per mm^3 of blood) and differential (percentage of cell types) are needed to determine whether an infective or malignant process is occurring. These three tests can be performed with approximately five drops of blood. They are commonly obtained by a finger-prick or venipuncture. In addition to the CBC, a platelet count (number of platelets per mm^3 of blood) may be performed to check a patient's tendency to bleed.*

Leukemia is characterized as a malignancy in one of the types of white cells. In leukemia, the total white cell count in the peripheral blood is usually increased above the normal range, sometimes to thirty or forty times the normal number of white cells. At other times, especially following leukemia therapy, the total white cell count is below the normal range.

Leukemia may be suspected from a patient's clinical symptoms. It is the findings from the peripheral blood, and from a bone marrow examination, however, which confirm the diagnosis of leukemia. Table 2 gives the initial blood findings for Eric and Meredith before diagnosis.

Both children showed an anemia as evidenced by the low

*Blood is composed of 45% cellular elements, and 55% plasma. Included in the cellular elements are red cells (erythrocytes), white cells (leukocytes), and platelets. The relationship of cells to plasma can be determined using the photograph in Figure 1. The main function of these cellular elements follows:

Red cells—oxygen transfer via the hemoglobin component contained within
White cells—control of infection
Platelets—control of bleeding through coagulation

The white cells are of five major types: neutrophils, lymphocytes, monocytes, eosinophils, and basophils. The relative normal values (child and adult) for the cellular components of blood are found in Table 1.

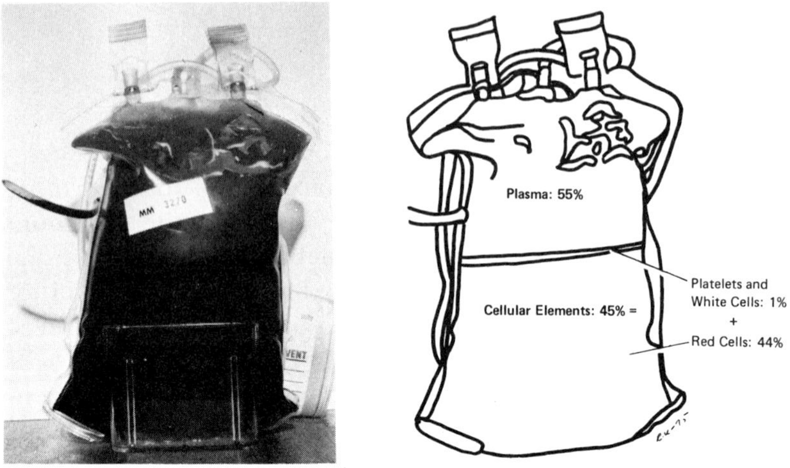

FIG. 1. Constituents of the blood.

hemoglobin values. The anemia was secondary to the leukemic process. Most dramatic, however, were the numbers of lymphoblasts and immature lymphocytes in each of these children's white cell differentials. Blasts and immature forms should *not* be present normally. In addition, Meredith had a decreased platelet count, which evidenced itself clinically by easy bruising.

A bone marrow examination is the best confirmation for leukemia. Except for the lymphocytes, blood-cell formation occurs almost exclusively in the bone marrow. Thus, one can examine bone marrow to determine the number, types, and degree of maturity of the cells produced there. Meredith did not have a bone marrow examination until November 1969, and initial diagnosis was made only on symptomology and blood findings. A bone marrow aspiration on Eric confirmed the suspicion of acute lymphocytic leukemia soon after the initial symptoms were recognized.

There are many theories about blood-cell production. One theory that is accepted for the development of these cells is described in Figure 2.

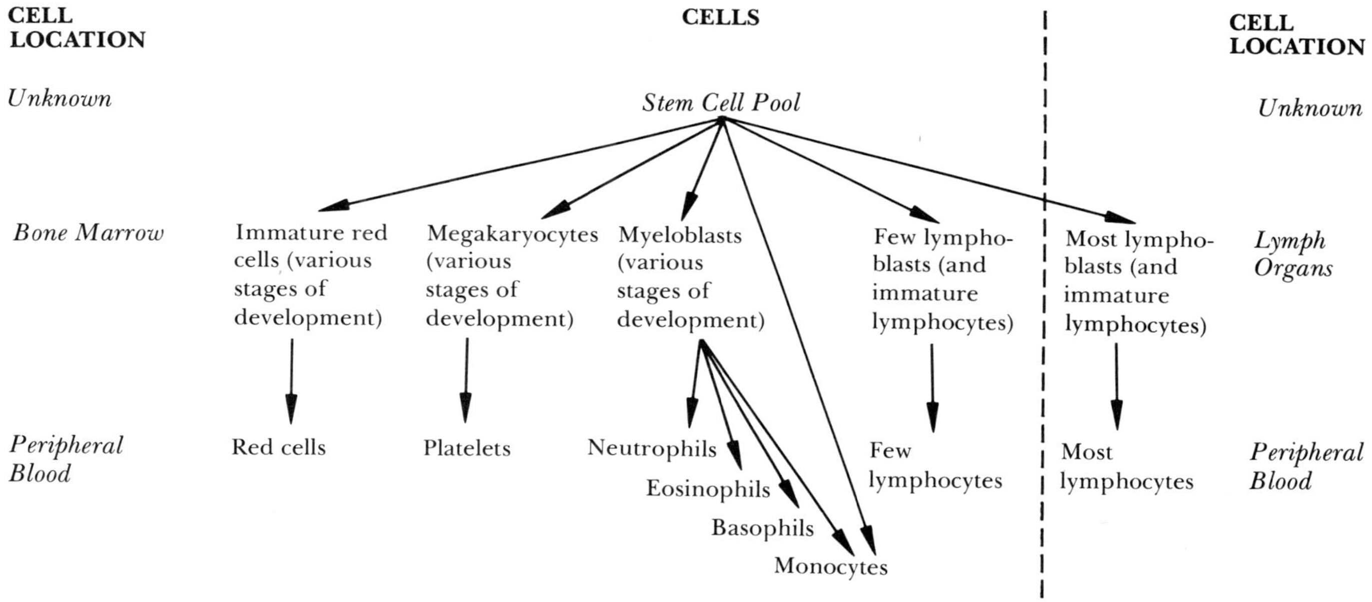

FIG. 2. Schematic diagram illustrating one theory of the normal production of blood cells (red cells, white cells, and platelets). In normal production, cells originate from a "stem cell pool" of unknown location. These stem cells seed the bone marrow and lymph organs. Red cells, platelets, and most white cells (neutrophils, eosinophils, basophils, monocytes, and a few lymphocytes) originate in the bone marrow. When these cells mature, they migrate into the peripheral blood. Most lymphocytes are formed in the lymph organs (spleen and lymph nodes), and then migrate into the peripheral blood. Researchers believe that monocytes may originate from both the stem cell pool and myelocytic precursors.

Of the cell types shown in Table 1 and Figure 2, leukemia usually affects two cells, the neutrophils and lymphocytes. The majority of leukemias, therefore, are either *myelogenous* (also called granulocytic) or *lymphocytic.**

Normally, most lymphocytes are produced by lymphoid tissues, such as the spleen and lymph nodes. In lymphocytic leukemia, however, lymphoblasts are believed to infiltrate the bone marrow and establish centers of production of lymphocytic cells. Thus, examination of the bone marrow may be used to diagnose (or monitor) all leukemic processes.

Leukemia occurs at any stage in the developmental sequence of blood cells. Generally, the earlier the stage of cell maturation at which the malignancy occurs, the poorer is the prognosis for the patient. In other words, a patient whose predominant cell is the lympho*blast* has a poorer prognosis than one whose predominant cell is the mature lympho*cyte.*†

Two other terms are also used in a discussion of leukemia, acute and chronic. Originally, an acute leukemia was defined as leukemia, which if left untreated would, on the average, give a patient a lifespan of less than six months. Chronic leukemia was one which, if left untreated, would give a patient a life span of more than one year. Presently, however, the terms "acute" and "chronic" are used to denote the predominant cell type present: immature *(blast),* or mature *(cyte).* Thus, an acute leukemia is one with a predominance of blasts, while chronic leukemia has a predominance of the more mature forms, cytes. Complicating the nomenclature is the "subacute" form which falls between the acute and chronic forms; unfortunately, hematologists vary in their criteria for classification of the subacute leukemias. A summary of the four major types of leukemia follows:

*The terms myelogenous or granulocytic indicate that the cells involved are primarily in the neutrophilic series. There *are* other types such as aleukemic leukemia, stem-cell leukemia, monocytic leukemia, etc. However, only the major types—lymphatic (or lymphocytic) and myelogenous (or granulocytic) are discussed in this chapter.

†A blast form of a cell indicates a very immature cell, while a cyte indicates a more mature form.

*General Term Used in Classification**	*Lymphatic*	*Myelogenous*
Acute form	Acute lymphoblastic leukemia	Acute myeloblastic leukemia
Chronic form	Chronic lymphocytic leukemia	Chronic myelocytic leukemia

Research to determine the correlation between age of patients and types of leukemia has found that in childhood the most common leukemia is acute (or subacute) lymphoblastic leukemia, (ALL or SLL), the type both Eric and Meredith had. In older adults, the most common types are chronic lymphocytic leukemia (CLL), and chronic myelocytic leukemia (CML). Acute myeloblastic leukemia (AML) appears to affect all age groups equally. It is ironic, therefore, that the acute forms, with their poorer prognosis, affect children primarily, while the chronic forms, with their better prognosis, affect adults. More leukemia is found in males than in females, with a male–female ratio of 5:4 in children who have ALL, to 2:1 in adults who have CLL. For purposes of comparison, the photographs in Figure 3 show gross differences among these four major types, as seen from blood smears under 450× and 1000× magnification.

There are three causes of death usually associated with leukemia: infection, bleeding, and infiltration of leukemic cells into the central nervous system (CNS). Presently, infection is the major cause of death. It is strange that while in leukemia a proliferation of white cells generally occurs, these cells are not effective disease fighters. Consequently, leukemics are more prone to infections. Because of advances in coagulation therapy, bleeding is not as serious a problem as it once was. Because therapy has lengthened the total life span of leukemics, however, infiltration of cells to the central nervous system has become more common.

The laboratory, then, is involved in monitoring the status of a person who has leukemia to determine whether any of

*Note: Differences in terminology do exist. An acute lymphoblastic leukemia may also be written as acute lymphatic leukemia, or chronic myelocytic leukemia may be written as chronic granulocytic leukemia.

A B C D E

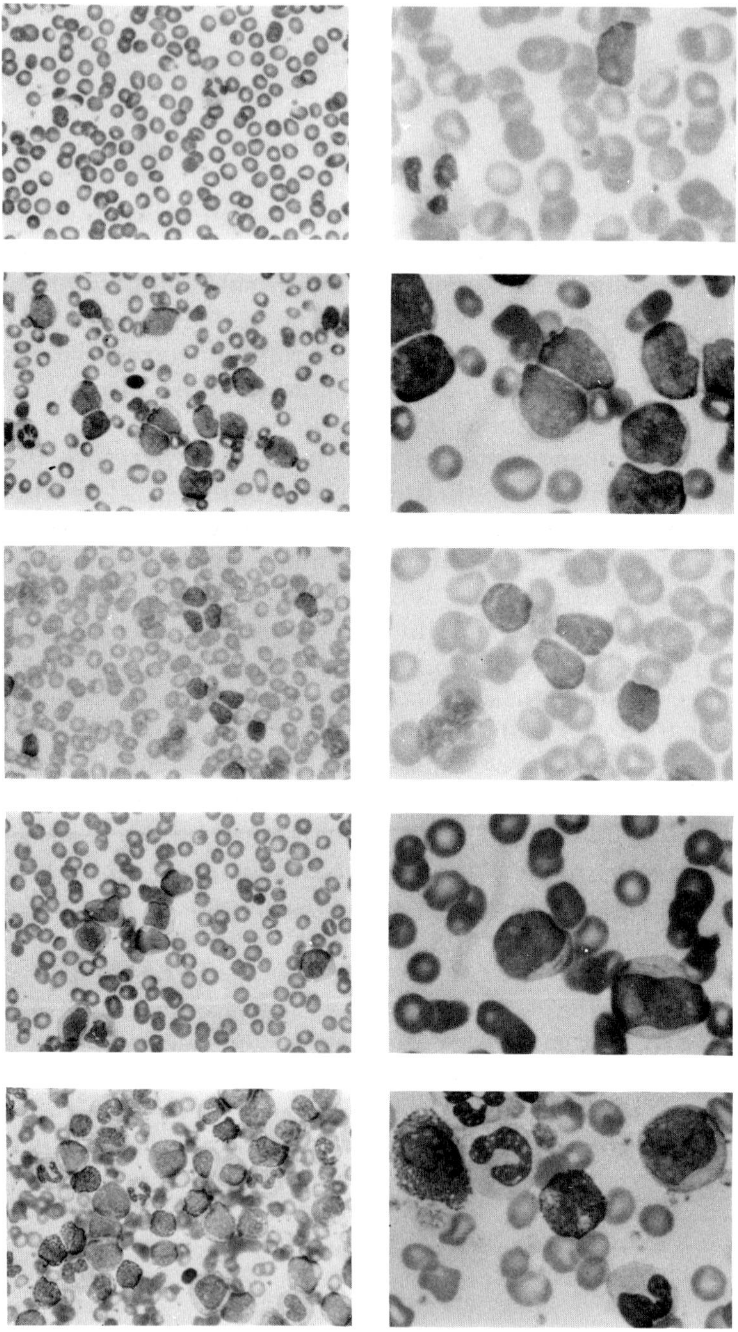

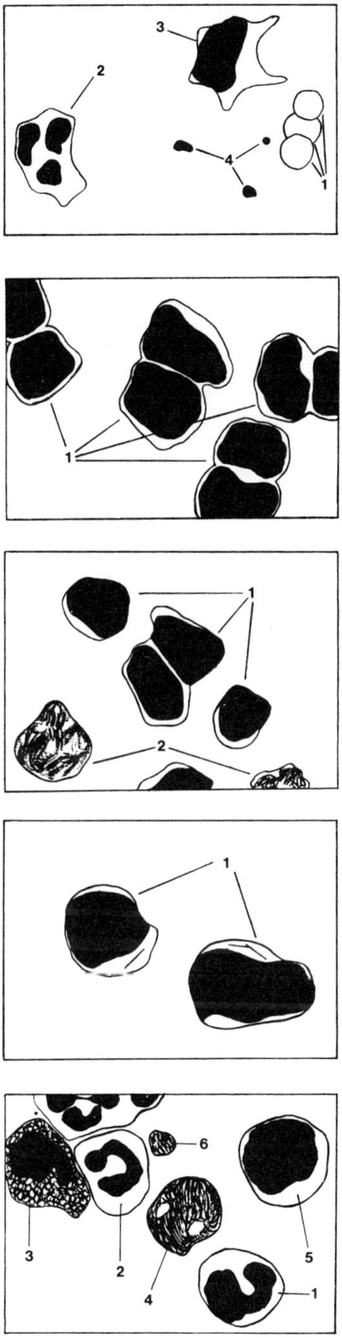

FIG. 3. Series of photographs and drawings showing normal and leukemic blood pictures (opposite page: left column, ×450; right column, × 1000; this page: drawings from × 1000 photographs). A. Normal (WBC count, 6100/mm³): (1) normal red cells, (2) normal neutrophil, (3) normal lymphocyte, (4) normal platelets. B. Acute lymphoblastic leukemia (ALL) (WBC count, 59,000/mm³): (1) lymphblasts. Note the absence of platelets. C. Chronic lymphocytic leukemia (CLL) (WBC count, 46,000/mm³): (1) mature lymphocytes, (2) damaged lymphocytes. Note the increase of damaged cells. D. Acute myeloblastic leukemia (AML) (WBC count, 24,700/mm³): (1) myeloblasts. Note the presence of Auer rods, red-staining structures in the cytoplasm of myeloblasts, characteristic of AML. E. Chronic myelocytic leukemia (CML) (WBC count, 187,000/mm³): (1) neutrophil, (2) neutrophil, band-form, (3) eosinophil, (4) basophil, (5) myeloblast, (6) giant platelet. Note the variety of cell types characteristic of CML.

these three processes could be occurring: infection, bleeding, or infiltration of cells to the CNS. Usually, if an infection is suspected, cultures for bacteria (or viruses or fungi) are taken. Platelet counts are used to establish an individual's tendency to bleeding, and, finally, examination of cerebrospinal fluid is made to determine whether leukemic cells are present.

To illustrate further the laboratory's function in monitoring this disease, data are presented on Eric and Meredith (Tables 3 and 4). These data show the numbers of hospitalizations and numbers and types of laboratory tests employed in trying to monitor a leukemic patient.

From these data, one can see the vast number and variety of tests performed on leukemic patients. Meredith had a greater number of tests performed because of the greater length of her illness. She was also subjected to additional laboratory testing which has become customary in recent years.

Why, then, are all of these procedures necessary? In hematology, the CBC is used, as described before, to determine whether the total numbers of white cells are within normal range, to determine whether they are of the normal type (the appearance of blasts for example, is not a good sign), and to determine whether an anemia may be occurring along with the leukemia. Unfortunately, when a leukemic process occurs, the proliferation of white cells in the marrow takes place at the expense of the red cells and platelets. Thus, their numbers are often decreased. Fewer red cells (anemia) is not as serious as fewer platelets. The body can adjust to the decrease in red cells; however, the decrease in platelets can lead to bleeding. Such bleeding, if it occurs, is most serious when it happens in the brain. Thus, platelet counts are usually requested along with a CBC to determine whether they, like the white cells, are within normal limits.

A bone marrow examination is done to determine the numbers, types, and degree of maturation of developing cells in the marrow. This is not a routine laboratory procedure because of the nature of the examination, but is essential in leukemia to monitor the disease. In an adult, the sternum and the posterior iliac crests are used most frequently as sources from which bone marrow material can be obtained.

In children, the posterior iliac crest or upper end of the tibia are usually used. (See Figure 4 for location of the posterior iliac crest which is used most commonly with children.)

In a bone marrow "aspiration," a physician introduces a needle into a sterile, anesthetized area until the point of the needle reaches the bone. Then the needle is rotated through the bone. Sudden loss of resistance usually indicates the needle has entered the marrow cavity. Then a 10 to 20 ml syringe is attached, and approximately 0.3 ml of material is quickly removed. At this point, the patient usually experiences a momentary sharp pain. From the aspirate, a technologist makes bone marrow films immediately; marrow particles can also be used for preparation of "imprints." Then the marrow aspirate is usually centrifuged to determine its composition (by layering) and clotted marrow fragments can be used to make histologic sections. When carefully handled, all of these tests are performed with less than 1 ml of bone marrow aspirate.

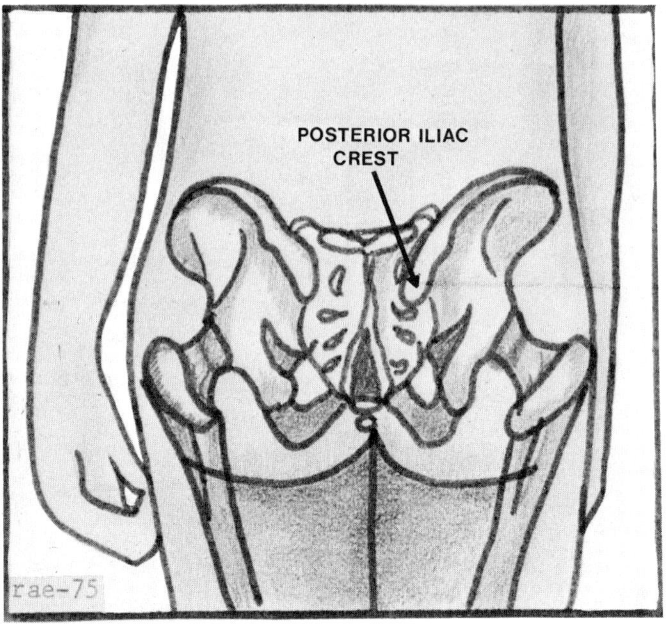

FIG. 4. Location of the posterior iliac crest, the common source of bone marrow material in children.

Table 3
Basic Medical Data on Eric and Meredith

	Eric		*Meredith*	
Diagnosis	Acute lymphoblastic leukemia		Acute (or subacute) lymphoblastic leukemia	
Length of illness	2½ years (1970–72)		7¾ years (1966–74) (complete remission from 1966–70)	
Number of hospitalizations	5		9	
		Length of stay (days)		Length of stay (days)
Reasons for hospitalizations	1. Diagnosis, bone marrow biopsy, fever, antibiotics	23	1. CNS leukemia, bone marrow and spinal fluid examination	1
	2. CNS leukemia, radiation therapy	6	2. CNS leukemia, radiation therapy, laparotomy, right oophorectomy and radiation therapy	52

	3. Relapse of CNS leukemia, radiation therapy	12	3. Herpes infection, antibiotics	3
	4. Pneumocystis carinii pneumonitis, antibiotics, CNS leukemia, intrathecal methotrexate	16	4. Bone lesions (leukemic), biopsies	8
	5. CNS leukemia, left hemiparesis, therapy	8	5. CNS leukemia, radiation therapy,	27
			6. Bleeding, blood component therapy, sepsis, antibiotics	24
			7. CNS leukemia, "VAMP" treatment, bleeding, component therapy, sepsis, antibiotics	29
			8. Sepsis, antibiotics, bone pain, medication	8
			9. Pancreatitis, low fat diet, bone pain, medication	6
Total length of hospitalizations		65		158

Table 4
Laboratory Tests Performed Over the Course of Childrens' Illness

Area	*Eric*			*Meredith*		
HEMATOLOGY	Inpatient	Outpatient	Total	Inpatient	Outpatient	Total
Complete blood count (CBC)	40	107	147	114	135	249
Platelet count	31	105	136	86	124	210
Hematocrit	35	4	39	25	1	26
Special hematology report—white cell differential	1	0	1	4	3	7
Bone marrow examination	1	15	16	5	16	21
Other (eg, red cell indices, reticulocyte count, erythrocyte sedimentation rate, etc.)	2	0	2	100	25	125
SPINAL FLUID ANALYSIS	(Number of Spinal Taps = 18)			(Number of Spinal Taps = 30)		
Cells (red cells, white cells)	1	17	18	25	5	30
Protein	1	10	11	20	4	24
Glucose	1	9	10	17	3	20
Culture—bacteria	1	17	18	4	1	5
Viral studies	—	—	—	2	—	2
MICROBIOLOGY						
Blood culture	12	—	12	17	6	23
Throat culture	5	1	6	11	4	15
Wound culture	—	3	3	1	4	5

Stool culture	1	—	1	5	1	6
Urine culture	2	—	2	14	8	22
Viral studies	—	—	—	12	—	12
Fungal studies	—	—	—	3	1	4
Sensitivities	—	—	—	5	—	5
Other	—	—	—	2	—	2
CHEMISTRY						
Alkaline phosphatase	4	3	7	6	2	8
Ornithine carbamyl transferase (OCT)	3	5	8	2	2	4
Serum glutamic oxalacetic transaminase (SGOT)	3	5	8	5	3	8
Protein (total)	—	—	0	7	—	7
Protein electrophoresis	2	1	3	7	—	7
Bilirubin	1	—	1	3	—	3
Blood urea nitrogen (BUN)	8	—	8	11	2	13
Creatinine	8	—	8	11	1	12
Uric Acid	8	—	8	9	—	9
Electrolytes						
Na	2	—	2	15	1	16
K	2	—	2	15	1	16
Cl	2	—	2	15	1	16
CO_2	2	—	2	13	1	14
Calcium	2	—	2	1	1	2
Phosphorus	1	—	1	3	1	4
Glucose	1	—	1	10	—	10

Table 4 *(cont.)*

Area	*Eric*			*Meredith*		
CHEMISTRY (*cont.*)	Inpatient	Outpatient	Total	Inpatient	Outpatient	Total
Amylase	—	—	0	4	1	5
Routine urinalysis	10	—	10	16	9	25
Other (eg, cholesterol, VMA, pH, P_{CO_2}, P_{O_2})	23	1	24	19	1	20
COAGULATION						
Prothrombin time	3	—	3	3	1	4
Partial thromboplastin time	3	—	3	2	1	3
Thrombin time	3	—	3	3	—	3
BLOOD BANK—IMMUNOLOGY						
ABO and Rh type	1	—	1	4	—	4
Antibody screening	—	—	—	1	—	1
Australia antigen-antibody studies	—	—	—	—	1	1
Cold agglutinins	—	—	—	1	—	1
Heterophil test	—	—	—	1	—	1
Cross-match	—	—	—	2	—	2
PATHOLOGY						
Spinal fluid for malignant cells	—	1	1	3	—	3
Urine for malignant cells	—	—	—	1	1	2
Total	226	304	530	665	372	1037

In addition to a bone marrow aspiration, a bone marrow "biopsy" can be made in which a core of the marrow is obtained for smears, imprints, and sections.

Bone marrows are not dangerous to perform; however, they do require skill and they can be painful. Many patients, especially children, view them with apprehension.

More dangerous and uncomfortable than a bone marrow aspiration, however, is a spinal fluid aspiration, which is done to determine abnormalities, especially leukemic cells, in cerebrospinal fluid (CSF). Cerebrospinal fluid is secreted by the choroid plexuses of the brain, and fills the ventricles and subarachnoid cavities of the brain and spinal cord. Normally, CSF is a clear, colorless fluid with a volume (adult) of 90 to 150 ml. It does not contain cells, causing one to believe there is a blood–CSF barrier, similar to a blood-brain barrier.

In leukemia, however, leukemic cells can find their way into spinal fluid and also into the brain. Thus, when symptoms which involve the central nervous system appear (headache, dizziness, nausea) spinal fluid may be aspirated and analyzed.

The procedure (spinal tap) involves lumbar puncture into the subarachnoid space of the spinal cord, performed by a physician under sterile conditions at the third, fourth, or fifth lumbar interspace. When done on a child, the child lies on his side with his back exactly vertical to the table. A local anesthetic is used and lumbar puncture needle is inserted exactly in the midsagittal plane of his body. The needle is advanced slowly and the stylet withdrawn until CSF drips out. When fluid is dripping, a three-way stopcock and manometer are attached and CSF pressure is obtained. Then, appropriate aliquots of CSF are obtained (by drop); these usually consist of three 1-ml samples for laboratory analysis. The needle is removed, pressure is applied, and the child is encouraged to rest for a time. Again, a skilled physician can make a spinal tap almost painless, but poor punctures can be uncomfortable, painful, and even fatal.

In the laboratory, spinal fluid is examined most commonly for:

1. Gross appearance
2. Presence of cells (red cells & white cells)
3. Total protein
4. Glucose
5. Presence of infectious agents (bacterial, viral and fungal)

As an example, Table 5 shows a comparison of the values for CSF from normal children, with that obtained from Meredith, when CNS involvement by leukemic cells was evident.

Because leukemics have increased susceptibility to infectious agents, they have more frequent infections and heal from them more slowly. Both Eric and Meredith had numerous bacterial cultures done on them for pathogenic bacteria. Meredith, in fact, had three relapses with sepsis (bacteria in the blood). Viral cultures were negative for each child. Stool cultures were also requested, since the antibiotics used in leukemia causes suppression of normal bacterial flora of the bowel, which in turn allows certain yeasts to grow. Meredith also had "thrush," a *Candida* (yeast) infection of the mouth caused by a normal inhabitant, *Candida,* overgrowing the other normal flora of the oral cavity. Eric had a *Pneumocystis carinii* infection of the lungs—an infection caused by an organism classified as a tiny parasite. Pneumocystis infection may result also from extensive chemotherapy.

Because the disease is treated with chemotherapy, the chemistry section of the laboratory is also used. The chemistry laboratory is especially important in determining a patient's liver function, which may be affected by drugs. Elevated levels of certain liver enzymes such as alkaline phosphatase, ornithine carbamyl transferase (OCT), and serum glutamic oxalacetic transaminase (SGOT) will indicate liver involvement. Measurements of protein and bilirubin levels may also be made to determine liver function. In addition, if kidney involvement occurs, determinations of blood urea nitrogen (BUN) and creatinine, as well as uric acid, are made. Again, elevated values of these tests reflect kidney impairment because the kidneys are unable to clear these products. Other testing, especially in the relapse phases of the dis-

Table 5
Normal CSF Values in Children Compared with Those for Meredith

CSF	*Normal Values*	*Meredith's Values (8/30/73)*
Pressure	60–150 mm	Unknown
Gross appearance	Clear, colorless	Slightly turbid, colorless
Red cells	0	5
White cells	$0–5/mm^3$	$136/mm^3$ (97% mononuclear—lymphocytic)
Total protein	15–40 mg/100 ml	96 mg/100 ml
Glucose	45–75 mg/100 ml	20 mg/100 ml
Microbial agents (bacteria, viruses, or fungi)	None	None

ease, includes determination of electrolyte values (sodium, potassium, chloride, CO_2), as well as other determinations of calcium, phosphorus, and so on.

The blood bank was not required extensively for these children. However, in some cases of leukemia, the typing and cross-matching of blood and blood components to elevate the hemoglobin and to control bleeding are required. During Meredith's sixth hospitalization, she did require platelet packs and red cell transfusions to control extensive bleeding.

Both children had tests performed in the pathology laboratory. Meredith had three spinal fluid determinations—all positive—for malignant cells. The diagnosis of Pneumocystis infection was made by special staining of a lung biopsy from Eric.

Thus, the laboratory is used extensively in this disease; first in the diagnosis of leukemia, and then in following the patient throughout the course of his illness.

The primary role of the laboratory, therefore, is to provide information obtained from the analysis of body fluids and secretions. The medical technologist is, for the most part, often in the background, with actual patient contact limited to the drawing of specimens, or assisting at bone marrow aspirations.

Nevertheless, in a more personal way, the medical

technologist is involved in the health team, especially the team of patient, family, and physician. Even in a large hospital setting, the technologist comes to know most of the leukemia patients and their families, due primarily to their clinic visits, as well as to the volume of laboratory tests that are required. During this time, the leukemic becomes a "professional" patient. A professional patient is one who requires close monitoring, and thus is seen regularly and often at a clinic or hospital. "Professionals" also come to understand the testing that is being done, and are able to tolerate uncomfortable or painful procedures.

Both Eric and Meredith were professionals. Their parents as well as the staff, often marveled at their ability to control themselves under stress. In addition, like many leukemic children, they were curious about the disease itself, and Eric, for example, requested and obtained his own blood films to examine under a microscope at home.

In working with leukemics, then, we have come to admire their patience, steadfastness, and courage, as well as that of their families who have become professionals in their own way. This is especially so in the support they give, whether it be in obtaining a specimen, or in soothing an apprehensive child.

It is difficult for all health professionals when a leukemic patient dies. And, unfortunately, it is often the technologist who first detects the downward trend which signals the final period of life. Yet, there are rewards in this work. They are in having a child smile with appreciation when a procedure is done skillfully, or having a very sick patient in relapse, through the use of therapy, go into continued remission.

Whether a cure will be found for leukemia is speculative. Nevertheless, progress is being made, and the technologist shares in the hopes of all humankind that someday leukemia will not be a word of dread.

The hospital setting for the leukemic child is discussed here from two perspectives. The first considers the psychologic aspect of the child and his care, including the development of interpersonal relationships between the child and his family and the hospital staff in the face of death. The second perspective deals with the technical aspect of the nursing care given the leukemic child.

18

THE HOSPITAL SETTING FOR THE CHILD WITH CANCER

Sue N. Sauer

PSYCHOLOGIC ASPECTS OF THE NURSING CARE

Caring for dying children and their families in the hospital setting presents a challenging and enlightening experience. It taxes one's skill and ingenuity to give complex physical and emotional care, but one can witness the adaptability, courage, and strength of the family in reacting to the traumatic crises of illness and death. At no other time in life are needs so great or defenses so low, and patients become uniquely vulnerable and open to emotional hurt and devastation. This imparts a special responsibility to all hospital personnel to support and protect the family, and to aid in their growth and well-being during the hospitalization.

HOSPITAL SETTING

It is overwhelmingly agreed that the best place for children is at home with parents, siblings, pets, and the familiar environment. The decision to keep the child either at home or in the hospital is made by the parents and doctor with consultation from family members and nursing staff. In general, most parents wish to keep their child home as long as possible, utilizing outpatient facilities for necessary care and equipment. When the care needed by the child becomes so complex or difficult, when pain control measures increase, or when the family can no longer handle the situation, then hospitalization is necessary. This need not be radically different from the home life and normal functioning that children love, but should provide an atmosphere which he or she finds familiar and comforting.

There are many facets of hospital care that can enhance the unity of the family and provide a desirable place for them to spend their last days together. The transition from home to hospital need not be great if the primary desires of the child are placed foremost. What a child craves most besides love and honesty is the security and contentment of a normal life. We believe that most time-honored hospital rules should not exist for the dying child or the family. Grieving people have a right to be protected from a "business-as-usual" atmosphere.[1] Relaxing most hospital rules is the very thing that aids the closeness of the family unit.

Years of listening to parents have taught hospital personnel that it is the small things that make the difference for children and parents alike during this time. An understanding of the little worries and concerns can be an unmistakable message of interest and kindness to the apprehensive parents and child, and is a reflection of a hospital that cares.

A normal atmosphere begins in the hospital by having the whole family together whenever possible. This would be the usual situation at home and moving to the hospital should not sever the normal interplay between the child and the mother, father, and siblings. There should be no defined visiting hours; rather, parents and siblings should have the freedom to come and go as desired and be with the child when they wish and when their child needs them. The transmission of an active infection or the desires of parents and sick child need be the only limiting restrictions on visitation. The child needs the closeness of loved ones more during hospitalization than at any other time. Relatives offer silent companionship and support and hospital personnel should not feel that relatives are in the way. Consideration and caution must be exercised so that the family and child are not bombarded with well-meaning people wanting to help but only adding further to the stress and burden of the family. Persons important to the family should be close by.

Almost without exception, no hospital quarters are too small to accommodate the family members and objects from home that the child wishes to have nearby. Room should always be made for the child's own wagon, special chair or potty chair, and phonograph. When the child's condition is stable, parents should be urged to go home at night or to other accommodations made for the family. There are two reasons for this: first, to enhance the relationship between mother and father and to have them spend time with their other children; secondly, to enable the parents to acquire proper rest so that they may cope and handle the complexities of the next day. When the condition of the child becomes grave and parents do not wish to leave the bedside, they care little how elaborate the accomodations are so long as a roll-away bed, cot, chair lounger, or makeshift bed is made for them at the bedside where they can remain in continual close contact with their child. There seems to be some unwritten rule that only the child can occupy the hospital bed, so parents need to be told that it is all right for them to lie in bed, close to the child, with their arms around him. This practice is almost always employed at home and is comforting and soothing for the child depending on his age and size. All physical care can usually be managed, and parents very willingly reposition themselves when it becomes necessary to administer some form of treatment. We feel strongly that all avenues should be investigated to foster comfort and closeness between child and parents at this time.

An occasion may arise when the child has a strong need to

see and hold a pet. Because pets have not been brought to the hospital before does not mean that it cannot be done. Usually, it can be easily arranged. Just a few moments with a pet may bring long periods of happiness for the child. On one occasion a very large pet goose was brought into the hospital for the child to see and touch. The joy was evident.

Most children desire to be out of the hospital whenever possible and therefore a liberal pass policy must be established. Many desires and wishes are accomplished by the child and pleasurable moments remembered by the family when the child is permitted to be out of the hospital for even as short a time as an hour or two. The family's wishes, feelings, and fears should always be explored before the decision is made to send the child home or on pass. Dying children quite often wish this very strongly and usually it can be managed even if the child's condition is poor. A child generally knows when it is time to return to the hospital. It may necessitate sending a nurse along with the patient and family, not only to care for the child physically, but also to be of support for the family if the patient's condition worsens. A nurse in accompaniment may also add a measure of security to the situation and make the time happier and more relaxed for the family. When a child's condition is not grave and he or she wishes to go out on pass, there are few limiting factors other than great distance from the hospital. Intravenous fluids and poles, portable oxygen, and feeding tubes need not stand in the way if a child strongly wishes the trip and the family welcomes the opportunity. A precious nine-year-old girl accompanied me home for the evening, stopping on the way at the supermarket to buy her favorite delicatessen chicken. The intravenous pole and infusion shocked some shoppers, but bothered the girl not at all.

If as a care-giver to the child our gut reaction indicates that something is right for that patient, then we pursue it, and try to make it happen. An attitude such as this has enabled many children to do what mattered most to them before they died. One boy bought his Christmas presents for the family on an October afternoon, the day before he died. Another slept beside the Christmas tree holding his dog just hours before he died. Another teenage boy, Jim, who was in grave condition, went to his grandfather's house daily for an hour to watch him build the kayak that Jim, himself, had dreamed of making. His family even managed to have him spend a few minutes in the kayak on the water when it was finished. Still another four-year-old boy slept between his mother and father in their big bed at home as his last wish. These are the memories that parents carry with them after the child is gone.

Many environmental aids can be utilized to make the hospital atmosphere more like home. We feel telephones are necessary beside each bed. They serve as a device for helping the child keep in touch with the family and feel reassured that he has links with his everyday world. We believe hospitalized sick children should be dressed in their own clothes, be up and about, and outdoors whenever possible. They should be treated as much like well children as is reasonable and be encouraged to attend hospital school, occupational and recreational therapy programs, and other activities. It is important to keep active until the last possible moment. Often adaptation of their activity, such as participation for short time intervals or on a limited scope, permits some normal functions to continue.

Another aspect that helps maintain normalcy are considerations for special foods. They are generally easy to obtain and mothers can be aided in their efforts to prepare familiar favorites. Withholding request for food because of the child's physical condition should be assessed carefully by the medical and nursing staff. If death is imminent, then perhaps the Spanish peanuts and bing cherries should be allowed even to the child with a bowel obstruction. This wish was granted to a little six-year-old boy the afternoon of his death. Outdoors in a reclining wheelchair, he ate cherries, delightedly spitting the pits at any nearby target. His joy will long be remembered. These are times for considerate assessment of small concerns.

Uniforms of hospital personnel are gradually being modified, since white is often a symbol of authority and pain. A colorful uniform enables the child to see the nurse as an individual more easily and think of him/her as a friend and person. This also relaxes the atmosphere. When the atmosphere is relaxed, loving, romping, and physical contact are more freely displayed. We see children spontaneously hugging the personnel and shedding their wigs, exposing bald heads without worry that they will not be accepted.

Children in the hospital need to feel that there is one safe place for them, usually their bed and room. Therefore, we attempt to have all invasive procedures or traumatic treatments done in the treatment room of the hospital ward, leaving their own rooms as a retreat—a safe environment. We encourage the parents if they wish to do so, to accompany their children through all procedures and treatments. Parents and siblings need to be actively involved in the care and to participate in every aspect possible. Children and relatives derive a sense of closeness through touch, and often participation in the care can enhance this dimension.

All health disciplines must function in a coordinated effort to meet the changing needs of the patient and family, and to ensure that things go smoothly in the hospital setting. If things do not go smoothly, it is an added frustration to an already trying situation. If a doctor decides that a patient can have a change in diet or therapy, the order should be written promptly, everyone informed, and the changes carried out quickly.

The question of segregating dying children on the hospital ward usually arises. This should be handled by considering the child's condition, and exploring the wishes of the parents and the other patients in the room. Often the dying child wishes to remain in a ward, not bothered by the noise and comforted by the friendship and association with roommates. Parents often request this, having formed a bond with the other parents and wishing to share the last hours with them and receive support from them. The other patients may express a wish to be moved or to remain in the room. Quite often, if the roommates are old enough, they relate the situation to themselves, consider their closeness with the dying child, and base their decisions on these feelings. Parents of roommates when they make their decision consider their children's emotional involvement and their coping abilities. A private room may enable the dying child and his family more freedom of expression, and certainly the desire or need for privacy should always be respected. The following experience showed us that where the dying child is situated is not as important as how people feel.

> Four teen-age girls all fighting a malignancy shared a four bed ward. It became very evident after exploratory surgery that one girl did not have long to live. The statement that children do not schedule talks about death became very clear to me as I was having a casual discussion with the dying girl the day after her surgery. I asked her if she was depressed because her colostomy had not been closed. She replied, "yes," and asked me why it was not. Her parents and surgeon assumed she would know automatically that the cancer had spread when she discovered the colostomy was still present. I replied that they were unable to close her colostomy because of the obstructing cancer. Her reaction was screaming panic. "That means that the cancer is all over my belly. That means I'm going to die. Tell me I'm not going to die. Tell me!" "I can't tell you that, Lori," I said. She screamed, "I can't die yet. Mom and dad can't take it. Grandma just died. I can't die yet. I just got my horse. I don't want to die. I'm scared." My gut reaction was, "I'm scared too, Lori." She then yelled, "Get out of here. Pull the window shades. Leave me alone." My regrets about having handled this poorly and worry that I had wounded this child were paramount as I watched her silent anger through the next day. The other three girls in the room all witnessed this outbreak. They chose to stay in the ward and all three began relating the dying girl's feelings to themselves. One girl openly accepted her own death. The second girl spoke about it as a very distant inevitability, and the third reacted with some denial and guarded optimism. As Lori broke her angry silence and began speaking freely about her feelings to her parents, aunt, and staff she gained a peaceful acceptance. On the second day after the outbreak she told me she wasn't mad any longer and that things were ok. She turned to religious meaning. An uncle priest performed a mass in the ward with all three roommates, their families, and the nursing staff participating despite religious differences. This priceless sharing had a profound effect on all present, especially the three girls. As Lori lapsed into a coma and her condition worsened, the girls requested to be moved because it was difficult for them to see their loved friend deteriorate. At this point the family also appreciated the privacy in order to very openly express their sadness when Lori died.

CHILDREN

Children's fears and feelings encompass a wide gamut of emotion and present the most difficult aspect of care. No matter what the age or condition of the children, all considerations are aimed at allowing them to be themselves. Hospitalization brings about a drastic alteration of the children's normal patterns of functioning. Staff personnel should try to keep in mind that children have a right to an open expression of all feelings, including fear, pain and anger, and that regression must be accepted and the children supported until they can maintain a more advanced level of functioning.

Children exhibit their need to control the environment in many ways; and with sensitive understanding, they can be allowed to take an active role in their own care and, within limits, make choices and decisions which keep the environment consistent. All children derive security from having consistent limits set for them. By fostering decision making and active participation in care, we do not strip children of their independence. What is achieved, in fact, is that we add a measure of respect for them as people.

It is important to alleviate discomfort and employ any measures of pain control, because physical distress enhances emotional discomfort and adds to a child's fears and concerns about the safety of his or her body. Most often the body-fears that children display in the hospital revolve around bleeding, deterioration of a body part, hurt, or death. Children must know what reactions to expect from an anticipated treatment and must feel confident that every maneuver or treatment is designed to help them. It has often been helpful to relate the treatment back to the fear; for example, statements like, "You are getting the blood transfusion to help control your bleeding," or, "You know that you are very sick but that we are doing everything possible to help you," lets children know that you are giving them truthful reality but not stripping them of the hope and optimism that are so necessary. This gives them the courage to keep fighting. Referring to children's conditions in their own terms gives them a measure of confidence in the honesty of the care giver. Usually some form of active treatment is continued, such as intravenous fluids or oxygen, to the very end so that both parents and children will feel that everything is being done to help and comfort them.

Regardless of the age, children derive a sense of closeness through touch. Touch reduces the bleakest feelings of isolation. By the tender communication that touching offers, a close bond is formed with the child, and a rapport develops that is of inestimable value in supporting the child in particular emotional needs.

Children select those with whom they feel most comfortable and those who create an environment that permits conversation and questioning. It is a good idea to consult with the parents early in the hospitalization about their attitudes toward death, what they are comfortable telling the child, and how much they wish of the staff in order to help prepare the staff member to be responsive to the child's orientation and coping games and mechanisms.

Admittedly, the hardest questions to deal with are those that ask, "Am I going to die?" Generally, children express three fundamental concerns by their behavior, by direct questions, and by questions expressed indirectly: First, am I safe? Second, will there be a trusted person to keep me from feeling helpless and alone, and to overcome pain? Third, will you make me feel all right?[2] Kubler-Ross once stated, "It doesn't really matter what you say or what you do as much as how you feel inside."[3]

Sharing our feelings and gut reactions with children and families enables them to talk more openly about their own concerns, since they realize that we, too, are human beings with similar fears. Children often understand "how" things are said better than "what" is said; they need to know that we are comfortable with the mechanisms they use in coping, be it denial, anger, or acceptance.

An example of this was a fifteen-year-old dying boy telling me of his plans to get his driving permit the next summer. His next sentence shifted to reminiscing: "Didn't we used to have fun squirting water with syringes at each other behind the nursing desk? Maybe we can do that again just one more time." Complete comfort in the listener allows children to go in whatever direction they wish. Children will generally not push the listener beyond what he or she can handle, and, of course, the child should not be pushed either.

Listening to children educates us in awareness. They are perceptive and sensitive to the feelings of others and can quickly pick up anxiety, see through dishonesty, evasiveness, undue optimism, false cheeriness, and a smile that is not reflected in a person's eyes. A child can forgive almost anything except untruthfulness.

Children share many feelings with each other in the hospital and in this way may be able to help another child cope with his or her emotions. Children in their natural beauty offer each other simple understanding and uncomplicated responses. They have a natural concern about the well-being of the other children on the ward, and a child's anxieties about his own welfare are most poignantly revealed in the question, "What happened to Susie?" When a death occurs on a ward, deception and manipulation are impossible and the true nature of the event must be honestly shared with every child. Evasion of the truth does little except to deny children a chance to talk about their fears. These hospital-wise children quickly learn to interpret the signals in the environment and the feelings of all the personnel. They learn to interpret the meaning of the missing name tag on the door, the sudden cessation of hustle, and the missing relatives. We find an opportunity to share a bond with the child by revealing our own sadness. At the same time, it also helps to add some sort of statement like, "He was a very sick child." It is also important to share with the children experiences of another child recovering from a trying or critical happening; this can give support and another measure of hope. Life is intolerable without hope, but it is important not to project one's own hope or a false hope on the child and the family.

The following true example illustrates the importance of following one's gut reactions. It concerns a death occuring on the ward and its effects on the other children.

> Peggy died very suddenly one morning at 6AM and all attempts to revive her were instituted. Another child in the room, six-year-old Carl, apparently heard and witnessed much of the efforts despite the curtains being pulled around his bed before he was removed from the room. Carl was affected with an illness that has left him severely crippled and unable to speak but for a few, barely audible words. Approximately two hours after Peggy's death as all staff members

> were involved in comforting the family, Carl began acting very bizarre and became belligerent. His movements and cries showed fear and anger, and although his mother attempted to console him on another part of the ward, he could not be comforted. Barely audible we thought we heard him utter, "Jesus." We summoned the minister who was comforting the dead child's parents, thinking he might help calm Carl. Carl continued his irrational behavior, flailing his arms and crying. Stymied and confused we brainstormed our gut reactions and felt perhaps Carl had been affected by the resuscitation efforts more than we thought. We weighed the risks of taking Carl to see the dead girl. After consulting with Carl's mother and the dead girl's parents we carried Carl into the room and put him on his mother's lap where she had seated herself close beside the dead girl. He hugged his mother's chest and crying, muttered "Does she hurt?" The minister replied, "No, Carl, she doesn't hurt anymore. She is with Jesus." He picked Carl up, carried him to his own bed and rocked him in his arms as Carl's mother and I held each other trembling, tears running down our cheeks. Carl stopped crying and looked up at us over the minister's shoulder and smiled.

PARENTS

The fears and concerns of parents take on a new dimension and can only be handled with complete honesty and warmth. If the staff stresses an open-minded policy of freedom, freedom to ask, to help, to be there, then strength and stability are built up in the parents.

We support parent groups and meetings scheduled for parents of children with cancer, and also for groups comprised of all parents on the ward. Meetings are informal and unstructured. They are focused primarily on providing a supportive environment for the expression of feelings related to the child's hospitalization, and on helping parents find ways for the family to cope with the emotional aspects of the child's illness.

Parents also need the staff to support their decisions and to maintain an optimistic and encouraging outlook without giving unwarranted reassurance or promising too much. Many times the promise is for "good times" for the child; this may vary widely from a child contentedly lying on a bed coloring a picture to a few extra sunshine days spent at home with the family. Part of our role is to help the parents understand what may constitute a realistically happy life at this stage with "good times" for the child, emphasizing the needs of the child for love, security, and indulgence without sacrificing discipline and limit-setting.

The natural reaction of parents during the time that they are hurting so badly is to pull apart from one another, not wishing to burden the other with their overwhelming emotions. We attempt to bring them together early in the hospitalization, explaining that by sharing their hurt with each other they become closer, help themselves as well as their mates, and are better able to cope with the devastation of losing their child.

Parents often state that humor and conversations about completely unrelated subjects can ease the heaviness during the trying days. They confess that they can't live with the thought of their dying child twenty-four hours a day. One father told of a meaningful conversation he had with a staff member about canoes shortly before the child died.

As death draws near, parents may worry that their child will suffer more. Honest reassurance must be given to them that their child will not suffer unduly and that you are doing and will continue to do everything possible to make him comfortable. Perhaps such comforting will be to sit on the child's bed, hold his hand, and speak softly to him throughout the long, dark night as his mother and father catch a few minutes of needed sleep.

Parents are comforted and relieved in knowing that another person also loves their child. When leaving the child, they often feel an added security in the knowledge that he will be cared for by someone who loves him. The nurse or staff member can feel far more comfortable with the child if a close bond and involvement exists with the family.

Parents worry about how they will react at the last moment. Questions such as "Will they bleed? Will they just stop breathing? How much warning will I have?" signal their fears about what death might be like. They know the last moment is coming, but they don't want it to arrive. Honestly sharing your perceptions, explaining what they might expect, and telling them, "It is going to be all right, try not to worry—we understand," reassures parents that there is no standard by which their behavior will be judged. Parents also need the closeness of those persons who matter most. The presence of a caring, sensitive, familiar person is of the utmost importance at the moment of death. This person must communicate in any way possible, "I care deeply." It is very difficult to describe the unique and beautiful bond that is created with these parents through the death of their child. The bond is nourished because all barriers and walls are down, true feelings and reactions are bared, and there is a sharing of total understanding of what the persons involved are experiencing through the shattering experience of the child's death. There are very few special moments one can share with another person in life, and being able to share the last few moments of a child's life is a rare and special privilege.

STAFF

To combine nursing skills with love, understanding, caring, and empathy is not easily or quickly achieved. Staffs working with dying children should be handpicked. They are not expected to be amateur psychiatrists, but simply people who try to understand, care deeply about children, and are kind in thoughtful ways. Such attitudes foster a comfortable environment of hope, love, acceptance, and caring. It is of extreme importance how the staff members feel about the patients. Display of emotion then becomes a natural expression.

We feel that deep involvement is the way to go. To remain emotionally isolated from the patients and families is detrimental to their care. Personal involvement and love of the child helps sustain the family throughout the long and trying ordeal. We stress involvement of several staff members with each family, for no single person can be sure of being present when needed. The questions of overinvolvement and overavailability always arise. Where does the loss of ability to give support come into play? We feel that we are able to maintain this delicate balance by keeping foremost in mind—"Whose needs are being met? Mine or the child's and his family's?"

Gratifying moments are experienced when one feels he or she has truly helped a family.

The ability to become deeply involved depends on support among staff members. They must communicate freely and have confidence in each other; they must share feelings and gut reactions and display emotion. Sharing dilutes the misery, and silent support through caring eyes can ease the pangs of hurt.

Some very beautiful bonds are created among staff members through this mutual love of a child and the understanding of what the other is experiencing in the loss. This closeness was recently experienced and cherished by three staff members as they stood at a grave site crying and holding hands during the funeral service for a child they had loved.

Going to funerals is a therapeutic way to resolve grief. It also tells many other people that there is nothing unprofessional about becoming involved. To be seated in front with the family at the funeral, and to share in their grieving is an honor brought about by the unique bond formed through involvement.

Our greatest gifts come from loving the dying child and his family, caring for them, and helping them. Thus we reach our own stages of acceptance and personal growth and are able to continue the challenge.

Our struggle is to place the human endeavor in proper perspective. From sunrise to sunset and through the dark hours, we participate in the living of a day and night. The beauty of the day culminates in the splendor of a sunset and the peace of the night. And so too with living and dying—our challenge is to bring dignity and peace to the twilight hours and into the night which follows.[4]

TECHNICAL ASPECTS OF THE NURSING CARE

Nursing care of the child with cancer is very specific and complex. It requires a high degree of skill and knowledge, not only about leukemia and solid tumors, but also about cell destruction, drug and tissue effects, and hematologic conditions and marrow depression.

Because care of the child with cancer covers such a wide range of nursing principles and considerations, the author will discuss only briefly some of the more pertinent aspects of management. Several recent articles (see Refs. 5,6), describe the nursing care in detail. In addition, Chapter 16 of this book reviews more completely treatment, chemotherapy, and drug toxicity. Most of the following nursing implications revolve around the therapy outlined in that chapter.

Observation is the key nursing principle involved in the management and care of the child. Astute observation and prompt reporting of any symptoms or suspicions can help prevent the serious consequences of overwhelming infections, bleeding, or complications of the drugs or other therapy.

Due to the abnormal cell proliferation, marrow infiltration, and marrow depression from chemotherapy, conditions such as thrombocytopenia and leukopenia occur.

THROMBOCYTOPENIA

Nursing observations pertinent to thrombocytopenia include checking the child for petechiae and ecchymotic areas, including skin, gingivial, conjunctivial, nasal, and rectal tissue, and examining for any evidence of bleeding. All urine, stool, and emesis are tested for blood. Stool softeners are routinely used to prevent any trauma to the rectal mucosa.

Nursing precautions include avoiding injections unless absolutely necessary; when they are given, pressure should be applied for several minutes after to prevent hematomas. Similarly, pressure is applied following venipunctures, not only to control bleeding, but to preserve the vessel, since the child's debilitated condition often makes veins fragile and difficult to find.

The nurse needs to know that nosebleeds may be caused not only by low platelet counts, but also by environmental conditions drying the nasal passages. Only sterile, closed-system humidity should be used as a preventive measure in the hospital. The nurse should also know that platelet administration is usually necessary when ordinary means of pressure and application of topical thrombin fail to stop bleeding. We caution strongly against packing the nasal cavity to control bleeding; it has been our observation that the bleeding continues in the nasopharynx, forming clots on the back of the packing with continued oozing. This packing may also constitute a threat of infection.

Blood pressure cuffs should not be pumped too high and padding should be placed against the skin under a tourniquet so that unwarranted petechiae do not result. Skin should not be rubbed vigorously, since this may result in small hemorrhages. Routine oral care includes brushing with a soft bristled brush to prevent trauma to tissue, while eliminating bacteria, and frequent mouth washes are encouraged.

It is necessary for the nurse to monitor the hemoglobin, hematocrit, and platelet determinations which are done routinely (the frequency dependent on the patient's condition), so that she may be aware of falling counts and relate them to the peak effects of the chemotherapy. Awareness of these measures sharpens her observations.

NEUTROPENIA

Neutropenia and depressed immunologic responses leave the child very susceptible to infection. Routine nursing procedures, such as observation of vital signs, take on a new dimension. Temperatures are monitored frequently because the fever spike indicating the infection often appears suddenly. The child is usually cultured as the rise in temperature is occurring. In conjunction with the blood cultures, the nasal pharyngeal area, throat, urine, and stool are also cultured.

Auscultation of the chest and observation of respirations are very important as the child is often unable to mount a white cell response great enough to show on x-ray. The presence of rales or any symptoms such as cyanosis, tachypnea, dyspnea, grunting, flaring, retracting, congestion, or coughing must be reported immediately.

The nurse needs to understand that any break in the integrity of the skin or mucous membrane permits the introduction of microorganisms and thus creates a potential situation for infection. The nurse must examine all body parts for any sign of infection (redness, swelling, heat, pain, discharge), tissue breakdown or potential problems, and report signs or symptoms immediately. Again, it is important to remember that the child may not be able to mount a WBC response; therefore, the usual symptoms of pus or exudate may not be present. A culture of any suspicious area is usually done. The nurse must also be aware that areas of the body where cells are dividing rapidly are the most susceptible to the drugs and tissue breakdown. The following areas must be examined: skin, nails and surrounding tissue of both hands and feet, and the conjunctiva of both upper and lower lids. Frequent examination of the mouth, including pharynx, tonsilar area, tongue sides of cavity and gingivial area should be done. Loose or decayed teeth should be looked for. Anal and genital examination includes separating the buttocks and spreading the folds. The child should be examined for warts or an increasing number of them and other skin lesions. The neurologic status should be evaluated with respect to neck stiffness and other abnormal neurologic signs.

The nurse must be aware of general symptoms such as chilling, malaise, or irritability, as these may be early clues of the presence of an infection. Monitoring the WBC count and differential help the nurse to be aware of the child's susceptibility to infection.

Some routine nursing precautions include no rectal temperatures, suppositories, or digital examinations unless absolutely necessary in order to prevent infection transference or the possible formation of lesions, fissures, or abscesses from developing in the area. Should the child develop any of these conditions, measures such as sitz baths, one-half strength peroxide and sterile water irrigations, and heat-lamp treatments may be helpful.

There are other nursing measures practiced in order to

prevent infection. For instance, paper tape is used instead of adhesive to prevent skin erosion and breakdown; butterflys are used for intravenous lines in lieu of Medicuts or Angiocaths; I.V. solutions, buretrols, or collecting flasks and tubing are changed at least every 24 hours; blood culture preparation of Betadine and alcohol are used on the skin before every venipuncture or fingerstick; microlances are used in place of #11 knife blades for finger punctures; Band-Aids are discouraged and all dressings are removed from bone marrow and lumbar puncture sites after 24 hours.

Aspirin is never used for temperature control because it interfers with platelet function. Tylenol is discouraged but used in lieu of aspirin for temperature control when the child is very uncomfortable or when the temperature is very high. Our observation has been that children are more comfortable at a steady elevated temperature (eg, 102F) than vascillating from elevated to normal temperature (eg, 102 to 99 to 102F, and so forth).

Last but not least, meticulous hair, skin, nail, and oral care are employed to reduce the threat of infection.

CHEMOTHERAPY IMPLICATIONS

General Comments. A variety of protocols are used along with various combinations of pharmacologic agents to treat childhood cancer. Because of the broad spectrum of drugs used today, a nurse must have as her guide a handbook complete with the drug actions, side effects, and toxic reactions. The following guide will briefly outline some specific nursing measures indicated with the use of certain drugs; their specific actions and complications are discussed in Chapter 16.

Nursing measures involved in chemotherapy management center around prevention of toxic reactions as well as management of complications.

Many of the drugs cause some common symptomatology such as alopecia, marrow suppression, nausea, and vomiting. Any symptom such as abdominal pain, jaundice, edema, fever, stomatitis, renal, bladder, pulmonary, and vaginal complaints should be reported promptly.

Nausea and vomiting problems may be helped by premedication with drugs, such as Emeticon, before chemotherapy is administered.

Specific Comments. Several of the chemotherapy agents are cleared by the kidneys. Strict monitoring of both I.V. and oral intake and output becomes very important to ensure proper hydration and that elimination is adequate for the specific drug effects. For example, very large amounts of fluids are administered with Cytoxan to prevent hermorrhagic cystitis. Methotrexate, especially in large doses, requires high fluid levels for renal excretion and, in addition, urine must be alkalinized often with sodium bicarbonate, to prevent the crystals from causing renal damage. Uric acid, a compound that forms as a result of cell breakdown, is controlled with allopurinol, and alkaline diuresis. This is extremely important in order to prevent renal shutdown and is usually indicated for children with markedly elevated white counts or those with enlarged organs harboring malignant cells. Nurses should check urine pH frequently and monitor changes closely. Prompt reporting of nonalkaline urine states helps the physician correct the condition immediately. Protein and glucose are also checked by Combistix, since positive determinations may be an indication of renal damage. The serum blood, urea, nitrogen, and creatinine are watched and urine creatinine clearances and protein collections are also carried out to detect nephrotoxicity.

Urine glucose checks are used to monitor the possible effects on the pancreas from L-asparginase; in addition, the presence of fever and abdominal pain may signal toxicity to abdominal organs. The nurse must be attuned to note any fever spikes and pain symptoms associated with the pancreas. Coagulation factors are also monitored, since L-asparginase has also been associated with coagulopathies. L-Asparginase administration requires additional nursing measures. Anaphalactic reactions may arise from the drug; therefore, after administration of the agent, a nurse monitors the vital signs every 15 minutes for one hour, and stays with the child constantly for the first half-hour. Benadryl and epinephrine are placed by the bedside as a precautionary measure. Other drugs requiring blood pressure monitoring are 5-azacytidine and VP 16-213.

The nurse must be aware that drugs such as Adriamycin, Daunomycin, Cytoxan (cyclophosphamide), may cause cardiac arrythmias. Depending on the dosage of the drug or the cumulative amount given, the child may be placed on a cardiac monitor during administration.

Several symptoms may occur with vincristine therapy. Jaw pain is a common complaint of children after one or two doses, and warns the nurse to be aware of other manifestations of peripheral neuropathy such as areflexia, weakness, leg pain, foot drop, and numbness and tingling of fingers. The frequency and consistency of stools are monitored closely, including observation for paralytic ileus. Electrolytes are measured to detect significant changes such as the development of hyponatremia.

Should infiltration of any of the chemotherapy agents occur during administration, we have found that the application of ice packs immediately and continuing applications frequently for 24 hours helps prevent tissue necrosis.

The nurse must understand the significance of rescue drugs such as Calcium Leucovorin or citrovorum factor. These drugs are administered to provide a salvage pathway for cell metabolism and to rescue normal cells. Failure to administer them exactly at specific rescue times could cause very serious complications for the child.

Supportive therapy throughout the course of chemotherapy and maintenance is often indicated. The nurse must familiarize herself with specific implications associated with the use of leukophoresed WBC transfusions. She must report shaking, chilling, and fever spikes and understand that treatment with corticosteroid (Solu Cortef) and antihistamine (Benadryl) administration are sometimes necessary to prevent reactions from the cells themselves, or from pyrogens released during cell collection.

Nurses monitor whole blood, packed cells, and platelet transfusions. The nurse often has to employ many I.V. aids such as hotpacks, I.V.A.C. or Harvard pumps to enable the cells to pass through the small needles that are used for the I.V. infusion. The nurse must also know the specific filter, mini- or maxidrip size used for each product, and last but not least, adhere to the usual blood and blood product administration precautions.

Supportive therapy also includes a long list of antibiotics to combat infections and sepsis. Each drug has specific requirements for dilution, mixing, administration, and time viability. Close observation is also necessary for any side effects of these drugs.

Emotional support and understanding of the child and his parents throughout treatment and chemotherapy is vital. Children fear the drugs, the support products, and procedures. Physical discomfort also adds to their fears. Parents and children should be given complete information regarding their condition and the purpose and side effects of the various drugs and therapies since this decreases their apprehension. Additionally, they should be taught to report any sign, symptom, or change in their condition. They may then watch their blood counts with interest and derive a sense of satisfaction if they begin to rise. The nurse's greatest role is to assist the child and the family through the emotional and physical trials of treatment with compassion, love, and understanding.

From this brief outline, the complex nature of the care involved when a child is undergoing treatment for cancer becomes obvious. Additionally, protocols for chemotherapy are constantly changing, adding to the nurse's task of attempting to give the most up-to-date care. Thus, all aspects of nursing knowledge and skill are continually challenged in an effort to maintain optimal care for the child with cancer.

REFERENCES

1. Petrillo M, Sanger S: Emotional Care of Hospitalized Children. Philadelphia, Lippincott, 1972, p 205
2. Green M: Care of the dying child. Pediatr 40:3, 1967
3. Kübler-Ross E: How you can help the dying. In Wintz JA: Interview in St. Anthony Messenger

4. Krant M: In the context of dying. In Shoenberg B et al (eds): Psychosocial Aspects of Terminal Care. New York, Columbia Univ Press, 1972, p 209
5. Keaveny ME et al: Creative nursing care for acute leukemia. Nursing 73:19, 1973
6. Lunceford JL: Leukemia. Disease process, chemotherapeutic approach, and nursing care. Nurs Clin North Am 2:635, 1967

BIBLIOGRAPHY

Barckley V: Families facing cancer. Cancer News. American Cancer Society Publication, Spring/Summer 1970

Bright F, France ML: The nurse and the terminally ill child. Nurs Outlook 15:39, 1967

Green T: Administration of Cancer Chemotherapeutic Agents. A Manual for the Pediatric Housestaff and Nursing Staff. North Carolina Memorial Hospital, Chapel Hill, North Carolina

Hardgrove CB, Dawson RB: Parents and Children in the Hospital: The Family's Role in Pediatrics. Boston, Little, Brown, 1972

Lunceford JL: Leukemia. Disease process, chemotherapeutic approach, and nursing care. Nurs Clin North Am 2:635, 1967

Northrup FC: The dying child. Am J Nurs 74:1066, 1974

Prattes OR: Helping the family face an impending death. Nursing 73:1, 1973

Kübler-Ross E: Questions and Answers on Death and Dying. New York, Collier, 1974

Vernick J, Karon M: Who's afraid of death on a leukemia ward? Am J Dis Child 109:393, 1965

In this chapter the author shows the importance of a positive relationship between the child as patient and the adult members of the clinic staff.

19

THE NATURE OF THE CHILD'S INTERACTIONS WITH ADULTS IN THE CLINIC*

Romana Urueta

Contacts with adults elicit mixed reactions from many children. In the child's past, adults have been associated with both positive and negative events. An example of this might be a child's relationship to a teacher. The teacher may praise a child for the good work he has done (a positive aspect), but she also may discipline him for the disturbance he has created (a negative aspect). Thus, when a child meets a new adult labeled "teacher," the reactions to that adult will be strongly influenced by his past experience with other adults having the same title.

Because the child's past interactions with adults have been both positive and negative, the child approaches each adult stranger with some apprehension. According to a study done by McCoy and Ziegler, the responses an adult makes may ac-

*Supported in part by Faculty Research Facilitation Grant (USPHS IR-NV 00475-01).

tivate a variety of responses from the child.[1] Of the possible responses to an adult stranger, the one which the child chooses to make is apparently determined by a very complex, and as yet not completely understood, process. McCoy and Ziegler, however, made the assumption that the strength of each of these response tendencies is affected by the general quality of the relationship existing between the child and the adult. The adult stranger, then, may become a positive or a negative person for the child.

The general quality of the relationship between the two is basically the responsibility of the adult. If the relationship is to develop to the point where the adult becomes a positive person in the child's eyes, the adult must continuously strive to be warm, helpful, and responsive to the child's needs regardless of the child's behavior.

If the goal of achieving a good relationship is pursued, time becomes extremely important. It is essential that the health care staff get to know both the child and the parents as quickly as possible. Too frequently the staff focuses on the child to the exclusion of the parents. But the parents are very significant people for the establishment of a desirable relationship between the child and the staff member, since the parents can influence the child's first reactions to the new adult. In addition, parents—especially the mother—have seen the child in health, illness, and convalescence; that is, deviating from the norm both bodily and mentally, and returning once more to it. Thus, in unfamiliar settings or situations, the parent becomes a highly valuable resource person for the health professional.

When children are under stress they frequently will use ritualized behaviors to help them cope with the event. This type of behavior is frequently displayed by children in the outpatient clinic; the young ones may keep a Kleenex covering their eyes during a treatment; others ask for their mothers' direct contact to massage legs or back; others may ask direct questions of parents or health agents; and others may express their feelings: "I never get use to the needles," "put it in my right hand," "Mom, it hurts," "perhaps today Dr. T. will miss the vein," "leave me alone," "doctor tell Mom, about my sports."

Preadolescents and adolescents are less likely to communicate their feelings, concerns, and attitudes than are the younger children. There is a tendency to exclude adults from their private world. They keep their feelings and thoughts to themselves, a normal development, since this is a part of the process of the child's establishing control of his developing ego. In view of this, the adult must curb this tendency to encourage the venting of feelings related to the diagnosis, because the client-child may choose not to share these feelings.

The experience of children in the outpatient clinic described below show the importance of the relationships among parents, children, and health care personnel.

> Peter, a red-haired adolescent, came to the clinic feeling tired and listless. His appetite was poor and he had a fever. He had been unable to attend school for four days. The medical laboratory assessment revealed that he was going through a relapse. The physician had the responsibility of conveying this news to the patient. The approach the physician used was one of openness and directness coupled with warmth and understanding. The mother's actions were crucial to the boy's acceptance of what he was being told. In this particular example, the response of the nurse was that of silence.
>
> The physician began by saying, "I have bad news for you, Peter. It means you are to be hospitalized in order to get some medications. The effect of these medications requires close medical supervision." Then he directed a question to Peter's mother about when Peter could be hospitalized. Peter had kept his composure up to that point. His face then turned so red that the freckles disappeared. His long, well-formed fingers turned from pale to bluish and his whole body started to shake. Although Peter's mother was unable to talk, she embraced her son. Peter turned over and buried his face in the pillow. When the nurse gave him some Kleenex, he rejected them, throwing them on the floor. The physician's warmth was present in the tone of his voice and when he rubbed Peter's legs while giving the news; his helpfulness was also apparent when he explained clearly the physical progress of the disease and the medical plan.

There are some patients who, in spite of pain and discouragement, react at times with surprising maturity for their years. They seem able to accept the limitations of their disease and to relate to the health professionals as friends who are trying to help them. Then again they may respond as miserable children who demand a mother's comforting presence as well as the nurses' professional support. Nancy, a slender thirteen-year-old, was an example of such a patient.

> During the time that Nancy was seen at the clinic, her behavior alternated between positive and negative tendencies. There were days when Nancy's responses and verbal expressions to the nurse related to regular activities: "I wonder if my white dress will fit now that I've gained weight. I'd like to wear it to my brother's confirmation on Sunday." "I've been playing with my brothers and they're really rough but I get back at them."
>
> At other times Nancy expressed both concern about and interest in her medical treatment: "Here he comes [referring to the doctor]; I wonder which vein he'll use this time. Do you think he'll miss? He's pretty good. He told me the other time that I'm in remission now." When the medication was injected into her spinal cord, Nancy lost her composure and expressed her pain openly. She cried loudly and was restless for about fifteen minutes. She needed her mother to comfort her. This need was expressed openly, too. "That pain in my back; rub my leg, Mom. No, not there, up here. Oh Mom, it hurts so much. Can't you do something?" At this point she looked with tearful eyes to the nurse and asked, "When do I get the pain reliever medication?" Nancy reached for the container to vomit and said, "I hurt all over. Oh, my head, my head!"
>
> On another occassion, Nancy had remained very still in an awkward position, something that was very helpful to the attending physician. Both the doctor and the nurse praised her for helping them in this way.
>
> That Nancy viewed the members of the health care team positively was shown by her asking the nurse to rub her legs to help ease the pain from the medication. Another time she brought the nurse a "God's Eye," a frame of yarn she had made. She smiled and called the nurse by her first name.

In all contacts with patients, health care personnel in the outpatient clinic use simple but proper terminology (eg, lymphatic leukemia, platelet count). They are careful to explain to the patients, in terms they can understand, exactly what is being done ("I'm going to swab your arm before I give this injection. It may feel a little cool.") and how the child's behavior helps ("Your sitting up like that really helps me.") or how it could help ("If you don't move when I insert the needle, it will hurt less.").

These examples are illustrative of the attempts of the health care professionals to establish and maintain warm relationships with the patients in order that they may be viewed positively by the patients as people who care about them and want to help them. If this occurs, then the care agent can exert a greater influence on the patient and that could help the patient cope with the disease.

Good relationships between health care professionals and patients will be established if the professionals become truly aware of the patient. If, as one writer has stated, they can identify with his hopes, dreams, fears, and his longings.

REFERENCE

1. McCoy N, Ziegler E: Social reinforcer effectiveness as a function of the relationship between child and adult. J. Pers Soc Psy 1:604, 1965

During the dying process certain body changes occur of which the child with cancer is aware. This chapter reports the impact on the child of the loss of hair which occurs early in the treatment. The effect of such a change suggests the significance of more extensive alterations that will occur later.

20

HEALTH CARE APPROACHES TO HAIR LOSS IN CHILDREN WITH CANCER

Janice M. Anderson

A recent study of current practices of health care for leukemic children in the Netherlands, Great Britain, and the United States suggests that the health care systems of those two European nations give more attention to the importance of the hair loss usually expected during the course of leukemia and its treatment than do the health care systems of the United States.[1] In the Netherlands, health care focuses on maintaining the patient's usual body image and quality of life during the course of treatment. The health care system in Great Britain recognizes the disruptive body changes, such as loss of head hair, as important to patients. In the United States, less importance is attached to the loss of head hair. According to one Dutch person, the patient might be discharged from the hospital with his disease under control, but experiencing significant body change resulting from his treatment.

The relationship of body image to the concept of self is discussed by several authors. Rosen et al[2] report that satisfaction with body image and satisfaction with self-concept are positively related and that their measurement can be refined if the subjective importance of component aspects is given consideration.

Higgins[3] reports two main concepts that are complementary: first, that the body surface serves as a boundary, and secondly, that the body surface serves as a plane of contact. According to Fisher,[4] the individual's manner of distributing attention to his body is intimately related to the traits, inner conflicts, and personality defenses characterizing him.

The fact that age and/or body awareness can be factors in one's concept of his body image is alluded to by several authors. Easson[5] suggests that normally the body image is well established before the age of three, perhaps by the end of the first year. The results of Buck's[6] study in relationship to consciousness seem to suggest that individuals have a relatively enduring conception of their body image. This conception, he states, serves as a frame of reference for a variety of situations. Pasqua and Beltrani[7] report personality studies in an eight-year-old subject with total alopecia areata of two years' standing. Investigation of the patient's family and school background showed a close relationship between his lack of adaptation and the alopecia.

It could be concluded that hair might be an important aspect of one's body image. Gellert et al[8] did a study to determine factors associated with body perception in order to explore children's awareness of their bodily appearance. They found that when head portions of the figures were visible, self-recognition was perfect from the anterior view and nearly so from side views. Self-recognition from the back view improved with age. They stated that hair style was one of the cues that might be utilized to guide the subject's awareness.

Nash[9] reported on a study in which recognition of the upper one-half of the head seemed to have been determined more by hair cues than by eye cues. He stated that the head and face are regions in which the experience of selfhood is frequently said to be most localized. This is perhaps associated, Nash continued, with the fact that interpersonal relations are so often of a face-to-face nature.

Plutchnik, Weiner, and Conte's[10] studies included two relevant findings. The first was that body discomforts and body worries are highly correlated, and the second was that bodily worries and discomforts are not related to age per se, but reflect special life circumstances. The data showed that the head is an area of a good deal of discomfort for nine of eleven groups. The importance of hair to the body image was noted in several ways: hair style is a cue to self-recognition, hair is an area of little discomfort for six of eleven groups, and recognition of the upper one-half of one's head is determined more by hair cues than by eye cues.

Several studies have been done to assess the interruption and changes in hair growth. Hurley[11] reported that x-irradiation and various cytotoxic drugs are responsible for hair loss. According to Counce[12] this reversible hair loss results from metals and cancer therapeutics. As Rook[13] stated, the alopecia resulting from use of antimitotic drugs in the treatment of neoplastic disease is easily overlooked. Patients show differing reactions to this hair loss. For some patients, as shown by Whitelaw et al[14], the alopecia side effect of cancer therapy is extremely upsetting, even though they had been warned in advance about its possible occurrence. Conversely, others seem less disturbed and adjust to the use of wigs and kerchiefs. It appears then, that hair loss has an effect upon one's emotions, but this effect is not yet clearly delineated.

In the United States, medicine focuses on the basic disease process, as evidenced in many medical reports.[15–20] The pharmocologic focus is on the desired action of drugs.[21–26] Very little has been written documenting the side effects, in terms of body changes and of life, which the leukemic child must endure during the course of his disease and its treatment.

In the Netherlands, for example, it is made clear to patients that body changes such as hair loss will occur. According to Frau Molendijk, district nurse supervisor, Rotterdamsch Radio-Therapeutisch Institute, Dutch nurses encourage these patients who lose head hair to maintain their body integrity by providing them with a wig. Many of these patients choose wigs of their own hair color and hair style. Regular hair clinics are held which deal with concerns such as hair growth and scalp care during this time of alopecia. It seems that, in thus attending to the value of head hair and recognizing the importance of body changes to the individual, the patient's care is approached from a holistic perspective.

In a recent study, pertinent data relative to the patient's perception of hair loss was revealed. The investigator had identified certain areas to be covered during each interview for this study. Among these were the financial—that is, how much will it cost to look the way I want to; the social—how do I seem to others; the emotional—how do I feel about myself; the physical—how do I take care of my scalp. If the subject did not mention an area voluntarily, he was asked directly whether that particular factor was relevant to his experience.

For example, one young boy in the Netherlands indicated that his life style had changed. He was not doing as much swimming, and he was doing "more standing in front of the mirror to hide this space of no (head) hair."

The content analysis revealed three variables related to the perception of hair loss: prior expectations, current control, and present feelings. The variable of "prior expectation" includes both the expectation that the hair loss would occur, and the complete lack of any such expectation. Subjects from the Netherlands tended to experience the hair loss in accordance with their expectations. For subjects from Great Britain or the United States[27] this was not true.

The variable of "current control" of hair loss included "control" (the subject describes self as acting upon, contradicting, or manipulating activities and materials related to dealing with the hair loss) and lack of control (the subject describes self as being acted upon, being manipulated or controlled by activities and materials related to the hair loss). Subjects from the Netherlands tended to describe current control; those from the United States tended to describe lack of current control; and those from Great Britain tended to describe both control and lack of control.[28]

The variable of "present feelings" regarding hair loss included negative feelings or neutral feelings. Positive feelings were not included. Subjects from the Netherlands, tended to express neutral feelings regarding hair loss; those from the United States, negative feelings; and those from Great Britain both negative and neutral feelings.

In the Netherlands the feelings about a child's hair loss due to therapy are dealt with in a positive way. Frau Molendijk, by way of a comparison of treatment in the United States and the Netherlands, states that, "You Americans treat the patient's cancer and leave him on the door steps of the hospital, discharged to go home dealing with body changes from the cancer treatment, being without hair." Nursing must show an interest in these body changes and provide appropriate alternatives for the patient.

There is a lack of nursing literature which describes and documents the responses of patients to their body changes. At present little is known about how children perceive their body changes due to cancer therapy. There is a need to know at what stages these changes become manifest, how long they persist, and how they affect the patient, his family, and his peers. Nursing research of these questions could contribute much. Data derived from such research would be an invaluable asset for health care professionals in preparing patients to understand their illness and its treatment. In a recent study, the following recommendations were made by parents about their child's hair loss: (1) Parents should be helped to understand certain aspects of hair loss, (2) should be informed of the possible need for a wig, and (3) should be assured that in time hair will grow again.

Children's attitudes are largely dependent on their parents' attitude. Children need to know that the hair loss does not affect the parents' love. Parents must show understanding and patience, and share with the children the idea that "this too will pass."

The child should make the decision whether to wear a wig or not.

Girls of about 12 years of age are usually self-conscious about their hair, and fear that people will ridicule them because of their hair loss. If they have always had long hair, this is especially true. Thus it is wise to provide wigs for these girls.

If parents know where children's wigs may be obtained, it would be helpful to give this information to a clinic for others to check into. If some have wigs that are no longer needed, these could be made available for purchase by other parents in similar circumstances.

Attending to the patient's symptoms of the disease and its treatment will facilitate finding alternatives for improving the patient's quality of life during the course of therapy.

It is possible that current practices in other health care systems, such as in the Netherlands, will influence positively current practice in the United States. The question of which variables regarding symptoms of therapy are left unattended remains a challenge. American nurses might well consider whether Frau Molendijk's indictment is still valid. An approach to cancer therapy which includes focusing on the body changes and what they mean to the patient appears to be important to the patient's quality of life.

REFERENCES

1. Anderson Janice M: Patient perception of hair loss: An exploratory cross-cultural study. Master's thesis, University of Minnesota, School of Nursing, 1975
2. Rosen GM et al: Relationship of body image to self concept. J Consult Clin Psy 32: 100, 1968
3. Higgins R: The perception of the body surface. Br J Med Psychol 36: 261, 1963
4. Fisher S: Body attention patterns and personality defenses. Psychol Monogr 80: 9: 1, 1966
5. Easson WM: Body image and self image in children. Arch Gen Psychiat 4: 619, 1961
6. Buck LA, Barden M: Body image scores and varieties of consciousness. J Pers Asses 35: 309, 1971
7. Pasqua MC, Beltrani G: Personality studies and attempted psychological treatment in a case of total alopecia areata. G Ital Dermatol 46: 210, 1971

8. Gellert E et al: Children's awareness of their bodily appearance. Genet Psychol Monogr 79: 297, 1971
9. Nash H: Recognition of body surface regions. Genet Psychol Monogr 79: 297, 1969
10. Plutchnik R, Weiner MB, Conte H: Studies of the body image: I. Body worries and body discomforts. J Gerontol 26: 344, 1971
11. Hurley HJ: Hair growth and alopecia with special references to children. Penn Med J 64: 371, 1967
12. Counce JH, Wise LJ, Burks JW: Hair loss: Some current concepts. Louisiana State Med Soc J 114: 233, 1962
13. Rook A: Some chemical influences on hair growth and pigmentation. Br J Derm 77: 115, 1965
14. Whitelaw, D.M. et al: Vincristine in the treatment of neoplastic disease. Can Med Assoc J 90: 1385
15. Donnenberg A et al: Evaluation of Intravenous Allopurinol (NSC-1390) in Pediatric Neoplasia. Cancer Chemother Rep 58: 737, 1974
16. Geiser CF et al: Adverse Effects of Intratheral Methotrexate in Children with Acute Leukemia in Remission. Blood 45: 189, 1975
17. Humphrey B, Fernbach DJ, Razek AA et al: Evaluation of Daunorubicin (NSC-82151) and Methotrexate (NSC-740) in combination as a remission maintenance regimen in the treatment of Acute Leukemia. Cancer Chemother Rep 59: 395, 1975
18. Price RA, Jameson PA: The Central Nervous System in Childhood Leukemia. III Subacute Leukoencephalopathy. Cancer 35: 306, 1975
19. Sullivan MP, Humphrey GB, Vietti TJ, Haggard ME, Lee E: Superiority of Conventional Intrathical Metholrexate Therapy with Maintenance over intensive intrathical Methotrexate Therapy. Unmaintained, or radiotherapy (2000-2500 Radio tumor dose) in Treatment of Meningeal Leukemia. Cancer 35: 1066, 1975
20. Wehinger JS et al: Prophylactic central nervous system therapy with cranial irradiation and intratheral metholrexate in acute lymphoblastic leukemia of Childhood. Strathlentherapic 148: 590, 1974
21. Cope, L: Adrenal Steroids and Disease. London, Pitman Medical, 1972, pp 488–489
22. Evam AE: Vincristine in the treatment of Children with Acute Leukemia. Cancer Chemother Rep 52: 469, 1968
23. Haggard Mary Ellen: Vincristine (NSC-67574) Therapy for Acute Leukemia in Children. Cancer Chemother 52: 477, 1968
24. Holton CP, Burrington JD, Hatch EJ: A Multiple Chemotherapeutic Approach to the Management of Hepatoblastoma. A Preliminary Report. Cancer 35: 1033, 1975.
25. Sutow Wataru W: Vincristine (NSC-67574) Therapy for Malignant Solid Tumors in Children (Except Welmi Tumor). Cancer Chemother 52: 485, 1968

26. Pratt CB, James David HJ, Holton CP, Pinkel D: Combination Therapy Including Vincristine (NSC-67574) for Malignant Solid Tumors in Children. Cancer Chemother Rep 52: 489, 1968.
27. Anderson JM: Patient Perception of Hair Loss
28. Anderson JM: Unpublished study, University of Minneapolis, School of Nursing, August 1975.

PART V

THEORETICAL CONSIDERATIONS FOR HEALTH PROFESSIONALS

This writer discusses a preliminary model for home care of the dying as an extension of hospital services.

21

A MODEL FOR CARE OF THE DYING AT HOME*

Evelyn Peterson

In the health care services—a large, widely diversified professionally-controlled system,—changes come about through what clients want from health care professionals and through what health care professionals themselves want to give. The following chapter addresses itself to an experiment in delivering home care to dying leukemic children carried out at the University of Minnesota School of Nursing. In this project faculty work with parents who have dying children and wish to have their children at home during the last few weeks or days of their lives—often through the dying process itself.

Out of this still limited experience with children dying at home, the writer proposes a model for giving care to persons who are dying or critically ill and wish to be cared for in the home. A model is a conceptual tool developed to organize

*Supported in part by Faculty Research Facilitation Grant (USPHS IR02-NU 00475-01).

ideas about a subject, in this case, the care of dying children or adults who want to return to their homes after hospitalization. It will attempt to take into account the extreme variability and complexity of situations having to do with patients going home still quite ill. The model speaks only to the care of dying persons who wish to return to their homes after a period of hospitalization. The model attempts to establish a means by which one worker, the professional nurse, can take primary responsibility for coordinating the patient's care.

The project from which the model developed had the following overall objectives: one, identification of the feasibility and desirability of the home as an alternative care facility for the terminally ill; and two, evaluation of the role of the professional nurse as the primary care giver and liaison agent in assisting the patient, family, and physician during the experience. Individual faculty members, because of personal interest, volunteered to work with children in the terminal phase of leukemia who had been or were to be discharged from the hospital and who were to be cared for by their parents in the home. The faculty met regularly to support each other, and to receive support from the originator of the project, Ida Martinson, and from various physicians from the University of Minnesota School of Medicine faculty.

The writer was a participant in the seminar in a research capacity. The research goal was to collect data from this experience to construct a viable model which could serve for a larger demonstration. The writer also served as a resource person to faculty in recording their work with the parents and the sick child. This recording experience was to serve as an introduction to methods of recording and analyzing large amounts of descriptive data, and as a beginning of an understanding of field work methodology. As individual members of the faculty made visits to the homes to aid parents with problems that arose in the home care of their dying child, recordings of the visits were made and shared. It was from this data that the following model, and the rationale supporting it, were formed.

Another contributor to the seminar was the nurse who headed the Home Care Program at the University of Minnesota Hospitals. At this hospital there had been an interest by nursing management and by individual nurses in some type of follow-up care for patients who left the hospital still acutely ill. Thus while data was limited, it was collected from three sources or perspectives: the parents and sometimes the ill child, the faculty person caring for the child in the home, and the home care department of the university hospital.

From the data collected on interactions with parents in care of the sick child, some problems have been identified which are crucial to the success of the new approach to care proposed here. As an example, parents find that the first days, and particularly the first day, at home with the sick child are "almost overwhelming." This is the time during which they feel most helpless and in need of help. During this crucial period ready access to the nurse was most important. In the project reported here, the faculty member who was responsible for the patient care received the most calls for help during this period. This occurred even when preparation for caring for the child had been given parents by the hospital nursing staff.

These first days at home constitute a small crisis within a larger, longer crisis period for the family. Our data indicate that parents faced problems for which they had not developed coping mechanisms—fortunately, having a child die of leukemia is rarely an experience families must cope with more than once in their lifetime. During these first days at home, the parent was in a state of great emotional turmoil over the child's condition and had difficulty taking action to solve problems without some outside support. For example, there were complicated problems that arose from the prescribed medical care, possibly entailing such technological features as giving injections for pain. Nursing support at this time was crucial to parents so they could reestablish their equilibrium and care for their child. As one parent said to the nurse about this period, "the most important value that we got of your being available was that you were." The model proposed here attempts to meet this expression of need.

One type of referral service that has been attempted in many urban communities in the United States by health care services is the hospital referral either to public health agencies or visiting nurse associations. There have been difficulties with such referral programs. One problem has been the time lag in getting referral information from the hospital to the community nurse. There are reasons for this. One is the complicated effort of getting a form through the bureaucracies of both the hospital and the agency. For example, there is the effort of processing a patient's discharge which requires obtaining the signatures of all the professionals involved in the care. Even the postal service is not as efficient as one would like in getting mail from one section of the city to another, and most referral forms are mailed.

Another problem with immediate referral to community agencies for nursing care of acutely ill patients is that of keeping the community nurses expert in all the new treatments. When one thinks of the quickly changing, complicated, and varied types of treatments utilized for acutely ill patients in hospitals, one can understand why the nurse in a community agency may not be able to constantly update her expertise in all types of acute care. Granted the treatments lessen when the patient goes home, but for the first few days or weeks at home there is a carry-over of the hospital-originated treatments, some of which remain in force for as long as the patient lives. Because of the inherent difficulty of setting up a system which would allow for immediate transmission of all chart information to the nurse in the community and of constantly updating her expertise in acute-illness care, the problem of home care for the critically ill and dying might be better solved by having a nurse from the hospital continue the care in the home for a period of two to three weeks. There would be no break in the institutional accountability for care during the crucial first days in the home. The hospital nurse would know and have access to much of the information necessary to care for the patient. She also has ready access to persons who have contributed to the care of the patient while in the hospital.

Logically, the professional nurse in the hospital could reach out into the community to give care to the client in the first days or weeks at home and, at the same time, communication could begin with an appropriate agency in the community to take over the support of the family and care of the patient. The patient's condition may stabilize and his care require less intense supervision, making it easier for community nurses to handle. If the patient's condition deteriorates, the care responsibility could be returned to the hospital nurse or the patient could return to the hospital. The hospital nurse, because of her work with the patient in the community, would have an understanding of what happened in the home, facilitating nursing care in the hospital. This continuity of care would give comfort to the patient.

What then are the impediments to extending hospital nursing care to patients in the community for a short period of time?

In the process of preparing even comparatively well patients for discharge from the hospital, many problem arise. In planning for the discharge of dying persons to return to their homes, these problems are magnified. Intensive planning for home care has not been given top priority in the hospital hierarchy of work with patients. However, there is now an attempt to integrate such planning into patient care, beginning with admission to the hospital, since such has been mandated by the Federal law covering Professional Standards and Review Organizations.

Article after article in health care literature states that no person should leave the hospital without discharge planning. All the rhetoric and planning has been concerned with persons who are able to eventually care for themselves once they have returned home. What to do about dying patients who return home, still requiring care has not been attended to. To begin such a service as discharge planning in as complex an organization as the hospital is fraught with problems. The hospital, as it was historically set up to function and still continues to function, cares for persons during acute illness or acute phases of an illness. It has not been programmed for planning home care. That is not to say that such planning has not occurred, but it has been sporadic and incidental to the primary goal of the hospital which is the treatment of conditions which are nondeferrable.

Picture the leukemic child in the hospital: critically ill and in great pain, receiving new drugs which necessitate constant monitoring by the nursing staff, with parents who are upset and needing both information about their child and physical and emotional support themselves from the nursing staff. Meeting these needs, however, is only a portion of the nurse's work. She is also responsible for juggling all the other necessary care activities, such as physician's visits, laboratory and x-ray examinations, occupational therapy, in short, all the people and forces which ebb and flow around critically ill patients. Additionally, the work of the nurse requires a special alertness to problems which demand immediate attention. There is little tolerance for error or ambiguity in the care of acutely ill patients, and so the work carries heavy moral and professional responsibility.

Families of patients who wish to die at home may not be ready to make the intensive preparations home care requires while their relative is still in the hospital. Family members are husbanding their emotional and physical energies in supporting the dying person and contending with the immediate, complicated hospital world. They are little able to attend to new learning, since they are absorbed with the care the child is receiving and with their feelings about what is happening to them. Hospital equipment is usually more sophisticated and available than that which will be in the home, and families may become frustrated in this knowledge. The hospital experience is stressful and learning theorists tell us that learning does not take place under excessively stressful situations. So what can be done? Extension of hospital services outside the hospital for the first crucial days when the patient goes home should be considered.

Why is the hospital suggested as the agency to extend home care services for critically ill patients into the community? One, the hospital is already recognized in communities as the major center for the delivery of health care, since hospitals employ a large number of health professionals and have the instrumentalities needed to support professionals in their work. Employed by the hospital are nurses most knowledgeable of the newest and often experimental treatments which critically ill patients receive. It is in the hospital environment that new and unusual medical technology is first introduced. Here nursing personnel are constantly being oriented to new medical technology which sets some of the parameters for nursing care. However, the nurse who works in home care or public health agencies learns of these treatments later—after they have been tested. In the case of leukemic children involved in the project reported here, the hospital nurses were the most knowledgeable of new treatments and medications. Because the critically ill leukemic child was usually in the midst of or finishing such treatments when he/she went home, the nursing faculty who worked with the children utilized the hospital nursing staff as resource persons in planning for care at home. Also, as interminable articles on continuity of nursing care have chronicled, the follow-through from the hospital to the community either by a primary nurse or by some institutional means is emotionally supportive to the patients and families.

Hospitals are accustomed to intramural transfer of patients, that is, from intensive care to regular hospital care to ambulatory care; extending such service to the home is not an introduction of a new concept but simply its extension. Also the mechanism for record transfers is also part of hospital routine. Historically, interest in care of patients outside the hospital has been the interest of professional nurses. There have always been nursing professionals who have been employed in the care of patients in the home. The hospital nurses concerned with hospital care of the leukemic children in this study had for many years, out of personal interest and compassion, followed the progress of children who had left their hospital wards. They made telephone calls, many of which were long-distance calls, visited homes, and always welcomed parents when they returned to the ward "just to talk about what had happened to them."

Professional nurses employed in hospitals are programmed to 24-hour responsibility and activities concerned with patient care. In fact, they are the only professional in the hospital carrying out that responsibility. All other professionals interact with patients and families on a daily, but sporadic basis. The hospital itself functions to provide 24-hour access to its services. Its doors and switchboard do not close as public health and visiting nurses' associations do. The families who have critically ill persons at home need the assurance of such a back-up agency or a specified professional, because problems in care can arise at any hour of the day or night. At one time the "old family physician" filled this role, but he no longer exists as such. In our project, the faculty person who became the "family" nurse functioned in this capacity. This is possible for one or two cases at infrequent intervals, but is physically exhausting if it continues over an extended period of time when one must also function in another full-time position. Such responsibility should be institutionalized so that it becomes shared. The hospital seems the most appropriate agency to provide services to families caring for very ill persons at home.

Can the hospital do it? Is it feasible? There are certain characteristics of a hospital which conspire to make the hospital the agency most capable of managing such a task. Hospitals have the support system—the facilities, equipment, supplies and medicines—which are necessary to the professional working in the community. At this time, no other community agency can supply such support without a costly expansion of its services and duplication of what is already available through the hospital. During the care for one of the leukemic children in this study, the nurse was called in the middle of the night by parents who were badly frightened because their child's jaw had locked. The nurse gave the parents information of possible dangers to the child and directions on what to do. Then she told the parents that if the jaw did not relax the child would need to be taken to the hospital where the treatment of last resort was available—giving of an anesthesia. Fortunately, in this case, the child's jaw did relax. But because the hospital has the equipment and experienced staff capable of giving sophisticated care twenty-four hours a day, it will remain the focus for health care delivery.

The logistics of such an extended service, maybe a problem for hospitals but with hospital management increasingly using centralized, computerized staffing, the goal of staffing for extramural care becomes more attainable. Use of the more advanced techniques of record-keeping and transference makes one think that the problem is not insurmountable. One conundrum for hospital management is how to finance such a service. The method should be one compatible with present methods of patient-care financing.

While documentation is needed on the comparative costs of home versus hospital care, the emphasis on the humanitarian aspects of patient care should not be lost. The humanitarian approach is not necessarily the most economical. If the financers of health care lose sight of the emotional needs of patients and their families, the professional nurse must help to keep the humanitarian approach to care in constant focus. While the answer must come from a combination of both factors, health care service must have as its paramount aim satisfaction of the patient's needs.

A model for persons dying in their homes under care of their families is proposed. The model was suggested by experiences of professional nurses supporting parents of children dying of leukemia who were taken home to be cared for during the last days and months of their lives. The hospital with all its services and facilities, its twenty-four-hour functioning, and its ready access to professional expertise is suggested as the agency of immediate help for such families. The extramural extension of nursing care to such patients and families is probably logistically and economically possible. But more important in human terms, it gives continuous support and help to families in great need. The professional nurses who have begun the care for the patient and support of the family during the crisis period in the hospital would extend the same services for the first crucial days at home, since it is at this time that the family and dying person are most in need of the consistent, expert, and humane relationship provided by a caring professional.

The literature dealing with the child's general knowledge of death as well as his reactions to his impending death is reviewed by this author. The inadequacy of our knowledge in these areas is readily apparent.

22

CHILDREN'S CONCEPTS OF DEATH

Delores M. Krause

What is the child's concept of death? What is meant when an author states that he is writing about a child's understanding of death? Is the child's cognitive, rational understanding of death being discussed? His reaction to the death of another person? The child's ability to handle his own dying? Is the writer approaching the subject from the position of a person reacting to the death of a child? Or is the writer looking at the child's fears and anxieties as they relate to his own death and/or serious illness?

There are many ways to approach the study of a child's perception of death. Each focuses on a different aspect of the problem; each is valid in its own area of concern; each adds to our understanding of the topic. Unfortunately, too frequently persons who have written about the phenomenon of death have failed to specify their approach. Therefore, the reader who wants to study a child's concerns about death must determine the approach the writer utilized and how it was—or could be—related to children.

This chapter will first deal with the child's understanding of death as a general concept. The second section will discuss the child's reaction to his own dying and his knowledge of that event. The implications for health care personnel of the child's view of death will be treated in the third section.

GENERAL CONCEPTS

What do children understand about death? In this area, as in so many others, the behavior of adults indicates that they believe they know what children understand. The assumption seems to be that young children must not be confronted with the reality of death. And so, when someone the child knows dies, the child frequently is told the person has taken a long trip or that he has gone away. If a member of the family dies, the young child is quickly sent off to the home of a relative where he usually stays until the funeral is past and things "return to normal." As Harrison et al point out, "American culture seems involved in a conspiracy to remove death from conscious awareness."[1]

Although there is as yet no true body of literature concerned with the child and death, the number of publications has increased markedly in recent years. It is surprising, therefore, that no new investigations of children's beliefs concerning death have been done. In fact, only two studies treating a child's understanding of death were found; one was done in Hungary in 1948, the other in England in 1940. Not available to this writer were two studies conducted earlier by the authors of the studies reviewed in this section. Maria Nagy, well known for her 1948 article "The child's theories concerning death," referred in that article to her earlier (1936) book which apparently was never translated from the original Hungarian.[2] Sylvia Anthony's *The Child's Discovery of Death*, the other study not available, has long been out of print.[3] Both Nagy and Anthony indicated that the findings reported earlier are incorporated into their later works. In fact, Anthony apparently gathered little new data for her 1971 book.[4] However, whether American children in the 1970s understand death in the same way that European children did in the late 1930s and the early 1940s is a moot point.

The measurement of children's understanding of complex concepts such as death is a task fraught with methodologic problems. All too frequently investigators seem to have assumed that if a child did not verbalize his understanding of a concept in a direct way, he lacked understanding of it. Neither Nagy nor Anthony made such an assumption. Both used projective techniques (Nagy used pictures drawn by the children; Anthony used a standardized story-completion task), as well as the more structured approach of word definition. Nagy also discussed death with her children using the instructions "Tell me all you can think of about death," and Anthony had available to her parent diaries of their children's spontaneous comments regarding death.

The findings of the two studies support the general hypothesis that there are definite stages in the child's understanding of death. Nagy's stages illustrate the development in children of the meaning of "death," while Anthony's stages or categories deal with the development of the childs concept of "dead."

Nagy reported three stages in the development of the child's theory of death. In the first stage, characteristic of children from three to five, death is denied as a regular and final process. These children see death as temporary; in fact, they make distinctions in degrees of death. To die, for these children, means the same as living except under changed circumstances.[5] For instance, the dead person's eyes are closed to keep the dirt out, and they do not move because the coffin restricts their mobility. Or, the dead "feel a tiny little bit [and when] he is quite dead he no longer feels anything."

The personification of death is the dominant theme in the second stage of development.[6] In general, children between five and nine belong to this group. For them, death is perceived as a distinct personality or as a person. The belief is that only those people who were carried off by the deathman died. Unlike children in the first stage, children in this second stage accept the reality of death, but it exists outside the child and consequently is not seen as inevitable.

Only after the age of nine, Nagy stated, does the child recognize death as a process operating within all living things and therefore universal. This represents the third and final stage in the child's theory concerning death. The child now sees death realistically; it is inevitable and results in the dissolution of bodily life.

Nagy concluded her study by stating that

> . . . the theory the child makes of death faithfully reflects at each stage a general picture of its world. To conceal death from the child is not possible and is also not permissible.[7]

In the second stage, the child exhibits interest in death but the interest is combined with a very limited concept which may be erroneous.

Children in the third stage do not show or express an inability to understand the word, but they refer it only to people or to associated but nonessential phenomena.

The fourth stage is much like the third in that the child apparently understands the meaning of "dead" and he sometimes referred only to humanity. However, the reference would be combined with logical or biologic essentials or with generalizations.

The child's concept of death, Anthony stated, seemed to reach intellectual maturity when "dead" was defined logically and physiologically, the characteristics of stage five.

Anthony pointed out that the way the child conceived of death depended largely upon his age, intelligence level, and cultural background.

Table 1 indicates some of this influence. According to Anthony's data, chronologic age had a correlation of 0.47 with category or stage, whereas mental age correlated a little higher (r=0.67). Unfortunately, Nagy did not provide this type of information about subjects.

One of the more interesting differences between the two studies was the failure of the English children to pesonify death. It was prcisely this personification which characterized

Table 1
Meaning Given to "Dead" by Average Chronologic and Mental Age*

Concept Category	*Average Chronological Age*†	*Average Mental Age*
1	5.6	4.9
2	5.8	5.9
3	8.0	8.2
4	10.2	10.1
5	10.4	11.8

*Adapted from Anthony: *The Discovery of Death in Childhood and After.*
†Does not include persons classified by Anthony as "educationally subnormal."

Nagy's second stage. This difference, Anthony concludes, "... appears to be a function of the language and general environment of the Hungarian children."[9] (In Hungary, the figure of Death was commonly portrayed pictorially as a reaper in white.) Anthony also believed that the almost invariable human reference of the English children in her third stage corresponded to the pesonification of the Hungarian children in Nagy's second stage.

The part of Anthony's study reported here focused on the development of the child's logical thinking about death. But she pointed out the following about when that concept reaches intellectual maturity:

> [It] ... is only the beginning of the meaning of death. ... The idea is developing continually, linking with the concepts of time and cause ... and with the concept of man himself, which is the concern of us all.[10]

THE MEANING OF PERSONAL DEATH

What is the reaction of a child to his own death? As is true of any other life experience, the person experiencing death reacts to it in a manner consistent with his understanding of that experience and the emotional strength available to him. Thus, children respond to their own deaths with reactions appropriate and natural to persons of that age.

As there are stages or levels in the cognitive understanding of death, so too, it is theorized, are there stages in the understanding of personal death. In *The Dying Child,* Easson hypothesized the following six stages in this understanding.[11] The first stage is really not one of understanding as such; rather it is a response to dying and is present at birth. There is in every human being a physiologic mechanism that strives to maintain life. Whether the person is consciously aware of it or not, that struggle—what Easson has called the "death agony"—is probably the most intolerable physical sensation a human can experience. And all persons living, even infants, must face this reality.

The next aspect of death to which the child is capable of responding is that of physical changes that result from disease or the treatment procedures. The changes may make the child physically repulsive, irritable, and more difficult to be with, or they may take the form of symptoms such as vomiting. The child does not react to the physical changes themselves so much as he responds to the reactions of persons around him. Even the very young infant of five or six months can sense when something about him makes others tense or angry. He then becomes anxious and more hesitant about "reaching out" for comfort. This, of course, means that he receives less consoling from others—and so a vicious circle begins. It ends with the stunting of the infant's emotional growth, making him less able to cope with his approaching death.

At about four years of age, Easson stated, the young child begins to view himself as a separate and unique person. As his sense of identity grows, so does the gnawing knowledge that he might cease to exist. This third stage in the child's reaction to death, the awareness of possible nonexistence, brings with it unbearable psychologic pain, pain akin to that of the death agony. The child automatically responds to this threat using age-appropriate defenses—usually denial and repression. However, as death draws nearer, he is less able to control his fears; frequently they break through into consciousness and are seen in the child's disturbed and disturbing behavior.

Adding to the child's burden is the enforced dependency

that accompanies many types of fatal illness. For the child who so recently was reveling in his new-found independence, the absolute dependent state creates frustration and anger.

The fourth and fifth stages of the child's reaction to personal death—the significance of diagnosis and prognosis—are greatly influenced by the child's intellectual and cognitive growth as well as by social and cultural factors. Through antismoking campaigns aimed at ever younger audiences, for example, children are learning from the electronic media the meaning of words such as "cancer" and "heart disease." Soap operas, too, teach the young child about various diagnoses and diseases. In fact, by the time a child is five he may well understand the personal significance of a specific diagnosis.

But in order for a child to understand his prognosis, he must be able to grasp the abstract concept of time. Time future has little real meaning for a child under seven; he lives in the present. If such a child learns his disease has a six-months' survival prognosis, he could react in one of two ways: he could be very unconcerned because "six months" is the same as never; or he could become very upset because "six months" is tonight or tomorrow. However, a child who has grasped the concept of future time may react to his prognosis as an inescapable fate, an execution order. As time passes, and the date approaches, such a child's anxiety could grow to the point where it would exhaust him emotionally and physically, making him less able to deal with his illness.

The final aspect of death to which the child reacts is related to the impending change in his social relationships and role. A young child, unable to comprehend the fact that death is irreversible and means separation from his family and loved ones, is relatively unconcerned about discussions of his death. But by the age of seven the child is well aware that his dying means losing all those he loves. Being told that the impending separation will be only temporary does little to appease him. The thought of his approaching death makes him both sad and angry, two very realistic reactions to his situation.

The dying child also has to come to grips with the new role given him—that of a dying person. Each culture has a socially acceptable way of dying and the child quickly learns from the reactions of adults around him what their expectations are. He learns that certain feelings and thoughts must be hidden because they cause discomfort in health care personnel, fellow patients, and his family. He learns that if people are uncomfortable when they are around him, they will soon avoid him and he will be left alone. And he learns to die "a good death." The child who in life has been open and outgoing learns in dying to be reticent and withdrawn, playing the part given him by his family and his culture.

Health care personnel who attempt to assist the child toward a truly good death are confronted by the question of the dying child's awareness of his death. If encouraging the dying child to share his fears, anger, and sadness about his impending death is viewed as a necessary part of caring for the child, it would seem imperative that the child's awareness of his death be ascertained.

Does a terminally ill child really know he is dying? In situations where fatally ill children were not told their diagnoses or prognoses, some researchers have reported that not until the age of ten did the children show fear of death.[12] From this they argued that children younger than ten were unaware of their impending deaths. Other researchers have claimed that the anxiety of adults was conveyed to the dying children via the altered emotional climate surrounding them.[13]

Two carefully designed studies attempting to answer the question concerning a fatally ill child's awareness of death have been completed recently.[14,15] The findings of the Waechter and Spinetta et al studies suggested that even from the very first hospitalization, fatally ill six- to ten-year-old children are aware that theirs is no ordinary illness. Not only did they have more generalized anxiety than did chronically ill children, they also showed a much greater concern about body integrity than did the comparison groups. To ask if a child should be told he has a fatal illness is, therefore, meaningless. The focus, rather, should be on what can be done to help these children feel less isolated and alienated from their parents and other meaningful adults.

HEALTH CARE PERSONNEL

What can health care personnel do to help meet the needs of the dying child? Perhaps the most good would come from their remembering that the fatally ill child is just that: a child with a terminal illness. He has the same needs as other children of his age group, in addition to the needs unique to his situation.

Easson has pointed out that when a very young child is dying, he really does need his mother if he is to cope with the experience. Therefore, to meet the needs of this age patient, health care personnel must work through the child's family. They must remember that a child of this age has no real awareness of the meaning of personal death except as he reacts to the emotions of those around him. The task for the health care team, then, becomes one of helping the family deal with their emotional struggles about the approaching death of the child. One very concrete way of helping the family is that of letting them assist in the care of their child and/or other children. Frequently, parents feel less anxious if they participate in the treatment program in a meaningful way. If the family can learn to handle their feelings productively, the youngster may be much better able to face the task of dying.

The child of two or three is just discovering independence and mastery. He may view hospitalization with its painful procedures and its separation from his home as punishment. A child at this stage needs a great deal of reassurance that hospitalization is neither punishment nor rejection. His thwarted independence drive may result in anger which frequently is directed against the staff or the parents. In such instances, the child needs help in channeling his anger in as productive a fashion as possible.

At four or five the dying child, having just gained his independence, is threatened with nonexistence. Health care personnel can assist him by letting him know when various aspects of his treatment program will occur. This knowledge gives him some security and certainty in addition to allowing him to feel in control of at least part of his situation. When and if the child asks about his illness, he should be told only what he asks and in words that he can understand. The hallmarks of assistance to children of this age are a present orientation and truthfulness of response. If, as death approaches, the child can regress emotionally to a more dependent stage, the regression should be supported by the staff for it makes dying much easier for the child.

The grade school child of six or seven frequently will view death as punishment for something bad he has done or said. Therefore, he needs assurance that he is not being punished nor are his parents rejecting him. This older child is happiest when he is actively involved in his own treatment or is helping others. If he asks about his illness, he should be told the truth. He can grasp and cope with the meaning of his diagnosis; however, his prognosis, if given at all, should be stated only in very general terms. It is one thing for the child to know he is going to die; it is an entirely different matter for him to think he knows when that will occur.

Health care personnel who want to be of greatest assistance to the dying child must be aware of three things in their dealings with these children. First, although health care personnel may pride themselves on their clinical detachment, they also have an emotional investment in their patients. They must learn to recognize their involvement and deal with it in a manner which will enable them to be therapeutically helpful to other dying patients.[17] Second, persons dealing with these children must remember that they have the same general needs as other children at a comparable developmental stage. Third, the dying child has needs unique to his situation and those who would help him must be aware of his level of understanding so that the proffered help can be received.

If everyone who deals with the dying child remembers these things, they can help him "achieve in his dying the maximum comfort, the greatest security and the deepest closeness."[18]

REFERENCES

1. Harrison SI et al: Children's reactions to bereavement. Arch Gen Psychiat 17:593, 1967

2. Nagy M: The child's theories concerning death. J Gen Psy 73:3, 1948.
3. Anthony S: The Child's Discovery of Death. London, Routledge and Kegan Paul, 1940
4. Anthony S: The Discovery of Death in Childhood and After. London, Penguin, 1971, p 47
5. Nagy M: *op cit*, pp 7–16
6. *Ibid*, pp 17–25
7. *Ibid*, p 27
8. Anthony S: *op cit*, pp 50–54
9. *Ibid*, p 75
10. *Ibid*, p 253
11. Easson M: The Dying Child. Springfield, Thomas, 1970, pp 6–18
12. Natterson J, Knudson A: Observations concerning fear of death in fatally ill children and their mothers. Psychosom Med 22:456, 1960
13. Binger C et al: Childhood leukemia: Emotional impact on patient and family. N Engl J Med 280:414, 1969
14. Waechter E: Children's awareness of fatal illness. A J N 71:1168, 1971
15. Spinetta J, Rigler D, Karon M: Anxiety in the dying child. Pediatr 52:841, 1973
16. Easson: *op cit*, pp 23–49
17. Easson W: Management of the dying child. J Clin Child Psy 3:25, 1974
18. Easson W: The Dying Child, p 18

Paul Martinson seeks to view the health professionals in a broader social-cultural context, in an attempt to see how the various participants provide a meaningful contribution to the whole.

23

THE HEALTH PROFESSIONAL AND THE DYING CHILD: TOWARD A THEORETICAL FRAMEWORK

Paul V. Martinson

This writer can hardly be considered a health professional; however, he is married to one and, as all of us in society, he has some investment in the way health professionals relate to him personally and to his family. Having been theologically trained, moreover, the death and dying of old and young is a matter of considerable and direct professional relevance. This triple investment prompts the following reflections.

In its least sense, death is an event of transition from one psychosomatic state to another unspecified state. It is basically an uncontrollable event not amenable to the efforts of human technology to prevent. It is both universal and inevitable, as well as being an intensely individual experience. It is an event that does not give up its secrets and cannot be understood for what it is by the living, nor, so far as we know empirically, by the dead. This means that the only way we can understand death is by bringing it into some meaningful relationship with the totality of the human life experience—unless one chooses to ignore it.

If death is inscrutable, and if dying is an intensely individual process, it can hardly be expected that, whether parent or professional, one can penetrate the soul of the dying child and adequately comment upon that experience. Indeed, for the parent or professional to attempt this, and make the dying child a kind of subject for experimental psychology, nothing less than a violation of that child's humanity would be involved. One cannot, and must not, presume to experience for the child, but only *alongside* the child, and each in his or her own capacity—as parent or sibling, as doctor, nurse, or chaplain. Let us, then, attempt to investigate this "living alongside the dying," each in his separate way, and see how this kind of experiencing by kin and professional has implications for our total understanding of life and society. Perhaps in this way we shall be led by the hand of a dying child to a richer understanding of life, and in the end to our own better death.

THE SITUATION

The persons we shall isolate for comment are the parent, the doctor, the nurse, and chaplain, and, of course, the child. Each has a significant part to play, and each does so in a distinctive way. The doctor, nurse, and chaplain do so above all in terms of a specific personal involvement. It is the course of the disease that largely determines events and that calls forth appropriate action and response on the part of all.

The parent and the doctor, in that order, are the first to become involved. It may well be that the parent will pick up certain signs or symptoms that seem to suggest that all is not well with the child physically. At some point it is likely that the child will be brought to a doctor. The doctor will examine the child, take note of any symptoms that may point to a pathologic condition, and if this is so, attempt to arrive at some kind of determination with respect to the underlying pathology, prognosis, and treatment. Both parent and doctor have become involved in a direct way with the child, and this will continue and intensify as the disease progresses. However, the nature of this direct involvement is very different in each case. For the doctor, the involvement is more strictly physical, and requires the utilization of the doctor's technical competence and skills. For the parent, the involvement rather than being physical is biological, for the child is "bone of bone" and "flesh of flesh." But more than being a merely biologic, kinship involvement—though normally building upon this—it is also an affective, interpersonal involvement in which the parent senses an intense commitment. For the time being let us move no further than this in the event of illness and dying, but instead use it as the starting point for reflection and comment.

DOCTOR AND PARENT AS TECHNICAL AND SOCIAL AGENTS

This initial phase in what will likely be a rather long and drawnout process already introduces us to some rather significant complexities. The doctor with a specific technical competence stands immediately in a kind of opposition or contrast to the parent. It is a necessary opposition of a supportive, not adversary, kind, but an opposition nonetheless. The parent, in contrast to the doctor, has no claim to technical competence, but is simply a hapless and involuntary participant in the event. Though the child may be entirely unaware of anything critical at the initial stage, the parent may already be in a crisis of emotion, for nothing less than the wholeness of the family and the life of an individual member is threatened.

If the doctor with a technical competence represents culture in this situation, the parent with a familial commitment represents society, for the parent together with the child constructs the basic unit of all human society. Culture is, so to speak, external, made by society, "out there," ready to be used (eg, medicine) or enjoyed (eg, art) as the case may be. As such, culture stands outside of and in contrast to society. In the situation before us, the doctor is the principal representative of this realm. In contrast to culture, the family as the nuclear form of society is not "out there" but is "right here." It is in the family that we find ourselves, develop personhood, become people. Our social experience is a far more primal reality than is our cultural experience. It is the precondition for culture; it is the locus of our human identity and our human experience. Technological culture can be given up—we could conceivably revert to premodern existence, even to "barbaric" existence—but society in its most basic form cannot be given up—to do so would cause us to cease to be recognizably human. The parent and the doctor, as chief representatives of these two spheres of our humanness, though in a supportive, symbiotic relation, nevertheless stand in contrast to one another. This opposition lies at the root of many of the tensions and dilemmas that develop in the health care situation before us.

The nature of these potential difficulties can be made more explicit if we speak about the cultural and sociological involvements separately. There are certain commitments inherent in the cultural involvement of the doctor. The first and most fundamental commitment, as expressed in the Hippocratic oath, is to the preservation of life. A strange commitment, one might think, for death is the way of all men—none excepted. Yet the medical profession intercedes between mankind and death as if to slow down, if not halt, that inevitable process. This may seem strange, but if humankind were to cease to affirm life in some such way the very existence of the race would be at stake. This commitment, this affirmation, is programmed into our very humanity. Culture, second only to the biologic level of reproduction, is the most convincing evidence of this affirmation.

In this cultural role the doctor may well be spoken of as a modern, secularized version of an archaic mythical figure. Prometheus, so the tale goes, stole fire from the gods for the benefit of humanity. The doctor is in the direct line of this mythic image, for the doctor is the cultural agent *par excellence* of the human effort to achieve life. So also the doctor is the direct descendant of Utnapishtim, that Noah of Babylonian myth who sought for the herb of immortality. The doctor is also the descendant of the alchemist who sought by physical manipulation to reverse the processes of death. Perhaps the modern, secular doctor has a more realistic appraisal of what is possible (at least in the short term), but as cultural agent and technical expert the doctor today still needs the boldness of Prometheus, the questing determination of Utnapishtim, and the manipulative inquisitiveness of the alchemist. To fail in this is to deny one's own personal-professional identity. But even as the doctor acts, beneath the daring lurks the awareness that the struggle between culture (man's attempt to construct life) and nature (the ecological process that always returns life to death) is an uneven one—Prometheus was punished, Utnapishtim returned empty-handed, the alchemist produced but fool's gold. The doctor's commitment is a difficult one indeed. We now see that to the culture-society dichotomy earlier disclosed, we find another level of complexity, that of a culture-nature opposition.

But let us return to the parent, the social agent in this situation. As with the doctor's involvement, so are there special forms of commitment in the parental involvement. The parental familial commitment can perhaps best be expressed in spatiotemporal categories. There is a spatial dimension to the nuclear social unit of the family. It is the locus where human community is experienced in a particularly focal way. Here communication takes place in as primal and complete a way as possible (from the somatic level of nursing to the more abstract linguistic level). Within the network of relations built up, the child is able to locate and identify itself. The human being is a "locative" creature, needing a location in space, physical and social. It is the parent that initiates creation of not merely the physical but also the interpersonal space, and it is the parent, moreover, who is primarily responsible for the shape it shall take. Spatially speaking, the prime commitment of the parent is to the development of this community. This nuclear group is the sociological base for all other forms of community, and if community is communication, the parental commitment is to the nurturing and fostering of such a reality—the family.

At the same time this structured community with its internal network of relations is a process that goes on through time. Life requires time in order to be lived. The family network of relations is not created for its own sake, important though it be. The relations so carefully fostered in the early life of the child will eventually undergo transformation, for the family exists finally for the sake of the future of the child. That family will end; the child will live on. The parent mediates the past to the child through an ongoing present so as to make as rich and full a future for the child as is possible. Temporally speaking, the prime parental commitment is to the future of the child, not to its present or the family's present, and it is this element of hope, expectancy, and anticipation that conditions all meaning and relationship within the family.

The advent of terminal illness strikes a lethal blow, so it would seem, to this spatiotemporal unit. The all-pervasive element of hope is shattered at a single stroke. The experience of sharing in community is cruelly threatened. Slowly but surely, imminent separation looms as the child's energies are increasingly depleted. Nothing can prevent the ultimate rending of the fabric. Nonetheless, parental commitment does not shatter, it does not suddenly end. To be sure, the future of the child has been greatly foreshortened, and the breadth of its experience all at once severely restricted. In the parent this foreshortening and confining to narrower limits can only intensify the original familial commitment.

At this point some tension can develop between the representative of culture (doctor) and that of society (parent). The doctor's commitment is to the prolongation of physical life by the application of a technical competence; the parental commitment is to the quality of life in the foreshortened period of time. A predominantly quantitative commitment runs counter to a predominantly qualitative one. To be sure, this dual commitment is present in both doctor and parent (for doctor may also be or is potentially a parent), but in the situation before us the dominating commitments will naturally focalize in this way. Probably the issue in which these commitments are most clearly brought to the fore is the question of home care for the dying—a consideration we shall come back to shortly.

NURSE AS ECOLOGIC AGENT

The province of the nurse in this situation is quite different from that of both doctor and parent. There are many indicators of this differing role, and they can be readily quantified. In terms of the time of initial involvement, the nurse is normally brought in only subsequent to the involvement of parent and doctor. In terms of the numbers of persons to whom one relates, the child is only one of many patients with whom the doctor is currently dealing, whereas for the parents this is likely the only individual for whom they are thus concerned, and for the nurse the child is one of a limited number of similar patients. In terms of contact hours, the same differential holds—the doctor, brief and intermittent contact; the parent, frequent and prolonged contact; the nurse, less frequent and less prolonged contact than the parent but considerably more than the doctor.

To point out these quantifiable differences does not yield us much by way of qualifying the differences, but this can be done. We have described the doctor as a representative of culture in his or her predominantly technologic role; we have described the parent as a representative of society in his or her predominantly nurturing and social role; we would now suggest that we describe the nurse as being a representative of nature in his or her predominantly ecologic role. Let us expand on this.

In contrast to the doctor, the nurse takes no Hippocratic oath. Performing an ecologic role it would be rather incongruous to do so. Rather than standing over against nature so as to control it, as both culture and technology do, the nurse seeks to be sensitive to the natural processes and to respond to these in ways deemed appropriate. The nurse relates above all to the total environment, seeking to enhance that which is desirable within the natural setting; unlike the doctor, the nurse is not preoccupied with obstructing the natural processes, even those of death. As such the nurse can never be seen as an extension of the doctor's primarily technologic commitment. Indeed, the nurse could well have ecologic commitments that might be in potential tension with the technologic commitments of the doctor, and there might well arise situations in which the nurse should act as advocate of the parent over against the doctor.

On the other hand, the role of nurse is by no means to be understood as that of a parental substitute. The primarily ecologic concerns of the nurse are very different from the predominantly social and nurturing concerns of the parent. Difference does not spell incompatibility, however. In fact, in many cases the concern of the nurse to provide the best possible environment within which the process of dying is to take place will precisely coincide with the concerns of the parent; however, in other settings this will not be so and the nurse will have to act as the doctor's advocate before the parent.

It is clear that we are trying to outline a distinctive, indeed pivotal, role for the nurse which cannot be reduced to any other role or become merely the function of another actor in this total situation. The nurse's role is to be defined from within, not from without. The nurse has a specific commitment. The nurse above all recognizes the processes of nature for what they are, will not deny them, does not have a professional commitment to control them, may often anticipate them, and continually adjusts the environment to accommodate them. The prior commitment is neither cultural nor technologic, but natural. So long as there is life the commitment is to provide the best of all possible environments within which the process of healing or dying can take place. But with this commitment the nurse does not let the affective and personal involvements of the parent become a priority. The role is ecologic, not social. This ecologic role requires a certain kind of detachment lest it collapse into the parental role. Consequently, in the best sense of the word a nurse needs to be a good "meditator," one who has practiced the Zen art of detached involvement. Though practicing a kind of Zen detachment, the original motivation is one of compassion; though compassionately active, this activity does not lead to self-defeating attachment. The myth figure of the Bodhisattva perhaps best characterizes the ecologic role of the nurse.

The potential conflict between doctor and parent, culture and society, technology and nurture is perhaps best exemplified in the health care field by the hospital/home dichotomy. Since this is treated in detail elsewhere, we need not go into it at length. It may be stated in this way. Our civilization has created a unique institutional complex with a technologically sophisticated health care system. This system has been organized around the institution of the hospital. Here we have a concentrated health care infrastructure—including personnel and equipment—that is prepared to deal with every conceivable health care problem in the quickest, most efficient and effective way that modern science and technology make possible. Technologically (or culturally) speaking, there is no more efficient and total way to care for the diseased, or to prolong physical life, than in the hospital. All that we have said about the role of the doctor in relation to technology applies here to the hospital and the modern institutionalization of medicine.

But with this commitment to technology—and this is a good and right commitment—we see the health care system enter into a potential conflict situation with the base of society: hospitalization requires removal from the home. Hospitalization says that the critically ill cannot be dealt with adequately in the home by the family. At best, the family performs a minimal constructive role, such as through occasional visits at the convenience of health care professionals and the institution. At other times the family proves to be an obstacle to the health care system, especially if procedures are questioned. In some cases it may even be considered irrelevant. This separation and isolation takes place at a time when the family with its organic network of relationships is the most critically needed. Clearly, culture enters into conflicts with the society of which it is the product.

The nurse has a somewhat ambivalent role in this conflict—and it is this ambivalence that makes possible the nurse's mediating, pivotal function. When hospitalized, the patient is under the constant, watchful eye of the nurse; when at home, the patient is, where situations permit, in the continual care of kith and kin. The nurse's ecologic commitment to providing a natural environment conducive to the greatest wholeness possible, tips the scales whenever possible in the favor of home care. In the case of the dying child where technology has less and less of a curative role and more and more of a merely life-sustaining role, the ecologic commitment would seem to suggest that the home environment may well be the most desirable. A satisfying environment is more precious than whatever benefits sophisticated but "unnatural" technology can provide. The only serious question becomes that of feasibility. As studies in this volume suggest and demonstrate, the ecologic commitment of the nurse can lead to innovations making possible the most desirable environment. A key element in this is whether the nursing role is to be carried out by direction (direct nursing care) or indirection (direct care carried out by others, such as family members, the nurse performing a supportive role). As demonstrated in an earlier chapter, nursing care by indirection returns the maximum of environmental control to the family, where it was in the first place, prior to the onset of illness, and thus fosters the natural participation of the family in the overall dying process. If one were to place the types of commitments on a scale of priorities, they would probably fall into the order of sociologic, ecologic, and technologic. The health-care system exists for the family, not the family for the system. Culture fulfills itself instrumentally, not through domination, for it is the instrument created by society to foster its own well-being; beyond this culture becomes opposed to society. The ecologic commitment must mediate between the two. In the industrial sphere events of our own day have indicated that technology is ultimately a child of nature, and must be responsive to nature, for if technology ignores ecology the result is self-destruction; that is, the final triumph of nature over culture, the end of man. This potential chain of events in the industrial world has its counterpart in the realm of health care. Disease is not only a somatic manifestation, but psychologic and sociologic as well. Technology can deal with the somatic, but not with the psychologic or sociologic factors. This, the basic social unit is normally best able to deal with. Among the professionals it is the nurse who is above all concerned that the technologic and sociologic elements in the environment are balanced in the most effective way possible. But in terms of priority, it is home care for the dying that remains the more desirable, and it is the nursing profession's ecologic commitment to work towards its increasing feasibility.

CHILD AS PROTAGONIST

We also have the child—the protagonist of the dying event. Let us not be too bold or say too much. We wish to remember our earlier caution. But we must attempt to see the dying child in the proper perspective within this total situation. Perhaps the child's experience can best be described as a passage into unfamiliarity. There are sudden moments of passage, such as into the doctor's office or into a hospital ward. These changes in the external situation can be dealt with relatively easily and may be momentary of temporary. Only if hospitalization becomes permanent does this passage constitute a major difficulty. The factors that are most decisive for the child's passage are those internal to the child's own experience: physical strength gradually diminishes; organic harmony begins to be disrupted so that unnatural bleeding or other disabilities increasingly show themselves; immobility gradually replaces mobility. In short, the dynamics of disease replace the dynamics of growth. This unfamiliar physical condition gradually brings an alteration in social relations and in the psychologic outlook of the child. Increasingly, the familiar world of action and interaction recedes and is replaced by an unfamiliar world within which the child seemingly plays a strictly passive role.

If the child's experience can be described as a passage into unfamiliarity, the corollary is that the familiar becomes correspondingly more important. Absolute unfamiliarity is total nonsense; it is insanity. It is only by means of analogy, which is essential to the human mental and psychologic processes, that we can safely negotiate the passage into the unfamiliar. The child may wonder what is happening to his or her body. Only by some analogy (your body is getting tired) can the unfamiliar be understood. Such questions as, "What is death like?" and the response, "It is like sleep." Or, "What is heaven like?" "It is like home." As the child passes into unfamiliarity (ie, beyond the family), the familiar (for the familiar is the family) becomes even more important as the base for the child's psychological development. For it should be noted that for the physically incapacitated child, such as the leukemic, where mental impairment is not a part of the disease process, the physical decline may well be measured by a corresponding increase in psychologic growth. The base unit of society, the family, provides the richest analogical resources that can be used to bridge the increasing gap between familiar and unfamiliar, and may thereby foster a rich psychologic growth right up to the end.

CHAPLAIN AS THE SYMBOLIC AGENT

We have one othe participant in the death event—the chaplain. If the doctor, the nurse, the parent, and the child represent in some particular way the cultural, ecologic, sociologic, and psychologic spheres in the total event of the dying child, how then shall we discuss the chaplain? Is the chaplain an appendage, a luxury that some may wish to have?

This essay began with the statement that the particular human way to deal with death is "by bringing it into some meaningful relationship with the totality of one's life experience." If the quest for meaning and the quest for experiencing wholeness in the life-death nexus is a luxury or a misguided dream that the human animal alone indulges in, then the chaplain is indeed a luxury. If society is no more than a function of biology, if culture is only an inert material extension of a biologic organism, if death is the ultimate significance of nature, and if the psychologic growth of a dying child is a cruel ecologic joke, and if meaning is simply the sum of all these parts and the mythologic has no ultimate significance in rendering the whole greater than the sum of its parts, then for a certainty the chaplain can be considered an odd species, extinct while still existing. And if meaning be thus quickly exhausted and the chaplain thus readily forgot, then there hardly need be a doctor, a nurse, a parent or child—significance lacks for all. Yet human society has always argued otherwise. No society has existed or developed culture without a mythos, without a reason-for-being that is greater than that particular society itself; none has existed without an inward necessity, an articulated meaning given expression through various symbolic constructions. If we can argue for an irreducible symbolic core at the heart of human existence—be it understood mythically, theologically, or morally—then the dynamics of the health care situation as we have been discussing it require a taking of this dimension into account. The chaplain as professional is preeminently the representative of this symbolic or mythic order that gives to all the parts a share in a greater wholeness.

In performing a religious or symbolic function the principal commitment of the chaplain can be described as a commitment to wholeness. It is the symbolic order that provides a point of reference that renders it possible to speak of wholeness—wholeness in the sense of both totality and well-being. In carrying out this commitment, the chaplain functions on at least two levels.

The first level is the sociologic level. Physical illness can threaten to disrupt the wholeness of the family. No family exists that is an ideal network of ideal relationships. It is the laboratory, so to speak, wherein one learns the meaning of both functional and dysfunctional relationships. Though this be true of all families, the whole family is able to creatively contain if not eliminate dysfunctional relations. But with the unwelcome advent of terminal illness the shock and disruption might be so great as to place unbearable stress upon actual or potential dysfunction. Parents may disagree on procedures or attitudes. Work demands may conflict with increased home demands. Social pressures from sources outside the immediate kin group may press in. Different kinds of response—fear, anger, bewilderment, sympathy—may be generated in siblings. The ability of individuals to deal with ultimate questions thrown up by the disastrous event may differ, and levels of acceptance may vary markedly. These and other factors complicate the internal structure of the family. In addition, any conflicts that might arise in family relating to professionals may only exacerbate the difficulties.

Whether the situation becomes as bleak as all this suggests is not the question. Whatever the case, the first field of activity for the chaplain is just here—to foster the wholeness of the family group. The goal will be reconciled relationships. It is obvious that, in this, the chaplain's primary relation is with the family as the critical unit in the total situation. Secondarily, the chaplain will also relate to other participating health professionals. Wholeness requires this.

But the chaplain must be equally prepared to function at another level, the less concrete, though no less immediate and urgent, symbolic level. If reconciled relationships are the goals on the sociologic level, reconciliation with reality and the self is the goal at this level. At least two things should be said as to the way this function is carried out.

First, the chaplain is not a source of readymade explanations served out as occasion demands. Any such conception on the part of the chaplain would be fatal. Some questions ought not to be answered but ought rather to be lived with. The chaplain seeks to enhance the ability of persons to live with the unanswerable and inexpressible. Further, in performing this function the chaplain relates principally to the parents, not the child. As with the nurse, the most desirable mode of action is by indirection. This assumes that the family is the basic social unit within which meaning is experienced and found. The parents might need help addressing themselves to the unpredictable questions of the child just as they need help to know how to meet the unpredictable physical needs. Only after relating to the parents does the chaplain relate to the dying child. Meanwhile, the chaplain maintains contact with the other health professionals. Just as the chaplain ought to be free to inquire about the prognosis and care, so the other professionals should inquire about the questions of meaning and how the chaplain addresses the symbolic as well as social needs. But a second thing must also be said. The chaplain is not a partisan advocate of a specific faith, although his or her own religious commitment ought to be made clear. The chaplain does not prescribe right symbols, confessions, or beliefs to the participants, but assists each one to make an adequate and significant use of the symbolic and religious resources already available to them. The participants in this event might well be Buddhist, Christian, Jew, or secularist. The chaplain will be a participant as one who holds a religious option, but it is not the chaplain's intent to impose this option. The intent is that each will expand the option already held and on this basis contribute to a meaningful, functioning whole. This is not to suggest, however, that the chaplain adopt a pseudo religious attitude of noncommitment. A noncommitted attitude is a nonmeaningful attitude and a poor way to provide significant symbolic resources. Rather, the chaplain is always prepared to make available those religious resources that are his own whenever and wherever these resources are sought. Just as a doctor must "own" a technology so also the chaplain must "own" a faith. A faith-less chaplain is a useless chaplain.

SUMMING UP

We come, finally, to some kind of a summing up. It may have been noticed that we have been speaking of two groups of persons—the family members who have met with misfortune, and the professionals. We have described the situation as a process and as an event. We have tried to locate some of the major participants in terms of their creative role in this process, and have intentionally limited this discussion to what we consider to be focal points. We have discussed three of the professionals—the doctor, the nurse, the chaplain. The doctor, we have suggested, represents culture and technology, the human quest for control of nature, and the life–death processes. This quest and its fruits are an essential part of what it means to be human. The nurse, we have suggested, performs a mediating role between family and technology, in a way that the doctor should not, and in a way that the family could not. The nurse affirms the inevitability of death and the natural, ecologic rhythms of nature, while at the same time affirming the life that has come from nature and that shall return to it. In adjusting to the rhythms of nature, affirming both life and death, the nurse seeks to direct the environment in a way that will enhance life so long as it continues. This requires a delicate balancing of the commitments of culture or technology (doctor) and social unit or family (parent and child) in such a way that both are maximized; yet, when a choice must be made, the prior commitment to the ecologic will assert itself. The chaplain, we have said, performs an integrating function derived from an assumption that the dying process or event is more than the mere sum of its parts or phases. The chaplain's function provides resources for the family that neither technology nor ecology can provide. At the sociologic level, the chaplain functions to enhance the preexistent strengths of the family so as to guarantee continued relations of wholeness; at the symbolic level, the participants are encouraged to build upon their prior moral and religious resources so as to continue to move towards the reconcilitation of self with society and final reality.

It might be noted in conclusion that these three professional roles are not unique to modern society. What is unique is that they have been so clearly differentiated and so highly specialized. In many primal societies these roles have had a more compact existence in the single figure of the shaman. Such a figure will often apply medicinal herbs and indigenous medical technology, will control the environment within which dying is to take place, will articulate in mythologic and ritual terms the meaning of the event, and will often inquire as well into the animosities and tensions within society and seek through various means to effect reconcilitation. In our complex society this kind of compactness of professional role is hardly possible, and probably not even desirable. What is desirable, however, is an awareness of this original compactness so that as professionals they carry out their specialist functions and do so not antagonistically or competitively, but harmoniously.

APPENDIXES

APPENDIX I: RECOLLECTIONS OF A NURSE*

Ida Marie Martinson

Thinking back on my basic nursing experience, I can still remember seeing a dying patient, wiping his feverish brow with a damp washcloth, holding his hands, trying to comfort the crying relatives as well as the patient but not really knowing how, frequently going off duty to cry to myself about how inadequate I felt in the face of death and dying.

Then nearly four years ago my father-in-law had cancer. During his last hospitalization he asked to "come home" to the cabin where we as a family were gathered. I knew the entire family wanted to honor his request, but wondered if it would be possible to give him the same high quality of nursing care that was available in the hospital. When the youngest brother checked with the attending physician regarding the request, the physician agreed to send my father-in-law home. With this information, and the decision made by the family

*Adapted from the chapter of the same title in Martinson I, Kuhlenkamp E, Fredlund D: *Eric*. Monograph. Minneapolis, University of Minnesota, School of Nursing, 1973

to bring him home, I began to establish a system of resources. The physician himself told me that this would be his own wish if he had cancer, and that nothing could be better than being at home with one's family during the last days. The doctor was instrumental in making available the resources found in a small town hospital, as well as the resources available from a public health nursing service and the local drug stores.

We as a family had a few crisis situations, but we were there the night he died. When I was awakened to give the pain medication that night, I noted the absence of restlessness; there seemed to be no need for pain medication. His feet were cool, evidencing circulatory failure, and his eyes, which had been glassy for the last day, were now clear. There may have been other signs, but these were enough. I awakened the family members who were sleeping and they were with him for the last five to ten minutes of his life.

Now, three years later, this event of his dying and death is still very meaningful and very precious to all of us who were with him. This difficult experience brought us closer together as a family. Since then I have wondered whether this was an experience unique to us because there were three nurses in the family. Do people really want their loved ones to die in the hospital? Is there a proper support system available to the patient and family at home? Could not dying and death become a meaningful and perhaps healthful experience, even facilitating the grief process?

Recently in discussion with John Kersey, who treats children with cancer at the Masonic Clinic, the topic came up of how to help families in similar situations. As a result of this conversation, Dr. Kersey mentioned to a family that I was interested in identifying the problems involved in home care for children with cancer. Within twenty-four hours the mother had called Dr. Kersey back saying she was interested, because it appeared her other child, the daughter, was ill. Dr. Kersey called me at home around 5:00 P.M. on a Friday with this message, and I called the mother. She said that if the daughter was not ill, she wouldn't need me on Saturday morning, but agreed readily when I said I would come

Saturday morning and stay as long as I could be of assistance to her.

This began a series of home visits of which only excerpts of the interactions are recorded. In the last 17 days of Eric's life, I made eight home visits and five phone calls and one visit with the family at the Masonic Clinic.

The mother welcomed me and seemed most receptive when I made my initial visit. She said she would be willing to help me identify what her problems were in the home care of Eric who was dying from leukemia.

One of her first areas of concern and one that continued throughout the experience was drug management. She was quite concerned about using a drug like codeine too early because of the possibility of its losing its effectiveness. My response was that by encouraging him to take the codeine, the energy he would otherwise use to handle the pain could be conserved for coping with the demands of living and of his own creativity.

Another area of concern was learning the abnormal reactions to the medication or to the disease process which would require contacting the physician. This suggested to me, as a professional, the need to develop guidelines for parents caring for the dying child at home. I was reminded of my own hesitancy in calling a physician. The mother did not want to be a bother; she did not want to call the physician unnecessarily. This is perhaps a more common experience than health professionals realize. We have more frequent contact with those clients who persist in their calls, but if the parents wait too long to call the problem may become graver.

I spent just a few minutes with Eric, wanting only to introduce myself and to let Eric decide how much he wanted to discuss with me. I wanted him to know I would listen to him. I believed it was important to let him know he was in charge of our conversation. It was important to me that on this first contact I explain to him that I was interested in his problems and concerns, and would try to help him to the best of my ability.

Following the three to five minute meeting with Eric, the mother and I sat around the kitchen table discussing some of her concerns. One of these was the relationship between the parents and the child. In the past, the family had been very close-knit, and this family style continued during the illness and even during the final phase of dying. During the terminal stages there were, however, times when the child wanted to be alone and somewhat apart from the parents.

My nursing background helped me throughout the discussion. I attempted to explain the implications of Eric's being on prednisone, a steroid that affects the emotions. A person who has been on this medication over an extended time tends to have changes in mood. The medical term used for this is "labile." Referring to the Kübler-Ross book,[1] I also explained that there tends to be a desire to be more alone at the end; this is not a rejection, but rather may be considered a preparatory phase for both the patient and the family for the final separation.

During my next visit, three days later, the discussion centered on the relationships with people who were not part of the immediate family. The mother said that the telephone seemed to ring constantly, and she was considering an answering service to give her some relief. Most of the callers were well-meaning friends, asking how things were and whether they could be of help. In the resulting discussion, I encouraged her to make use of every offer of help in order to conserve her energy. If someone offered to bring over supper, I advised, let them; now was the time to take advantage of the help friends were eager to give. However, if the friend bringing supper intended to stay for a two-hour visit, then perhaps making supper herself would be easier. I emphasized the necessity to conserve her own strength, for the situation was going to become more difficult. And since the family wanted to keep Eric at home, all supporting resources should be used to their fullest in helping her and her husband withstand the coming days. She should take only one day at a time, conserving as much energy as possible for the next. None of us was certain how close Eric was to the end of his life.

I told her of the Public Health Home Visiting Nurse Services. She responded that she didn't want a nurse coming in during the day; she wanted to care for Eric herself. Although

I left the name and number to call, she expressed the opinion that she didn't want a nurse to come in and take over. From this I perceived that my role must be one of supporting the parents rather than giving any physical care to Eric. It seemed important for the mother to see for herself that she was managing, and managing so well that there was no need for me to come in and take over. This would support the mother in giving her full confidence. She and her husband were in full control and managing beautifully.

In a telephone call the mother reported that there were sores developing in Eric's mouth and she wondered if he should eat only soft foods. I reassured her that she was absolutely right, that soft foods would help the sores heal more quickly. I also suggested that following eating he rinse his mouth with a mild sugar water solution.

On my third visit, I spent a little longer time with Eric. He was crying. When I asked him why, he said he was afraid that if he took the codeine he might become immune to it. This was a surprise to me and to his mother, and we both reassured him there was no danger of that! He then agreed to take the codeine his mother offered, and asked us to stay and talk with him.

He told us then that he didn't like soft foods, so I suggested that he eat whatever he wanted. If the mouth should get too sore, he could change his mind. From a professional point of view, I felt that since the end was near, it was more important that Eric have the enjoyment of eating foods he liked than that he and his mother worry about interference with the healing of mouth sores.

We spent close to 45 minutes talking about his hobbies. Being an avid stamp collector, he even teased me into offering to bring him stamps from Hong Kong, where I had once lived. Our conversation ranged from caviar to insects. This was interesting, for following the initial conversation about the ulcers and concerns of immunity we spent the rest of the time talking of his hobbies. He led the conversation, keeping me alert and teaching me; he certainly knew much more than I did about stamps and insects!

On the fourth visit, eight days before Eric's death, we went up almost immediately to see Eric. He was sitting up in bed because, he said, he could breathe more easily that way. I said, "That's fine."

This time he had many questions for me, all of which were about his condition. The questions came out, one right after another: "What is causing the spots?" "Can I stop taking prednisone?" "Can I get a muscle attachment for my right arm?" We discussed the questions and decided that since we were going to the Masonic Clinic shortly, we would ask these questions and any others he may wish of Dr. Kersey. This was the day he could finally ask me about some of these thoughts, which I suspect had been of concern to him for a long time. He seemed to enjoy our discussion very much. It had been one in which I found I could not give full answers to any of the questions he was asking. While there, he mentioned how tight his shirt was. I was receptive to this.

The things he discussed possibly reflected his thoughts about his body image. Changes were occuring. How much a ten-year-old child thinks. How much he perceives. What a most amazing child this was.

His mother commented that she appreciated my coming and that I was someone who "understood both sides." She mentioned that her husband had suggested Eric's possible readmission to the hospital, for they were both feeling there wasn't much more they could do for him at home. I reassured them that he was getting the best care possible; that care in the hospital could hardly be any better than what they were giving. I also mentioned that when it became too much, Eric could of course be readmitted.

On the next visit Eric was fascinated as I explained to him how cells in the mouth turn over. He seemed relieved to hear this and reported to me that one sore in his mouth was much better, although another one was starting.

There was a noticeable change in Eric's coloring; he was gray. There was difficulty in his breathing now, and for the first time he showed signs of becoming tired when he talked with me.

As we went downstairs, his mother and I discussed what to do if Eric died at home. She said they were willing to have an autopsy in the hope of helping to prevent this disease in the future for other children. I was exhausted when I reached home.

I arrived at the clinic at 9:00 A.M. the next day. While waiting for the family, I checked with the staff to find out what to do if Eric died at home and how to arrange for an autopsy. After several contacts were made, we found out that a doctor could come to the home to verify the death. An ambulance could then be called to bring the body to the hospital for an autopsy, which could be covered financially through insurance.

By this time the family had arrived and seemed happy to see me. Dr. Kersey, Eric, the parents, and I met together. Eric asked if he could discontinue taking prednisone, but the doctortold him he would onlyu feel worse. Then the question arose about controlling the nausea. Dr. Kersey suggested coeine be used as necessary for neauea, pain, or discomfort. Eric asked about cobalt, but the doctor replied it would not be helpful at this time. When his mother asked Eric if he wanted to inquire about the muscle attachment, Eric replied in the negative. It seemed to me that because of what had already been said, he knew there was no use in asking for a muscle attachment and decided not to bother with that question.

We took Eric to the nurses' station, after which Dr. Kersey and I continued discussion with the parents. The father wondered whether he was making it harder for Eric by carrying him downstairs for meals, having noticed more bruises under Eric's arms from being carried. Dr. Kersey replied that there was nothing they could do to hurt the child and that the child was receiving good care at home. In discussing the possibility of bleeding, I suggested a supply of towels, thus when bleeding took place, the towels could easily be removed without Eric seeing the accumulation of blood. Dr. Kersey mentioned that since the end was near, the bleeding would continue and Eric's condition would deteriorate further. It was his opinion that about a week remained of Eric's life. The mother asked what to do if her boy died at home. Dr. Kersey told the parents to call him at any time. She also asked Dr. Kersey about memorials, as they wanted memorial gifts given to leukemia research. Hearing this question, I was sure that they both were facing the fact that death was imminent. Dr. Kersey reassured the parents that readmission was possible at any time and that they should feel free to call on either him or me whenever they needed help.

The next day when I arrived for my visit Eric's mother met me, saying how glad she was to see me. She said she was in the middle of adjusting the large lamb's wool pad under Eric and would appreciate a little help. He thanked me for suggesting that he sleep without pajamas because they had become too tight. Since he quit wearing them, he had slept much better.

After moving Eric in bed, he related to me some family experiences. His dad had come into his room three times the previous night without even being called. He seemed in a good mood and was laughing during the conversation

Sensing Eric was getting tired, we only stayed with him about 15 minutes. His mother spoke of how much Eric looked forward to my coming. She thought this made him feel that the doctor and the hospital personnel were still interested and concerned about him. Secondly, she felt it was important for him to have a professional person to whom he could talk and who understood his problems so well.

She asked if there was any possibility of Eric going into a coma. We talked about coma, and I mentioned that there was no pain involved then, but that since hearing appears to be one of the last senses to go, one should be careful of conversation. She had gotten a large supply of towels in preparation for bleeding. I again reminded her to call me at any time, day or night.

My impression was that this mother was quite strong and holding up very well under this constant stress. I felt she would have the strength to face the coming days and I sensed that she found her time with Eric very precious. My assessment as a professional was that the care they were giving Eric possibly surpassed what could be given in a hospital. The approach now was how to support both Eric and family in this, their experience. How well the parents were managing. Everything I said and did was to support them.

When the mother called me three days later, I could tell she was upset. Eric was unable to swallow the codeine. I suggested that among other things they raise the head of the bed to see if this would help Eric swallow. I promised to come to the home that afternoon as soon as I could cancel my scheduled appointments. I was very concerned and called their home at noon to find that they had just finished calling Dr. Kersey. Eric was having pain and the father would give the shots if I could bring the medication. I immediately contacted Dr. Kersey who made arrangements for me to get a small supply of pain medication and syringes to take to the home.

By the time I arrived that afternoon Eric had fallen asleep looking very peaceful and showing no sign of pain. For over an hour and a half we waited to see how Eric would be on waking. While we were watching him, he opened his eyes and recognized his mother and father. Then he had to vomit. There was no blood in the emesis, only the undigested food from the supper he had eaten the night before. The mother gave him some mouth care. He didn't moan, and when we asked him if he had any pain, he said, "No, no, no." We said we had an injection for pain, but he said he did not want that. It was hard to tell whether he had pain or not when he was resting. It appeared that he had pain only when he moved. In walking with his mother outside for a few minutes we talked about the possibility of his swallowing a codeine pill, for he apparently did not want the injection.

Eric's father was not going to work that day or the next. His aunt was there to take care of Betsy, Eric's sister, who had asked on the previous Saturday if Eric was going to die. Her father had said that Eric was very sick. On this day, her mother had told her that Eric was going to die.

Eric's mother wanted to manage at home for that is what Eric wanted. When I brought up the possibility of hospitalization, she said that she had managed this long and wanted to manage it to the end; she would feel she had failed if she did not. I told her that she had not failed, that she had done a wonderful job of nursing, making Eric's days as full as possible. "I've managed up to now," she said, "but now I feel I'm falling all to pieces."

That noon Eric apparently had pain. Apart from the medication we had just obtained, there was nothing to ease it. At 6:00 P.M. Eric's mother called and asked me to come back since Eric needed an injection, so I returned to their home.

Eric, upon seeing me, said "No, no," although I had come to help him be more comfortable. He again vomited, and we decided that he definitely needed the injection for pain. The father prepared it, 50 mg or 1 cc of Demerol, and gave it to Eric under my supervision, as the doctor had ordered,—for it had been a long time since he had given an injection. Finally, at about 6:50 P.M. Eric said that he was "feeling much better now." Apparently the medicine was helping him for he went to sleep.

I called Dr. Kersey to ask if it would be possible for Demerol to be available for them the next morning at the drug store nearby.

Everyone and everything seemed under control. However, I had trouble sleeping. I worried about what was happening. Was Eric all right? Was he in much pain? I wondered if I had been too supportive of caring for the child at home. I worried about the family. Would they be able to manage? Would they hold up under this strain? I worried about what would happen since the child was not on prednisone. I wondered if the doctor knew this. I worried about the father having to give the pain medication injection. I worried about what the reaction would be when Eric died, for I was sure Eric would not live through the night. What would happen after the doctor came?

After a sleepless night, I waited until close to 9:00 A.M. before I called the family. The daughter Betsy, answered and said, "Yes, mommy's here." I asked the mother how Eric was, and she said he had died.

She had been able to sleep from midnight until 4:00 A.M. while her husband had been with Eric. At 4:00 A.M. she had gone in and held Eric's hand until he got comfortable. Then, having lain down on the floor beside him to rest, she suddenly wondered if he had died, and getting up to check, she found him dead. She went on to thank me for all the help that I had given her, saying that they would never have been able to manage if I had not been there.

She said that Dr. Kersey had come and had suggested that we get together in three or four weeks to talk about this experience, but that I could come earlier if I wanted to discuss these events with them first. Again she thanked me and mentioned that the memorial service would be the following Thursday. She expressed deep gratitude that Eric had passed away peacefully—there was no hemorrhage, no sudden emergency. Their pastor was with them that morning.

This, of course, encouraged me, making me realize that this family had wanted to take care of Eric at home. Eric did not want to be returned to the hospital. The family was willing to care for him, and whatever service I had brought to them they had found supportive. They were then able to cope with this crisis of death in the home.

I debated about going to the memorial service since I didn't want to make it more difficult for them. Yet I felt that it might help if they knew that we did care enough to come. So my husband and I went. I first introduced my husband to Eric's father, who told him that it had been a help for me to be there, that I had been such a help to the whole family, and especially to his wife! I was embarrassed by these comments, but I understood them. She told me it seemed she had known me for a long, long time and wanted again to thank me. They seemed genuinely pleased that we had come.

In looking back over this experience, it seems to me that one of the strengths of the home is the interpersonal relationships that have already been established. In a family where these relationships are relatively healthy—ie, where communication is relatively open and there is a mutual trust with an anticipatory hope for the future—the crises of illness and even death can result in a more integrated family or a reintegrated family. In the common experience of the closeness one has with a friend when going through a difficult period of life, a bond is formed that is meaningful.

Also, human beings have a need to feel they are productive, that they are having an impact, and that there is still hope. We all want to feel that we are creating our destiny rather than simply reacting to it.[1]

REFERENCES

1. Kübler-Ross E: On Death and Dying. New York, Macmillan, 1969
2. Picard M: Intrusion Into the Soul of a Child, Modern Age 16:339, 1972

APPENDIX II: A NURSE'S PERSPECTIVE*

Ida Marie Martinson

I first met Meredith on Friday, April 19, 1974. Dr. John Kersey had called to tell me of a child with leukemia, now nearing the end of medical treatment. The parents, having heard of the Home Care Program, were interested in caring for their child at home and would like her to die at home as well.

I went immediately to the University of Minnesota hospital where I met Meredith and her father, David Wetzel. As Mr. Wetzel stepped out to call his wife, Jodi, I asked Meredith when her birtday was. "May 8th," she replied quietly. She would be ten-years-old, and she would like to play birthday games at her party. Noticing she was trying to move her arm, I asked how it was working. "Not so good any more," she replied, solemn and unsmiling.

When Mr. Wetzel returned with his wife, we left Meredith for a while in order to talk together over coffee in the cafeteria. Meredith's illness, they said, had been diagnosed when she was two. For three years she had had a complete remission, but now her relapses were more and more frequent, and the treatment given had become as difficult for Meredith as the disease itself. The parents were now making a difficult decision. Rather than having Meredith suffer any more from treatments, they themselves wanted to care for her at home. They had realized home care would be possible only a short time ago when reading about Eric in the University of Minnesota *Report.* They hoped very much that I would help them to prepare for their own child's death at home. To make this possible, Mr. Wetzel would be home three days a week and Mrs. Wetzel two days; over the weekend, both would be home.

We talked about many things over that cup of coffee—about the difficult days ahead for which they both must conserve their energy and time in order to help Meredith enjoy her last days as much as possible; about Meredith's partial loss of movement, which would increase; about possible death from hemorrhage; about practical details, such as mouth care and the use of a lamb's wool pad. They were also concerned about a report that tension within families with a leukemic child was so great that following the death of the child 80 percent of marriages ended in divorce. We talked of Meredith's artistic ability, and how her artwork around the home would be a precious memory of her. Meredith has a healthy younger brother, 20 months old. Fortunately, the Wetzels did have capable relatives and friends who would be able to help in caring for Meredith and babysitting for her little brother.

Before we said goodbye, I asked them to call me when Meredith was to leave the hospital and assured them that they must feel free to telephone me at any time, day or night. This would be essential if I was to be able to help them. As I left, I thought to myself: What will these parents need? Certainly both a hospital bed and a wheelchair, available perhaps through the American Cancer Society.

Several days later I visited Meredith and her parents in their home. The rather new house is conveniently arranged with two bedrooms and a bath as well as a large living room, dining room and kitchen on the main floor. Meredith's bedroom adjoins both the kitchen and the bathroom. A hospital bed and a wheelchair, obtained through the American Cancer Society, were there; Meredith had been up in the wheelchair that afternoon, happily manipulating it around the room. I had brought with me two lamb's wool pads which Eric's mother, Mrs. Kulenkamp, had bought to give them.

Meredith seemed happy to see me. We talked about her coming birthday. She showed me her doll collection from *Little Women* and told me how much she enjoyed the book. Smiling and relaxed, she related some of her activities at home—viewing the family's home movies and watching the little gerbil one grandmother had given as an early birthday gift. She even expressed interest in having someone from school come to help her keep up with her classes.

After visiting awhile I examined her briefly. Her skin was good and there was very little bleeding of the gums. However, she looked somewhat moon-faced now from the medications, and her thighs were quite swollen from the injections. Packs had been made with hot washcloths wrapped in plastic. Fortunately, there was no sign of infection.

During the hour and a half in their home, I had very little opportunity for visiting alone with Mr. and Mrs. Wetzel, because Meredith was anxious for us to be with her. But they did share with me that upon first bringing Meredith home from the hospital, they had felt it to be an almost overwhelming burden. After two or three days, however, Meredith seemed to be feeling and looking better; she even seemed to enjoy eating. The Wetzels had coped very well with their difficult situation.

The next time I met the Wetzels was at the hospital in the Masonic Clinic. Meredith seemed happy to see me again, which pleased us all. She had received an injection for pain relief, which, by her request, had been given by her mother—a unique experience in the clinic. Now she was very alert and talkative. She suggested that although her birthday was on Wednesday, I could still bring her a present on Thursday! It was a pleasant visit for us all.

On Thursday, May 9th, I brought Meredith's gift to her home, but when I arrived Meredith was sleeping and her parents seemed tired and discouraged. As we sat together in the living room, they told me that Meredith had been having a great deal of pain, needing Demerol as frequently as every two hours; and that since last Monday when I had met them at the hospital, Meredith's itching had become quite a problem. She had not been eating much solid food, but was still able to drink quite well and enjoyed pop. They also mentioned that during a visit a friend had told of a relative who had died from cancer. Because Meredith did not seem to be "wasting away" in the same way, they suggested it would be a long time yet before Meredith's death. We discussed then the different types of cancer and the different disease courses. Of course, we couldn't know how long it would be for Meredith yet, but I doubted that she would live even three or four months. I think we all felt this opportunity to sit down and talk together was helpful. With the pressures of Meredith's care and their own fatigue, Mr. and Mrs. Wetzel had had very little time to share their concerns and feelings with each other. At times, Mrs. Wetzel said, she felt she could "no longer perk herself up."

By this time, Meredith had awakened and we went in to see her. She was quiet but seemed to appreciate the gift I had brought. The pain in her leg seemed continuous, but that in her arms was spasmodic. I tried to show the parents how to pull the shoulder muscle up and forward for an injection, but this was painful for Meredith. Nevertheless, brightening a little, she offered me a can of "nuts." As I opened the can, a "snake" popped out at me and across the bed. I jumped, and we all had a good laugh. Then abruptly Meredith said she needed an injection for pain—immediately. (It had been three hours since her last injection.) When it was ready she changed her mind. "Oh, let's wait awhile," she said. So we helped turn her on her side, though she moved quite a bit by herself as well. She tried bravely to keep her mind off the pain. Then we concentrated for some time on her itching, as she first directed her father to the various "itchy" spots, and then decided to use the soft toothbrush her mother had cleverly thought of for reaching these spots herself. Finally, she asked again for the shot and one of her parents gave it to her. We talked then of her birthday; she showed me her new doll and told me what she had done that day.

After spending about 20 minutes with Meredith, we went into the kitchen to discuss the call we planned to make to Dr. Kersey. What about antihistamine, for example, to control the itching? Which would more likely be effective for pain, Seconal or Demerol? When I had finished talking with Dr. Kersey, Mrs. Wetzel asked him a few questions while I visited with Meredith's grandmother who had recently come from Geneva, Switzerland on a visit. During our discussion of the possible medications I had used the term "snowed." She asked just what I meant by that. I explained that if a child is given Seconal plus Demerol plus Benadryl, the child could become confused. In all honesty and with deep feeling for Meredith's suffering, she asked whether this would really be a bad thing? We both realized, I think that this question was a very difficult one—even unanswerable. However, I did explain that one benefit of keeping Meredith alert as long as possible was that we would then be able to hear and understand her wants and needs. As we talked she broke down and cried. Mr. Wetzel joined us then and we discussed together how difficult it is to see a child suffer and how difficult it is to have control of pain.

Meanwhile, Mrs. Wetzel finished her conversation with Dr. Kersey. They had decided to stop temporarily the Seconal and to use Demerol and antihistamine. She asked me then if it would be at all possible for me to come more than once a week now. I said, "Certainly," and arranged to come again Monday evening at seven o'clock. Though I would be out of town Tuesday and Wednesday, a colleague had agreed to take my place temporarily. On Thursday, I would come again at about four o'clock.

I hoped that our discussion of very concrete problems that afternoon and our sharing of thoughts and feelings had been helpful. Meri's grandmother was to return to Geneva the next day. As I was leaving she told me how deeply she appreciated being listened to and, in her grief over never being able to see Meredith again, being able to cry. Ten days after her departure, Mrs. Wetzel's sister would arrive.

By Saturday, May 11th, Meredith seemed to be much freer of pain. Because the Demerol was no longer effective for her, she was on morphine sulphate. Her parents called the next day to say that her breathing had slowed to about eighteen respirations per minute from the morphine. Would it be necessary to give her oxygen? I reassured them that the slow respiration needn't alarm them, and in fact, within a short time it returned to normal—a great relief for them. That evening I stopped by their home for a brief visit. I noticed the more rapid deterioration in Meredith's condition, which was causing them to worry. Because her gums were bleeding more now, I gave some suggestions on mouth care: on cleaning the mouth, moistening it by periodically putting in a few ice chips, soothing and moistening her lips with vaseline or a lip balm. Then we talked about what the next few days would likely bring for them and Meredith.

On Monday, the 13th, the Wetzels had planned to bring Meredith in to Masonic Clinic. They were considering canceling these plans, which, I assured them, would be fine. Nevertheless, I stopped over at the clinic. They had not come in, so I left a message requesting Dr. Kersey to call them. When later I saw him, he was calling the Wetzels regarding a prescription for additional morphine and the possibility of death within the next 48 hours.

That evening at about seven o'clock I stopped by the Wetzel home. A few friends were there with them. During the morning one had helped Mr. Wetzel make funeral arrangements. The burial itself would be in Utah, where Mrs. Wetzel's parents live.

We went in a couple times to be with Meredith. She would moan and open her eyes and seemed to know we were there. Mrs. Wetzel told how during the day she would go in to Meredith and frequently tell her, "I love you; I'm right here with you." Meredith would respond with a little moan and then drop off to sleep. I was glad when both Mrs. and Mr. Wetzel said they felt they were holding up well under the strain, and that they were grateful to be able to continue giving Meredith care at home.

Then on Tuesday, May 14th, at four o'clock in the morning, my phone rang. Because a friend was with Meredith, the parents had been sleeping in the other bedroom, but a change in Meredith's breathing had wakened them both and they found that her jaw was clenched and could not be opened. As we talked, she relaxed her jaw and was able to breathe through her mouth again. Though I offered to go over, they declined, saying that they would be able to manage now.

At six-fifteen Mrs. Wetzel called again to say that Meredith's breathing had greatly changed. "Can you come?" she asked, "My knees are shaking." I said I would be over immediately, but when I arrived at six-thirty, Meredith had just died. Though heartbeat and breathing had both ceased, her body was still warm. She had died peacefully, had seemingly just stopped breathing. Mr. Wetzel commented that these last two hours had passed by extremely fast. Mrs. Wetzel pulled the pad up over Meredith's body and said, "Can't I keep her warm?" We stayed by the bedside quite awhile, then left and sat around the dining room table. Mrs. Wetzel returned to the room once more and cried; her husband joined her for a moment and they returned together. This experience, he said, was as profoundly moving as the birth of a child.

Around the table we talked of what that day would hold for them. All these weeks these parents had cared for their daughter, Meredith, in such a wonderful way that I had felt happy to be able to learn to know them and to work with them as a family. I mentioned this to them before leaving.

On Thursday when I met Dr. Kersey, he commented that again in this experience the parents had found deep meaning in having their child die at home with them. He also suggested I return the unused morphine, which the parents had given to me, to the outpatient pharmacy, which I did.

Mr. and Mrs. Wetzel had invited me to Meredith's memorial service Monday afternoon in Theodore Wirth Park. It is a beautiful location on top of a hill. A group of friends—about 30 to 40—had gathered. Meredith's teacher first sang a children's fun song which Meredith would have enjoyed. There were several readings. As the scripture was read, the sun came out from behind the clouds and shone brightly. A friend read a moving poem by Meredith's father, seemingly written after her death. The group sang a few more songs before leaving for dinner together.

Tuesday morning, Mrs. Wetzel called to say that she was returning the lamb's wool pads and other equipment which she would like to pass on to other families who are sharing a similar experience of caring for their dying child at home. "Let me know if there is any way I can help," she offered, and thanked me again for the help I had given to them.

INDEX